The Baby Boom

AMERICANS
BORN 1946 to 1964

The Baby Boom

AMERICANS
BORN 1946 to 1964

4th EDITION

BY CHERYL RUSSELL

New Strategist Publications, Inc.
Ithaca, New York

New Strategist Publications, Inc.
P.O. Box 242, Ithaca, New York 14851
800/848-0842; 607/273-0913
www.newstrategist.com

ISBN 1-885070-51-9

Printed in the United States of America

Table of Contents

Chapter 5. Labor Force

Chapter 6. Living Arrangements

Chapter 7. Population

Chapter 8. Spending

Chapter 9. Wealth

Tables

Chapter 3. Housing

Chapter 4. Income

Illustrations

Introduction

The mood of the nation—our problems and concerns, hopes and fears—are influenced by the age structure of the population. For the past fifty years, the Baby-Boom generation has been one of the most important—if not *the* most important—factor shaping the age structure. The enormous size of the Baby-Boom generation ensures that its obsessions become national obsessions, its concerns national concerns. Those who want to know where the nation stands today hold in their hands the key to doing so. *The Baby Boom: Americans Born 1946 to 1964* is your strategic guide, revealing the unique characteristics of Boomers and explaining how those characteristics are remaking our society.

Boomers today are decidedly middle aged, focused on work, parenting, and homeownership. Most have passed important milestones on the way to middle age, according to an AARP survey. Eighty-eight percent have married, and 83 percent are parents. But Boomers are just now reaching other important milestones. Most have yet to become grandparents, about half say their father has died, but only 30 percent have experienced the death of their mother. Twenty-nine percent have had a major illness, and 51 percent have made a major career change, according to AARP.

Those two issues—health care and work/retirement—will be the top concerns of Boomers in the years ahead. Businesses and politicians are already wrestling with the problems of health care cost and coverage. As Boomers age and confront serious health problems for the first time, health care policy will become even more important, a political firestorm for the unwary. Most Boomers will postpone retirement, forced by their lack of retirement savings, to work well into their sixties. It will frustrate those who hoped to retire early, but some will enjoy the sense of discovery a second career will bring.

It is not easy to study the nation's 78 million Boomers, born from 1946 through 1964. Few government surveys focus solely on the generation, and the ages of Boomers usually do not fit neatly into the traditional five- or ten-year age categories. In 2004, for example, Boomers spanned the ages from 39 to 58. To analyze Boomer lifestyles, then, most of the tables in the book approximate the Baby-Boom generation. Single-year-of-age data are shown whenever they are available, but five-year age groups are most common. When five-year age categories are shown, Boomers are included in the relatively youthful 35-to-39 age group all the way up to the much older 55-to-59 age group. In a few tables, data are available only for much broader age groups, forcing a more general analysis of trends among the middle aged.

Whether Boomer age groups are exact or approximate, however, the results are clear. Boomers are in their peak earning and spending years. They account for the majority of

Critical Life Events Experienced by the Baby-Boom Generation, 2002

(percent of people aged 38 to 56 who have ever experienced selected life events, by age, 2002)

		Boomers (aged 38 to 56)	
	total	38 to 45	46 to 56
Gotten married for the first time	88%	86%	89%
Become a parent for the first time	83	83	84
Gotten a divorce	40	38	43
Remarried	29	26	32
Had last child move out of the house	31	15	45
Had spouse die	5	3	6
Become a grandparent	35	18	50
Had an adult child move back home	26	17	34
Moved back into parents' home	21	23	20
Provided child care or daycare to a grandchild on a regular basis	14	9	19
Had father die	49	35	61
Had mother die	30	18	39
Experienced a midlife crisis	24	18	29
Survived a major illness	29	27	30
Made major changes in diet because of a medical condition	28	26	31
Made a major career change	51	53	49
Lost a job	36	37	35

Source: © 2002, AARP. Reprinted with permission. Boomers at Midlife: The AARP Life Stage Study. A National Survey Conducted for AARP by Princeton Survey Research Associates, November 2002; Internet site http://www.aarp.org

households with incomes of $100,000 or more. They spend more than any other age group on most products and services. Many are the parents of teenagers while millions are becoming empty nesters. Most are feeling pressured to save for retirement and college tuition at the same time. Health problems are increasing and more are on the way. These are the issues of importance to Baby Boomers, and they are our top domestic concerns as well. *The Baby Boom: Americans Born 1946 to 1964* is your guide to Boomers and to the nation.

How to use this book

The Baby Boom: Americans Born 1946 to 1964 is designed for easy use. It is divided into nine chapters, organized alphabetically: Education, Health, Housing, Income, Labor Force, Living Arrangements, Population, Spending, and Wealth.

This edition of *The Baby Boom* includes the latest statistics on the labor force participation, living arrangements, incomes, health, spending, and wealth of this all-important generation. The socioeconomic estimates presented here reflect 2000 census results, which counted 6 million more Americans than demographers had estimated. *The Baby Boom* presents labor force data for 2003, including the government's updated occupational classifications. It contains new data on the health of the population, including updated estimates of the overweight and the obese. The Census Bureau's latest population projections—the first released by the bureau in years—are also included in the book, revealing the enormous expansion of the 45-to-64 age group as it fills with Boomers during the next decade. *The Baby Boom* also presents the latest data on wealth from the Survey of Consumer Finances. And because the government now breaks out the Asian population separately in its estimates, most of the racial and ethnic breakdowns include Asians for the first time, along with blacks, Hispanics, and non-Hispanic whites. New to this book is a chapter on housing, revealing the surprising finding that homeownership among Boomers is lower today than it was for their counterparts twenty years ago.

Most of the tables in *The Baby Boom* are based on data collected by the federal government, in particular the Census Bureau, the Bureau of Labor Statistics, the National Center for Education Statistics, the National Center for Health Statistics, and the Federal Reserve Board. The federal government is the best source of up-to-date, reliable information on the changing characteristics of Americans.

While most of the tables in this book are based on data collected by the federal government, they are not simply reprints of government spreadsheets—as is the case in many reference books. Instead, each table is individually compiled and created by New Strategist's editors, with calculations designed to reveal the trends. Each chapter of *The Baby Boom* includes the demographic and lifestyle data most important to researchers. Each table tells a story about Boomers, a story amplified by the accompanying text and chart, which analyze the data and highlight future trends. If you need more information than tables and text provide, you can plumb the original source listed at the bottom of each table.

The book contains a lengthy table list to help you locate the information you need. For a more detailed search, see the index at the back of the book. Also at the back of the book is the glossary, which defines the terms and describes the surveys commonly used in the tables and text. A list of telephone and Internet contacts also appears at the end of the book, allowing you to access government specialists and web sites.

Boomers continue to be the most influential of generations. They are now in their peak earning and spending years. With *The Baby Boom: Americans Born 1946 to 1964* in your hands, you have a guide not only to Boomers but to the nation as well.

1

Education

■ Men aged 50 to 59—the age group now filling with the oldest Boomers—are the most highly educated of all Americans. One-third have a college degree.

■ Baby-Boom women are better educated than older generations of women. Twenty-eight percent have a college degree compared with just 13 percent of women aged 65 or older.

■ Asians are by far the best-educated Boomers. Half of Asian men and 43 percent of Asian women born between 1946 and 1964 have a college degree.

■ At the undergraduate level, people aged 35 to 54 account for 32 percent of part-time students. At the graduate level, they account for 48 percent of part-timers.

■ The 54 percent majority of 45-to-54-year-olds participated in adult education courses in 2001, up fully 22 percentage points since 1991.

Boomer Men Are the Best Educated

One-third of men in their fifties have a bachelor's degree.

Men aged 50 to 59—the age group filling with the oldest Boomers—are the most highly educated of all Americans. One-third have a college diploma, and 14 to 15 percent have an advanced degree. Behind this high level of education is the Vietnam War. To avoid being drafted during the 1960s and early 1970s, many young men opted for college deferments. Those men are now in their fifties.

When the war ended, so did the incentive to stay in school. Consequently, among men, younger Boomers are less educated than their older counterparts. Still, more than half of men aged 40 to 49 have college experience and 29 to 30 percent have a college degree.

■ The educational attainment of Boomers has transformed lifestyles in middle age, driving the demand for Internet service, cell phones, GPS devices, travel, gourmet foods, and other sophisticated products and services.

Men aged 50 to 59 are the best educated

(percent of men aged 40 to 59 with a college degree, 2002)

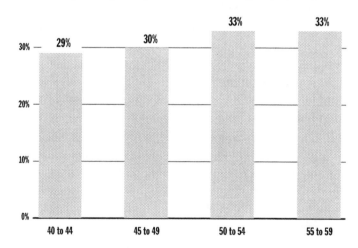

Table 1.1 Educational Attainment of Baby-Boom Men, 2002

(number and percent distribution of men aged 25 or older, aged 38 to 56, and aged 35 to 59 in five-year age groups, by highest level of education, 2002; numbers in thousands)

	total aged 25 or older	38 to 56 exactly	five-year age groups				
			35 to 39	40 to 44	45 to 49	50 to 54	55 to 59
Total men	**86,996**	**38,020**	**10,698**	**11,124**	**10,256**	**9,075**	**7,091**
Not a high school graduate	14,095	4,541	1,387	1,354	1,175	994	1,048
High school graduate	26,947	11,948	3,466	3,767	3,323	2,576	2,067
Some college, no degree	14,661	6,626	1,843	1,820	1,843	1,661	1,141
Associate's degree	6,466	3,295	918	980	846	828	504
Bachelor's degree	15,925	7,117	2,095	2,073	1,903	1,711	1,298
Master's degree	5,595	2,804	644	717	698	846	678
Professional degree	1,795	946	208	228	270	245	186
Doctoral degree	1,514	731	138	185	199	215	169
High school graduate or more	72,903	33,467	9,312	9,770	9,082	8,082	6,043
Some college or more	45,956	21,519	5,846	6,003	5,759	5,506	3,976
Bachelor's degree or more	24,829	11,598	3,085	3,203	3,070	3,017	2,331
Total men	**100.0%**	**100.0%**	**100.0%**	**100.0%**	**100.0%**	**100.0%**	**100.0%**
Not a high school graduate	16.2	11.9	13.0	12.2	11.5	11.0	14.8
High school graduate	31.0	31.4	32.4	33.9	32.4	28.4	29.1
Some college, no degree	16.9	17.4	17.2	16.4	18.0	18.3	16.1
Associate's degree	7.4	8.7	8.6	8.8	8.2	9.1	7.1
Bachelor's degree	18.3	18.7	19.6	18.6	18.6	18.9	18.3
Master's degree	6.4	7.4	6.0	6.4	6.8	9.3	9.6
Professional degree	2.1	2.5	1.9	2.1	2.6	2.7	2.6
Doctoral degree	1.7	1.9	1.3	1.7	1.9	2.4	2.4
High school graduate or more	83.8	88.0	87.0	87.8	88.6	89.1	85.2
Some college or more	52.8	56.6	54.6	54.0	56.2	60.7	56.1
Bachelor's degree or more	28.5	30.5	28.8	28.8	29.9	33.2	32.9

Source: Bureau of the Census, Educational Attainment in the United States: March 2002, *detailed tables (PPL-169); Internet site http://www.census.gov/population/www/socdemo/education/ppl-169.html; calculations by New Strategist*

Most Boomer Women Have Been to College

More than one in four is a college graduate.

Unlike their male counterparts, Boomer women did not have the threat of being drafted and sent to Vietnam as an incentive to keep them in college. Consequently, women in their fifties are less educated than men in the age group. Among people aged 50 to 59, 29 percent of women and 33 percent of men have a college degree.

Baby-Boom women are much more educated than older generations of women, however. Twenty-eight percent of Baby-Boom women have a college degree compared with just 13 percent of women aged 65 or older. Younger women are even better educated than Boomers. Thirty-three percent of women aged 30 to 34 have a college degree.

■ Because people marry those with similar educational backgrounds, college-educated Boomers tend to be married to one another. With earnings closely linked to education, these couples are now the nation's income elite.

Among Boomer women, those aged 45 to 54 are the best educated

(percent of women aged 40 to 59 with a college degree, 2002)

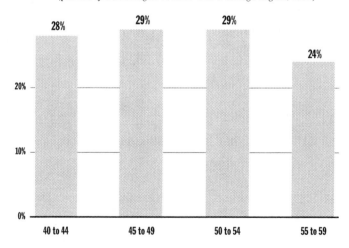

Table 1.2 Educational Attainment of Baby-Boom Women, 2002

(number and percent distribution of women aged 25 or older, aged 38 to 56, and aged 35 to 59 in five-year age groups, by highest level of education, 2002; numbers in thousands)

	total aged 25 or older	38 to 56 exactly	five-year age groups				
			35 to 39	40 to 44	45 to 49	50 to 54	55 to 59
Total women	**95,146**	**39,526**	**10,950**	**11,512**	**10,732**	**9,482**	**7,575**
Not a high school graduate	14,854	4,267	1,201	1,199	1,093	1,052	1,114
High school graduate	31,509	12,756	3,388	3,688	3,441	3,091	2,666
Some college, no degree	16,330	7,063	1,997	2,098	1,977	1,621	1,332
Associate's degree	8,585	4,359	1,210	1,340	1,159	1,008	674
Bachelor's degree	16,357	7,312	2,253	2,268	2,007	1,638	1,055
Master's degree	5,893	3,041	655	720	856	913	582
Professional degree	942	399	144	127	106	86	79
Doctoral degree	676	328	102	75	92	75	75
High school graduate or more	80,292	35,258	9,749	10,316	9,638	8,432	6,463
Some college or more	48,783	22,502	6,361	6,628	6,197	5,341	3,797
Bachelor's degree or more	23,868	11,080	3,154	3,190	3,061	2,712	1,791
Total women	**100.0%**	**100.0%**	**100.0%**	**100.0%**	**100.0%**	**100.0%**	**100.0%**
Not a high school graduate	15.6	10.8	11.0	10.4	10.2	11.1	14.7
High school graduate	33.1	32.3	30.9	32.0	32.1	32.6	35.2
Some college, no degree	17.2	17.9	18.2	18.2	18.4	17.1	17.6
Associate's degree	9.0	11.0	11.1	11.6	10.8	10.6	8.9
Bachelor's degree	17.2	18.5	20.6	19.7	18.7	17.3	13.9
Master's degree	6.2	7.7	6.0	6.3	8.0	9.6	7.7
Professional degree	1.0	0.1	1.3	1.1	1.0	0.9	1.0
Doctoral degree	0.7	0.8	0.9	0.7	0.9	0.8	1.0
High school graduate or more	84.4	89.2	89.0	89.6	89.8	88.9	85.3
Some college or more	51.3	56.9	58.1	57.6	57.7	56.3	50.1
Bachelor's degree or more	25.1	28.0	28.8	27.7	28.5	28.6	23.6

Source: Bureau of the Census, Educational Attainment in the United States: March 2002, *detailed tables (PPL-169); Internet site http://www.census.gov/population/www/socdemo/education/ppl-169.html; calculations by New Strategist*

Among Boomer Men, Asians Are the Best Educated

Hispanics are the least educated.

Asians are by far the best-educated Baby-Boom men. Sixty-nine percent of Asian men born between 1946 and 1964 have some college experience and half have a college degree. Among non-Hispanic white men, the figures are 61 and 34 percent, respectively.

Non-Hispanic black men are less educated than Asian and non-Hispanic white men, but the great majority (83 percent) are high school graduates and nearly half (47 percent) have college experience. Only 17 percent have a college degree, however.

Hispanic men are by far the least educated. Only 59 percent of Hispanic men of the Baby-Boom generation are high school graduates. Just 32 percent have college experience, and 14 percent have a bachelor's degree. One reason for the low educational level of Hispanics is that many are immigrants from countries that offer little educational opportunity.

■ Educational attainment is directly linked to income. The gap in the education of men by race and Hispanic origin translates into occupational and income differences.

Half of Asian Baby-Boom men are college graduates

(percent of men aged 38 to 56 with a college degree, by race and Hispanic origin, 2002)

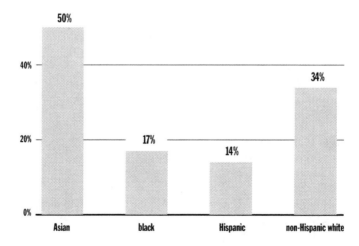

Table 1.3 Educational Attainment of Baby-Boom Men by Race and Hispanic Origin, 2002

(number and percent distribution of men aged 38 to 56 by educational attainment, race, and Hispanic origin, 2002; numbers in thousands)

| | | non-Hispanic | | |
	Asian	black	white	Hispanic
Total men	**1,585**	**3,978**	**28,412**	**3,728**
Not a high school graduate	139	664	2,159	1,530
High school graduate	352	1,446	8,993	1,021
Some college, no degree	179	863	5,069	466
Associate's degree	115	319	2,624	210
Bachelor's degree	467	441	5,843	337
Master's degree	187	180	2,335	92
Professional degree	52	32	813	46
Doctoral degree	86	24	585	30
High school graduate or more	1,438	3,305	26,262	2,202
Some college or more	1,086	1,859	17,269	1,181
Bachelor's degree or more	792	677	9,576	505
Total men	**100.0%**	**100.0%**	**100.0%**	**100.0%**
Not a high school graduate	8.8	16.7	7.6	41.0
High school graduate	22.2	36.3	31.7	27.4
Some college, no degree	11.3	21.7	17.8	12.5
Associate's degree	7.3	8.0	9.2	5.6
Bachelor's degree	29.5	11.1	20.6	9.0
Master's degree	11.8	4.5	8.2	2.5
Professional degree	3.3	0.8	2.9	1.2
Doctoral degree	5.4	0.6	2.1	0.8
High school graduate or more	90.7	83.1	92.4	59.1
Some college or more	68.5	46.7	60.8	31.7
Bachelor's degree or more	50.0	17.0	33.7	13.5

Note: Numbers will not add to total because not all races are shown and Hispanics may be of any race.
Source: Bureau of the Census, Educational Attainment in the United States: March 2002, *detailed tables (PPL-169); Internet site http://www.census.gov/population/www/socdemo/education/ppl-169.html; calculations by New Strategist*

Among Boomer Women, Hispanics Lag in Education

Asian women have the highest level of education.

Among women born between 1946 and 1964, Asians are by far the best educated. Fully 64 percent have college experience and 43 percent have a bachelor's degree. Interestingly, however, Asian women are less likely to have a high school diploma than non-Hispanic white women. The explanation lies in the socioeconomic differences within the Asian-American community itself, with some being immigrants from countries with little educational opportunity such as Vietnam.

Sixty-one percent of non-Hispanic white women of the Baby-Boom generation have college experience, while 31 percent have a college degree. Among black women in the age group, the figures are a smaller 50 and 19 percent, respectively. Hispanics are the least educated, with only 61 percent having a high school diploma and just 12 percent having a college degree.

■ Since earnings are directly linked to education, Asian women should reap the biggest rewards in the job market thanks to their high level of educational attainment.

Among Boomer women, Asians are the best educated

(percent of women aged 38 to 56 with a college degree, by race and Hispanic origin, 2002)

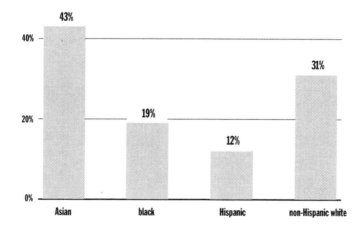

Table 1.4 Educational Attainment of Baby-Boom Women by Race and Hispanic Origin, 2002

(number and percent distribution of women aged 38 to 56 by educational attainment, race, and Hispanic origin, 2002; numbers in thousands)

| | | non-Hispanic | | |
	Asian	black	white	Hispanic
Total women	**1,809**	**4,821**	**28,749**	**3,753**
Not a high school graduate	238	749	1,722	1,489
High school graduate	413	1,650	9,483	1,068
Some college, no degree	199	987	5,299	495
Associate's degree	168	498	3,400	249
Bachelor's degree	584	625	5,746	318
Master's degree	141	260	2,528	98
Professional degree	26	27	312	30
Doctoral degree	35	20	257	11
High school graduate or more	1,566	4,067	27,025	2,269
Some college or more	1,153	2,417	17,542	1,201
Bachelor's degree or more	786	932	8,843	457
Total women	**100.0%**	**100.0%**	**100.0%**	**100.0%**
Not a high school graduate	13.2	15.5	6.0	39.7
High school graduate	22.8	34.2	33.0	28.5
Some college, no degree	11.0	20.5	18.4	13.2
Associate's degree	9.3	10.3	11.8	6.6
Bachelor's degree	32.3	13.0	20.0	8.5
Master's degree	7.8	5.4	8.8	2.6
Professional degree	1.4	0.6	1.1	0.8
Doctoral degree	1.9	0.4	0.9	0.3
High school graduate or more	86.6	84.4	9.4	60.5
Some college or more	63.7	50.1	61.0	32.0
Bachelor's degree or more	43.4	19.3	30.8	12.2

Note: Numbers will not add to total because not all races are shown and Hispanics may be of any race.
Source: Bureau of the Census, Educational Attainment in the United States: March 2002, detailed tables (PPL-169); Internet site http://www.census.gov/population/www/socdemo/education/ppl-169.html; calculations by New Strategist

More than Two Million Boomers Are Still in School

Of the nation's 72 million students, 2.8 million are aged 35 to 54.

Three percent of people aged 35 to 54 were enrolled in school in 2002 (Baby Boomers were aged 38 to 56 in that year). While this percentage is small, the number of middle-aged Americans attending school has expanded enormously over the past few decades.

Among Boomers in school, women outnumber men—1.7 million to 1 million. While 2.5 percent of men aged 35 to 54 are in school, the proportion is 4.0 percent among women in the age group—peaking at 5.7 percent among women aged 35 to 39.

■ As well-educated Boomers age into their fifties and sixties, expect to see school enrollment rise among older Americans.

Women outnumber men in school

(number of people aged 35 to 54 enrolled in school, by sex, 2002)

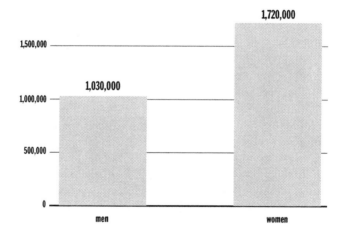

Table 1.5 School Enrollment of People by Sex and Age, 2002

(total number of people aged 3 or older, and number and percent enrolled in school by sex and age, 2002; numbers in thousands)

	total	enrolled number	percent
Total people	**270,919**	**74,046**	**27.3%**
Under age 35	122,906	70,809	57.6
Aged 35 to 54	83,740	2,751	3.3
Aged 35 to 39	21,174	982	4.6
Aged 40 to 44	22,553	790	3.5
Aged 45 to 49	21,206	632	3.0
Aged 50 to 54	18,807	347	1.8
Aged 55 to 59	15,150	153	1.0
Aged 60 or older	45,466	139	0.3
Total females	**139,061**	**37,266**	**26.8**
Under age 35	62,761	35,381	56.4
Aged 35 to 54	42,828	1,720	4.0
Aged 35 to 39	10,797	618	5.7
Aged 40 to 44	11,509	493	4.3
Aged 45 to 49	10,864	419	3.9
Aged 50 to 54	9,658	190	2.0
Aged 55 to 59	7,807	97	1.2
Aged 60 or older	25,665	68	0.3
Total males	**131,858**	**36,779**	**27.9**
Under age 35	63,800	35,622	55.8
Aged 35 to 54	40,914	1,030	2.5
Aged 35 to 39	10,378	364	3.5
Aged 40 to 44	11,044	297	2.7
Aged 45 to 49	10,342	212	2.1
Aged 50 to 54	9,150	157	1.7
Aged 55 to 59	7,343	56	0.8
Aged 60 or older	19,801	71	0.4

Source: Bureau of the Census, School Enrollment—Social and Economic Characteristics of Students: October 2002, detailed tables; Internet site http://www.census.gov/population/www/socdemo/school/cps2002.html; calculations by New Strategist

Most Middle-Aged College Students Attend School Part-time

With families to support, Boomers cannot afford to go to school full-time.

As the number of older college students has grown, so has the number of students attending college part-time. Most Boomers have families to support and cannot afford the luxury of full-time study, juggling daytime jobs and nighttime classes. In 2002, 73 percent of college students aged 35 to 54 attended school part-time.

Overall, 2.7 million people aged 35 to 54 are in college, accounting for a significant 17 percent of total college enrollment. At the undergraduate level, people aged 35 to 54 are just 5 percent of full-time students, but a 32 percent share of part-timers. At the graduate level, they account for 48 percent of part-timers.

■ Because highly educated people are the ones most likely to seek even more education, boomers will continue to enroll in college even as they age into their sixties.

Boomers account for one-third of undergraduates who attend college part-time

(people aged 35 to 54 as a share of total students, by attendance status, 2002)

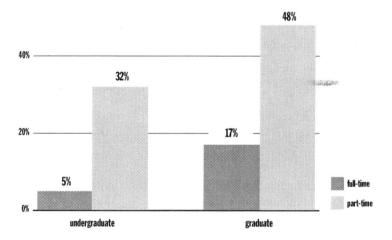

Table 1.6 College Students by Age and Attendance Status, 2002

(number and percent distribution of people aged 15 or older enrolled in institutions of higher education, by age and full- or part-time attendance status, 2002; numbers in thousands)

| | total | undergraduate | | | graduate | | |
		total	full-time	part-time	total	full-time	part-time
Total enrolled	**16,497**	**13,425**	**9,735**	**3,690**	**3,072**	**1,406**	**1,666**
Under age 35	13,505	11,606	9,207	2,399	1,899	1,146	753
Aged 35 to 54	2,739	1,689	498	1,191	1,050	243	807
Aged 35 to 39	954	600	191	409	354	115	239
Aged 40 to 44	724	470	136	334	254	57	197
Aged 45 to 49	591	353	101	252	238	44	194
Aged 50 to 54	324	188	50	138	136	18	118
Aged 55 to 59	146	78	20	58	68	9	59
Aged 60 or older	107	52	10	42	55	8	47

PERCENT DISTRIBUTION BY ATTENDANCE STATUS

| | total | undergraduate | | | graduate | | |
		total	full-time	part-time	total	full-time	part-time
Total enrolled	**100.0%**	**81.4%**	**59.0%**	**22.4%**	**18.6%**	**8.5%**	**10.1%**
Under age 35	100.0	85.9	68.2	17.8	14.1	8.5	5.6
Aged 35 to 54	100.0	61.7	18.2	43.5	38.3	8.9	29.5
Aged 35 to 39	100.0	62.9	20.0	42.9	37.1	12.1	25.1
Aged 40 to 44	100.0	64.9	18.8	46.1	35.1	7.9	27.2
Aged 45 to 49	100.0	59.7	17.1	42.6	40.3	7.4	32.8
Aged 50 to 54	100.0	58.0	15.4	42.6	42.0	5.6	36.4
Aged 55 to 59	100.0	53.4	13.7	39.7	46.6	6.2	40.4
Aged 60 or older	100.0	48.6	9.3	39.3	51.4	7.5	43.9

PERCENT DISTRIBUTION BY AGE

| | total | undergraduate | | | graduate | | |
		total	full-time	part-time	total	full-time	part-time
Total enrolled	**100.0%**	**100.0%**	**100.0%**	**100.0%**	**100.0%**	**100.0%**	**100.0%**
Under age 35	81.9	86.5	94.6	65.0	61.8	81.5	45.2
Aged 35 to 54	16.6	12.6	5.1	32.3	34.2	17.3	48.4
Aged 35 to 39	5.8	4.5	2.0	11.1	11.5	8.2	14.3
Aged 40 to 44	4.4	3.5	1.4	9.1	8.3	4.1	11.8
Aged 45 to 49	3.6	2.6	1.0	6.8	7.7	3.1	11.6
Aged 50 to 54	2.0	1.4	0.5	3.7	4.4	1.3	7.1
Aged 55 to 59	0.9	0.6	0.2	1.6	2.2	0.6	3.5
Aged 60 or older	0.6	0.4	0.1	1.1	1.8	0.6	2.8

Source: Bureau of the Census, School Enrollment—Social and Economic Characteristics of Students: October 2002, *detailed tables; Internet site http://www.census.gov/population/www/socdemo/school/cps2002.html; calculations by New Strategist*

More than Half of Boomers Participate in Adult Education

Life-long learning has been eagerly embraced by the best-educated generation.

Educated Americans are more likely to go back to school than those with less education; as is apparent in statistics on participation in adult education. Those most likely to take educational courses outside of postsecondary institutions are people under age 55—Boomers and younger generations of Americans.

The percentage of all Americans involved in adult education grew substantially between 1991 and 2001, rising from 32 to 47 percent of people aged 16 or older. Today, the majority of people under age 55 participate in adult education. The 54 percent majority of 45-to-54-year-olds participated in adult education courses in 2001, up fully 22 percentage points since 1991.

■ Look for the percentage of 55-to-64-year-olds who participate in adult education to soar in the years ahead as the Baby-Boom generation fills the age group.

Big gains in adult education are in store for the 55-to-64 age group

(percent of people aged 16 or older participating in adult education, by age, 2001)

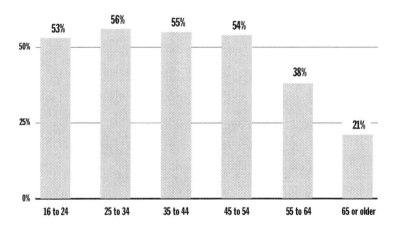

Table 1.7 Participation in Adult Education by Age, 1991 and 2001

(percent of people aged 16 or older participating in adult education activities, by age, 1991 and 2001; percentage point change, 1991–2001)

	2001	1991	percentage point change 1991–01
Total people	**47%**	**32%**	**15**
Aged 16 to 24	53	33	20
Aged 25 to 34	56	37	19
Aged 35 to 44	55	44	11
Aged 45 to 54	54	32	22
Aged 55 to 64	38	23	15
Aged 65 or older	21	10	11

Note: Adult education activities include apprenticeships, courses for basic skills, personal development, English as a second language, work-related courses, and credential programs in organizations other than postsecondary institutions. Excludes full-time participation in postsecondary institutions leading to a college degree, diploma, or certificate.
Source: National Center for Education Statistics, Adult Education and Lifelong Learning Survey of the National Household Education Surveys Program; Internet site http://nces.ed.gov/programs/coe/2003/section1/tables/t08_2.asp; calculations by New Strategist

2

Health

■ The percentage of Americans reporting excellent or very good health declines substantially within the 35-to-54 age group as chronic conditions become common.

■ Baby Boomers have a weight problem. Two-thirds are overweight and nearly one-third are obese.

■ Only 14 percent of the 4 million babies born to American women in 2002 had mothers aged 35 or older.

■ One in four Baby Boomers smokes cigarettes. Nearly half have tried to quit smoking during the past twelve months.

■ Among all Americans, 15 percent do not have health insurance. The figure is an even higher 18 percent among 35-to-44-year-olds and a slightly smaller 14 percent among 45-to-54-year-olds.

■ Thirty-five percent of Americans aged 45 to 64 have experienced lower back pain in the past three months, making it the most common health condition in this age group. Hypertension ranks second and arthritis third.

■ Among people aged 35 to 44, 9 percent had a work disability. The figure is a larger 13 percent among 45-to-54-year-olds and rises to 22 percent among those aged 55 to 64.

■ Heart disease and cancer are the leading causes of death in the United States. Among 35-to-64-year-olds, however, cancer is the number-one cause of death.

Most Middle-Aged Americans Feel Excellent or Very Good

The proportion declines significantly in the 45-to-54 age group, however.

Overall, the 55 percent majority of Americans aged 18 or older say their health is excellent or very good. The figure peaks at 64 percent in the 25-to-34 age group, then declines with age. The percentage of people reporting excellent or very good health declines substantially within the 35-to-54 age group, from 61 percent among 35-to-44-year-olds to just 54 percent among 45-to-54-year-olds. Behind the decline is the rise of chronic conditions as people age into their fifties.

Fewer than half of people aged 55 or older report that their health is excellent or very good. Nevertheless, the proportion of Americans who say they are in poor health remains below 10 percent regardless of age. The proportion of people aged 65 or older who say their health is excellent or very good (36 percent) surpasses the proportion saying their health is only fair or poor (28 percent).

■ Medical advances that allow people to manage their chronic conditions more easily should boost the number of people reporting excellent or very good health in the years ahead.

The majority of people aged 35 to 54 say their health is excellent or very good

(percentage of people aged 18 or older who say their health is excellent or very good, by age, 2002)

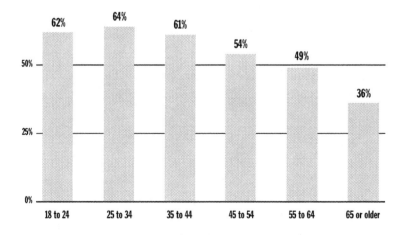

Table 2.1 Health Status by Age, 2002

(percent distribution of people aged 18 or older by self-reported health status, by age, 2002)

	excellent	very good	good	fair	poor
Total people	**21.4%**	**33.8%**	**29.8%**	**10.4%**	**3.9%**
Aged 18 to 24	25.4	37.0	29.5	6.0	0.8
Aged 25 to 34	26.6	37.5	27.4	5.8	1.2
Aged 35 to 44	24.8	35.8	27.6	8.1	2.4
Aged 45 to 54	21.1	32.6	29.6	10.7	4.1
Aged 55 to 64	18.8	30.0	30.2	13.5	6.5
Aged 65 or older	11.4	25.0	33.6	19.7	8.7

Source: Centers for Disease Control and Prevention, Behavioral Risk Factor Surveillance System Prevalence Data, 2002; Internet site http://apps.nccd.cdc.gov/brfss/index.asp

Weight Problems Are the Norm for Boomers

Four out of ten are trying to lose weight.

Americans have a weight problem. The 64 percent majority of people aged 20 or older are overweight, and 30 percent are obese, according to the latest data from the National Center for Health Statistics. Within the 35-to-54 age group, approximately the age of the baby-boom generation in 2000, the shares of people who are overweight and obese are about the same as the national average. Sixty-eight to 71 percent of boomer men are overweight, including 25 to 30 percent who are obese. Among boomer women, 64 to 65 percent are overweight, including 34 to 38 percent who are obese.

Not surprisingly, many Americans are trying to lose weight. Nationally, 38 percent are trying to shed pounds, a figure that tops 40 percent in the 35-to-54 age group. Twenty-eight percent of the middle aged say they are eating less fat to lose or maintain their weight, and a slightly larger proportion say they are eating fewer calories. Six out of ten claim to be exercising to lose or maintain their weight. Despite their weight problems, only 11 to 16 percent of boomers have been advised by a health professional to lose weight.

Although many people claim to exercise, only 31 percent of adults participate in regular leisure-time physical activity, according to government data. The figure ranges from a high of 40 percent among 18-to-24-year-olds to a low of 16 percent among people aged 75 or older. Among 45-to-64-year-olds, only 29 percent participate in regular leisure-time physical activity.

■ Most Baby Boomers lack the willpower to eat less or exercise more—fueling a diet and weight loss industry that never lacks customers.

Two-thirds of Boomers are overweight

(percent of people aged 35 to 54 who are overweight, by sex, 1999–2000)

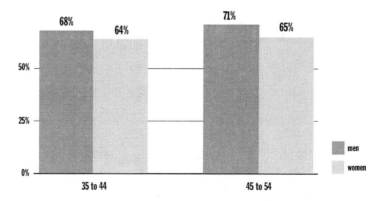

Table 2.2 Overweight and Obese by Sex and Age, 1999–2000

(percent of people aged 20 or older who are overweight or obese, by sex and age, 1999–2000)

	overweight	obese
TOTAL PEOPLE*	**64.3%**	**30.3%**
Total men*	**66.5**	**27.5**
Aged 20 to 34	58.0	24.1
Aged 35 to 44	67.6	25.2
Aged 45 to 54	71.3	30.1
Aged 55 to 64	72.5	32.9
Aged 65 to 74	77.2	33.4
Aged 75 or older	66.4	20.4
Total women*	**62.0**	**34.0**
Aged 20 to 34	51.5	25.8
Aged 35 to 44	63.6	33.9
Aged 45 to 54	64.7	38.1
Aged 55 to 64	73.1	43.1
Aged 65 to 74	70.1	38.8
Aged 75 or older	59.6	25.1

* Aged 20 to 74.
Note: Being overweight is defined as having a body mass index of 25 or higher. Obesity is defined as having a body mass index of 30 or higher. Body mass index is calculated by dividing weight in kilograms by height in meters squared.
Source: National Center for Health Statistics, Health, United States, 2003, Internet site http://www.cdc.gov/nchs/hus.htm

Table 2.3 Weight Loss Behavior by Age, 2000

(percent of people aged 18 or older engaging in selected weight loss behaviors, by age, 2000)

	total	18 to 24	25 to 34	35 to 44	45 to 54	55 to 64	65 or older
Trying to lose weight	38.0%	30.2%	38.0%	40.4%	44.7%	42.6%	30.6%
Trying to maintain weight	58.9	51.9	56.9	59.8	63.1	60.8	58.4
Eating fewer calories to lose/maintain weight*	13.5	11.4	12.1	13.9	15.2	13.2	12.0
Eating less fat to lose/maintain weight*	27.4	25.3	25.8	27.7	28.3	29.1	29.4
Eating fewer calories and less fat to lose/maintain weight*	29.6	25.5	27.0	30.1	32.6	33.0	29.0
Using physical activity or exercise to lose/maintain weight*	60.7	74.7	67.7	64.0	60.5	55.4	43.3
Advised by health professional to lose weight	11.7	4.0	8.4	11.3	16.0	17.7	11.2

* Among those trying to lose or maintain weight.
Source: Centers for Disease Control and Prevention, Behavioral Risk Factor Surveillance System Prevalence Data, 2000; Internet site http://apps.nccd.cdc.gov/brfss/index.asp

Table 2.4 Leisure-Time Physical Activity Level by Sex and Age, 1999–2001

(percent distribution of people aged 18 or older by leisure-time physical activity level, percent participating in regular leisure-time physical activity by level, and percent participating in strengthening activities, by sex and age, 1999–2001)

	total	physically inactive	at least some physical activity	regular physical activity			strengthening activities
				any	light-moderate	vigorous	
Total people	**100.0%**	**38.4%**	**61.6%**	**31.4%**	**15.5%**	**22.6%**	**23.2%**
Aged 18 to 24	100.0	29.9	70.1	39.7	17.8	31.7	36.5
Aged 25 to 44	100.0	33.7	66.3	34.3	15.4	26.6	27.2
Aged 45 to 64	100.0	40.5	59.5	29.3	15.1	19.9	18.6
Aged 65 to 74	100.0	46.6	53.4	26.3	17.0	13.4	12.4
Aged 75 or older	100.0	60.8	39.2	15.6	11.2	6.2	9.2
Total men	**100.0**	**35.4**	**64.6**	**35.1**	**16.8**	**26.6**	**27.5**
Aged 18 to 24	100.0	25.3	74.7	46.6	20.6	39.1	45.3
Aged 25 to 44	100.0	31.4	68.6	37.0	16.3	29.9	31.6
Aged 45 to 64	100.0	39.8	60.2	31.5	15.7	22.5	20.5
Aged 65 to 74	100.0	42.1	57.9	30.4	18.7	16.9	14.3
Aged 75 or older	100.0	54.4	45.6	20.7	14.5	9.4	11.9
Total women	**100.0**	**41.2**	**58.8**	**28.0**	**14.3**	**18.9**	**19.3**
Aged 18 to 24	100.0	34.4	65.6	32.8	15.1	24.5	27.8
Aged 25 to 44	100.0	36.0	64.0	31.7	14.6	23.3	23.0
Aged 45 to 64	100.0	41.3	58.7	27.3	14.5	17.4	16.9
Aged 65 to 74	100.0	50.3	49.7	22.9	15.6	10.6	10.9
Aged 75 or older	100.0	65.0	35.0	12.3	9.1	4.2	7.4

Note: "Physically inactive" means no light-moderate or vigorous leisure-time physical activity. "At least some" includes light-moderate or vigorous leisure-time physical activities. "Regular physical activity" includes activities done at least three to five times per week. Regular "light-moderate" activity is defined as engaging in light-moderate activity at least five times per week for at least 30 minutes each time. Regular "vigorous" activity is defined as engaging in vigorous activity at least three times per week for at least 20 minutes each time. "Any" regular activity is defined as meeting either criterion or both critera. Light-moderate activity is leisure-time physical activity that causes only light sweating or a light to moderate increase in breathing or heart rate and is done for at least 10 minutes per episode. Vigorous activity is leisure-time physical activity that causes heavy sweating or large increases in breathing or heart rate and is done for at least 10 minutes per episode. "Strengthening" activities are those designed to strengthen muscles such as weight lifting or calisthenics. Minimum duration and frequency were not asked. Those engaging in strengthening activities may be included in the physically inactive if they did not engage in any other type of physical activity. Numbers will not add to 100 because people may be in more than one category.
Source: National Center for Health Statistics, Health Behaviors of Adults: United States, 1999–2001, *Vital and Health Statistics, Series 10, No. 219, 2004*

Few New Mothers Are Aged 35 or Older

With the youngest Boomers turning 38 in 2002, most are finished with childbearing.

Only 14 percent of the 4 million babies born to American women in 2002 had mothers aged 35 or older. Although the birth rate rose among older women during the past decade, most babies were born to women in their twenties. Women aged 35 or older account for only 8 percent of first births and 14 percent of second births. Even among fourth and higher-order births, a 29 percent minority are to women aged 35 or older.

Sixty-five percent of women aged 35 or older who gave birth in 2002 were non-Hispanic white. This percentage is much higher than the non-Hispanic white share of all births, which stood at 56 percent.

Older mothers are more likely to be married than younger mothers. In 2002, only 15 percent of babies born to women aged 35 or older were out-of-wedlock. In contrast, fully 37 percent of babies born to women under age 35 were out-of-wedlock.

Overall, 36 percent of births to women aged 35 or older in 2002 were by Caesarean section. Among women aged 40 or older, 40 percent of births are Caesarean. The figure for women under age 35 is only 24 percent.

■ As the large and vocal Baby-Boom generation ages beyond the childbearing years, menopause has replaced infertility as the hot topic in the reproductive arena.

Most babies are born to women under age 35

(percent distribution of newborns by age of mother, 2002)

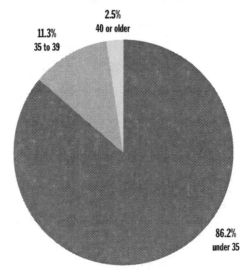

2.5%
40 or older

11.3%
35 to 39

86.2%
under 35

Table 2.5 Birth Rates by Age of Mother, 1990 to 2002

(number of live births per 1,000 women in age group and percent change in rate, 1990–2002)

	15 to 19	20 to 24	25 to 29	30 to 34	35 to 39	40 to 44	45 to 49
2002	43.0	103.6	113.6	91.5	41.4	8.3	0.5
2001	45.3	106.2	113.4	91.9	40.6	8.1	0.5
2000	47.7	109.7	113.5	91.2	39.7	8.0	0.5
1999	48.8	107.9	111.2	87.1	37.8	7.4	0.4
1998	50.3	108.4	110.2	85.2	36.9	7.4	0.4
1997	51.3	107.3	108.3	83.0	35.7	7.1	0.4
1996	53.5	107.8	108.6	82.1	34.9	6.8	0.3
1995	56.0	107.5	108.8	81.1	34.0	6.6	0.3
1994	58.2	109.2	111.0	80.4	33.4	6.4	0.3
1993	59.0	111.3	113.2	79.9	32.7	6.1	0.3
1992	60.3	113.7	115.7	79.6	32.3	5.9	0.3
1991	61.8	115.3	117.2	79.2	31.9	5.5	0.2
1990	59.9	116.5	120.2	80.8	31.7	5.5	0.2

Percent change

1990 to 2002	−28.2%	−11.1%	−5.5%	13.2%	30.6%	50.9%	150.0%

Source: National Center for Health Statistics, Revised Birth and Fertility Rates for the 1990s and New Rates for the Hispanic Populations 2000 and 2001: United States, *National Vital Statistics Report, Vol. 51, No. 12, 2003; calculations by New Strategist*

Table 2.6 Births to Women by Age and Birth Order, 2002

(number and percent distribution of births by age of mother and birth order, 2002)

	total births	first child	second child	third child	fourth or later child
Total births	**4,021,726**	**1,594,921**	**1,306,786**	**675,270**	**434,527**
Under age 35	3,466,524	1,470,943	1,129,611	548,882	308,584
Aged 35 or older	555,202	123,978	177,175	126,388	125,943
Aged 35 to 39	453,927	102,180	148,922	105,468	96,042
Aged 40 to 44	95,788	20,433	26,902	19,991	28,091
Aged 45 to 49	5,224	1,302	1,284	884	1,724
Aged 50 to 54	263	63	67	45	86
PERCENT DISTRIBUTION BY AGE					
Total births	**100.0%**	**100.0%**	**100.0%**	**100.0%**	**100.0%**
Under age 35	86.2	92.2	86.4	81.3	71.0
Aged 35 or older	13.8	7.8	13.6	18.7	29.0
Aged 35 to 39	11.3	6.4	11.4	15.6	22.1
Aged 40 to 44	2.4	1.3	2.1	3.0	6.5
Aged 45 to 49	0.1	0.1	0.1	0.1	0.4
Aged 50 to 54	0.0	0.0	0.0	0.0	0.0
PERCENT DISTRIBUTION BY BIRTH ORDER					
Total births	**100.0%**	**39.7%**	**32.5%**	**16.8%**	**10.8%**
Under age 35	100.0	42.4	32.6	15.8	8.9
Aged 35 or older	100.0	22.3	31.9	22.8	22.7
Aged 35 to 39	100.0	22.5	32.8	23.2	21.2
Aged 40 to 44	100.0	21.3	28.1	20.9	29.3
Aged 45 to 49	100.0	24.9	24.6	16.9	33.0
Aged 50 to 54	100.0	24.0	25.5	17.1	32.7

Note: Numbers will not add to total because not stated is not included.
Source: National Center for Health Statistics, Births: Final Data for 2002, *National Vital Statistics Reports, Vol. 52, No. 10, 2003; calculations by New Strategist*

Table 2.7   Births by Age, Race, and Hispanic Origin of Mother, 2002

(number and percent distribution of births by age, race, and Hispanic origin of mother, 2002)

		race				Hispanic origin	
	total	American Indian	Asian	black	white	Hispanic	non-Hispanic white
Total births	**4,021,726**	**42,368**	**210,907**	**593,691**	**3,174,760**	**876,642**	**2,298,156**
Under age 35	3,466,524	38,660	171,031	533,284	2,723,549	789,586	1,935,239
Aged 35 or older	555,202	3,708	39,876	60,407	451,211	87,056	362,917
Aged 35 to 39	453,927	2,976	32,730	48,388	369,833	71,480	297,436
Aged 40 to 44	95,788	701	6,716	11,443	76,928	14,809	61,853
Aged 45 to 49	5,224	30	397	562	4,235	751	3,444
Aged 50 to 54	263	1	33	14	215	16	184
PERCENT DISTRIBUTION BY AGE							
Total births	**100.0%**	**100.0%**	**100.0%**	**100.0%**	**100.0%**	**100.0%**	**100.0%**
Under age 35	86.2	91.2	81.1	89.8	85.8	90.1	84.2
Aged 35 or older	13.8	8.8	18.9	10.2	14.2	9.9	15.8
Aged 35 to 39	11.3	7.0	15.5	8.2	11.6	8.2	12.9
Aged 40 to 44	2.4	1.7	3.2	1.9	2.4	1.7	2.7
Aged 45 to 49	0.1	0.1	0.2	0.1	0.1	0.1	0.1
Aged 50 to 54	0.0	0.0	0.0	0.0	0.0	0.0	0.0
PERCENT DISTRIBUTION BY RACE AND HISPANIC ORIGIN							
Total births	**100.0%**	**1.1%**	**5.2%**	**14.8%**	**78.9%**	**21.8%**	**57.1%**
Under age 35	100.0	1.1	4.9	15.4	78.6	22.8	55.8
Aged 35 or older	100.0	0.7	7.2	10.9	81.3	15.7	65.4
Aged 35 to 39	100.0	0.7	7.2	10.7	81.5	15.7	65.5
Aged 40 to 44	100.0	0.7	7.0	11.9	80.3	15.5	64.6
Aged 45 to 49	100.0	0.6	7.6	10.8	81.1	14.4	65.9
Aged 50 to 54	100.0	0.4	12.5	5.3	81.7	6.1	70.0

Note: Numbers will not add to total because Hispanics may be of any race.
Source: National Center for Health Statistics, Births: Final Data for 2002, National Vital Statistics Reports, Vol. 52, No. 10, 2003;
calculations by New Strategist

Table 2.8 Births by Age, Marital Status, Race, and Hispanic Origin of Mother, 2002

(total number of births and number and percent to unmarried women aged 35 or older, by race and Hispanic origin of mother, 2002)

	total	race American Indian	Asian	black	white	Hispanic origin Hispanic	non-Hispanic white
Total births	**4,021,726**	**42,368**	**210,907**	**593,691**	**3,174,760**	**876,642**	**2,298,156**
Under age 35	3,466,524	38,660	171,031	533,284	2,723,549	789,586	1,935,239
Aged 35 or older	555,202	3,708	39,876	60,407	451,211	87,056	362,917
Aged 35 to 39	453,927	2,976	32,730	48,388	369,833	71,480	297,436
Aged 40 or older	101,275	732	7,146	12,019	81,378	15,576	65,481
BIRTHS TO UNMARRIED WOMEN							
Total births	**1,365,966**	**25,297**	**31,344**	**404,864**	**904,461**	**381,466**	**528,535**
Under age 35	1,282,456	23,823	28,493	381,146	848,994	358,407	495,742
Aged 35 or older	83,510	1,474	2,851	23,718	55,467	23,059	32,793
Aged 35 to 39	66,036	1,176	2,218	18,958	43,684	18,566	25,472
Aged 40 or older	17,474	298	633	4,760	11,783	4,493	7,321
PERCENT OF BIRTHS TO UNMARRIED WOMEN							
Total births	**34.0%**	**59.7%**	**14.9%**	**68.2%**	**28.5%**	**43.5%**	**23.0%**
Under age 35	37.0	61.6	16.7	71.5	31.2	45.4	25.6
Aged 35 or older	15.0	39.8	7.1	39.3	12.3	26.5	9.0
Aged 35 to 39	14.5	39.5	6.8	39.2	11.8	26.0	8.6
Aged 40 or older	17.3	40.7	8.9	39.6	14.5	28.8	11.2

Note: Births by race and Hispanic origin will not add to total because Hispanics may be of any race, and not all races are shown.
Source: National Center for Health Statistics, **Births: Final Data for 2002,** *National Vital Statistics Reports, Vol. 52, No. 10, 2003; calculations by New Strategist*

Table 2.9 Birth Delivery Method by Age, 2002

(number and percent distribution of births by age of mother and method of delivery, 2002)

	total	vaginal total	vaginal after previous Caesarean	Caesarean total	Caesarean first	Caesarean repeat
Total births	**4,021,726**	**2,958,423**	**59,248**	**1,043,846**	**634,426**	**409,420**
Under age 35	3,466,524	2,605,532	46,686	844,830	528,716	316,114
Aged 35 or older	555,202	352,891	12,562	199,016	105,710	93,306
Aged 35 to 39	453,927	293,251	10,278	158,005	82,497	75,508
Aged 40 or older	101,275	59,640	2,284	41,011	23,213	17,798
PERCENT DISTRIBUTION BY AGE						
Total births	**100.0%**	**100.0%**	**100.0%**	**100.0%**	**100.0%**	**100.0%**
Under age 35	86.2	88.1	78.8	80.9	83.3	77.2
Aged 35 or older	13.8	11.9	21.2	19.1	16.7	22.8
Aged 35 to 39	11.3	9.9	17.3	15.1	1.3	18.4
Aged 40 or older	2.5	2.0	3.9	3.9	3.7	4.3
PERCENT DISTRIBUTION BY DELIVERY METHOD						
Total births	**100.0%**	**73.6%**	**1.5%**	**26.0%**	**15.8%**	**10.2%**
Under age 35	100.0	75.2	1.3	24.4	15.3	9.1
Aged 35 or older	100.0	63.6	2.3	35.8	19.0	16.8
Aged 35 to 39	100.0	64.6	2.3	34.8	18.2	16.6
Aged 40 or older	100.0	58.9	2.3	40.5	22.9	17.6

Note: Numbers will not add to total because not stated is not included.
Source: National Center for Health Statistics, Births: Final Data for 2002, *National Vital Statistics Reports, Vol. 52, No. 10, 2003;*
calculations by New Strategist

About One in Four Boomers Smokes, Two-Thirds Drink

Among those who smoke, many have tried to quit.

The percentage of Americans who smoke cigarettes is down sharply from what it was a few decades ago. Nevertheless, in 2002, 23 percent of people aged 18 or older were current smokers. The figure peaks among 18-to-24-year-olds at 31 percent. Among Baby Boomers, 25 to 27 percent are smokers. Nearly half of smokers aged 35 to 54 have tried to quit on at least one day in the past twelve months.

Drinking alcohol is much more popular than smoking. Overall, 63 percent of people aged 18 or older are current drinkers, with men much more likely than women to drink (69 versus 57 percent). The proportion of people who drink alcohol peaks in the 25-to-44 age group, then declines with age. A minority of people aged 65 or older are drinkers.

Although many Boomers have experience with illicit drugs, particularly marijuana, few continue to use them. Only 3 to 9 percent of people aged 35 to 54 have used illicit drugs in the past month. But the majority has used them at some point, and more than 10 percent have done so in the past year.

■ As Boomers age and health concerns become increasingly important, the proportions of smokers and drinkers will decline.

Many Boomers have tried to quit smoking

(percent of people aged 35 to 54 who smoke cigarettes and share of smokers who have tried to quit in the past twelve months, 2002)

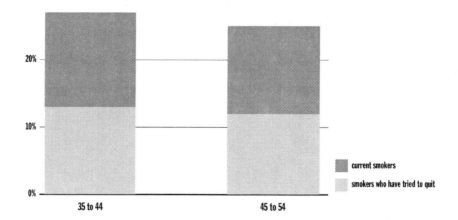

Table 2.10 **Cigarette Smoking and Attempts to Quit by Ae, 2002**

(percent of people aged 18 or older who currently smoke cigarettes and percent of smokers who quit smoking for at least one day in the past twelve months, by age, 2002)

	current smokers	smokers who quit on one or more days
Total people	**23.0%**	**51.8%**
Aged 18 to 24	31.2	65.4
Aged 25 to 34	25.9	56.9
Aged 35 to 44	27.2	49.3
Aged 45 to 54	24.8	47.9
Aged 55 to 64	20.8	44.2
Aged 65 or older	10.0	42.0

Source: Centers for Disease Control and Prevention, Behavioral Risk Factor Surveillance System Prevalence Data, 2002; Internet site http://apps.nccd.cdc.gov/brfss/index.asp

Table 2.11 Alcohol Use by Age, 2001

(percent of people aged 18 or older who are current drinkers, by age and sex, 2001)

	total	men	women
Total people	**62.5%**	**68.8%**	**56.8%**
Aged 18 to 24	63.6	69.6	57.7
Aged 25 to 44	70.8	76.8	65.0
Aged 45 to 54	65.6	70.1	61.2
Aged 55 to 64	57.6	64.2	51.6
Aged 65 or older	42.0	50.9	35.5
Aged 65 to 74	45.8	55.2	38.2
Aged 75 or older	37.6	45.1	32.6

Source: National Center for Health Statistics, Health, United States, 2003, *Internet site http://www.cdc.gov/nchs/hus.htm*

Table 2.12 Drug Use by Age, 2002

(percent of people aged 12 or older who ever used any illicit drug, who used an illicit drug in the past year, and who used an illicit drug in the past month, by age, 2002)

	ever used	used in past year	used in past month
Total people	**46.0%**	**14.9%**	**8.3%**
Aged 12 to 17	30.9	22.2	11.6
Aged 18 to 25	59.8	35.5	20.2
Aged 26 to 29	57.4	22.4	12.8
Aged 30 to 34	59.0	17.2	8.8
Aged 35 to 39	61.0	15.5	8.6
Aged 40 to 44	66.4	14.4	7.8
Aged 45 to 49	60.9	12.3	7.5
Aged 50 to 54	51.1	6.5	3.4
Aged 55 to 59	35.0	3.3	1.9
Aged 60 to 64	23.7	4.1	2.5
Aged 65 or older	9.2	1.3	0.8

Note: Illicit drugs include marijuana/hashish, cocaine (including crack), heroin, hallucinogens, inhalants, or any prescription-type psychotherapeutic used nonmedically.
Source: SAMHSA, Office of Applied Studies, National Survey on Drug Use and Health, 2002; Internet site http://www.samhsa.gov/

Many 35-to-54-Year-Olds Lack Health Insurance

Thirteen million 35-to-54-year-olds are not covered by health insurance, accounting for 32 percent of the nation's uninsured.

Among all Americans, 44 million lacked health insurance in 2002, or 15 percent of the population. The figure is an even higher 18 percent among 35-to-44-year-olds, while it's 14 percent among 45-to-54-year-olds.

Seventy-two percent of 35-to-54-year-olds have employment-based health insurance coverage, a figure that has been slipping as fewer employers offer such coverage. Only 10 percent of 35-to-54-year-olds have government health insurance, including 6 percent with Medicaid coverage and 3 percent with military insurance.

Middle-aged Americans without health insurance are vulnerable to financial catastrophe. Chronic illness becomes much more common as people enter their fifties. With one in seven 45-to-54-year-olds lacking insurance, a financial crisis looms for many.

■ Baby Boomers have never suffered silently. As the generation enters the age of vulnerability, expect to hear increasingly strident demands for reform in health care financing.

Many Americans do not have health insurance coverage

(percent of people aged 18 or older without health insurance coverage, by age, 2002)

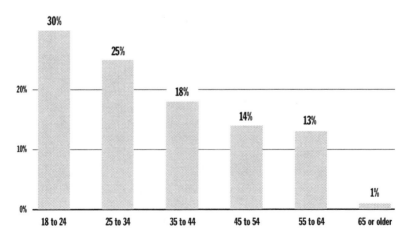

Table 2.13 Health Insurance Coverage by Age, 2002

(number and percent distribution of people by age and health insurance coverage status, 2002; numbers in thousands)

	total	covered by private or government health insurance							not covered
		private health insurance			government health insurance				
		total	total	employment based	total	Medicaid	Medicare	military	
Total people	285,933	242,360	198,973	175,296	73,624	33,246	38,448	10,063	43,574
Under age 18	73,312	64,781	49,473	46,182	19,662	17,526	524	2,148	8,531
Aged 18 to 24	27,438	19,310	16,562	13,429	3,738	2,909	183	779	8,128
Aged 25 to 34	39,243	29,474	26,492	24,800	3,944	2,801	455	922	9,769
Aged 35 to 44	44,074	36,292	33,240	31,180	4,240	2,728	881	1,121	7,781
Aged 45 to 54	40,234	34,648	31,724	29,617	4,345	2,227	1,382	1,351	5,586
Aged 55 to 64	27,399	23,879	20,797	18,505	4,882	1,773	2,392	1,482	3,521
Aged 65 or older	34,234	33,976	20,685	11,583	32,813	3,283	32,631	2,259	258
PERCENT DISTRIBUTION BY AGE									
Total people	100.0%	100.0%	100.0%	100.0%	100.0%	100.0%	100.0%	100.0%	100.0%
Under age 18	25.6	26.7	24.9	26.3	26.7	52.7	1.4	21.3	19.6
Aged 18 to 24	9.6	8.0	8.3	7.7	5.1	8.7	0.5	7.7	18.7
Aged 25 to 34	13.7	12.2	13.3	14.1	5.4	8.4	1.2	9.2	22.4
Aged 35 to 44	15.4	15.0	16.7	17.8	5.8	8.2	2.3	11.1	17.9
Aged 45 to 54	14.1	14.3	15.9	16.9	5.9	6.7	3.6	13.4	12.8
Aged 55 to 64	9.6	9.9	10.5	10.6	6.6	5.3	6.2	14.7	8.1
Aged 65 or older	12.0	14.0	10.4	6.6	44.6	9.9	84.9	22.4	0.6
PERCENT DISTRIBUTION BY TYPE OF COVERAGE									
Total people	100.0%	84.8%	69.6%	61.3%	25.7%	11.6%	13.4%	3.5%	15.2%
Under age 18	100.0	88.4	67.5	63.0	26.8	23.9	0.7	2.9	11.6
Aged 18 to 24	100.0	70.4	60.4	48.9	13.6	10.6	0.7	2.8	29.6
Aged 25 to 34	100.0	75.1	67.5	63.2	10.1	7.1	1.2	2.3	24.9
Aged 35 to 44	100.0	82.3	75.4	70.7	9.6	6.2	2.0	2.5	17.7
Aged 45 to 54	100.0	86.1	78.8	73.6	10.8	5.5	3.4	3.4	13.9
Aged 55 to 64	100.0	87.2	75.9	67.5	17.8	6.5	8.7	5.4	12.9
Aged 65 or older	100.0	99.2	60.4	33.8	95.8	9.6	95.3	6.6	0.8

Note: Numbers may not add to total because some people have more than one type of health insurance coverage.
Source: Bureau of the Census, 2003 Current Population Survey, Internet site http://www.census.gov/hhes/hlthins/historic/hihistt2.html; calculations by New Strategist

Health Problems Increase in the 45-to-64 Age Group

Lower back pain is the most common health condition among the middle-aged, but hypertension and arthritis are not far behind.

Thirty-five percent of Americans aged 45 to 64 have experienced lower back pain for at least one full day in the past three months, making it the most common health condition in this broad age group. Hypertension is second, with 29 percent of 45-to-64-year-olds having been told by a health professional that they have this problem. Arthritis is a close third, at 27 percent.

The percentage of people experiencing health problems rises, sometimes steeply, in the 45-to-64 age group. Only 7 percent of 18-to-44-year-olds have hypertension, for example, versus 29 percent of those aged 45 to 64. Arthritis rises from 12 percent among younger adults to 27 percent in the age group. The prevalence of hearing problems rises from 9 percent among younger adults to 21 percent among 45-to-64-year-olds.

As Americans became more aware of the problems associated with high cholesterol over the past few decades, rates have dropped in most age groups. The same cannot be said for high blood pressure. More than 30 percent of men and women aged 45 to 54 had high blood pressure in 1999–2000, significantly more than in 1988–94.

■ As the Baby-Boom generation ages into its fifties and sixties, the number of people with heart disease, arthritis, and hearing problems will rise.

The percentage of people with arthritis rises with age

(percent of people with arthritis, by age, 2001)

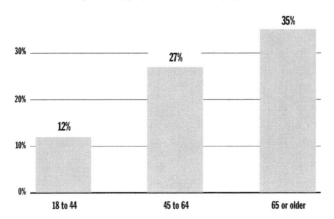

Table 2.14 Number of People Aged 18 or Older with Selected Health Conditions, 2001

(number of people aged 18 or older with selected health conditions, by type of condition and age, 2001; numbers in thousands)

	total	18 to 44	45 to 64	65 or older
Total people	**203,832**	**108,436**	**62,531**	**32,864**
Heart disease	23,482	4,996	8,173	10,313
Coronary	12,719	1,057	4,748	6,914
Hypertension	41,764	7,604	17,900	16,260
Stroke	4,836	478	1,416	2,942
Emphysema	2,984	200	1,100	1,684
Asthma	22,169	12,795	6,508	2,866
Hay fever	20,405	10,834	7,218	2,353
Sinusitis	35,462	17,203	13,281	4,979
Chronic bronchitis	11,199	4,913	4,074	2,211
Cancer	14,003	2,379	5,151	6,473
Breast cancer	2,256	176	987	1,092
Cervical cancer	1,172	597	423	151
Prostate cancer	1,499	3	225	1,274
Diabetes	13,006	2,167	5,834	5,005
Ulcers	18,901	7,025	7,211	4,665
Kidney disease	3,301	1,019	1,124	1,158
Liver disease	2,697	927	1,337	432
Arthritic symptoms	41,185	12,987	16,850	11,348
Migraines, severe headaches	33,899	21,616	10,027	2,255
Pain in neck	34,084	15,801	13,117	5,167
Pain in lower back	63,253	30,783	22,010	10,460
Pain in face or jaw	10,789	5,991	3,657	1,141
Hearing				
Good	168,207	99,096	49,678	19,433
A little trouble	28,411	8,199	10,822	9,389
A lot of trouble or deaf	6,996	1,116	1,988	3,893
Vision				
No trouble	183,272	101,587	54,778	26,907
Trouble	20,378	6,786	7,675	5,917
Absence of teeth	17,211	2,370	5,793	9,047
Sadness				
All or most of the time	6,862	3,455	2,337	1,070
Some of the time	19,529	9,692	6,319	3,519
Hopelessness				
All or most of the time	4,377	2,275	1,491	611
Some of the time	9,038	4,937	2,900	1,202
Worthlessness				
All or most of the time	3,850	1,824	1,432	594
Some of the time	7,031	3,516	2,442	1,073

	total	18 to 44	45 to 64	65 or older
Everything is an effort				
All or most of the time	11,464	6,319	3,596	1,549
Some of the time	18,362	10,285	5,455	2,622
Nervousness				
All or most of the time	9,147	4,540	3,177	1,431
Some of the time	28,279	15,921	8,671	3,687
Restlessness				
All or most of the time	11,171	6,187	3,563	1,421
Some of the time	26,962	15,001	8,387	3,573

Note: From heart disease through arthritic symptoms, respondents were asked whether they had been told by a doctor or other health professional in the past twelve months whether they had the condition; from migraines through pain in face or jaw, respondents were asked whether they had experienced pain for one full day or more during the past three months; from sadness through restlessness, respondents were asked how often they had the feeling in the past thirty days; numbers will not add to total because people may have more than one condition.
Source: National Center for Health Statistics, Summary Health Statistics for U.S. Adults: National Health Interview Survey, 2001, *Series 10, No. 218, 2004; calculations by New Strategist*

Table 2.15   Percent of People Aged 18 or Older with Selected Health Conditions, 2001

(percent of people aged 18 or older with selected health conditions, by type of condition and age, 2001)

	total	18 to 44	45 to 64	65 or older
Total people	**100.0%**	**100.0%**	**100.0%**	**100.0%**
Heart disease	11.5	4.6	13.1	31.4
Coronary	6.2	1.0	7.6	21.0
Hypertension	20.5	7.0	28.6	49.5
Stroke	2.4	0.4	2.3	9.0
Emphysema	1.5	0.2	1.8	5.1
Asthma	10.9	11.8	10.4	8.7
Hay fever	10.0	10.0	11.5	7.2
Sinusitis	17.4	15.9	21.2	15.2
Chronic bronchitis	5.5	4.5	6.5	6.7
Cancer	6.9	2.2	8.2	19.7
Breast cancer	1.1	0.2	1.6	3.3
Cervical cancer	0.6	0.6	0.7	0.5
Prostate cancer	0.7	0.0	0.4	3.9
Diabetes	6.4	2.0	9.3	15.2
Ulcers	9.3	6.5	11.5	14.2
Kidney disease	1.6	0.9	1.8	3.5
Liver disease	1.3	0.9	2.1	1.3
Arthritic symptoms	20.2	12.0	26.9	34.5
Migraines, severe headaches	16.6	19.9	16.0	6.9
Pain in neck	16.7	14.6	21.0	15.7
Pain in lower back	31.0	28.4	35.2	31.8
Pain in face or jaw	5.3	5.5	5.8	3.5
Hearing				
Good	82.5	91.4	79.4	59.1
A little trouble	13.9	7.6	17.3	28.6
A lot of trouble or deaf	3.4	1.0	3.2	11.8
Vision				
No trouble	89.9	93.7	87.6	81.9
Trouble	10.0	6.3	12.3	18.0
Absence of teeth	8.4	2.2	9.3	27.5
Sadness				
All or most of the time	3.4	3.2	3.7	3.3
Some of the time	9.6	8.9	10.1	10.7
Hopelessness				
All or most of the time	2.1	2.1	2.4	1.9
Some of the time	4.4	4.6	4.6	3.7
Worthlessness				
All or most of the time	1.9	1.7	2.3	1.8
Some of the time	3.4	3.2	3.9	3.3

	total	18 to 44	45 to 64	65 or older
Everything is an effort				
All or most of the time	5.6%	5.8%	5.8%	4.7%
Some of the time	9.0	9.5	8.7	8.0
Nervousness				
All or most of the time	4.5	4.2	5.1	4.4
Some of the time	13.9	14.7	13.9	11.2
Restlessness				
All or most of the time	5.5	5.7	5.7	4.3
Some of the time	13.2	13.8	13.4	10.9

Note: From heart disease through arthritic symptoms, respondents were asked whether they had been told by a doctor or other health professional in the past twelve months whether they had the condition; from migraines through pain in face or jaw, respondents were asked whether they had experienced pain for one full day or more during the past three months; from sadness through restlessness, respondents were asked how often they had the feeling in the past thirty days; numbers will not add to total because people may have more than one condition.
Source: National Center for Health Statistics, Summary Health Statistics for U.S. Adults: National Health Interview Survey, 2001, *Series 10, No. 218, 2004; calculations by New Strategist*

Table 2.16 Percent Distribution of People Aged 18 or Older with Selected Health Conditions, 2001

(percent distribution of people aged 18 or older with selected health conditions, by type of condition and age, 2001)

	total	18 to 44	45 to 64	65 or older
Total people	**100.0%**	**53.2%**	**30.7%**	**16.1%**
Heart disease	100.0	21.3	34.8	43.9
Coronary	100.0	8.3	37.3	54.4
Hypertension	100.0	18.2	42.9	38.9
Stroke	100.0	9.9	29.3	60.8
Emphysema	100.0	6.7	36.9	56.4
Asthma	100.0	57.7	29.4	12.9
Hay fever	100.0	53.1	35.4	11.5
Sinusitis	100.0	48.5	37.5	14.0
Chronic bronchitis	100.0	43.9	36.4	19.7
Cancer	100.0	17.0	36.8	46.2
Breast cancer	100.0	7.8	43.8	48.4
Cervical cancer	100.0	50.9	36.1	12.9
Prostate cancer	100.0	0.2	15.0	85.0
Diabetes	100.0	16.7	44.9	38.5
Ulcers	100.0	37.2	38.2	24.7
Kidney disease	100.0	30.9	34.1	35.1
Liver disease	100.0	34.4	49.6	16.0
Arthritic symptoms	100.0	31.5	40.9	27.6
Migraines, severe headaches	100.0	63.8	29.6	6.7
Pain in neck	100.0	46.4	38.5	15.2
Pain in lower back	100.0	48.7	34.8	16.5
Pain in face or jaw	100.0	55.5	33.9	10.6
Hearing				
Good	100.0	58.9	29.5	11.6
A little trouble	100.0	28.9	38.1	33.0
A lot of trouble or deaf	100.0	16.0	28.4	55.6
Vision				
No trouble	100.0	55.4	29.9	14.7
Trouble	100.0	33.3	37.7	29.0
Absence of teeth	100.0	13.8	33.7	52.6
Sadness				
All or most of the time	100.0	50.3	34.1	15.6
Some of the time	100.0	49.6	32.4	18.0
Hopelessness				
All or most of the time	100.0	52.0	34.1	14.0
Some of the time	100.0	54.6	32.1	13.3

	total	18 to 44	45 to 64	65 or older
Worthlessness				
All or most of the time	100.0%	47.4%	37.2%	15.4%
Some of the time	100.0	50.0	34.7	15.3
Everything is an effort				
All or most of the time	100.0	55.1	31.4	13.5
Some of the time	100.0	56.0	29.7	14.3
Nervousness				
All or most of the time	100.0	49.6	34.7	15.6
Some of the time	100.0	56.3	30.7	13.0
Restlessness				
All or most of the time	100.0	55.4	31.9	12.7
Some of the time	100.0	55.6	31.1	13.3

Note: From heart disease through arthritic symptoms, respondents were asked whether they had been told by a doctor or other health professional in the past twelve months whether they had the condition; from migraines through pain in face or jaw, respondents were asked whether they had experienced pain for one full day or more during the past three months; from sadness through restlessness, respondents were asked how often they had the feeling in the past thirty days; numbers will not add to total because people may have more than one condition.
Source: National Center for Health Statistics, Summary Health Statistics for U.S. Adults: National Health Interview Survey, 2001, *Series 10, No. 218, 2004; calculations by New Strategist*

Table 2.17 High Cholesterol by Age, 1988–1994 and 1999–2000

(percent of people aged 20 or older who have high serum cholesterol, by sex and age, 1988–1994 and 1999–2000; percentage point change, 1988–1994 to 1999–2000)

	1999–00	1988–94	percentage point change
TOTAL PEOPLE	**17.8%**	**19.6%**	**–1.8**
Total men	**16.7**	**17.7**	**–1.0**
Aged 20 to 34	11.0	8.2	2.8
Aged 35 to 44	21.1	19.4	1.7
Aged 45 to 54	22.9	26.6	–3.7
Aged 55 to 64	16.5	28.0	–11.5
Aged 65 to 74	19.2	21.9	–2.7
Aged 75 or older	10.1	20.4	–10.3
Total women	**18.7**	**21.3**	**–2.6**
Aged 20 to 34	9.3	7.3	2.0
Aged 35 to 44	12.8	12.3	0.5
Aged 45 to 54	23.7	26.7	–3.0
Aged 55 to 64	26.2	40.9	–14.7
Aged 65 to 74	37.4	41.3	–3.9
Aged 75 or older	27.6	38.2	–10.6

Note: High cholesterol is defined as 240 mg/dL or more.
Source: National Center for Health Statistics, Health, United States, 2003, Internet site http://www.cdc.gov/nchs/hus.htm; calculations by New Strategist

Table 2.18 High Blood Pressure by Age, 1988–1994 and 1999–2000

(percent of people aged 20 or older who have hypertension, by sex and age, 1988–1994 and 1999–2000; percentage point change, 1988–1994 to 1999–2000)

	1999–00	1988–94	percentage point change
TOTAL PEOPLE	**28.9%**	**24.1%**	**4.8**
Total men	**27.4**	**23.8**	**3.6**
Aged 20 to 34	9.8	7.1	2.7
Aged 35 to 44	17.1	17.1	0.0
Aged 45 to 54	32.3	29.2	3.1
Aged 55 to 64	44.1	40.6	3.5
Aged 65 to 74	59.9	54.4	5.5
Aged 75 or older	68.8	60.4	8.4
Total women	**30.3**	**24.4**	**5.9**
Aged 20 to 34	–	2.9	–
Aged 35 to 44	16.0	11.2	4.8
Aged 45 to 54	30.5	23.9	6.6
Aged 55 to 64	53.0	42.5	10.5
Aged 65 to 74	70.3	56.1	14.2
Aged 75 or older	84.1	73.5	10.6

Note: A person with hypertension is someone with systolic pressure of at least 140 mmHg or diastolic pressure of at least 90 mmHg, or who takes antihypertensive medication. (–) means sample is too small to make reliable estimate.
Source: National Center for Health Statistics, Health, United States, 2003 (updated tables), Internet site http://www.cdc.gov/nchs/hus.htm; calculations by New Strategist

Millions of Working-Age Americans Are Disabled

Overall, one in five Americans of working age has a disability.

Population surveys and censuses measure disability in many different ways, but the results are the same: The percentage of Americans who are disabled rises with age. According to the 2000 census, 19 percent of the U.S. population is disabled in some way. Among children under age 16, the figure is just 6 percent. It rises to 19 percent among people aged 16 to 64, and reaches 42 percent among people aged 65 or older.

A survey by the National Center for Health Statistics finds the percentage of people who have limited physical functioning stands at 17 percent among those aged 18 to 44, rises to 34 percent in the 45-to-64 age group and peaks at 64 percent among those aged 65 or older. But the proportion of Americans who are severely limited is much smaller, ranging from 5 to 36 percent.

The Census Bureau's Current Population Survey reports that 9 percent of people aged 35 to 44 had a work disability in 2002—meaning a health problem that prevented them from working or limited the amount or kind of work they can do. The figure is a larger 13 percent among 45-to-54-year-olds and rises to 22 percent among those aged 55 to 64. The more educated the worker, the less likely he or she is to have a work disability.

People with AIDS are often counted among the nation's disabled. As of mid-2002, more than 800,000 people had been diagnosed with AIDS, most of them Baby-Boom men. Fully 59 percent of those with AIDS are men aged 30 to 49.

■ Although Boomers are more health conscious than older generations of Americans, many are already experiencing disabilities. As they age, the percentage of Boomers with disabilities will only increase.

Work disabilities rise in middle age

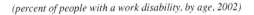

(percent of people with a work disability, by age, 2002)

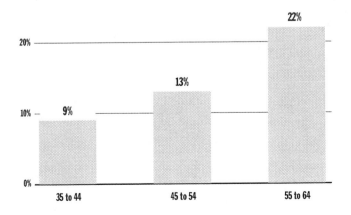

Table 2.19 Disability Status of People by Age, 2000 Census

(total number of people aged 5 or older and number and percent with disabilities, by age and type of disability, 2000)

	total		female		male	
	number	percent	number	percent	number	percent
TOTAL PEOPLE	257,167,527	100.0%	132,530,702	100.0%	124,636,825	100.0%
With any disability	49,746,248	19.3	25,306,717	19.1	24,439,531	19.6
TOTAL AGED 5–15	45,133,667	100.0	22,008,343	100.0	23,125,324	100.0
With any disability	2,614,919	5.8	948,689	4.3	1,666,230	7.2
Sensory	442,894	1.0	200,689	0.9	242,706	1.0
Physical	455,461	1.0	203,609	0.9	251,852	1.1
Mental	2,078,502	4.6	691,109	3.1	1,387,393	6.0
Self-care	419,018	0.9	174,194	0.8	244,824	1.1
TOTAL AGED 16–64	178,687,234	100.0	91,116,651	100.0	87,570,583	100.0
With any disability	33,153,211	18.6	16,014,192	17.6	17,139,019	19.6
Sensory	4,123,902	2.3	1,735,781	1.9	2,388,121	2.7
Physical	11,150,365	6.2	5,870,634	6.4	5,279,731	6.0
Mental	6,764,439	3.8	3,329,808	3.7	3,434,631	3.9
Self-care	3,149,875	1.8	1,686,691	1.9	1,463,184	1.7
Difficulty going outside the home	11,414,508	6.4	5,845,146	6.4	5,569,362	6.4
Employment disability	21,287,570	11.9	9,913,784	10.9	11,373,786	13.0
TOTAL AGED 65+	33,346,626	100.0	19,405,708	100.0	13,940,918	100.0
With any disability	13,978,118	41.9	8,343,836	43.0	5,634,282	40.4
Sensory	4,738,479	14.2	2,561,263	13.2	2,177,216	15.6
Physical	9,545,680	28.6	5,955,541	30.7	3,590,139	25.8
Mental	3,592,912	10.8	2,212,852	11.4	1,380,060	9.9
Self-care	3,183,840	9.5	2,138,930	11.0	1,044,910	7.5
Difficulty going outside the home	6,795,517	20.4	4,456,389	23.0	2,339,128	16.8

Note: Sensory disabilities are long-lasting impairments of vision and hearing; physical disabilities are limitations such as difficulty walking or climbing stairs; mental disabilities are difficulty with cognitive tasks such as learning, remembering, and concentrating; self-care disabilities are difficulty taking care of personal needs like dressing and bathing; employment disabilities are physical, mental, or emotional conditions making it difficult for people to work at a job; difficulty going outside the home is difficulty shopping or visiting the doctor.
Source: Bureau of the Census, Disability Status: 2000, *Census 2000 Brief, 2003*

Table 2.20 People with Limitations in Physical Functioning by Age, 2001

(number and percent distribution of people aged 18 or older with limitations in physical functioning, by type of limitation and age, 2001; numbers in thousands)

	total	18 to 44	45 to 64	65 or older
TOTAL PEOPLE	**203,832**	**108,436**	**62,531**	**32,864**
Total with any difficulty	**59,567**	**18,211**	**21,386**	**21,026**
Moderate	**32,951**	**12,646**	**11,622**	**9,150**
Severe	**26,616**	**5,565**	**9,764**	**11,876**
Mobility difficulty	41,217	10,476	14,593	16,704
Moderate	22,578	7,439	7,762	7,562
Severe	18,639	3,037	6,831	9,142
Flexibility/strength difficulty	50,496	14,377	18,356	18,509
Moderate	29,064	10,227	10,343	9,042
Severe	21,432	4,150	8,013	9,467
Social/leisure difficulty	19,706	6,439	7,819	5,856
Moderate	14,112	4,857	5,406	4,210
Severe	5,594	1,582	2,413	1,646
PERCENT DISTRIBUTION BY AGE				
TOTAL PEOPLE	**100.0%**	**53.2%**	**30.7%**	**16.1%**
Total with any difficulty	**100.0**	**30.6**	**35.9**	**31.8**
Moderate	**100.0**	**38.4**	**35.3**	**24.7**
Severe	**100.0**	**20.9**	**36.7**	**40.7**
Mobility difficulty	100.0	25.4	35.4	36.6
Moderate	100.0	32.9	34.4	30.0
Severe	100.0	16.3	36.6	44.8
Flexibility/strength difficulty	100.0	28.5	36.4	33.0
Moderate	100.0	35.2	35.6	27.5
Severe	100.0	19.4	37.4	40.8
Social/leisure difficulty	100.0	32.7	39.7	26.4
Moderate	100.0	34.4	38.3	26.0
Severe	100.0	28.3	43.1	27.5

PERCENT DISTRIBUTION BY TYPE OF LIMITATION	total	18 to 44	45 to 64	65 or older
TOTAL PEOPLE	100.0%	100.0%	100.0%	100.0%
Total with any difficulty	**29.2**	**16.8**	**34.2**	**64.0**
Moderate	**16.2**	**11.7**	**18.6**	**27.8**
Severe	**13.1**	**5.1**	**15.6**	**36.1**
Mobility difficulty	20.2	9.7	23.3	50.8
Moderate	11.1	6.9	12.4	23.0
Severe	9.1	2.8	10.9	27.8
Flexibility/strength difficulty	24.8	13.3	29.4	56.3
Moderate	14.3	9.4	16.5	27.5
Severe	10.5	3.8	12.8	28.8
Social/leisure difficulty	9.7	5.9	12.5	17.8
Moderate	6.9	4.5	8.6	12.8
Severe	2.7	1.5	3.9	5.0

Note: Mobility activities include walking a quarter of a mile or three city blocks; standing for two hours; and climbing 10 steps without resting. Flexibility/strength activities include stooping/bending/kneeling; reaching over one's head; using one's fingers to grasp or handle small objects; lifting or carrying a 10-pound object; and pushing or pulling a large object. Social/leisure activities include sitting for two hours; going shopping, to the movies, or attending sporting events; participating in social activities such as visiting friends, attending clubs or meeting; and activities to relax at home or for leisure (such as reaching, watching TV, etc.). Moderate difficulty includes the response categories "only a little difficult" or "somewhat difficult." Severe difficulty includes the categories "very difficult" or "can't do at all."
Source: National Center for Health Statistics, Summary Health Statistics for U.S. Adults: National Health Interview Survey, 2001, *Series 10, No. 218, 2004*

Table 2.21 People Aged 35 to 64 with a Work Disability, 2002

(number and percent of people aged 16 to 64 and 35 to 64 with a work disability, by education and severity of disability, 2002; numbers in thousands)

	total	with a work disability total number	total percent	not severe number	not severe percent	severe number	severe percent
Total aged 16 to 64	**183,018**	**18,120**	**9.9%**	**5,487**	**3.0%**	**12,632**	**6.9%**
Not a high school graduate	33,185	5041	15.2	801	2.4	4,240	12.8
High school graduate	54,676	6,579	12.0	1,878	3.4	4,701	8.6
Associate's degree or some college	50,118	4,442	8.9	1,776	3.5	2,666	5.3
Bachelor's degree or more	45,038	2058	4.6	1,032	2.3	1,026	2.3
Total aged 35 to 44	**44,003**	**3,839**	**8.7**	**1,174**	**2.7**	**2,665**	**6.1**
Not a high school graduate	5,138	946	18.4	131	2.5	817	15.9
High school graduate	14,258	1,495	10.5	448	3.1	1,047	7.3
Associate's degree or some college	12,077	1,004	8.3	398	3.3	606	5.0
Bachelor's degree or more	12,529	393	3.1	198	1.6	195	1.6
Total aged 45 to 54	**39,485**	**5,054**	**12.8**	**1,553**	**3.9**	**3,501**	**8.9**
Not a high school graduate	4,312	1,210	28.1	179	4.2	1,031	23.9
High school graduate	12,422	1,737	14.0	489	3.9	1,248	10.1
Associate's degree or some college	10,920	1,474	13.5	561	5.1	913	8.4
Bachelor's degree or more	11,831	634	5.4	324	2.7	310	2.6
Total aged 55 to 64	**25,867**	**5,678**	**22.0**	**1,556**	**6.0**	**4,122**	**15.9**
Not a high school graduate	4,254	1,865	43.8	239	5.6	1,536	36.1
High school graduate	8,799	1,984	22.5	541	6.1	1,444	16.4
Associate's degree or some college	6,070	1,189	19.6	426	7.0	763	12.6
Bachelor's degree or more	6,743	730	10.8	350	5.2	380	5.6

Note: A person is considered to have a work disability if one or more of the following conditions are met: 1) identified by the March supplement question "Does anyone in this household have a health problem or disability which prevents them from working or which limits the kind or amount of work they can do?"; 2) identified by the March supplement question "Is there anyone in this household who ever retired or left a job for health reasons?"; 3) identified by the core questionnaire as currently not in the labor force because of a disability; 4) identified by the March supplement as a person who did not work at all in the previous year because of illness or disability; 5) under 65 years old and covered by Medicare in previous year; 6) under 65 years old and received Supplemental Security Income in previous year; 7) received Veterans Administration disability income in previous year. If one or more of conditions 3, 4, 5, and 6 are met, the person is considered to have a severe work disability.
Source: Bureau of the Census. 2002 Current Population Survey Annual Demographic Supplement, Internet site http://www.census.gov/hhes/www/disable/cps/cps102.html

Table 2.22 AIDS Cases by Sex and Age, through June 2002

(cumulative number and percent distribution of AIDS cases by age at diagnosis and sex for those aged 13 or older, through June 2002)

	number	percent of total cases
Total cases	**831,112**	**100.0%**
Under age 1	3,249	0.4
Aged 1 to 12	5,558	0.7
Aged 13 to 19	4,627	0.6
Aged 20 to 29	134,170	16.1
Aged 30 to 39	365,924	44.0
Aged 40 to 49	223,467	26.9
Aged 50 to 59	68,988	8.3
Aged 60 or older	25,129	3.0
Females		
Aged 13 or older	145,696	17.5
Aged 13 to 19	1,995	0.2
Aged 20 to 29	29,996	3.6
Aged 30 to 39	63,504	7.6
Aged 40 to 49	35,168	4.2
Aged 50 to 59	10,243	1.2
Aged 60 or older	4,790	0.6
Males		
Aged 13 or older	676,609	81.4
Aged 13 to 19	2,632	0.3
Aged 20 to 29	104,174	12.5
Aged 30 to 39	302,420	36.4
Aged 40 to 49	188,299	22.7
Aged 50 to 59	58,745	7.1
Aged 60 or older	20,339	2.4

Source: National Center for Health Statistics, Health, United States, 2003; *calculations by New Strategist*

The Middle Aged Account for Half of Physician Visits

Among 25-to-64-year-olds, women make 62 percent of physician visits.

In 2001, Americans visited physicians a total of 880 million times. People aged 25 to 64 made 50 percent of the visits. Women account for the great majority of physician visits not only because of pregnancy and childbirth, but also because they outnumber men among older Americans—who visit physicians most frequently.

People aged 25 to 64 also account for more than half of visits to hospital outpatient departments. Among outpatients in the 25-to-44 age group, the largest share have an acute problem. Among outpatients in the 45-to-64 age group, the largest percentage are there on a routine visit for a chronic problem.

The 25-to-44 age group accounts for fewer than half the visits to hospital emergency departments (48 percent). Many people go to hospital emergency departments instead of health clinics or doctor's offices because they have no regular source of health care. Among emergency room visits by people aged 25 to 44, only 18 to 23 percent were classified as having "emergent" problems, or conditions that need to be addressed within 15 minutes.

■ As the Baby-Boom generation ages, older Americans will become the dominant health care consumers, boosting demand for physicians trained in geriatric medicine.

People aged 45 to 64 see doctors three to four times a year

(average number of physician visits per person per year, by age, 2001)

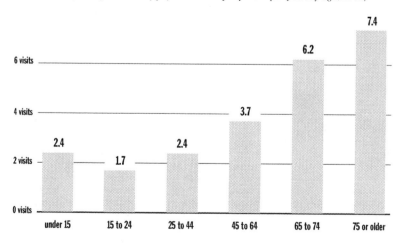

Table 2.23 Physician Office Visits by Sex and Age, 2001

(total number, percent distribution, and number of physician office visits per person per year, by sex and age, 2001; numbers in thousands)

	total	percent distribution	average visits per year
Total visits	**880,487**	**100.0%**	**3.1**
Under age 15	146,683	16.7	2.4
Aged 15 to 24	65,632	7.5	1.7
Aged 25 to 44	200,636	22.8	2.4
Aged 45 to 64	239,106	27.2	3.7
Aged 65 to 74	112,978	12.8	6.2
Aged 75 or older	115,452	13.1	7.4
Visits by females	**520,110**	**59.1**	**3.6**
Under age 15	69,614	7.9	2.4
Aged 15 to 24	42,071	4.8	2.2
Aged 25 to 44	131,664	15.0	3.1
Aged 45 to 64	142,657	16.2	4.3
Aged 65 to 74	64,029	7.3	6.5
Aged 75 or older	70,075	8.0	7.3
Visits by males	**360,377**	**40.9**	**2.6**
Under age 15	77,069	8.8	2.5
Aged 15 to 24	23,562	2.7	1.2
Aged 25 to 44	68,971	7.8	1.7
Aged 45 to 64	96,449	11.0	3.1
Aged 65 to 74	48,950	5.6	6.0
Aged 75 or older	45,376	5.2	7.6

Source: National Center for Health Statistics, National Ambulatory Medical Care Survey: 2001 Summary, *Advance Data No. 337, 2003*

Table 2.24 Hospital Outpatient Department Visits by Age and Reason, 2001

(number and percent distribution of visits to hospital outpatient departments by age and major reason for visit, 2001; numbers in thousands)

| | total | major reason for visit | | | | | |
		acute problem	chronic problem, routine	chronic problem, flare-up	pre- or post-surgery	preventive care	unknown
Total visits	**83,715**	**31,738**	**26,017**	**6,619**	**3,230**	**12,969**	**3,142**
Under age 15	18,319	7,970	4,258	1,106	588	3,936	460
Aged 15 to 24	9,834	3,881	1,977	663	272	2,737	304
Aged 25 to 44	20,576	8,790	5,243	1,643	795	3,267	838
Aged 45 to 64	21,590	7,128	8,750	2,033	911	1,831	938
Aged 65 to 74	7,299	2,190	3,044	665	376	661	363
Aged 75 or older	6,097	1,779	2,745	510	288	536	238
PERCENT DISTRIBUTION BY AGE							
Total visits	**100.0%**	**100.0%**	**100.0%**	**100.0%**	**100.0%**	**100.0%**	**100.0%**
Under age 15	21.9	25.1	16.4	16.7	18.2	30.3	14.6
Aged 15 to 24	11.7	12.2	7.6	10.0	8.4	21.1	9.7
Aged 25 to 44	24.6	27.7	20.2	24.8	24.6	25.2	26.7
Aged 45 to 64	25.8	22.5	33.6	30.7	28.2	14.1	29.9
Aged 65 to 74	8.7	6.9	11.7	10.1	11.6	5.1	11.6
Aged 75 or older	7.3	5.6	10.6	7.7	8.9	4.1	7.6
PERCENT DISTRIBUTION BY MAJOR REASON							
Total visits	**100.0%**	**37.9%**	**31.1%**	**7.9%**	**3.9%**	**15.5%**	**3.8%**
Under age 15	100.0	43.5	23.2	6.0	3.2	21.5	2.5
Aged 15 to 24	100.0	39.5	20.1	6.7	2.8	27.8	3.1
Aged 25 to 44	100.0	42.7	25.5	8.0	3.9	15.9	4.1
Aged 45 to 64	100.0	33.0	40.5	9.4	4.2	8.5	4.3
Aged 65 to 74	100.0	30.0	41.7	9.1	5.2	9.1	5.0
Aged 75 or older	100.0	29.2	45.0	8.4	4.7	8.8	3.9

Source: National Center for Health Statistics, National Hospital Ambulatory Medical Care Survey: 2001 Outpatient Department Summary, *Advance Data No. 338, 2003*

Table 2.25 Emergency Department Visits by Age and Urgency of Problem, 2001

(number of visits to emergency rooms and percent distribution by age and urgency of problem, 2001; numbers in thousands)

| | number | percent distribution | percent distribution by urgency of problem | | | | | |
			total	emergent	urgent	semiurgent	nonurgent	unknown
Total visits	**107,490**	**100.0%**	**100.0%**	**19.2%**	**31.7%**	**16.3%**	**9.1%**	**23.6%**
Under age 15	22,245	20.7	100.0	14.9	31.2	17.6	8.7	27.6
Aged 15 to 24	17,371	16.2	100.0	15.7	31.4	18.5	11.4	22.9
Aged 25 to 44	32,732	30.5	100.0	17.9	32.2	17.1	10.2	22.6
Aged 45 to 64	19,260	17.9	100.0	22.6	31.5	14.8	8.6	22.5
Aged 65 to 74	6,551	6.1	100.0	26.7	31.3	13.4	6.4	22.1
Aged 75 or older	9,332	8.7	100.0	29.0	32.0	11.4	5.0	22.6

Note: Emergent is a visit in which the patient should be seen in less than 15 minutes; urgent is a visit in which the patient should be seen within 15 to 60 minutes; semiurgent is a visit in which the patient should be seen within 61 to 120 minutes; nonurgent is a visit in which the patient should be seen within 121 minutes to 24 hours; unknown is a visit with no mention of immediacy or triage or the patient was dead on arrival.
Source: National Center for Health Statistics, National Hospital Ambulatory Medical Care Survey: 2001 Emergency Department Summary, *Advance Data No. 335, 2003*

Causes of Death Shift in Middle Age

Accidents become less important, while heart disease climbs to second place.

Heart disease and cancer are the leading causes of death in the United States. Among 35-to-64-year-olds, however, cancer is the number-one cause of death. Heart disease ranks third among 35-to-44-year-olds and rises to second place among 45-to-54-year-olds. Accidents rank second among 35-to-44-year-olds and fall to third place among 45-to-54-year-olds.

HIV infection has become much less important as a cause of death among the middle aged because new drug treatments have slowed the progress of the disease. HIV ranked third as a cause of death among 35-to-44-year-olds in 1996, and was in fifth place in 2001. Among 45-to-54-year-olds, HIV fell from fourth to eighth place during those years.

If middle age is defined as the point when people have lived half their lives, then 35-year-olds are not quite middle aged while 40-year-old men most definitely are. Men aged 40 can expect to live only 37.2 more years, on average. In contrast, women aged 40 can expect to live another 41.5 years—four years longer than their male counterparts.

■ As Boomers age, preventing heart disease and cancer will become an increasingly important focus of their daily life.

Most Baby Boomers have lived more years than they have remaining

(years of life remaining for people at selected ages, 2002)

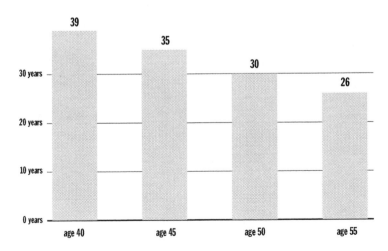

Table 2.26 Leading Causes of Death for People Aged 35 to 44, 2001

(number and percent distribution of deaths for the ten leading causes of death for people aged 35 to 44, 2001)

		number	percent
All causes		**91,674**	**100.0%**
1.	Malignant neoplasms (2)	16,569	18.1
2.	Accidents (5)	15,945	17.4
3.	Diseases of heart (1)	13,326	14.5
4.	Suicide (11)	6,635	7.2
5.	Human immunodeficiency virus infection	5,867	6.4
6.	Homicide (13)	4,268	4.7
7.	Chronic liver disease and cirrhosis (12)	3,336	3.6
8.	Cerebrovascular diseases (3)	2,491	2.7
9.	Diabetes mellitus (6)	1,958	2.1
10.	Influenza and pneumonia (7)	983	1.1
All other causes		20,296	22.1

Note: Number in parentheses shows rank for all age groups if the cause of death is among top fifteen.
Source: National Center for Health Statistics, Deaths: Leading Causes for 2001, National Vital Statistics Report, Vol. 52, No. 9, 2003; calculations by New Strategist

Table 2.27 Leading Causes of Death for People Aged 45 to 54, 2001

(number and percent distribution of deaths for the ten leading causes of death for people aged 45 to 54, 2001)

		number	percent
All causes		**168,065**	**100.0%**
1.	Malignant neoplasms (2)	49,562	29.5
2.	Diseases of heart (1)	36,399	21.7
3.	Accidents (5)	13,344	7.9
4.	Chronic liver disease and cirrhosis (12)	7,259	4.3
5.	Suicide (11)	5,942	3.5
6.	Cerebrovascular diseases (3)	5,910	3.5
7.	Diabetes mellitus (6)	5,343	3.2
8.	Human immunodeficiency virus infection	4,120	2.5
9.	Chronic lower respiratory disease (4)	3,324	2.0
10.	Homicide (13)	2,467	1.5
All other causes		34,395	20.4

Note: Number in parentheses shows rank for all age groups if the cause of death is among top fifteen.
Source: National Center for Health Statistics, Deaths: Leading Causes for 2001, National Vital Statistics Report, Vol. 52, No. 9, 2003; calculations by New Strategist

Table 2.28 Leading Causes of Death for People Aged 55 to 64, 2001

(number and percent distribution of deaths for the ten leading causes of death for people aged 55 to 64, 2001)

		number	percent
All causes		**244,139**	**100.0%**
1.	Malignant neoplasms (2)	90,223	37.0
2.	Diseases of heart (1)	62,486	25.6
3.	Chronic lower respiratory disease (4)	11,166	4.6
4.	Cerebrovascular diseases (3)	9,608	3.9
5.	Diabetes mellitus (6)	9,570	3.9
6.	Accidents (5)	7,658	3.1
7.	Chronic liver disease and cirrhosis (12)	5,750	2.4
8.	Suicide (11)	3,317	1.4
9.	Nephritis (9)	3,284	1.3
10.	Septicemia (10)	3,111	1.3
All other causes		37,966	15.5

Note: Number in parentheses shows rank for all age groups if the cause of death is among top fifteen.
Source: National Center for Health Statistics, Deaths: Leading Causes for 2001, *National Vital Statistics Report, Vol. 52, No. 9, 2003; calculations by New Strategist*

Table 2.29 Life Expectancy by Age and Sex, 2002

(years of life remaining at selected ages, by sex, 2002)

	total	females	males
At birth	77.4	79.9	74.7
Aged 1	76.9	79.4	74.3
Aged 5	73.0	75.5	70.4
Aged 10	68.1	70.6	65.4
Aged 15	63.1	65.6	60.5
Aged 20	58.3	60.7	55.8
Aged 25	53.6	55.9	51.1
Aged 30	48.8	51.0	46.5
Aged 35	44.1	46.2	41.8
Aged 40	39.4	41.5	37.2
Aged 45	34.9	36.8	32.7
Aged 50	30.4	32.2	28.4
Aged 55	26.2	27.8	24.2
Aged 60	22.0	23.5	20.3
Aged 65	18.2	19.5	16.6
Aged 70	14.7	15.8	13.3
Aged 75	11.6	12.5	10.4
Aged 80	8.9	9.5	8.0
Aged 85	6.7	7.0	5.9
Aged 90	4.9	5.1	4.4
Aged 95	3.7	3.8	3.3
Aged 100	2.8	2.8	2.6

Source: National Center for Health Statistics, **Deaths: Preliminary Data for 2002,** *National Vital Statistics Report, Vol. 52, No. 13, 2004*

3

Housing

■ Although the nation's homeownership rate is at a record high, homeownership among householders aged 35 to 54 is lower today than it was two decades ago.

■ During the past two decades the Baby-Boom generation filled the 35-to-54 age group, when homeownership rates climb sharply—fueling the boom in the housing industry.

■ Although married couples are most likely to own a home, the majority of householders aged 45 or older are homeowners regardless of household type.

■ Housing is most expensive for married-couple homeowners aged 30 to 44, with median monthly housing costs exceeding $1,000 in 2001—61 percent higher than average.

■ More than one in five married couples aged 35 to 64 own a home with a value of $250,000 or more.

Homeownership Is Down among the Middle Aged

Rate climbed significantly for older householders, however.

During most of the 1980s and 1990s, homeownership was below the 1982 peak of 64.8 percent. But homeownership began to climb in 1996, setting a new record each ensuing year. In 2003, 68.3 percent of householders owned their home. Although homeownership is up overall since 1982, the rate is still lower today than it was in the early 1980s among householders aged 35 to 54.

Homeownership among thirty- and forty-somethings fell as the age group filled with Baby Boomers. One reason for the decline is the high divorce rate among Boomers. For most families, it requires two incomes to make the mortgage payment, and as couples split apart fewer could afford to own a home.

Since 1990, the homeownership rate has been climbing for householders aged 35 to 54, thanks to the decade's booming economy and low mortgage interest rates. Still, the increase in homeownership among the middle aged is well below the average gain of 4.4 percentage points.

■ If today's low interest rates continue, it's likely Baby Boomers will catch up with the homeownership rates of their predecessors in another few years.

Homeownership is lower for 35-to-54-year-olds

(homeownership rates for householders aged 35 to 54, 1982 and 2003)

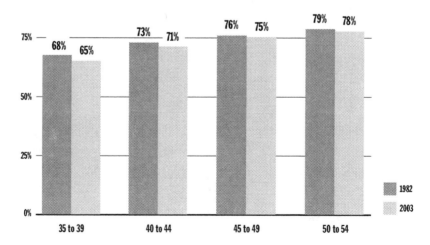

Table 3.1 Homeownership by Age of Householder, 1982 to 2003

(percentage of householders who own their home by age of householder, 1982 to 2003; percentage point change for selected years)

	2003	2000	1990	1982	percentage point change		
					2000–03	1990–03	1982–03
Total households	**68.3%**	**67.4%**	**63.9%**	**64.8%**	**0.9**	**4.4**	**3.5**
Under age 35	42.2	40.8	38.5	41.2	1.4	3.7	1.0
Aged 35 to 39	65.1	65.0	63.0	67.6	0.1	2.1	–2.5
Aged 40 to 44	71.3	70.6	69.8	73.0	0.7	1.5	–1.7
Aged 45 to 49	75.4	74.7	73.9	76.0	0.7	1.5	–0.6
Aged 50 to 54	77.9	78.5	76.8	78.8	–0.6	1.1	–0.9
Aged 55 to 59	80.9	80.4	78.8	80.0	0.5	2.1	0.9
Aged 60 to 64	81.9	80.3	79.8	80.1	1.6	2.1	1.8
Aged 65 or older	80.5	80.4	76.3	74.4	0.1	4.2	6.1

Source: Bureau of the Census, Housing Vacancy Surveys, Internet site http://www.census.gov/hhes/www/housing/hvs/annual03/ann03ind.html; calculations by New Strategist

Homeownership Rises with Age

People aged 55 or older are most likely to own a home.

The housing industry is booming because the Baby-Boom generation has reached the ages of home buying. The homeownership rate climbs steeply as people enter their thirties and forties. During the past two decades, Boomers have filled those age groups, fueling the real estate, construction, and home improvement industries.

Those least likely to own a home are young adults who have not yet accumulated the savings for a down payment and are not yet earning enough to qualify for a mortgage. Only 42 percent of householders under age 35 own a home. The homeownership rate peaks at more than 80 percent among Americans aged 55 or older.

■ Homeownership rates will continue to rise as Boomers age into their fifties and sixties.

Homeowners outnumber renters among 35-to-59-year-olds

(percent distribution of householders aged 35 to 59 by homeownership status, 2003)

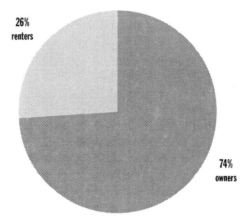

26%
renters

74%
owners

Table 3.2 Owners and Renters by Age of Householder, 2003

(number and percent distribution of householders by age and homeownership status, 2003; numbers in thousands)

		owners			renters		
	total	number	percent distribution	share of total	number	percent distribution	share of total
Total households	**105,560**	**72,054**	**100.0%**	**68.3%**	**33,506**	**100.0%**	**31.7%**
Under age 35	24,738	10,439	14.5	42.2	14,299	42.7	57.8
Aged 35 to 39	10,777	7,018	9.7	65.1	3,759	11.2	34.9
Aged 40 to 44	11,748	8,376	11.6	71.3	3,372	10.1	28.7
Aged 45 to 49	11,341	8,555	11.9	75.4	2,786	8.3	24.6
Aged 50 to 54	10,194	7,944	11.0	77.9	2,250	6.7	22.1
Aged 55 to 59	8,550	6,916	9.6	80.9	1,634	4.9	19.1
Aged 60 to 64	6,776	5,552	7.7	81.9	1,224	3.7	18.1
Aged 65 or older	21,436	17,253	23.9	80.5	4,183	12.5	19.5

Source: Bureau of the Census, Housing Vacancy Survey, Internet site http://www.census.gov/hhes/www/housing/hvs/historic/histt12.html; calculations by New Strategist

Married Couples Are Most Likely to Be Homeowners

Two incomes make homes more affordable.

The homeownership rate among all married couples was a lofty 83 percent in 2003, much higher than the 68 percent rate for all households. Among Boomer couples, the homeownership rate ranges from 79 percent in the 35-to-39 age group to fully 92 percent among couples aged 55 to 59.

Homeownership is much lower for other types of households and lowest among female-headed families, at slightly less than 50 percent in 2003. Regardless of household type, however, the majority of householders aged 45 or older are homeowners.

■ Although low mortgage interest rates have enabled more people to buy homes, they have not eliminated differences in homeownership rates by household type.

Most middle-aged couples own their home

(percent of married-couple householders aged 35 to 59 who own their home, 2003)

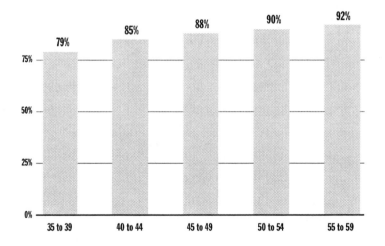

Table 3.3 Homeownership Rate by Age of Householder and Type of Household, 2003

(percent of households owning their home, by age of householder and type of household, 2003)

	total	family households			people living alone	
		married couples	female householder, no spouse present	male householder, no spouse present	females	males
Total households	**68.3%**	**83.3%**	**49.6%**	**57.9%**	**59.1%**	**50.0%**
Under age 25	22.8	32.8	23.1	40.4	12.7	16.0
Aged 25 to 29	39.8	57.9	23.0	39.0	23.8	28.2
Aged 30 to 34	56.5	71.6	33.3	49.2	37.3	38.1
Aged 35 to 39	65.1	78.9	43.2	53.5	45.2	44.6
Aged 40 to 44	71.3	84.9	51.6	63.7	49.8	49.6
Aged 45 to 49	75.4	88.3	60.0	69.6	54.2	50.4
Aged 50 to 54	77.9	90.2	61.1	71.5	60.9	55.4
Aged 55 to 59	80.9	91.6	65.8	75.2	65.4	58.7
Aged 60 to 64	81.9	92.2	71.3	75.0	68.6	61.4
Aged 65 or older	80.5	92.1	81.6	81.9	70.0	67.8

Source: Bureau of the Census, Housing Vacancy Survey, Internet site http://www.census.gov/hhes/www/housing/hvs/annual03/ann03t15.html

Non-Hispanic Whites Are Most Likely to Be Homeowners

Most older Boomers own their home regardless of race or Hispanic origin, however.

The homeownership rate of non-Hispanic whites stood at 72 percent, according to the 2000 census. The rate was a much lower 53 percent among Asians, and below the 50 percent majority among blacks and Hispanics. Regardless of race and Hispanic origin, however, homeownership rises with age as people acquire the savings and income needed to become homeowners.

Among younger Boomers, aged 35 to 44 in 2000, the majority of Asians and non-Hispanic whites are homeowners. Among black and Hispanic householders in the age group, however, only 44 to 49 percent own their home. The majority of older Boomers, aged 45 to 54 in 2000, are homeowners, regardless of race and Hispanic origin. The figure ranges from a high of 80 percent among non-Hispanic whites to a low of 55 percent among blacks.

■ Blacks are less likely to be homeowners because a smaller share of their households are headed by married couples.

Most older Boomers are homeowners

(homeownership rate of householders aged 45 to 54 by race and Hispanic origin, 2000)

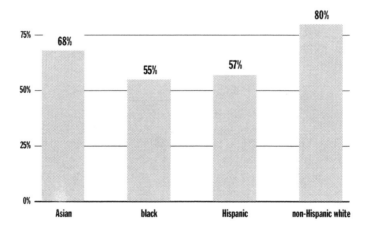

Table 3.4 Homeowners by Age, Race, and Hispanic Origin of Householder, 2000 Census

(percent of households owning their home by age, race, and Hispanic origin of householder, 2000)

	total	Asian	black	Hispanic	non-Hispanic white
Total households	**66.2%**	**52.8%**	**46.0%**	**45.7%**	**72.4%**
Under age 25	17.9	11.3	10.4	15.3	20.5
Aged 25 to 34	45.6	32.1	27.2	32.9	53.0
Aged 35 to 44	66.2	57.8	44.4	48.8	73.2
Aged 45 to 54	74.9	67.9	55.2	56.8	80.3
Aged 55 to 64	79.8	71.2	61.6	61.9	84.1
Aged 65 or older	78.1	62.0	64.3	62.8	80.6

Note: Each racial category includes those who identified themselves as being of the race alone and those who identified themselves as being of the race in combination with one or more other races. Hispanics may be of any race. Non-Hispanic whites include only those who identified themselves as white alone and non-Hispanic.
Source: Bureau of the Census, Census 2000, American Factfinder, Internet site http://factfinder.census.gov/home/saff/main.html?_lang=en

The Middle Aged Are Most Likely to Live in Single-Family Homes

Only 15 to 16 percent of householders aged 45 to 64 live in apartments.

The 63 percent majority of American households live in detached single-family homes. Householders aged 45 to 64 are most likely to live in this type of home, at 72 percent. The median age of householders living in detached single-family homes is 49.

Apartment living is most popular among younger adults. A 43 percent minority of householders under age 35 are in detached single-family homes, while nearly as many (40 percent) are in apartments. The median age of householders in multi-unit dwellings is 39— ten years younger than the median age of those in detached single-family homes. Interestingly, however, the median age of those living in the largest apartment buildings, with 50 or more units, is a much older 52. Behind this figure is the movement of older adults into multi-unit retirement complexes and assisted living facilities.

Overall, 7 percent of households live in mobile homes, a proportion that does not vary much by age. Householders aged 35 to 54 account for 41 percent of those living in mobile homes.

■ As Boomers fill the 55-to-64 age group, the market for detached single-family homes should remain strong.

Most of the middle aged are in single-family homes

(percent of households living in detached single-family homes, by age of householder, 2001)

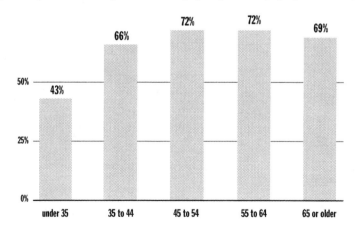

Table 3.5 Number of Units in Structure by Age of Householder, 2001

(number and percent distribution of households by age of householder and number of units in structure of home, 2001; numbers in thousands)

	total	one, detached	one, attached	multi-unit dwellings total	2 to 4	5 to 9	10 to 19	20 to 49	50 or more	mobile homes
Total households	106,261	67,129	7,305	24,609	8,200	4,994	4,620	3,253	3,543	7,219
Under age 35	24,803	10,724	2,382	9,937	3,297	2,273	2,171	1,256	942	1,761
Aged 35 to 54	45,528	31,298	2,807	8,453	3,008	1,725	1,671	1,096	953	2,970
Aged 35 to 44	23,882	15,803	1,541	4,900	1,789	975	1,034	607	496	1,638
Aged 45 to 54	21,646	15,495	1,266	3,553	1,219	750	637	489	457	1,332
Aged 55 to 64	14,117	10,125	889	2,077	723	423	288	262	381	1,026
Aged 65 or older	21,812	14,981	1,228	4,141	1,172	573	490	640	1,267	1,461
Median age	47	49	43	39	39	37	36	41	52	46

PERCENT DISTRIBUTION BY AGE OF HOUSEHOLDER

	total	one, detached	one, attached	multi-unit dwellings total	2 to 4	5 to 9	10 to 19	20 to 49	50 or more	mobile homes
Total households	100.0%	100.0%	100.0%	100.0%	100.0%	100.0%	100.0%	100.0%	100.0%	100.0%
Under age 35	23.3	16.0	32.6	40.4	40.2	45.5	47.0	38.6	26.6	24.4
Aged 35 to 54	42.8	46.6	38.4	34.3	36.7	34.5	36.2	33.7	26.9	41.1
Aged 35 to 44	22.5	23.5	21.1	19.9	21.8	19.5	22.4	18.7	14.0	22.7
Aged 45 to 54	20.4	23.1	17.3	14.4	14.9	15.0	13.8	15.0	12.9	18.5
Aged 55 to 64	13.3	15.1	12.2	8.4	8.8	8.5	6.2	8.1	10.8	14.2
Aged 65 or older	20.5	22.3	16.8	16.8	14.3	11.5	10.6	19.7	35.8	20.2

PERCENT DISTRIBUTION BY UNITS IN STRUCTURE

	total	one, detached	one, attached	multi-unit dwellings total	2 to 4	5 to 9	10 to 19	20 to 49	50 or more	mobile homes
Total households	100.0%	63.2%	6.9%	23.2%	7.7%	4.7%	4.3%	3.1%	3.3%	6.8%
Under age 35	100.0	43.2	9.6	40.1	13.3	9.2	8.8	5.1	3.8	7.1
Aged 35 to 54	100.0	68.7	6.2	18.6	6.6	3.8	3.7	2.4	2.1	6.5
Aged 35 to 44	100.0	66.2	6.5	20.5	7.5	4.1	4.3	2.5	2.1	6.9
Aged 45 to 54	100.0	71.6	5.8	16.4	5.6	3.5	2.9	2.3	2.1	6.2
Aged 55 to 64	100.0	71.7	6.3	14.7	5.1	3.0	2.0	1.9	2.7	7.3
Aged 65 or older	100.0	68.7	5.6	19.0	5.4	2.6	2.2	2.9	5.8	6.7

Source: Bureau of the Census. American Housing Survey for the United States in 2001, Internet site http://www.census.gov/hhes/ www/housing/ahs/ahs01/ahs01.html

Few Middle-Aged Householders Own New Homes

The youngest homeowners are most likely to live in new homes.

New homes are the province of the young. Overall, fewer than 6 percent of homeowners live in a new home—meaning one built in the past four years. The share is much greater among young homeowners, however. Fourteen percent of homeowners under age 35 live in a new home. The figure drops to 8 percent among those aged 35 to 44 and bottoms out at just 3 percent among householders aged 65 or older. Behind this pattern is the fact that older people are less likely to move and are aging in place, along with their homes.

Among renters, young adults account for the majority (57 percent) of those in rental units built in the past four years. People aged 35 to 54 account for only 26 percent of renters in newly constructed units.

■ The homeownership boom of the past few years is certain to have boosted the proportion of people living in recently built homes, but the pattern by age is likely to have remained unchanged.

Many young homeowners live in new homes

(percent of homeowners living in homes built in the past four years, by age of householder, 2001)

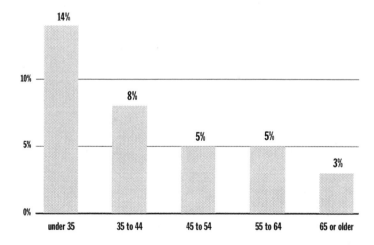

Table 3.6 Owners and Renters of New Homes by Age of Householder, 2001

(number of total occupied housing units, number and percent built in the past four years, and percent distribution of new units by housing tenure and age of householder, 2001; numbers in thousands)

	total	new homes		
		number	percent of total	percent distribution
Total households	**106,261**	**5,853**	**5.5%**	**100.0%**
Under age 35	24,803	2,118	8.5	36.2
Aged 35 to 54	45,528	2,461	5.4	42.1
Aged 35 to 44	23,882	1,502	6.3	25.7
Aged 45 to 54	21,646	959	4.4	16.4
Aged 55 to 64	14,117	680	4.8	11.6
Aged 65 or older	21,812	593	2.7	10.1
Owners	**72,265**	**4,690**	**6.5**	**100.0**
Under age 35	10,287	1,456	14.2	31.0
Aged 35 to 54	33,009	2,156	6.5	46.0
Aged 35 to 44	16,359	1,310	8.0	27.9
Aged 45 to 54	16,650	846	5.1	18.0
Aged 55 to 64	11,456	604	5.3	12.9
Aged 65 or older	17,513	474	2.7	10.1
Renters	**33,996**	**1,163**	**3.4**	**100.0**
Under age 35	14,516	663	4.6	57.0
Aged 35 to 54	12,520	304	2.4	26.1
Aged 35 to 44	7,524	191	2.5	16.4
Aged 45 to 54	4,996	113	2.3	9.7
Aged 55 to 64	2,661	76	2.9	6.5
Aged 65 or older	4,299	119	2.8	10.2

Source: Bureau of the Census. American Housing Survey for the United States in 2001, Internet site http://www.census.gov/hhes/www/housing/ahs/ahs01/ahs01.html

Housing Costs Are Highest for Homeowners Aged 30 to 44

Costs are lowest for homeowners aged 65 or older.

Monthly housing costs for the average household in 2001 stood at $658, including mortgage interest and utilities. For homeowners, the median monthly housing cost was $685, and for renters the figure was a slightly smaller $632.

Housing costs are highest for married-couple homeowners aged 30 to 44, not only because their homes are larger than average to offer room for children but also because many are recent homeowners with hefty mortgage interest charges. The median monthly housing cost for married-couple homeowners aged 30 to 44 exceeded $1,000 in 2001—61 percent higher than average.

Housing costs are lowest for homeowners aged 65 or older regardless of household type. For older renters, however, housing costs do not decline with age. Among married householders aged 65 or older, homeowners paid a median of $383 for housing while renters paid a median of $651.

■ The financial advantages of homeownership grow as householders age and pay off their mortgages.

Housing costs fall after age 45

(median monthly housing costs for married-couple homeowners, by age of householder, 2001)

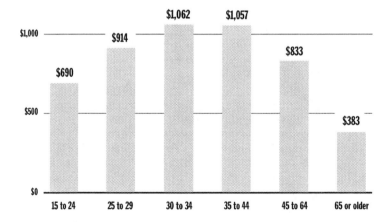

Table 3.7 Median Monthly Housing Costs by Household Type and Age of Householder, 2001

(median monthly housing costs and indexed costs by type of household, age of householder, and housing tenure, 2001)

	median monthly cost			indexed cost		
	total	owners	renters	total	owners	renters
Total households	**$658**	**$685**	**$632**	**100**	**104**	**96**
TWO-OR-MORE-						
PERSON HOUSEHOLDS	**734**	**775**	**682**	**112**	**118**	**104**
Married couples	**783**	**811**	**721**	**119**	**123**	**110**
Aged 15 to 24	638	690	622	97	105	95
Aged 25 to 29	796	914	691	121	139	105
Aged 30 to 34	928	1,062	737	141	161	112
Aged 35 to 44	979	1,057	775	149	161	118
Aged 45 to 64	815	833	740	124	127	113
Aged 65 or older	395	383	651	60	58	99
Other female householder	**639**	**648**	**634**	**97**	**99**	**96**
Aged 15 to 44	661	752	633	101	114	96
Aged 45 to 64	692	724	648	105	110	99
Aged 65 or older	404	365	609	61	56	93
Other male householder	**700**	**708**	**696**	**106**	**108**	**106**
Aged 15 to 44	724	789	703	110	120	107
Aged 45 to 64	690	719	661	105	109	101
Aged 65 or older	463	400	702	70	61	107
SINGLE-PERSON						
HOUSEHOLDS	**488**	**401**	**548**	**74**	**61**	**83**
Female householder	**455**	**374**	**538**	**69**	**57**	**82**
Aged 15 to 44	632	798	586	96	121	89
Aged 45 to 64	527	536	518	80	82	79
Aged 65 or older	318	284	473	48	43	72
Male householder	**531**	**478**	**557**	**81**	**73**	**85**
Aged 15 to 44	611	682	591	93	104	90
Aged 45 to 64	515	501	523	78	76	80
Aged 65 or older	339	298	445	52	45	68

Source: Bureau of the Census, American Housing Survey for the United States in 2001, Internet site http://www.census.gov/hhes/ www/housing/ahs/ahs01/ahs01.html; calculations by New Strategist

Middle-Aged Married Couples Have the Most Valuable Homes

Many are dual earners and can afford more expensive homes.

The median value of homes owned by married couples aged 35 to 44 stood at $147,327 in 2001, 18 percent greater than the $124,624 median value of all owned homes. More than one in five married couples aged 35 to 64 own a home with a value of $250,000 or more.

Among homeowning families headed by men or women without a spouse, the middle-aged also have the most valuable homes, although not as highly valued as the homes of middle-aged married couples. The median value of homes owned by female-headed family householders aged 45 to 64 stood at $110,821 in 2001, while the homes of their male counterparts were valued at a higher $118,762. Among men and women who live alone, the youngest homeowners (those under age 45) have the most valuable homes, with female householders owning homes of greater value ($110,798) than their male counterparts ($102,821).

■ Home values have been rising steadily and are now significantly higher than the 2001 figures shown in this table.

Home values are highest for 35-to-44-year-old couples

(median value of homes owned by married couples, by age of householder, 2001)

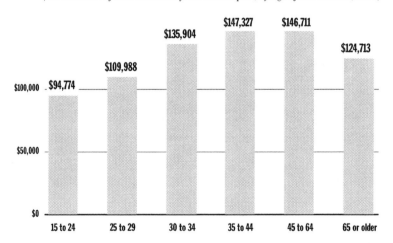

Table 3.8 Value of Owner-Occupied Homes by Type of Household and Age of Householder, 2001

(total number of homeowners and percent distribution by value of home, median value of housing unit, and indexed median value, by type of household and age of householder, 2001)

	total number (in 000s)	percent	under $100,000	$100,000 to $149,999	$150,000 to $199,999	$200,000 to $249,999	$250,000 to $299,999	$300,000 or more	median value of home	indexed median value
Total homeowners	72,265	100.0%	39.3%	21.6%	14.1%	7.9%	5.2%	11.8%	$124,624	100
TWO-OR-MORE-PERSON										
HOUSEHOLDS	56,867	100.0	36.2	21.7	14.8	8.6	5.7	13.0	131,805	106
Married couples	44,618	100.0	32.8	21.9	15.5	9.4	6.3	14.1	139,364	112
Under age 25	490	100.0	53.7	19.2	11.2	6.5	3.1	5.9	94,774	76
Aged 25 to 29	2,039	100.0	44.9	25.7	14.4	6.0	3.4	5.6	109,988	88
Aged 30 to 34	3,744	100.0	31.8	25.3	15.7	9.6	7.0	10.6	135,904	109
Aged 35 to 44	11,182	100.0	29.1	22.0	16.5	10.2	7.1	15.1	147,327	118
Aged 45 to 64	18,681	100.0	30.0	21.4	15.8	10.0	6.4	16.5	146,711	118
Aged 65 or older	8,482	100.0	39.8	20.6	14.1	8.3	5.4	11.8	124,713	100
Other female householder	7,829	100.0	50.8	20.8	11.8	5.6	3.4	7.7	98,944	79
Under age 45	3,290	100.0	56.6	19.5	10.7	4.7	2.6	5.9	92,177	74
Aged 45 to 64	2,927	100.0	45.3	21.7	12.4	7.1	4.1	9.4	110,821	89
Aged 65 or older	1,612	100.0	48.8	21.8	12.7	4.7	3.8	8.3	102,977	83
Other male householder	4,419	100.0	44.8	21.7	13.3	6.0	3.8	10.4	111,924	90
Under age 45	2,377	100.0	46.2	23.7	12.0	5.8	3.7	8.6	107,989	87
Aged 45 to 64	1,505	100.0	42.6	19.6	13.2	6.8	4.4	13.4	118,762	95
Aged 65 or older	537	100.0	44.5	19.0	18.6	4.8	2.8	10.1	113,887	91
SINGLE-PERSON										
HOUSEHOLDS	15,398	100.0	51.1	21.1	11.4	5.4	3.4	7.6	98,253	79
Female householder	9,448	100.0	51.8	21.4	11.8	5.1	3.0	6.9	97,337	78
Under age 45	1,295	100.0	43.9	28.4	11.4	6.0	3.3	7.0	110,798	89
Aged 45 to 64	2,890	100.0	48.7	21.4	12.9	5.1	3.6	8.3	103,018	83
Aged 65 or older	5,262	100.0	55.5	19.8	11.3	4.8	2.6	6.0	92,013	74
Male householder	5,950	100.0	50.1	20.6	10.6	5.9	4.1	8.8	99,898	80
Under age 45	2,228	100.0	48.7	22.8	10.1	5.6	3.6	9.2	102,821	83
Aged 45 to 64	2,103	100.0	50.2	19.3	10.7	6.3	5.2	8.3	99,693	80
Aged 65 or older	1,620	100.0	51.8	19.2	11.2	5.9	3.1	8.8	97,048	78

Source: Bureau of the Census, American Housing Survey for the United States in 2001, *Internet site http://www.census.gov/hhes/www/housing/ahs/ahs01/ahs01.html; calculations by New Strategist*

Mobility Rate Falls in Middle Age

Most of the middle aged move for housing-related reasons.

While 14 percent of Americans aged 1 or older moved between March 2002 and March 2003, the proportion was a smaller 10 percent among people aged 35 to 59. Within the age group, the mobility rate falls from 15 percent among 35-to-39-year-olds to just 7 percent among 55-to-59-year-olds. Among all movers, the majority stays within the same county. Only 19 percent move to a different state.

Housing is the primary motivation for moving among 30-to-64-year-olds. Most cite housing-related reasons, with one in five saying they moved because they wanted a better home or apartment. Family reasons rank second as a motivation for moving among 30-to-64 year olds, and job reasons rank third—despite the fact that people in the age group are typically at the peak of their career. Only 9 to 10 percent of movers in the 30-to-64 age group say they moved because of a new job or job transfer.

■ Americans are moving less than they once did. Several factors are behind the lower mobility rates, including the aging of the population, the rise in homeownership, and the proliferation of dual-income couples.

Mobility rate falls sharply in middle age

(percent of people who moved between March 2002 and March 2003, by age)

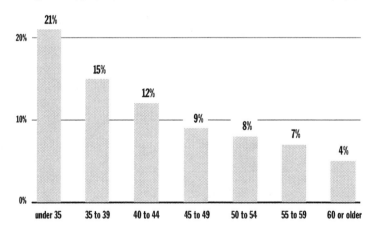

Table 3.9 Geographical Mobility by Age, 2002 to 2003

(total number and percent distribution of people aged 1 or older by mobility status between March 2002 and March 2003, by selected age groups; numbers in thousands)

	total	nonmovers	total movers	same county	different county, same state	different state, same division	different division, same region	different region	abroad
Total, aged 1 or older	282,556	242,463	40,093	23,468	7,728	3,752	1,181	2,695	1,269
Under age 35	136,614	109,030	27,581	16,544	5,217	2,365	780	1,775	900
Total aged 35 to 59	99,778	89,343	10,434	5,935	2,025	1,091	342	731	310
Aged 35 to 39	21,284	18,032	3,252	1,910	635	273	105	209	120
Aged 40 to 44	22,790	20,108	2,683	1,524	573	236	75	181	94
Aged 45 to 49	21,420	19,444	1,976	1,151	350	227	64	142	42
Aged 50 to 54	18,814	17,342	1,471	799	284	190	48	113	37
Aged 55 to 59	15,470	14,417	1,052	551	183	165	50	86	17
Aged 60 or older	46,163	44,090	2,073	988	485	296	57	189	58

PERCENT DISTRIBUTION BY AGE

	total	nonmovers	total movers	same county	different county, same state	different state, same division	different division, same region	different region	abroad
Total, aged 1 or older	100.0%	100.0%	100.0%	100.0%	100.0%	100.0%	100.0%	100.0%	100.0%
Under age 35	48.3	45.0	68.8	70.5	67.5	63.0	66.1	65.9	70.9
Total aged 35 to 59	35.3	36.8	26.0	25.3	26.2	29.1	29.0	27.1	24.4
Aged 35 to 39	7.5	7.4	8.1	8.1	8.2	7.3	8.9	7.8	9.5
Aged 40 to 44	8.1	8.3	6.7	6.5	7.4	6.3	6.4	6.7	7.4
Aged 45 to 49	7.6	8.0	4.9	4.9	4.5	6.1	5.4	5.3	3.3
Aged 50 to 54	6.7	7.2	3.7	3.4	3.7	5.1	4.1	4.2	2.9
Aged 55 to 59	5.5	5.9	2.6	2.3	2.4	4.4	4.2	3.2	1.3
Aged 60 or older	16.3	18.2	5.2	4.2	6.3	7.9	4.8	7.0	4.6

PERCENT DISTRIBUTION BY MOBILITY STATUS

	total	nonmovers	total movers	same county	different county, same state	different state, same division	different division, same region	different region	abroad
Total, aged 1 or older	100.0%	85.8%	14.2%	8.3%	2.7%	1.3%	0.4%	1.0%	0.4%
Under age 35	100.0	79.8	20.2	12.1	3.8	1.7	0.6	1.3	0.7
Total aged 35 to 59	100.0	89.5	10.5	5.9	2.0	1.1	0.3	0.7	0.3
Aged 35 to 39	100.0	84.7	15.3	9.0	3.0	1.3	0.5	1.0	0.6
Aged 40 to 44	100.0	88.2	11.8	6.7	2.5	1.0	0.3	0.8	0.4
Aged 45 to 49	100.0	90.8	9.2	5.4	1.6	1.1	0.3	0.7	0.2
Aged 50 to 54	100.0	92.2	7.8	4.2	1.5	1.0	0.3	0.6	0.2
Aged 55 to 59	100.0	93.2	6.8	3.6	1.2	1.1	0.3	0.6	0.1
Aged 60 or older	100.0	95.5	4.5	2.1	1.1	0.6	0.1	0.4	0.1

PERCENT DISTRIBUTION OF MOVERS BY TYPE OF MOVE

	total	nonmovers	total movers	same county	different county, same state	different state, same division	different division, same region	different region	abroad
Total, aged 1 or older	–	–	100.0%	58.5%	19.3%	9.4%	2.9%	6.7%	3.2%
Under age 35	–	–	100.0	60.0	18.9	8.6	2.8	6.4	3.3
Total aged 35 to 59	–	–	100.0	56.9	19.4	10.5	3.3	7.0	3.0
Aged 35 to 39	–	–	100.0	58.7	19.5	8.4	3.2	6.4	3.7
Aged 40 to 44	–	–	100.0	56.8	21.4	8.8	2.8	6.7	3.5
Aged 45 to 49	–	–	100.0	58.2	17.7	11.5	3.2	7.2	2.1
Aged 50 to 54	–	–	100.0	54.3	19.3	12.9	3.3	7.7	2.5
Aged 55 to 59	–	–	100.0	52.4	17.4	15.7	4.8	8.2	1.6
Aged 60 or older	–	–	100.0	47.7	23.4	14.3	2.7	9.1	2.8

Note: (–) means not applicable.
Source: Bureau of the Census, Geographical Mobility: March 2002 to March 2003, Detailed Tables for P20-549, *2003 Current Population Survey, Internet site http://www.census.gov/population/www/socdemo/migrate/p20-549.html; calculations by New Strategist*

Table 3.10 Reason for Moving by Age, 2002 to 2003

(number and percent distribution of movers between March 2002 and March 2003 by primary reason for move, and age; numbers in thousands)

	total	under 30	30 to 44	45 to 64	65 or older
TOTAL MOVERS	**40,093**	**23,524**	**9,996**	**5,203**	**1,371**
Family reasons	**10,548**	**6,675**	**2,322**	**1,151**	**401**
Change in marital status	2,679	1,504	752	358	65
To establish own household	2,814	2,018	540	224	33
Other family reason	5,055	3,153	1,030	569	303
Job reasons	**6,247**	**3,550**	**1,769**	**859**	**69**
New job or job transfer	3,546	2,015	1,048	460	23
To look for work or lost job	749	452	196	102	–
To be closer to work/easier commute	1,275	776	334	158	5
Retired	101	6	19	45	32
Other job-related reason	576	301	172	94	9
Housing reasons	**20,578**	**11,713**	**5,394**	**2,830**	**636**
Wanted own home, not rent	4,078	2,323	1,172	532	50
Wanted new or better home/apartment	7,942	4,653	2,074	1,034	181
Wanted better neighborhood/less crime	1,530	881	410	199	39
Wanted cheaper housing	2,622	1,463	684	358	116
Other housing reason	4,406	2,393	1,054	707	250
Other reasons	**2,722**	**1,587**	**509**	**364**	**261**
To attend or leave college	1,010	864	121	21	3
Change of climate	160	41	46	46	26
Health reasons	565	148	96	124	197
Other reasons	987	534	246	173	35

	total	under 30	30 to 44	45 to 64	65 or older
PERCENT DISTRIBUTION BY REASON					
TOTAL MOVERS	**100.0%**	**100.0%**	**100.0%**	**100.0%**	**100.0%**
Family reasons	**26.3**	**28.4**	**23.2**	**22.1**	**29.2**
Change in marital status	6.7	6.4	7.5	6.9	4.7
To establish own household	7.0	8.6	5.4	4.3	2.4
Other family reason	12.6	13.4	10.3	10.9	22.1
Job reasons	**15.6**	**15.1**	**17.7**	**16.5**	**5.0**
New job or job transfer	8.8	8.6	10.5	8.8	1.7
To look for work or lost job	1.9	1.9	2.0	2.0	–
To be closer to work/easier commute	3.2	3.3	3.3	3.0	0.4
Retired	0.3	0.0	0.2	0.9	2.3
Other job-related reason	1.4	1.3	1.7	1.8	0.7
Housing reasons	**51.3**	**49.8**	**54.0**	**54.4**	**46.4**
Wanted own home, not rent	10.2	9.9	11.7	10.2	3.6
Wanted new or better home/apartment	19.8	19.8	20.7	19.9	13.2
Wanted better neighborhood/less crime	3.8	3.7	4.1	3.8	2.8
Wanted cheaper housing	6.5	6.2	6.8	6.9	8.5
Other housing reason	11.0	10.2	10.5	13.6	18.2
Other reasons	**6.8**	**6.7**	**5.1**	**7.0**	**19.0**
To attend or leave college	2.5	3.7	1.2	0.4	0.2
Change of climate	0.4	0.2	0.5	0.9	1.9
Health reasons	1.4	0.6	1.0	2.4	14.4
Other reasons	2.5	2.3	2.5	3.3	2.6

PERCENT DISTRIBUTION BY AGE	total	under 30	30 to 44	45 to 64	65 or older
TOTAL MOVERS	**100.0%**	**58.7%**	**24.9%**	**13.0%**	**3.4%**
Family reasons	**100.0**	**63.3**	**22.0**	**10.9**	**3.8**
Change in marital status	100.0	56.1	28.1	13.4	2.4
To establish own household	100.0	71.7	19.2	8.0	1.2
Other family reason	100.0	62.4	20.4	11.3	6.0
Job reasons	**100.0**	**56.8**	**28.3**	**13.8**	**1.1**
New job or job transfer	100.0	56.8	29.6	13.0	0.6
To look for work or lost job	100.0	60.3	26.2	13.6	–
To be closer to work/easier commute	100.0	60.9	26.2	12.4	0.4
Retired	100.0	5.9	18.8	44.6	31.7
Other job-related reason	100.0	52.3	29.9	16.3	1.6
Housing reasons	**100.0**	**56.9**	**26.2**	**13.8**	**3.1**
Wanted own home, not rent	100.0	57.0	28.7	13.1	1.2
Wanted new or better home/apartment	100.0	58.6	26.1	13.0	2.3
Wanted better neighborhood/less crime	100.0	57.6	26.8	13.0	2.5
Wanted cheaper housing	100.0	55.8	26.1	13.7	4.4
Other housing reason	100.0	54.3	23.9	16.1	5.7
Other reasons	**100.0**	**58.3**	**18.7**	**13.4**	**9.6**
To attend or leave college	100.0	85.5	12.0	2.1	0.3
Change of climate	100.0	25.6	28.7	28.7	16.2
Health reasons	100.0	26.2	17.0	21.9	34.9
Other reasons	100.0	54.1	24.9	17.5	3.5

Note: (–) means number is less than 500 or sample is too small to make a reliable estimate.
Source: Bureau of the Census, Geographical Mobility: March 2002 to March 2003, Detailed Tables for P20-549, *2003 Current Population Survey, Internet site http://www.census.gov/population/www/socdemo/migrate/p20-549.html; calculations by New Strategist*

Income

■ Between 2000 and 2002, median household income fell for householders aged 35 to 54. Nevertheless, median household income remains higher than its level in 1980 or 1990.

■ Household income peaks in middle age, topping out at $59,845 among householders aged 45 to 49—far above the $42,409 national median.

■ Among the nation's 16 million households with incomes of $100,000 or more, fully 61 percent are headed by married couples aged 35 to 59.

■ Between 2000 and 2002, the median income of men aged 35 to 54 fell 4 percent, continuing a decline that has been ongoing for the past two decades. In contrast, the incomes of women have surged since 1980, regardless of age.

■ Among men aged 35 to 54 who work full-time, those with professional degrees had the highest earnings, a median of $100,000 or more. Among women aged 35 to 54 who work full-time, earnings were highest for those with doctorates.

■ The poverty rate bottoms out in the 45-to-54 age group, now entirely filled with the Baby-Boom generation. As Boomers age, the poverty rate may rise.

Incomes Are Down for Middle-Aged Householders

The decline has been especially steep for householders aged 35 to 44.

Between 2000 and 2002, median household income fell 3.3 percent after adjusting for inflation. Behind the drop was recession, followed by a lengthy jobless recovery. For householders aged 35 to 44 (Boomers were aged 38 to 56 in 2002), the decline in median household income was an even steeper 4.7 percent during those years. For those aged 45 to 54, median household income fell 1.9 percent. The oldest Boomers are entering the 55-to-64 age group, which has seen its income rise slightly—by 0.8 percent—since 2000. Behind the rise is the postponement of retirement among men in their early sixties.

Median household income was higher in 2002 than in 1990 or 1980, despite its decline since 2000. The gains made by householders aged 35 to 54 have been below average, however, while householders aged 55 to 64 have seen above average increases in median income during those time periods.

■ The incomes of householders aged 55 to 64 are likely to rise faster than average during the next decade as million of Boomers are forced to postpone retirement.

Householders aged 55 to 64 are the only ones with growing incomes

(percent change in median income of total households and households headed by people aged 35 to 64, 2000–02; in 2002 dollars)

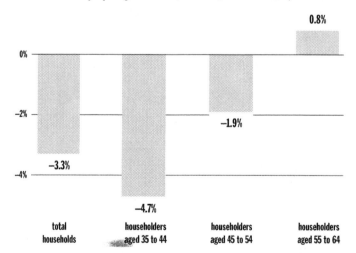

Table 4.1 **Median Income of Households Headed by People Aged 35 to 64, 1980 to 2002**

(median income of total households and households headed by people aged 35 to 64, 1980 to 2002: in 2002 dollars)

	total households	35 to 44	45 to 54	55 to 64
2002	$42,409	$53,521	$59,021	$47,203
2001	42,899	54,168	58,968	46,593
2000	43,848	56,142	60,193	46,838
1999	44,044	54,897	61,419	48,125
1998	42,844	53,384	59,661	47,561
1997	41,346	51,798	57,961	46,208
1996	40,503	50,690	57,598	45,436
1995	39,931	50,932	56,314	44,619
1994	38,725	50,012	56,726	42,288
1993	38,287	50,078	56,628	41,024
1992	38,482	50,060	55,817	42,699
1991	38,790	50,666	56,334	42,882
1990	39,949	51,447	55,931	43,181
1989	40,484	52,709	58,154	43,163
1988	39,766	53,394	55,817	42,218
1987	39,453	53,266	56,324	41,722
1986	38,975	51,326	55,824	41,916
1985	37,648	49,520	52,959	40,739
1984	36,921	49,059	51,913	39,687
1983	35,774	47,411	51,990	39,016
1982	35,986	47,045	49,926	39,383
1981	36,042	47,966	51,103	39,759
1980	36,608	48,839	51,927	40,405
Percent change				
2000–2002	–3.3%	–4.7%	–1.9%	0.8%
1990–2002	6.2	4.0	5.5	9.3
1980–2002	15.8	9.6	13.7	16.8

Source: Bureau of the Census, data from the Current Population Survey Annual Demographic Supplements, Internet site http://www.census.gov/hhes/income/histinc/h10.html; calculations by New Strategist

Household Income Peaks in Late Forties

Householders aged 45 to 49 have the highest incomes.

Household income peaks in middle age because so many middle-aged householders are dual-income married couples at the height of their career. Median household income tops out at $59,845 among householders aged 45 to 49, far above the $42,409 national median.

Among the nation's most affluent households—those with incomes of $100,000 or more in 2002—the 40 to 59 age group accounts for the 60 percent majority (Boomers were aged 38 to 56 in that year). Fully 22 percent of households headed by 45-to-54-year-olds have incomes of $100,000 or more. The figure is almost as high (21 percent) among householders aged 55 to 59.

■ The incomes of householders aged 55 to 59 are likely to rise in the next few years as the dual-income couples of the Baby-Boom generation fill the age group.

The middle aged have the highest incomes

(median income of householders by age, 2002)

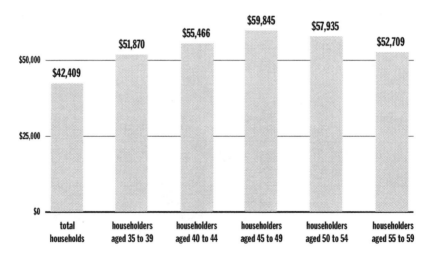

Table 4.2 Income of Households Headed by People Aged 35 to 59, 2002: Total Households

(number and percent distribution of total households and households headed by people aged 35 to 59 by income, 2002; households in thousands as of 2003)

	total	aged 35 to 44			aged 45 to 54			aged 55 to 59
		total	35 to 39	40 to 44	total	45 to 49	50 to 54	
Total households	**111,278**	**24,069**	**11,486**	**12,583**	**22,623**	**11,957**	**10,666**	**9,192**
Under $10,000	10,090	1,408	674	733	1,424	757	667	736
$10,000 to $19,999	15,063	1,944	982	962	1,614	791	823	909
$20,000 to $29,999	14,362	2,613	1,296	1,316	2,046	1,080	967	948
$30,000 to $39,999	12,795	2,569	1,250	1,320	2,245	1,166	1,077	908
$40,000 to $49,999	10,743	2,522	1,271	1,250	2,120	1,107	1,015	864
$50,000 to $59,999	9,226	2,321	1,146	1,177	2,012	1,091	922	784
$60,000 to $69,999	7,633	1,948	905	1,041	1,782	971	811	670
$70,000 to $79,999	6,695	1,867	893	974	1,697	929	767	591
$80,000 to $89,999	5,039	1,399	641	758	1,422	746	675	479
$90,000 to $99,999	3,952	1,132	504	628	1,194	640	553	389
$100,000 or more	15,676	4,346	1,921	2,425	5,069	2,679	2,390	1,914
Median income	$42,409	$53,521	$51,870	$55,466	$59,021	$59,845	$57,935	$52,709
Total households	**100.0%**	**100.0%**	**100.0%**	**100.0%**	**100.0%**	**100.0%**	**100.0%**	**100.0%**
Under $10,000	9.1	5.8	5.9	5.8	6.3	6.3	6.3	0.8
$10,000 to $19,999	13.5	8.1	8.5	7.6	7.1	6.6	7.7	9.9
$20,000 to $29,999	12.9	10.9	11.3	10.5	9.0	9.0	9.1	10.3
$30,000 to $39,999	11.5	10.7	10.9	10.5	9.9	9.8	10.1	9.9
$40,000 to $49,999	9.7	10.5	11.1	9.9	9.4	9.3	9.5	9.4
$50,000 to $59,999	8.3	9.6	10.0	9.4	8.9	9.1	8.6	8.5
$60,000 to $69,999	6.9	8.1	7.9	8.3	7.9	8.1	7.6	7.3
$70,000 to $79,999	6.0	7.8	7.8	7.7	7.5	7.8	7.2	6.4
$80,000 to $89,999	4.5	5.8	5.6	6.0	6.3	6.2	6.3	5.2
$90,000 to $99,999	3.6	4.7	4.4	5.0	5.3	5.4	5.2	4.2
$100,000 or more	14.1	18.1	16.7	19.3	22.4	22.4	22.4	20.8

Source: Bureau of the Census, data from the 2003 Current Population Survey Annual Social and Economic Supplement, Internet site http://ferret.bls.census.gov/macro/032003/hhinc/new02_000.htm; calculations by New Strategist

Among Boomers, Asians and Non-Hispanic Whites Have the Highest Incomes

Blacks and Hispanics have much lower median household incomes.

The median income of households headed by Asians and non-Hispanic whites in the broad 35-to-59 age group ranged from $57,000 to $66,000. In contrast, the household incomes of their black counterparts ranged from just $33,000 to $36,000. For Hispanics aged 35 to 59, median household income was only slightly higher than for blacks, ranging from $37,000 to $40,000.

Many Asian and non-Hispanic white middle-aged householders are in the most-affluent income group. From 24 to 29 percent of Asian households headed by 35-to-59-year-olds have incomes of $100,000 or more. Among non-Hispanic whites in the age group, the figure ranges from 20 to 26 percent. In contrast, among black householders aged 35 to 59, only 8 to 10 percent have incomes of $100,000 or more. The figures are similar for Hispanics, with 7 to 12 percent of householders aged 35 to 59 having incomes of $100,000 or more.

■ Black incomes are well below those of Asians and non-Hispanic whites because married couples—the most affluent household type—make up a much smaller share of black households. For Hispanics, incomes are lower because they are much less educated and, consequently, have little earning power.

Median household income varies by race and Hispanic origin

(median income of householders aged 45 to 54, by race and Hispanic origin, 2002)

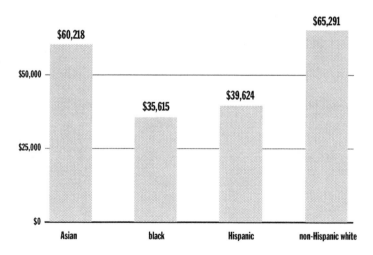

Table 4.3 Income of Households Headed by People Aged 35 to 59, 2002: Asian Households

(number and percent distribution of total Asian households and Asian households headed by people aged 35 to 59 by income, 2002; households in thousands as of 2003)

	total	aged 35 to 44			aged 45 to 54			aged 55 to 59
		total	35 to 39	40 to 44	total	45 to 49	50 to 54	
Total Asian households	**4,079**	**1,029**	**546**	**483**	**811**	**444**	**368**	**284**
Under $10,000	329	65	31	34	37	17	21	18
$10,000 to $19,999	379	79	50	31	31	17	14	29
$20,000 to $29,999	407	83	43	39	71	33	37	25
$30,000 to $39,999	436	97	55	43	83	48	36	21
$40,000 to $49,999	359	70	30	41	90	56	35	22
$50,000 to $59,999	355	80	39	41	92	54	37	23
$60,000 to $69,999	270	75	41	33	40	18	22	23
$70,000 to $79,999	261	80	46	35	49	26	22	28
$80,000 to $89,999	228	80	45	34	57	41	17	12
$90,000 to $99,999	166	41	20	21	50	29	19	15
$100,000 or more	889	279	145	134	212	106	106	71
Median income	$52,285	$65,246	$66,174	$63,086	$60,218	$57,334	$60,640	$63,587
Total Asian households	**100.0%**	**100.0%**	**100.0%**	**100.0%**	**100.0%**	**100.0%**	**100.0%**	**100.0%**
Under $10,000	8.1	6.3	5.7	7.0	4.6	3.8	5.7	6.3
$10,000 to $19,999	9.3	7.7	9.2	6.4	3.8	3.8	3.8	10.2
$20,000 to $29,999	10.0	8.1	7.9	8.1	8.8	7.4	10.1	8.8
$30,000 to $39,999	10.7	9.4	10.1	8.9	10.2	10.8	9.8	7.4
$40,000 to $49,999	8.8	6.8	5.5	8.5	11.1	12.6	9.5	7.7
$50,000 to $59,999	8.7	7.8	7.1	8.5	11.3	12.2	10.1	8.1
$60,000 to $69,999	6.6	7.3	7.5	6.8	4.9	4.1	6.0	8.1
$70,000 to $79,999	6.4	7.8	8.4	7.2	6.0	5.9	6.0	9.9
$80,000 to $89,999	5.6	7.8	8.2	7.0	7.0	9.2	4.6	4.2
$90,000 to $99,999	4.1	4.0	3.7	4.3	6.2	6.5	5.2	5.3
$100,000 or more	21.8	27.1	26.6	27.7	26.1	23.9	28.8	25.0

Note: Asian householders include those who identified themselves as Asian alone and those who identified themselves as Asian in combination with one or more other races.
Source: Bureau of the Census, data from the 2003 Current Population Survey Annual Social and Economic Supplement, Internet site http://ferret.bls.census.gov/macro/032003/hhinc/new02_000.htm; calculations by New Strategist

Table 4.4 Income of Households Headed by People Aged 35 to 59, 2002: Black Households

(number and percent distribution of total black households and black households headed by people aged 35 to 59 by income, 2002; households in thousands as of 2003)

	total	aged 35 to 44 total	aged 35 to 44 35 to 39	aged 35 to 44 40 to 44	aged 45 to 54 total	aged 45 to 54 45 to 49	aged 45 to 54 50 to 54	aged 55 to 59
Total black households	**13,778**	**3,187**	**1,524**	**1,663**	**2,836**	**1,541**	**1,295**	**1,022**
Under $10,000	2,432	397	176	221	437	231	205	158
$10,000 to $19,999	2,486	459	225	234	350	173	177	169
$20,000 to $29,999	2,111	488	245	243	399	204	195	142
$30,000 to $39,999	1,809	412	189	224	388	216	173	117
$40,000 to $49,999	1,190	351	174	176	253	146	107	95
$50,000 to $59,999	918	265	141	124	211	106	108	75
$60,000 to $69,999	698	201	96	105	168	112	57	61
$70,000 to $79,999	566	166	85	81	159	94	65	42
$80,000 to $89,999	384	104	37	68	111	70	41	36
$90,000 to $99,999	280	90	37	53	88	47	41	25
$100,000 or more	904	252	118	134	270	144	126	105
Median income	$29,177	$35,478	$35,811	$35,141	$35,615	$36,773	$33,382	$34,091
Total black households	**100.0%**	**100.0%**	**100.0%**	**100.0%**	**100.0%**	**100.0%**	**100.0%**	**100.0%**
Under $10,000	17.7	12.5	11.5	13.3	15.4	15.0	15.8	15.5
$10,000 to $19,999	18.0	14.4	14.8	14.1	12.3	11.2	13.7	16.5
$20,000 to $29,999	15.3	15.3	16.1	14.6	14.1	13.2	15.1	13.9
$30,000 to $39,999	13.1	12.9	12.4	13.5	13.7	14.0	13.4	11.4
$40,000 to $49,999	8.6	11.0	11.4	10.6	8.9	9.5	8.3	9.3
$50,000 to $59,999	6.7	8.3	9.3	7.5	7.4	6.9	8.3	7.3
$60,000 to $69,999	5.1	6.3	6.3	6.3	5.9	7.3	4.4	6.0
$70,000 to $79,999	4.1	5.2	5.6	4.9	5.6	6.1	5.0	4.1
$80,000 to $89,999	2.8	3.3	2.4	4.1	3.9	4.5	3.2	3.5
$90,000 to $99,999	2.0	2.8	2.4	3.2	3.1	3.1	3.2	2.4
$100,000 or more	6.6	7.9	7.7	8.1	9.5	9.3	9.7	10.3

Note: Black householders include those who identified themselves as black alone and those who identified themselves as black in combination with one or more other races.
Source: Bureau of the Census, data from the 2003 Current Population Survey Annual Social and Economic Supplement, Internet site http://ferret.bls.census.gov/macro/032003/hhinc/new02_000.htm; calculations by New Strategist

Table 4.5 Income of Households Headed by People Aged 35 to 59, 2002: Hispanic Households

(number and percent distribution of total Hispanic households and Hispanic households headed by people aged 35 to 59 by income, 2002; households in thousands as of 2003)

	total	aged 35 to 44			aged 45 to 54			aged 55 to 59
		total	35 to 39	40 to 44	total	45 to 49	50 to 54	
Total Hispanic households	**11,339**	**3,104**	**1,625**	**1,478**	**1,913**	**1,092**	**822**	**654**
Under $10,000	1,247	226	112	115	183	105	78	67
$10,000 to $19,999	1,879	435	237	198	236	124	109	98
$20,000 to $29,999	1,949	524	292	232	289	167	120	96
$30,000 to $39,999	1,574	479	245	234	257	149	108	88
$40,000 to $49,999	1,109	319	168	152	178	103	75	61
$50,000 to $59,999	945	310	165	145	170	104	66	37
$60,000 to $69,999	693	206	106	100	146	81	66	48
$70,000 to $79,999	505	175	84	91	94	49	45	29
$80,000 to $89,999	372	115	62	51	67	40	28	32
$90,000 to $99,999	249	68	42	26	68	37	32	19
$100,000 or more	815	246	113	134	223	131	92	80
Median income	$33,103	$37,228	$36,870	$37,731	$39,624	$39,827	$39,398	$37,193
Total Hispanic households	**100.0%**	**100.0%**	**100.0%**	**100.0%**	**100.0%**	**100.0%**	**100.0%**	**100.0%**
Under $10,000	11.0	7.3	6.9	7.8	9.6	9.6	9.5	10.2
$10,000 to $19,999	16.6	14.0	14.6	13.4	12.3	11.4	13.3	15.0
$20,000 to $29,999	17.2	16.9	18.0	15.7	15.1	15.3	14.6	14.7
$30,000 to $39,999	13.9	15.4	15.1	15.8	13.4	13.6	13.1	13.5
$40,000 to $49,999	9.8	10.3	10.3	10.3	9.3	9.4	9.1	9.3
$50,000 to $59,999	8.3	10.0	10.2	9.8	8.9	9.5	8.0	5.7
$60,000 to $69,999	6.1	6.6	6.5	6.8	7.6	7.4	8.0	7.3
$70,000 to $79,999	4.5	5.6	5.2	6.2	4.9	4.5	5.5	4.4
$80,000 to $89,999	3.3	3.7	3.8	3.5	3.5	3.7	3.4	4.9
$90,000 to $99,999	2.2	2.2	2.6	1.8	3.6	3.4	3.9	2.9
$100,000 or more	7.2	7.9	7.0	9.1	11.7	12.0	11.2	12.2

Note: Hispanics may be of any race.
Source: Bureau of the Census, data from the 2003 Current Population Survey Annual Social and Economic Supplement, Internet site http://ferret.bls.census.gov/macro/032003/hhinc/new02_000.htm; calculations by New Strategist

Table 4.6 Income of Households Headed by People Aged 35 to 59, 2002: Non-Hispanic White Households

(number and percent distribution of total non-Hispanic white households and non-Hispanic white households headed by people aged 35 to 59 by income, 2002; households in thousands as of 2003)

	total	aged 35 to 44 total	35 to 39	40 to 44	aged 45 to 54 total	45 to 49	50 to 54	aged 55 to 59
Total non-Hispanic white households	**81,166**	**16,553**	**7,702**	**8,851**	**16,875**	**8,795**	**8,080**	**7,130**
Under $10,000	5,977	702	342	359	758	402	357	479
$10,000 to $19,999	10,170	956	466	490	958	459	500	606
$20,000 to $29,999	9,797	1,512	715	797	1,272	663	608	673
$30,000 to $39,999	8,829	1,563	749	813	1,489	744	745	671
$40,000 to $49,999	7,982	1,746	883	862	1,584	796	786	672
$50,000 to $59,999	6,958	1,647	791	856	1,534	824	710	632
$60,000 to $69,999	5,926	1,448	658	790	1,418	754	662	535
$70,000 to $79,999	5,301	1,433	672	762	1,383	756	627	491
$80,000 to $89,999	4,034	1,090	492	598	1,181	597	584	398
$90,000 to $99,999	3,235	924	401	522	981	522	459	324
$100,000 or more	12,958	3,534	1,533	2,000	4,319	2,278	2,041	1,649
Median income	$46,900	$60,867	$58,424	$62,760	$65,291	$66,176	$64,307	$57,431
Total non-Hispanic white households	**100.0%**	**100.0%**	**100.0%**	**100.0%**	**100.0%**	**100.0%**	**100.0%**	**100.0%**
Under $10,000	7.4	4.2	4.4	4.1	4.5	4.6	4.4	6.7
$10,000 to $19,999	12.5	5.8	6.1	5.5	5.7	5.2	6.2	8.5
$20,000 to $29,999	12.1	9.1	9.3	9.0	7.5	7.5	7.5	9.4
$30,000 to $39,999	10.9	9.4	9.7	9.2	8.8	8.5	9.2	9.4
$40,000 to $49,999	9.8	10.5	11.5	9.7	9.4	9.1	9.7	9.4
$50,000 to $59,999	8.6	9.9	10.3	9.7	9.1	9.4	8.8	8.9
$60,000 to $69,999	7.3	8.7	8.5	8.9	8.4	8.6	8.2	7.5
$70,000 to $79,999	6.5	8.7	8.7	8.6	8.2	8.6	7.8	6.9
$80,000 to $89,999	5.0	6.6	6.4	6.8	7.0	6.8	7.2	5.6
$90,000 to $99,999	4.0	5.6	5.2	5.9	5.8	5.9	5.7	4.5
$100,000 or more	16.0	21.3	19.9	22.6	25.6	25.9	25.3	23.1

Note: Non-Hispanic white householders include only those who identified themselves as white alone and non-Hispanic.
Source: Bureau of the Census, data from the 2003 Current Population Survey Annual Social and Economic Supplement, Internet site http://ferret.bls.census.gov/macro/032003/hhinc/new02_000.htm; calculations by New Strategist

Married Couples Have the Highest Incomes

No other household type comes close to the affluence of married couples.

Among households headed by people ranging in age from 35 to 59 (Boomers were aged 38 to 56 in 2002), the median household income of married couples was far above the median of other household types. At the youngest end of the age range, married-couple household- ers aged 35 to 39 had a median income of $67,395 in 2002 versus a low of $26,853 for female- headed families in the age group. Among the nation's most affluent householders, aged 45 to 49, married couples had a median income of $79,089 versus a low of $30,492 for women living alone. The median income of men aged 45 to 49 who live alone was not much higher than that of their female counterparts, at $30,903.

Behind the higher incomes of married couples are dual earners. The more earners in a household, the higher the income. Female-headed families have low incomes, for example, because they often have only one earner in the home. The incomes of female-headed fami- lies rise through middle age as they become increasingly likely to have adult children at home—adding earners to the household. Men and women who live alone frequently have the lowest incomes because their household has only one earner.

■ Married couples aged 35 to 59 head fully 61 percent of the nation's 16 million house- holds with incomes of $100,000 or more.

Incomes peak among married couples aged 45 to 49

(median income of married couples, by age of householder, 2002)

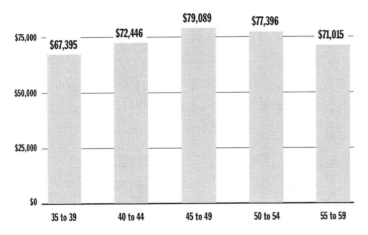

Table 4.7 Income of Households by Household Type, 2002: Aged 35 to 44

(number and percent distribution of households headed by people aged 35 to 44, by income and household type, 2002; households in thousands as of 2003)

| | | family households | | | nonfamily households | | | |
| | | | | | female householder | | male householder | |
	total	married couples	female hh, no spouse present	male hh, no spouse present	total	living alone	total	living alone
Total householders								
aged 35 to 44	**24,069**	**14,001**	**3,653**	**1,087**	**2,050**	**1,638**	**3,278**	**2,573**
Under $10,000	1,408	246	470	55	306	294	331	309
$10,000 to $19,999	1,944	507	722	102	236	218	375	325
$20,000 to $29,999	2,613	927	723	158	265	229	542	487
$30,000 to $39,999	2,569	1,094	499	182	340	306	451	376
$40,000 to $49,999	2,522	1,325	446	152	236	182	362	281
$50,000 to $59,999	2,321	1,450	272	120	169	119	309	234
$60,000 to $69,999	1,948	1,384	148	101	110	80	205	137
$70,000 to $79,999	1,867	1,401	110	66	98	67	194	130
$80,000 to $89,999	1,399	1,123	80	39	60	42	98	65
$90,000 to $99,999	1,132	919	49	22	68	33	74	45
$100,000 or more	4,346	3,624	133	89	162	71	338	185
Median income	$53,521	$70,405	$28,558	$42,087	$35,750	$31,763	$38,161	$34,352
Total householders								
aged 35 to 44	**100.0%**	**100.0%**	**100.0%**	**100.0%**	**100.0%**	**100.0%**	**100.0%**	**100.0%**
Under $10,000	5.8	1.8	12.9	5.1	14.9	17.9	10.1	12.0
$10,000 to $19,999	8.1	3.6	19.8	9.4	11.5	13.3	11.4	12.6
$20,000 to $29,999	10.9	6.6	19.8	14.5	12.9	14.0	16.5	18.9
$30,000 to $39,999	10.7	7.8	13.7	16.7	16.6	18.7	13.8	14.6
$40,000 to $49,999	10.5	9.5	12.2	14.0	11.5	11.1	11.0	10.9
$50,000 to $59,999	9.6	10.4	7.4	11.0	8.2	7.3	9.4	9.1
$60,000 to $69,999	8.1	9.9	4.1	9.3	5.4	4.9	6.3	5.3
$70,000 to $79,999	7.8	10.0	3.0	6.1	4.8	4.1	5.9	5.1
$80,000 to $89,999	5.8	8.0	2.2	3.6	2.9	2.6	3.0	2.5
$90,000 to $99,999	4.7	6.6	1.3	2.0	3.3	2.0	2.3	1.7
$100,000 or more	18.1	25.9	3.6	8.2	7.9	4.3	10.3	7.2

Source: Bureau of the Census, data from the 2003 Current Population Survey Annual Social and Economic Supplement, Internet site http://ferret.bls.census.gov/macro/032003/hhinc/new02_000.htm; calculations by New Strategist

Table 4.8 Income of Households by Household Type, 2002: Aged 45 to 54

(number and percent distribution of households headed by people aged 45 to 54, by income and household type, 2002; households in thousands as of 2003)

| | total | family households | | | nonfamily households | | | |
		married couples	female hh, no spouse present	male hh, no spouse present	female householder total	living alone	male householder total	living alone
Total householders aged 45 to 54	**22,623**	**13,297**	**2,644**	**923**	**2,790**	**2,303**	**2,970**	**2,516**
Under $10,000	1,424	213	276	42	471	453	422	401
$10,000 to $19,999	1,614	372	381	101	342	306	418	379
$20,000 to $29,999	2,046	701	365	123	416	387	441	404
$30,000 to $39,999	2,245	928	353	112	432	360	417	370
$40,000 to $49,999	2,120	1,044	326	133	337	295	281	240
$50,000 to $59,999	2,012	1,163	266	87	216	177	283	235
$60,000 to $69,999	1,782	1,158	203	84	174	92	164	116
$70,000 to $79,999	1,697	1,233	151	80	111	72	123	93
$80,000 to $89,999	1,422	1,130	86	31	62	43	113	88
$90,000 to $99,999	1,194	987	63	31	44	27	69	45
$100,000 or more	5,069	4,367	178	103	181	89	240	145
Median income	$59,021	$78,482	$37,871	$45,952	$33,293	$30,122	$35,058	$31,708
Total householders aged 45 to 54	**100.0%**	**100.0%**	**100.0%**	**100.0%**	**100.0%**	**100.0%**	**100.0%**	**100.0%**
Under $10,000	6.3	1.6	10.4	4.6	16.9	19.7	14.2	15.9
$10,000 to $19,999	7.1	2.8	14.4	10.9	12.3	13.3	14.1	15.1
$20,000 to $29,999	9.0	5.3	13.8	13.3	14.9	16.8	14.8	16.1
$30,000 to $39,999	9.9	7.0	13.4	12.1	15.5	15.6	14.0	14.7
$40,000 to $49,999	9.4	7.9	12.3	14.4	12.1	12.8	9.5	9.5
$50,000 to $59,999	8.9	8.7	10.1	9.4	7.7	7.7	9.5	9.3
$60,000 to $69,999	7.9	8.7	7.7	9.1	6.2	4.0	5.5	4.6
$70,000 to $79,999	7.5	9.3	5.7	8.7	4.0	3.1	4.1	3.7
$80,000 to $89,999	6.3	8.5	3.3	3.4	2.2	1.9	3.8	3.5
$90,000 to $99,999	5.3	7.4	2.4	3.4	1.6	1.2	2.3	1.8
$100,000 or more	22.4	32.8	6.7	11.2	6.5	3.9	8.1	5.8

Source: Bureau of the Census, data from the 2003 Current Population Survey Annual Social and Economic Supplement. Internet site http://ferret.bls.census.gov/macro/032003/hhinc/new02_000.htm; calculations by New Strategist

Table 4.9 Income of Households by Household Type, 2002: Aged 35 to 39

(number and percent distribution of households headed by people aged 35 to 39, by income and household type, 2002; households in thousands as of 2003)

	total	family households			nonfamily households			
					female householder		male householder	
		married couples	female hh, no spouse present	male hh, no spouse present	total	living alone	total	living alone
Total householders aged 35 to 39	**11,486**	**6,640**	**1,826**	**498**	**943**	**771**	**1,578**	**1,178**
Under $10,000	674	119	256	23	127	123	148	132
$10,000 to $19,999	982	283	392	45	95	90	168	145
$20,000 to $29,999	1,296	480	358	83	120	109	257	225
$30,000 to $39,999	1,250	551	244	81	172	152	204	163
$40,000 to $49,999	1,271	658	222	76	112	91	203	145
$50,000 to $59,999	1,146	679	152	63	85	62	167	111
$60,000 to $69,999	905	679	56	36	36	28	98	67
$70,000 to $79,999	893	696	41	27	53	37	78	50
$80,000 to $89,999	641	517	24	15	30	23	57	37
$90,000 to $99,999	504	429	18	8	23	3	26	11
$100,000 or more	1,921	1,552	65	42	89	53	173	90
Median income	$51,870	$67,395	$26,853	$41,725	$36,638	$33,393	$40,504	$35,771
Total householders aged 35 to 39	**100.0%**	**100.0%**	**100.0%**	**100.0%**	**100.0%**	**100.0%**	**100.0%**	**100.0%**
Under $10,000	5.9	1.8	14.0	4.6	13.5	16.0	9.4	11.2
$10,000 to $19,999	8.5	4.3	21.5	9.0	10.1	11.7	10.6	12.3
$20,000 to $29,999	11.3	7.2	19.6	16.7	12.7	14.1	16.3	19.1
$30,000 to $39,999	10.9	8.3	13.4	16.3	18.2	19.7	12.9	13.8
$40,000 to $49,999	11.1	9.9	12.2	15.3	11.9	11.8	12.9	12.3
$50,000 to $59,999	10.0	10.2	8.3	12.7	9.0	8.0	10.6	9.4
$60,000 to $69,999	7.9	10.2	3.1	7.2	3.8	3.6	6.2	5.7
$70,000 to $79,999	7.8	10.5	2.2	5.4	5.6	4.8	4.9	4.2
$80,000 to $89,999	5.6	7.8	1.3	3.0	3.2	3.0	3.6	3.1
$90,000 to $99,999	4.4	6.5	1.0	1.6	2.4	0.4	1.6	0.9
$100,000 or more	16.7	23.4	3.6	8.4	9.4	6.9	11.0	7.6

Source: Bureau of the Census, data from the 2003 Current Population Survey Annual Social and Economic Supplement, Internet site http://ferret.bls.census.gov/macro/032003/hhinc/new02_000.htm; calculations by New Strategist

Table 4.10 Income of Households by Household Type, 2002: Aged 40 to 44

(number and percent distribution of households headed by people aged 40 to 44, by income and household type, 2002; households in thousands as of 2003)

| | | family households | | | nonfamily households | | | |
| | | | | | female householder | | male householder | |
	total	married couples	female hh, no spouse present	male hh, no spouse present	total	living alone	total	living alone
Total householders aged 40 to 44	**12,583**	**7,361**	**1,826**	**589**	**1,108**	**867**	**1,700**	**1,395**
Under $10,000	733	127	214	32	177	169	183	177
$10,000 to $19,999	962	225	330	57	141	128	208	181
$20,000 to $29,999	1,316	446	364	76	143	119	285	262
$30,000 to $39,999	1,320	545	256	103	170	152	249	213
$40,000 to $49,999	1,250	667	224	76	124	91	159	136
$50,000 to $59,999	1,177	771	122	58	84	57	141	123
$60,000 to $69,999	1,041	705	91	64	74	53	107	69
$70,000 to $79,999	974	706	69	39	45	31	116	81
$80,000 to $89,999	758	606	57	24	30	19	40	27
$90,000 to $99,999	628	489	31	14	46	30	47	33
$100,000 or more	2,425	2,072	68	46	73	17	165	95
Median income	$55,466	$72,446	$30,134	$42,453	$34,472	$30,669	$36,399	$32,236
Total householders aged 40 to 44	**100.0%**	**100.0%**	**100.0%**	**100.0%**	**100.0%**	**100.0%**	**100.0%**	**100.0%**
Under $10,000	5.8	1.7	11.7	5.4	16.0	19.5	10.8	12.7
$10,000 to $19,999	7.6	3.1	18.1	9.7	12.7	14.8	12.2	13.0
$20,000 to $29,999	10.5	6.1	19.9	12.9	12.9	13.7	16.8	18.8
$30,000 to $39,999	10.5	7.4	14.0	17.5	15.3	17.5	14.6	15.3
$40,000 to $49,999	9.9	9.1	12.3	12.9	11.2	10.5	9.4	9.7
$50,000 to $59,999	9.4	10.5	6.7	9.8	7.6	6.6	8.3	8.8
$60,000 to $69,999	8.3	9.6	5.0	10.9	6.7	6.1	6.3	4.9
$70,000 to $79,999	7.7	9.6	3.8	6.6	4.1	3.6	6.8	5.8
$80,000 to $89,999	6.0	8.2	3.1	4.1	2.7	2.2	2.4	1.9
$90,000 to $99,999	5.0	6.6	1.7	2.4	4.2	3.5	2.8	2.4
$100,000 or more	19.3	28.1	3.7	7.8	6.6	2.0	9.7	6.8

Source: Bureau of the Census, data from the 2003 Current Population Survey Annual Social and Economic Supplement, Internet site http://ferret.bls.census.gov/macro/032003/hhinc/new02_000.htm; calculations by New Strategist

Table 4.11 Income of Households by Household Type, 2002: Aged 45 to 49

(number and percent distribution of households headed by people aged 45 to 49, by income and household type, 2002; households in thousands as of 2003)

| | | family households | | | nonfamily households | | | |
| | | | | | female householder | | male householder | |
	total	married couples	female hh, no spouse present	male hh, no spouse present	total	living alone	total	living alone
Total householders aged 45 to 49	**11,957**	**7,085**	**1,505**	**529**	**1,295**	**1,054**	**1,543**	**1,292**
Under $10,000	757	112	166	23	233	221	223	208
$10,000 to $19,999	791	179	205	56	140	128	211	194
$20,000 to $29,999	1,080	358	229	75	178	166	238	220
$30,000 to $39,999	1,166	468	215	67	207	174	212	187
$40,000 to $49,999	1,107	542	195	72	151	125	149	128
$50,000 to $59,999	1,091	620	148	48	130	105	146	118
$60,000 to $69,999	971	613	116	45	89	49	108	73
$70,000 to $79,999	929	719	63	48	45	22	54	44
$80,000 to $89,999	746	620	44	16	21	12	46	32
$90,000 to $99,999	640	545	26	20	20	10	29	20
$100,000 or more	2,679	2,312	98	60	84	41	126	68
Median income	$59,845	$79,089	$36,549	$45,721	$34,282	$30,492	$34,534	$30,903
Total householders aged 45 to 49	**100.0%**	**100.0%**	**100.0%**	**100.0%**	**100.0%**	**100.0%**	**100.0%**	**100.0%**
Under $10,000	6.3	1.6	11.0	4.3	18.0	21.0	14.5	16.1
$10,000 to $19,999	6.6	2.5	13.6	10.6	10.8	12.1	13.7	15.0
$20,000 to $29,999	9.0	5.1	15.2	14.2	13.7	15.7	15.4	17.0
$30,000 to $39,999	9.8	6.6	14.3	12.7	16.0	16.5	13.7	14.5
$40,000 to $49,999	9.3	7.6	13.0	13.6	11.7	11.9	9.7	9.9
$50,000 to $59,999	9.1	8.8	9.8	9.1	10.0	10.0	9.5	9.1
$60,000 to $69,999	8.1	8.7	7.7	8.5	6.9	4.6	7.0	5.7
$70,000 to $79,999	7.8	10.1	4.2	9.1	3.5	2.1	3.5	3.4
$80,000 to $89,999	6.2	8.8	2.9	3.0	1.6	1.1	3.0	2.5
$90,000 to $99,999	5.4	7.7	1.7	3.8	1.5	0.9	1.9	1.5
$100,000 or more	22.4	32.6	6.5	11.3	6.5	3.9	8.2	5.3

Source: Bureau of the Census, data from the 2003 Current Population Survey Annual Social and Economic Supplement, Internet site http://ferret.bls.census.gov/macro/032003/hhinc/new02_000.htm; calculations by New Strategist

Table 4.12 Income of Households by Household Type, 2002: Aged 50 to 54

(number and percent distribution of households headed by people aged 50 to 54, by income and household type, 2002; households in thousands as of 2003)

| | | family households | | | nonfamily households | | | |
| | | | | | female householder | | male householder | |
	total	married couples	female hh, no spouse present	male hh, no spouse present	total	living alone	total	living alone
Total householders aged 50 to 54	**10,666**	**6,212**	**1,139**	**393**	**1,494**	**1,249**	**1,428**	**1,224**
Under $10,000	667	103	109	19	238	233	199	193
$10,000 to $19,999	823	192	176	44	203	178	207	185
$20,000 to $29,999	967	343	135	47	239	221	203	183
$30,000 to $39,999	1,077	463	138	45	227	186	205	182
$40,000 to $49,999	1,015	503	131	61	188	170	132	112
$50,000 to $59,999	922	544	119	37	84	73	136	118
$60,000 to $69,999	811	545	86	39	86	43	55	43
$70,000 to $79,999	767	514	88	31	66	50	68	49
$80,000 to $89,999	675	510	43	14	43	30	68	57
$90,000 to $99,999	553	441	36	11	24	18	41	25
$100,000 or more	2,390	2,055	80	43	97	48	115	77
Median income	$57,935	$77,396	$40,649	$46,404	$32,478	$29,611	$35,354	$32,785
Total householders aged 50 to 54	**100.0%**	**100.0%**	**100.0%**	**100.0%**	**100.0%**	**100.0%**	**100.0%**	**100.0%**
Under $10,000	6.3	1.7	9.6	4.8	15.9	18.7	13.9	15.8
$10,000 to $19,999	7.7	3.1	15.5	11.2	13.6	14.3	14.5	15.1
$20,000 to $29,999	9.1	5.5	11.9	12.0	16.0	17.7	14.2	15.0
$30,000 to $39,999	10.1	7.5	12.1	11.5	15.2	14.9	14.4	14.9
$40,000 to $49,999	9.5	8.1	11.5	15.5	12.6	13.6	9.2	9.2
$50,000 to $59,999	8.6	8.8	10.4	9.4	5.6	5.8	9.5	9.6
$60,000 to $69,999	7.6	8.8	7.6	9.9	5.8	3.4	3.9	3.5
$70,000 to $79,999	7.2	8.3	7.7	7.9	4.4	4.0	4.8	4.0
$80,000 to $89,999	6.3	8.2	3.8	3.6	2.9	2.4	4.8	4.7
$90,000 to $99,999	5.2	7.1	3.2	2.8	1.6	1.4	2.9	2.0
$100,000 or more	22.4	33.1	7.0	10.9	6.5	3.8	8.1	6.3

Source: Bureau of the Census, data from the 2003 Current Population Survey Annual Social and Economic Supplement, Internet site http://ferret.bls.census.gov/macro/032003/hhinc/new02_000.htm; calculations by New Strategist

Table 4.13 Income of Households By Household Type, 2002: Aged 55 to 59

(number and percent distribution of households headed by people aged 55 to 59, by income and household type, 2002; households in thousands as of 2003)

	total	family households			nonfamily households			
					female householder		male householder	
		married couples	female hh, no spouse present	male hh, no spouse present	total	living alone	total	living alone
Total householders aged 55 to 59	**9,192**	**5,513**	**753**	**245**	**1,552**	**1,406**	**1,128**	**980**
Under $10,000	736	150	60	18	283	280	223	216
$10,000 to $19,999	909	250	148	27	272	257	211	197
$20,000 to $29,999	948	346	106	21	283	269	189	167
$30,000 to $39,999	908	464	106	31	205	181	102	92
$40,000 to $49,999	864	485	88	38	155	138	99	84
$50,000 to $59,999	784	504	76	31	107	93	67	56
$60,000 to $69,999	670	510	52	16	47	39	45	35
$70,000 to $79,999	591	436	22	19	67	57	47	40
$80,000 to $89,999	479	391	23	11	27	21	29	21
$90,000 to $99,999	389	326	23	5	11	11	24	13
$100,000 or more	1,914	1,649	50	29	97	58	89	60
Median income	$52,709	$71,015	$36,017	$46,386	$26,931	$25,730	$27,557	$24,674
Total householders aged 55 to 59	**100.0%**	**100.0%**	**100.0%**	**100.0%**	**100.0%**	**100.0%**	**100.0%**	**100.0%**
Under $10,000	8.0	2.7	8.0	7.3	18.2	19.9	19.8	22.0
$10,000 to $19,999	9.9	4.5	19.7	11.0	17.5	18.3	18.7	20.1
$20,000 to $29,999	10.3	6.3	14.1	8.6	18.2	19.1	16.8	17.0
$30,000 to $39,999	9.9	8.4	14.1	12.7	13.2	12.9	9.0	9.4
$40,000 to $49,999	9.4	8.8	11.7	15.5	10.0	9.8	8.8	8.6
$50,000 to $59,999	8.5	9.1	10.1	12.7	6.9	6.6	5.9	5.7
$60,000 to $69,999	7.3	9.3	6.9	6.5	3.0	2.8	4.0	3.6
$70,000 to $79,999	6.4	7.9	2.9	7.8	4.3	4.1	4.2	4.1
$80,000 to $89,999	5.2	7.1	3.1	4.5	1.7	1.5	2.6	2.1
$90,000 to $99,999	4.2	5.9	3.1	2.0	0.7	0.8	2.1	1.3
$100,000 or more	20.8	29.9	6.6	11.8	6.2	4.1	7.9	6.1

Source: Bureau of the Census, data from the 2003 Current Population Survey Annual Social and Economic Supplement, Internet site http://ferret.bls.census.gov/macro/032003/hhinc/new02_000.htm; calculations by New Strategist

Incomes for Many Middle-Aged Men Have Declined

Women's incomes have soared over the past two decades, and have climbed even since 2000.

Between 2000 and 2002, the median income of men aged 35 to 54 fell 4 percent, after adjusting for inflation (Boomers were aged 38 to 56 in 2002). While recession and the jobless recovery could be blamed for the decline, in fact men in this broad age group have experienced falling incomes for the past two decades. In contrast, the incomes of women have surged since 1980, regardless of age. Even in the 2000 to 2002 period, incomes continued to grow for women, although much more slowly—and they fell among women aged 35 to 44. Behind women's rising income is their growing labor force participation rate.

The median income gains experienced by men aged 55 to 64 stand in stark contrast to the losses experienced by men aged 35 to 54. These gains may continue as Boomer men fill the age group, postponing retirement until they reach age 65 or older.

■ With the incomes of Boomer men declining, the incomes of women are increasingly important to the financial well-being of the nation's middle-aged householders.

Among the middle aged, women are faring better than men

(percent change in median income of people aged 35 to 64 by age and sex, 2000–02; in 2002 dollars)

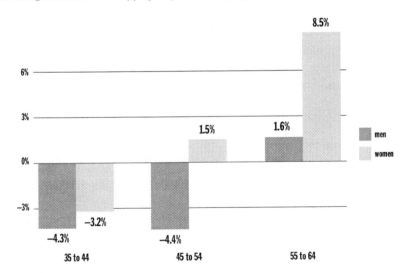

Table 4.14 Median Income of Men Aged 35 to 64, 1980 to 2002

(median income of men aged 15 or older and aged 35 to 64, 1980 to 2002; percent change for selected years; in 2002 dollars)

	total men	35 to 44	45 to 54	55 to 64
2002	$29,238	$37,892	$40,969	$36,277
2001	29,564	38,950	41,758	36,204
2000	29,597	39,600	42,855	35,702
1999	29,433	39,082	44,177	36,309
1998	29,189	38,759	42,884	36,113
1997	28,170	36,705	42,038	34,812
1996	27,199	36,709	41,347	33,694
1995	26,439	36,818	41,700	33,959
1994	26,070	36,857	41,929	32,498
1993	25,862	37,185	40,632	30,809
1992	25,694	37,044	40,423	32,176
1991	26,357	37,729	40,918	32,782
1990	27,075	39,723	41,369	33,093
1989	27,861	41,227	43,364	34,210
1988	27,618	41,695	43,204	33,080
1987	26,925	40,938	43,126	33,128
1986	26,791	40,971	43,450	32,927
1985	26,000	40,422	41,198	32,290
1984	25,696	40,464	40,502	32,164
1983	25,061	38,437	39,593	32,020
1982	24,888	38,623	38,434	31,806
1981	25,459	39,903	39,724	32,813
1980	25,900	41,418	41,288	32,896
Percent change				
2000–2002	−1.2%	−4.3%	−4.4%	1.6%
1990–2002	8.0	−4.6	−1.0	9.6
1980–2002	12.9	−8.5	−0.8	10.3

Source: Bureau of the Census, data from the Current Population Survey Annual Demographic Supplements, Internet site http:// www.census.gov/hhes/income/histinc/p08.html; calculations by New Strategist

Table 4.15   Median Income of Women Aged 35 to 64, 1980 to 2002

(median income of women aged 15 or older and aged 35 to 64, 1980 to 2002; percent change for selected years; in 2002 dollars)

	total women	35 to 44	45 to 54	55 to 64
2002	$16,812	$22,322	$25,165	$19,165
2001	16,878	22,828	24,519	18,106
2000	16,774	23,054	24,782	17,669
1999	16,523	22,319	24,375	17,176
1998	15,899	22,350	23,785	16,169
1997	15,311	20,900	22,943	16,062
1996	14,624	21,052	21,735	15,196
1995	14,215	20,386	20,768	14,508
1994	13,762	19,431	20,465	13,043
1993	13,537	19,418	20,006	13,272
1992	13,458	19,365	19,912	12,728
1991	13,489	19,475	18,959	12,750
1990	13,435	19,351	18,985	12,541
1989	13,479	19,335	18,407	12,833
1988	12,977	18,326	17,558	12,237
1987	12,558	18,159	17,051	11,416
1986	11,914	17,320	16,249	11,549
1985	11,504	16,378	15,333	11,434
1984	11,313	15,749	14,665	11,261
1983	10,823	15,177	14,054	10,498
1982	10,502	14,006	13,384	10,538
1981	10,313	13,919	13,284	10,157
1980	10,170	13,364	13,235	10,182
Percent change				
2000–2002	0.2%	–3.2%	1.5%	8.5%
1990–2002	25.1	15.4	32.6	52.8
1980–2002	65.3	67.0	90.1	88.2

Source: Bureau of the Census, data from the Current Population Survey Annual Demographic Supplements, Internet site http:// www.census.gov/hhes/income/histinc/p08.html; calculations by New Strategist

Men in Their Fifties Have the Highest Incomes

The incomes of non-Hispanic white men are much higher than those of Asians, blacks, and Hispanics.

Among men, income grows through middle age as they rise through the ranks in their career. Median income peaks among men aged 50 to 54, at $41,005 in 2002. But among men who work full-time, median income peaks in the older 55-to-59 age group, at $49,885 in 2002. The overall median income of men aged 55 to 59 is lower than that of younger men because a smaller proportion work full-time (64 percent versus 73 to 77 percent).

Non-Hispanic white men have the highest median income, peaking at $52,358 in 2002 for full-time workers aged 55 to 59. Among black men who work full-time, income also peaks in the 55-to-59 age group, but at a much lower median of $37,370. Median income peaks at $48,617 in the 45-to-49 age group among Asian men who work full-time. There is little difference by age in the incomes of Hispanic men who work full-time, with a median income of just $30,000 to $31,000 for those ranging in age from 40 to 59.

■ One in eight non-Hispanic white men aged 45 to 59 has an income of $100,000 or more.

Among men working full-time, those aged 55 to 59 have the highest median income

(median income of men working full-time, by age, 2002)

Table 4.16 Income of Men Aged 35 to 59, 2002: Total Men

(number and percent distribution of men aged 16 or older and aged 35 to 59 by income, 2002; median income by work status, and percent working year-round, full-time; men in thousands as of 2003)

	total	aged 35 to 44			aged 45 to 54			aged 55 to 59
		total	35 to 39	40 to 44	total	45 to 49	50 to 54	
TOTAL MEN	108,814	21,733	10,510	11,223	19,606	10,449	9,157	7,493
Without income	9,026	754	381	373	635	334	301	208
With income	99,788	20,979	10,129	10,850	18,971	10,115	8,856	7,285
Under $10,000	16,061	1,678	802	875	1,548	834	714	719
$10,000 to $19,999	18,536	2,548	1,317	1,232	2,237	1,192	1,045	1,013
$20,000 to $29,999	16,206	3,377	1,693	1,685	2,556	1,393	1,163	959
$30,000 to $39,999	13,528	3,340	1,640	1,702	2,793	1,458	1,335	987
$40,000 to $49,999	9,485	2,471	1,220	1,249	2,244	1,211	1,034	786
$50,000 to $59,999	7,048	1,995	945	1,050	1,858	1,023	835	658
$60,000 to $69,999	4,735	1,342	617	726	1,344	680	663	424
$70,000 to $79,999	3,769	1,152	508	644	1,104	601	502	461
$80,000 to $89,999	2,355	674	310	364	738	350	387	312
$90,000 to $99,999	1,512	458	208	250	460	264	196	164
$100,000 or more	6,556	1,943	867	1,076	2,090	1,108	983	801
Median income of men with income	$29,238	$37,892	$36,942	$39,371	$40,969	$40,938	$41,005	$39,538
Median income of full-time workers	40,507	43,099	41,956	45,115	47,652	47,276	48,332	49,885
Percent working full-time	54.0%	76.6%	75.9%	77.1%	74.5%	75.6%	73.2%	64.2%
TOTAL MEN	100.0%	100.0%	100.0%	100.0%	100.0%	100.0%	100.0%	100.0%
Without income	8.3	3.5	3.6	3.3	3.2	3.2	3.3	2.8
With income	91.7	96.5	96.4	96.7	96.8	96.8	96.7	97.2
Under $10,000	14.8	7.7	7.6	7.8	7.9	8.0	7.8	9.6
$10,000 to $19,999	17.0	11.7	12.5	11.0	11.4	11.4	11.4	13.5
$20,000 to $29,999	14.9	15.5	16.1	15.0	13.0	13.3	12.7	12.8
$30,000 to $39,999	12.4	15.4	15.6	15.2	14.2	14.0	14.6	13.2
$40,000 to $49,999	8.7	11.4	11.6	11.1	11.4	11.6	11.3	10.5
$50,000 to $59,999	6.5	9.2	9.0	9.4	9.5	9.8	9.1	8.8
$60,000 to $69,999	4.4	6.2	5.9	6.5	6.9	6.5	7.2	5.7
$70,000 to $79,999	3.5	5.3	4.8	5.7	5.6	5.8	5.5	6.2
$80,000 to $89,999	2.2	3.1	2.9	3.2	3.8	3.3	4.2	4.2
$90,000 to $99,999	1.4	2.1	2.0	2.2	2.3	2.5	2.1	2.2
$100,000 or more	6.0	8.9	8.2	9.6	10.7	10.6	10.7	10.7

Source: Bureau of the Census, data from the 2003 Current Population Survey Annual Social and Economic Supplement. Internet site http://ferret.bls.census.gov/macro/032003/perinc/toc.htm; calculations by New Strategist

Table 4.17 Income of Men Aged 35 to 59, 2002: Asian Men

(number and percent distribution of Asian men aged 16 or older and aged 35 to 59 by income, 2002; median income by work status, and percent working year-round, full-time; men in thousands as of 2003)

	total	aged 35 to 44			aged 45 to 54			aged 55 to 59
		total	35 to 39	40 to 44	total	45 to 49	50 to 54	
TOTAL ASIAN MEN	**4,688**	**1,010**	**534**	**476**	**752**	**401**	**351**	**253**
Without income	**549**	**52**	**23**	**28**	**27**	**6**	**21**	**11**
With income	**4,139**	**958**	**511**	**448**	**725**	**395**	**330**	**242**
Under $10,000	708	65	35	31	46	24	22	28
$10,000 to $19,999	701	114	75	39	98	48	50	41
$20,000 to $29,999	589	140	78	64	106	53	52	40
$30,000 to $39,999	536	137	62	75	98	51	45	29
$40,000 to $49,999	371	105	62	43	82	43	39	24
$50,000 to $59,999	235	75	39	37	53	34	19	5
$60,000 to $69,999	206	70	38	32	32	18	14	12
$70,000 to $79,999	199	61	28	33	45	28	17	21
$80,000 to $89,999	141	48	27	21	41	26	15	7
$90,000 to $99,999	95	29	15	12	29	16	13	9
$100,000 or more	360	114	53	61	94	50	44	24
Median income of men with income	$30,839	$41,657	$40,746	$43,298	$41,197	$45,316	$38,308	$33,386
Median income of full-time workers	42,448	46,375	45,843	47,306	46,559	48,617	43,839	40,476
Percent working full-time	56.2%	79.0%	78.1%	79.8%	78.5%	82.0%	74.6%	67.6%
TOTAL ASIAN MEN	**100.0%**	**100.0%**	**100.0%**	**100.0%**	**100.0%**	**100.0%**	**100.0%**	**100.0%**
Without income	11.7	5.1	4.3	5.9	3.6	1.5	6.0	4.3
With income	88.3	94.9	95.7	94.1	96.4	98.5	94.0	95.7
Under $10,000	15.1	6.4	6.6	6.5	6.1	6.0	6.3	11.1
$10,000 to $19,999	15.0	11.3	14.0	8.2	13.0	12.0	14.2	16.2
$20,000 to $29,999	12.6	13.9	14.6	13.4	14.1	13.2	14.8	15.8
$30,000 to $39,999	11.4	13.6	11.6	15.8	13.0	12.7	12.8	11.5
$40,000 to $49,999	7.9	10.4	11.6	9.0	10.9	10.7	11.1	9.5
$50,000 to $59,999	5.0	7.4	7.3	7.8	7.1	8.5	5.4	2.0
$60,000 to $69,999	4.4	6.9	7.1	6.7	4.3	4.5	4.0	4.7
$70,000 to $79,999	4.2	6.0	5.2	6.9	6.0	7.0	4.8	8.3
$80,000 to $89,999	3.0	4.8	5.1	4.4	5.5	6.5	4.3	2.8
$90,000 to $99,999	2.0	2.9	2.8	2.5	3.9	4.0	3.7	3.6
$100,000 or more	7.7	11.3	9.9	12.8	12.5	12.5	12.5	9.5

Note: Asians include those who identified themselves as Asian alone and those who identified themselves as Asian in combination with one or more other races.
Source: Bureau of the Census, data from the 2003 Current Population Survey Annual Social and Economic Supplement, Internet site http://ferret.bls.census.gov/macro/032003/perinc/toc.htm; calculations by New Strategist

Table 4.18 Income of Men Aged 35 to 59, 2002: Black Men

(number and percent distribution of black men aged 16 or older and aged 35 to 59 by income, 2002; median income by work status, and percent working year-round, full-time; men in thousands as of 2003)

	total	aged 35 to 44			aged 45 to 54			aged 55 to 59
		total	35 to 39	40 to 44	total	45 to 49	50 to 54	
TOTAL BLACK MEN	**12,188**	**2,492**	**1,211**	**1,281**	**2,121**	**1,165**	**956**	**659**
Without income	**2,092**	**222**	**116**	**107**	**165**	**94**	**71**	**48**
With income	**10,096**	**2,270**	**1,095**	**1,174**	**1,956**	**1,071**	**885**	**611**
Under $10,000	2,416	300	121	178	289	155	134	111
$10,000 to $19,999	2,254	406	203	204	418	229	189	123
$20,000 to $29,999	1,813	461	236	225	332	198	134	104
$30,000 to $39,999	1,373	391	207	184	330	161	169	90
$40,000 to $49,999	829	232	96	136	212	115	98	55
$50,000 to $59,999	527	181	85	96	124	70	54	36
$60,000 to $69,999	264	98	43	54	62	38	24	16
$70,000 to $79,999	214	76	46	32	64	33	32	29
$80,000 to $89,999	115	39	20	18	33	16	17	15
$90,000 to $99,999	70	28	11	17	19	10	8	6
$100,000 or more	221	56	28	28	70	46	24	26
Median income of men with income	$21,509	$28,846	$29,280	$28,213	$26,942	$26,563	$27,530	$26,869
Median income of full-time workers	31,966	34,989	33,886	35,619	35,408	35,713	34,858	37,370
Percent working full-time	45.2%	66.2%	67.5%	64.9%	61.8%	63.4%	59.7%	50.5%
TOTAL BLACK MEN	**100.0%**	**100.0%**	**100.0%**	**100.0%**	**100.0%**	**100.0%**	**100.0%**	**100.0%**
Without income	**17.2**	**8.9**	**9.6**	**8.4**	**7.8**	**8.1**	**7.4**	**7.3**
With income	**82.8**	**91.1**	**90.4**	**91.6**	**92.2**	**91.9**	**92.6**	**92.7**
Under $10,000	19.8	12.0	10.0	13.9	13.6	13.3	14.0	16.8
$10,000 to $19,999	18.5	16.3	16.8	15.9	19.7	19.7	19.8	18.7
$20,000 to $29,999	14.9	18.5	19.5	17.6	15.7	17.0	14.0	15.8
$30,000 to $39,999	11.3	15.7	17.1	14.4	15.6	13.8	17.7	13.7
$40,000 to $49,999	6.8	9.3	7.9	10.6	10.0	9.9	10.3	8.3
$50,000 to $59,999	4.3	7.3	7.0	7.5	5.8	6.0	5.6	5.5
$60,000 to $69,999	2.2	3.9	3.6	4.2	2.9	3.3	2.5	2.4
$70,000 to $79,999	1.8	3.1	3.8	2.5	3.0	2.8	3.3	4.4
$80,000 to $89,999	0.9	1.6	1.7	1.4	1.6	1.4	1.8	2.3
$90,000 to $99,999	0.6	1.1	0.9	1.3	0.9	0.9	0.8	0.9
$100,000 or more	1.8	2.2	2.3	2.2	3.3	3.9	2.5	3.9

Note: Blacks include those who identified themselves as black alone and those who identified themselves as black in combination with one or more other races.
Source: Bureau of the Census, data from the 2003 Current Population Survey Annual Social and Economic Supplement, Internet site http://ferret.bls.census.gov/macro/032003/perinc/toc.htm; calculations by New Strategist

Table 4.19 Income of Men Aged 35 to 59, 2002: Hispanic Men

(number and percent distribution of Hispanic men aged 16 or older and aged 35 to 59 by income, 2002; median income by work status, and percent working year-round, full-time; men in thousands as of 2003)

	total	aged 35 to 44			aged 45 to 54			aged 55 to 59
		total	35 to 39	40 to 44	total	45 to 49	50 to 54	
TOTAL HISPANIC MEN	14,353	3,061	1,653	1,408	1,768	993	775	591
Without income	1,729	131	76	55	95	47	48	22
With income	12,624	2,930	1,577	1,353	1,673	946	727	569
Under $10,000	2,395	294	152	141	228	134	93	99
$10,000 to $19,999	3,629	703	405	297	376	216	161	138
$20,000 to $29,999	2,715	743	414	330	357	206	149	98
$30,000 to $39,999	1,526	440	220	221	218	120	101	73
$40,000 to $49,999	869	269	151	117	155	85	70	50
$50,000 to $59,999	566	175	88	89	114	67	47	40
$60,000 to $69,999	304	106	55	52	60	36	25	20
$70,000 to $79,999	201	64	34	31	49	29	20	22
$80,000 to $89,999	104	33	18	15	24	13	11	8
$90,000 to $99,999	63	15	5	10	23	12	10	2
$100,000 or more	251	88	37	51	68	30	38	19
Median income of men with income	$20,702	$25,592	$24,867	$26,495	$25,941	$25,476	$26,487	$23,831
Median income of full-time workers	26,137	28,713	27,189	30,324	31,160	30,921	31,402	31,119
Percent working full-time	57.0%	74.1%	73.3%	75.1%	66.7%	66.9%	66.5%	64.1%
TOTAL HISPANIC MEN	100.0%	100.0%	100.0%	100.0%	100.0%	100.0%	100.0%	100.0%
Without income	12.1	4.3	4.6	3.9	5.4	4.7	6.2	3.7
With income	88.0	95.7	95.4	96.1	94.6	95.3	93.8	96.3
Under $10,000	16.7	9.6	9.2	10.0	12.9	13.5	12.0	16.8
$10,000 to $19,999	25.3	23.0	24.5	21.1	21.3	21.8	20.8	23.4
$20,000 to $29,999	18.9	24.3	25.1	23.4	20.2	20.7	19.2	16.6
$30,000 to $39,999	10.6	14.4	13.3	15.7	12.3	12.1	13.0	12.4
$40,000 to $49,999	6.1	8.8	9.1	8.3	8.8	8.6	9.0	8.5
$50,000 to $59,999	3.9	5.7	5.3	6.3	6.4	6.7	6.1	6.8
$60,000 to $69,999	2.1	3.5	3.3	3.7	3.4	3.6	3.2	3.4
$70,000 to $79,999	1.4	2.1	2.1	2.2	2.8	2.9	2.6	3.7
$80,000 to $89,999	0.7	1.1	1.1	1.1	1.4	1.3	1.4	1.4
$90,000 to $99,999	0.4	0.5	0.3	0.7	1.3	1.2	1.3	0.3
$100,000 or more	1.7	2.9	2.2	3.6	3.8	3.0	4.9	3.2

Note: Hispanics may be of any race.
Source: Bureau of the Census, data from the 2003 Current Population Survey Annual Social and Economic Supplement, Internet site http://ferret.bls.census.gov/macro/032003/perinc/toc.htm; calculations by New Strategist

Table 4.20 Income of Men Aged 35 to 59, 2002: Non-Hispanic White Men

(number and percent distribution of non-Hispanic white men aged 16 or older and aged 35 to 59 by income, 2002; median income by work status, and percent working year-round, full-time; men in thousands as of 2003)

	total	aged 35 to 44			aged 45 to 54			aged 55 to 59
		total	35 to 39	40 to 44	total	45 to 49	50 to 54	
TOTAL NON-HISPANIC WHITE MEN	**76,722**	**14,989**	**7,021**	**7,968**	**14,794**	**7,808**	**6,987**	**5,909**
Without income	**4,576**	**342**	**160**	**182**	**339**	**183**	**157**	**123**
With income	**72,146**	**14,647**	**6,861**	**7,786**	**14,455**	**7,625**	**6,830**	**5,786**
Under $10,000	10,338	983	480	503	967	512	455	472
$10,000 to $19,999	11,849	1,303	628	675	1,329	694	635	696
$20,000 to $29,999	10,984	2,017	957	1,059	1,732	923	810	705
$30,000 to $39,999	8,664	1,117	1,206	2,129	1,114	1,015	1,369	591
$40,000 to $49,999	6,633	901	942	1,786	968	819	1,074	426
$50,000 to $59,999	5,164	731	825	1,544	843	701	947	377
$60,000 to $69,999	3,841	776	558	797	947	548	618	326
$70,000 to $79,999	3,139	952	403	547	936	506	429	387
$80,000 to $89,999	1,973	546	243	304	627	288	339	282
$90,000 to $99,999	1,270	386	176	209	385	222	163	144
$100,000 or more	5,703	1,681	749	932	1,847	973	874	732
Median income of men with income	$32,034	$42,369	$41,809	$43,543	$45,343	$45,319	$45,370	$42,889
Median income of full-time workers	45,153	48,745	47,176	50,155	51,233	50,823	51,733	52,358
Percent working full-time	54.8%	78.8%	78.0%	79.4%	77.1%	78.4%	75.7%	65.7%
TOTAL NON-HISPANIC WHITE MEN	**100.0%**	**100.0%**	**100.0%**	**100.0%**	**100.0%**	**100.0%**	**100.0%**	**100.0%**
Without income	**6.0**	**2.3**	**2.3**	**2.3**	**2.3**	**2.3**	**2.2**	**2.1**
With income	**94.0**	**97.7**	**97.7**	**97.7**	**97.7**	**97.7**	**97.8**	**97.9**
Under $10,000	13.5	6.6	6.8	6.3	6.5	6.6	6.5	8.0
$10,000 to $19,999	15.4	8.7	8.9	8.5	9.0	8.9	9.1	11.8
$20,000 to $29,999	14.3	13.5	13.6	13.3	11.7	11.8	11.6	11.9
$30,000 to $39,999	11.3	7.5	17.2	26.7	7.5	13.0	19.6	10.0
$40,000 to $49,999	8.6	6.0	13.4	22.4	6.5	10.5	15.4	7.2
$50,000 to $59,999	6.7	4.9	11.8	19.4	5.7	9.0	13.6	6.4
$60,000 to $69,999	5.0	5.2	7.9	10.0	6.4	7.0	8.8	5.5
$70,000 to $79,999	4.1	6.4	5.7	6.9	6.3	6.5	6.1	6.5
$80,000 to $89,999	2.6	3.6	3.5	3.8	4.2	3.7	4.9	4.8
$90,000 to $99,999	1.7	2.6	2.5	2.6	2.6	2.8	2.3	2.4
$100,000 or more	7.4	11.2	10.7	11.7	12.5	12.5	12.5	12.4

Note: Non-Hispanic whites include only those who identified themselves as white alone and non-Hispanic.
Source: Bureau of the Census, data from the 2003 Current Population Survey Annual Social and Economic Supplement, Internet site http://ferret.bls.census.gov/macro/032003/perinc/toc.htm; calculations by New Strategist

Women's Incomes Are Flat through Middle Age

Among women who work full-time, income is highest in the 50-to-54 age group.

Women's incomes do not peak sharply in middle age, in contrast to the pattern for men. Among women who work full-time, the median income of those with the highest incomes, aged 50 to 54, is just $3,310 greater than the median for all women with full-time jobs. In contrast, among men the median income of those with the highest incomes, aged 55 to 59, is $9,378 greater than the median for all men who work full-time.

Also in contrast to men, women's incomes do not vary as much by race and Hispanic origin. The median income of non-Hispanic white women who work full-time ranges from $34,000 to $36,000 in the 35 to 59 age group. For their Asian counterparts, the figure ranges from $32,000 to $36,000. Among blacks, the median income of full-time workers aged 35 to 59 ranges from $28,000 to $31,000. Hispanic women have the lowest incomes. Among those working full-time, median income ranges from $23,000 to $25,000 in the 35-to-59 age group.

■ Women's incomes do not peak in middle age because many choose lower-paying jobs that allow them to spend more time with their family.

Among women working full-time, there is little difference in income by age

(median income of women working full-time, by age, 2002)

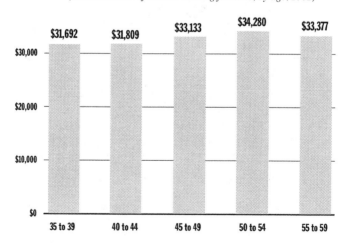

Table 4.21 Income of Women Aged 35 to 59, 2002: Total Women

(number and percent distribution of women aged 16 or older and aged 35 to 59 by income, 2002; median income by work status, and percent working year-round, full-time; women in thousands as of 2003)

| | total | aged 35 to 44 | | | aged 45 to 54 | | | aged 55 to 59 |
		total	35 to 39	40 to 44	total	45 to 49	50 to 54	
TOTAL WOMEN	116,436	22,341	10,774	11,567	20,627	10,971	9,657	7,977
Without income	13,949	1,854	974	880	1,533	770	764	758
With income	102,487	20,487	9,800	10,687	19,094	10,201	8,893	7,219
Under $10,000	33,026	4,873	2,489	2,383	4,011	2,106	1,906	1,872
$10,000 to $19,999	24,289	4,168	1,994	2,174	3,590	1,930	1,660	1,413
$20,000 to $29,999	16,626	3,891	1,781	2,110	3,550	1,919	1,633	1,271
$30,000 to $39,999	11,180	2,774	1,363	1,410	2,751	1,486	1,266	897
$40,000 to $49,999	6,784	1,851	858	991	1,915	1,057	858	614
$50,000 to $59,999	3,886	1,030	464	565	1,222	687	535	391
$60,000 to $69,999	2,264	578	232	347	700	340	360	241
$70,000 to $79,999	1,428	439	190	249	438	207	232	175
$80,000 to $89,999	787	257	119	137	269	150	119	82
$90,000 to $99,999	558	186	77	109	157	64	92	54
$100,000 or more	1,658	444	233	212	491	255	235	211
Median income of women with income	$16,812	$22,322	$21,726	$23,091	$25,165	$25,379	$24,854	$22,171
Median income of full-time workers	30,970	31,751	31,692	31,809	33,664	33,133	34,280	33,377
Percent working full-time	36.0%	51.6%	49.5%	53.5%	54.3%	55.6%	52.9%	45.7%
TOTAL WOMEN	100.0%	100.0%	100.0%	100.0%	100.0%	100.0%	100.0%	100.0%
Without income	12.0	8.3	9.0	7.6	7.4	7.0	7.9	9.5
With income	88.0	91.7	91.0	92.4	92.6	93.0	92.1	90.5
Under $10,000	28.4	21.8	23.1	20.6	19.4	19.2	19.7	23.5
$10,000 to $19,999	20.9	18.7	18.5	18.8	17.4	17.6	17.2	17.7
$20,000 to $29,999	14.3	17.4	16.5	18.2	17.2	17.5	16.9	15.9
$30,000 to $39,999	9.6	12.4	12.7	12.2	13.3	13.5	13.1	11.2
$40,000 to $49,999	5.8	8.3	8.0	8.6	9.3	9.6	8.9	7.7
$50,000 to $59,999	3.3	4.6	4.3	4.9	5.9	6.3	5.5	4.9
$60,000 to $69,999	1.9	2.6	2.2	3.0	3.4	3.1	3.7	3.0
$70,000 to $79,999	1.2	2.0	1.8	2.2	2.1	1.9	2.4	2.2
$80,000 to $89,999	0.7	1.2	1.1	1.2	1.3	1.4	1.2	1.0
$90,000 to $99,999	0.5	0.8	0.7	0.9	0.8	0.6	1.0	0.7
$100,000 or more	1.4	2.0	2.2	1.8	2.4	2.3	2.4	2.6

Source: Bureau of the Census, data from the 2003 Current Population Survey Annual Social and Economic Supplement, Internet site http://ferret.bls.census.gov/macro/032003/perinc/toc.htm; calculations by New Strategist

Table 4.22 Income of Women Aged 35 to 59, 2002: Asian Women

(number and percent distribution of Asian women aged 16 or older and aged 35 to 59 by income, 2002; median income by work status, and percent working year-round, full-time; women in thousands as of 2003)

	total	aged 35 to 44 total	35 to 39	40 to 44	aged 45 to 54 total	45 to 49	50 to 54	aged 55 to 59
TOTAL ASIAN WOMEN	5,131	1,062	565	497	895	487	408	289
Without income	994	142	68	73	108	54	54	41
With income	4,137	920	497	424	787	433	354	248
Under $10,000	1,373	239	127	112	158	81	78	54
$10,000 to $19,999	804	162	97	64	154	101	51	40
$20,000 to $29,999	642	157	72	85	152	90	62	56
$30,000 to $39,999	396	102	58	45	108	58	50	23
$40,000 to $49,999	291	79	39	40	69	39	31	18
$50,000 to $59,999	214	48	21	27	45	21	25	18
$60,000 to $69,999	118	32	20	13	28	7	21	15
$70,000 to $79,999	92	26	11	16	21	10	11	6
$80,000 to $89,999	45	19	16	3	13	7	5	5
$90,000 to $99,999	40	13	8	5	9	6	3	1
$100,000 or more	125	43	28	15	29	15	14	13
Median income of women with income	$17,898	$22,737	$23,510	$22,428	$24,940	$22,298	$26,926	$24,453
Median income of full-time workers	32,031	33,258	35,065	32,251	31,962	30,434	36,244	32,365
Percent working full-time	37.0%	50.3%	47.8%	53.1%	55.6%	55.6%	55.6%	53.3%
TOTAL ASIAN WOMEN	100.0%	100.0%	100.0%	100.0%	100.0%	100.0%	100.0%	100.0%
Without income	19.4	13.4	12.0	14.7	12.1	11.1	13.2	14.2
With income	80.6	86.6	88.0	85.3	87.9	88.9	86.8	85.8
Under $10,000	26.8	22.5	22.5	22.5	17.7	16.6	19.1	18.7
$10,000 to $19,999	15.7	15.3	17.2	12.9	17.2	20.7	12.5	13.8
$20,000 to $29,999	12.5	14.8	12.7	17.1	17.0	18.5	15.2	19.4
$30,000 to $39,999	7.7	9.6	10.3	9.1	12.1	11.9	12.3	8.0
$40,000 to $49,999	5.7	7.4	6.9	8.1	7.7	8.0	7.6	6.2
$50,000 to $59,999	4.2	4.5	3.7	5.4	5.0	4.3	6.1	6.2
$60,000 to $69,999	2.3	3.0	3.5	2.6	3.1	1.4	5.1	5.2
$70,000 to $79,999	1.8	2.4	1.9	3.2	2.3	2.1	2.7	2.1
$80,000 to $89,999	0.9	1.8	2.8	0.6	1.5	1.4	1.2	1.7
$90,000 to $99,999	0.8	1.2	1.4	1.0	1.0	1.2	0.7	0.3
$100,000 or more	2.4	4.1	5.0	3.0	3.2	3.1	3.4	4.5

Note: Asians include those who identified themselves as Asian alone and those who identified themselves as Asian in combination with one or more other races.
Source: Bureau of the Census, data from the 2003 Current Population Survey Annual Social and Economic Supplement, Internet site http://ferret.bls.census.gov/macro/032003/perinc/toc.htm; calculations by New Strategist

Table 4.23 Income of Women Aged 35 to 59, 2002: Black Women

(number and percent distribution of black women aged 16 or older and aged 35 to 59 by income, 2002; median income by work status, and percent working year-round, full-time; women in thousands as of 2003)

	total	aged 35 to 44			aged 45 to 54			aged 55 to 59
		total	35 to 39	40 to 44	total	45 to 49	50 to 54	
TOTAL BLACK WOMEN	**14,887**	**3,062**	**1,510**	**1,552**	**2,560**	**1,392**	**1,169**	**860**
Without income	**2,222**	**209**	**96**	**113**	**247**	**129**	**119**	**77**
With income	**12,665**	**2,853**	**1,414**	**1,439**	**2,313**	**1,263**	**1,050**	**783**
Under $10,000	4,069	539	264	274	522	276	245	174
$10,000 to $19,999	3,156	726	355	369	481	237	244	188
$20,000 to $29,999	2,196	618	310	309	477	275	202	153
$30,000 to $39,999	1,434	415	206	210	320	176	145	95
$40,000 to $49,999	774	237	117	118	201	125	76	77
$50,000 to $59,999	411	116	58	59	131	85	45	36
$60,000 to $69,999	260	74	36	38	83	49	31	20
$70,000 to $79,999	143	45	25	19	49	18	30	11
$80,000 to $89,999	71	26	12	16	16	4	12	11
$90,000 to $99,999	50	31	17	15	12	2	9	2
$100,000 or more	100	23	14	9	23	15	9	14
Median income of women with income	$16,671	$22,143	$22,607	$21,793	$23,001	$24,753	$21,371	$21,383
Median income of full-time workers	27,703	28,190	28,734	27,594	30,321	30,373	30,253	30,923
Percent working full-time	40.7%	61.7%	62.1%	61.3%	57.0%	60.5%	52.8%	47.3%
TOTAL BLACK WOMEN	**100.0%**	**100.0%**	**100.0%**	**100.0%**	**100.0%**	**100.0%**	**100.0%**	**100.0%**
Without income	**14.9**	**6.8**	**6.4**	**7.3**	**9.6**	**9.3**	**10.2**	**9.0**
With income	**85.1**	**93.2**	**93.6**	**92.7**	**90.4**	**90.7**	**89.8**	**91.1**
Under $10,000	27.3	17.6	17.5	17.7	20.4	19.8	21.0	20.2
$10,000 to $19,999	21.2	23.7	23.5	23.8	18.8	17.0	20.9	21.9
$20,000 to $29,999	14.8	20.2	20.5	19.9	18.6	19.8	17.3	17.8
$30,000 to $39,999	9.6	13.6	13.6	13.5	12.5	12.6	12.4	11.1
$40,000 to $49,999	5.2	7.7	7.7	7.6	7.9	9.0	6.5	9.0
$50,000 to $59,999	2.8	3.8	3.8	3.8	5.1	6.1	3.8	4.2
$60,000 to $69,999	1.7	2.4	2.4	2.4	3.2	3.5	2.7	2.3
$70,000 to $79,999	1.0	1.5	1.7	1.2	1.9	1.3	2.6	1.3
$80,000 to $89,999	0.5	0.8	0.8	1.0	0.6	0.3	1.0	1.3
$90,000 to $99,999	0.3	1.0	1.1	1.0	0.5	0.1	0.8	0.2
$100,000 or more	0.7	0.8	0.9	0.6	0.9	1.1	0.8	1.6

Note: Blacks include those who identified themselves as black alone and those who identified themselves as black in combination with one or more other races.
Source: Bureau of the Census, data from the 2003 Current Population Survey Annual Social and Economic Supplement, Internet site http://ferret.bls.census.gov/macro/032003/perinc/toc.htm; calculations by New Strategist

Table 4.24 Income of Women Aged 35 to 59, 2002: Hispanic Women

(number and percent distribution of Hispanic women aged 16 or older and aged 35 to 59 by income, 2002; median income by work status, and percent working year-round, full-time; women in thousands as of 2003)

| | total | aged 35 to 44 | | | aged 45 to 54 | | | aged 55 to 59 |
		total	35 to 39	40 to 44	total	45 to 49	50 to 54	
TOTAL HISPANIC WOMEN	13,607	2,866	1,535	1,331	1,903	1,072	831	602
Without income	3,589	537	313	224	354	174	180	143
With income	10,018	2,329	1,222	1,107	1,549	898	651	459
Under $10,000	3,822	621	344	278	416	230	186	176
$10,000 to $19,999	2,821	721	367	353	455	244	210	124
$20,000 to $29,999	1,602	445	232	214	289	179	111	69
$30,000 to $39,999	839	250	138	112	163	101	60	36
$40,000 to $49,999	444	138	70	69	104	64	39	22
$50,000 to $59,999	215	63	32	32	54	42	13	9
$60,000 to $69,999	110	33	10	23	26	13	13	7
$70,000 to $79,999	64	20	13	7	18	8	10	7
$80,000 to $89,999	30	14	8	6	7	6	1	5
$90,000 to $99,999	10	2	2	–	2	1	1	1
$100,000 or more	63	19	7	13	17	11	6	5
Median income of women with income	$13,364	$16,859	$16,633	$17,098	$16,891	$17,953	$15,950	$13,147
Median income of full-time workers	22,355	23,240	23,530	22,866	24,266	25,391	22,286	23,803
Percent working full-time	33.7%	47.5%	44.2%	51.3%	46.1%	49.4%	41.8%	36.4%
TOTAL HISPANIC WOMEN	100.0%	100.0%	100.0%	100.0%	100.0%	100.0%	100.0%	100.0%
Without income	26.4	18.7	20.4	16.8	18.6	16.2	21.7	23.8
With income	73.6	81.3	79.6	83.2	81.4	83.8	78.3	76.2
Under $10,000	28.1	21.7	22.4	20.9	21.9	21.5	22.4	29.2
$10,000 to $19,999	20.7	25.2	23.9	26.5	23.9	22.8	25.3	20.6
$20,000 to $29,999	11.8	15.5	15.1	16.1	15.2	16.7	13.4	11.5
$30,000 to $39,999	6.2	8.7	9.0	8.4	8.6	9.4	7.2	6.0
$40,000 to $49,999	3.3	4.8	4.6	5.2	5.5	6.0	4.7	3.7
$50,000 to $59,999	1.6	2.2	2.1	2.4	2.8	3.9	1.6	1.5
$60,000 to $69,999	0.8	1.2	0.7	1.7	1.4	1.2	1.6	1.2
$70,000 to $79,999	0.5	0.7	0.8	0.5	0.9	0.7	1.2	1.2
$80,000 to $89,999	0.2	0.5	0.5	0.5	0.4	0.6	0.1	0.8
$90,000 to $99,999	0.1	0.1	0.1	–	0.1	0.1	0.1	0.2
$100,000 or more	0.5	0.7	0.5	1.0	0.9	1.0	0.7	0.8

Note: Hispanics may be of any race. (–) means number is less than 500 or sample is too small to make a reliable estimate.
Source: Bureau of the Census, data from the 2003 Current Population Survey Annual Social and Economic Supplement, Internet site http://ferret.bls.census.gov/macro/032003/perinc/toc.htm; calculations by New Strategist

Table 4.25 Income of Women Aged 35 to 59, 2002: Non-Hispanic White Women

(number and percent distribution of non-Hispanic white women aged 16 or older and aged 35 to 59 by income, 2002; median income by work status, and percent working year-round, full-time; women in thousands as of 2003)

	total	aged 35 to 44			aged 45 to 54			aged 55 to 59
		total	35 to 39	40 to 44	total	45 to 49	50 to 54	
TOTAL NON-HISPANIC WHITE WOMEN	**81,851**	**15,173**	**7,104**	**8,070**	**15,076**	**7,922**	**7,155**	**6,148**
Without income	**7,037**	**953**	**491**	**463**	**797**	**394**	**404**	**482**
With income	**74,814**	**14,220**	**6,613**	**7,607**	**14,279**	**7,528**	**6,751**	**5,666**
Under $10,000	23,423	3,445	1,741	1,704	2,878	1,500	1,380	1,454
$10,000 to $19,999	17,326	2,537	1,175	1,363	2,463	1,323	1,139	1,060
$20,000 to $29,999	12,052	2,617	1,143	1,473	2,594	1,354	1,241	972
$30,000 to $39,999	8,440	1,992	957	1,035	2,139	1,149	991	736
$40,000 to $49,999	5,230	1,373	625	748	1,537	831	707	488
$50,000 to $59,999	3,018	790	347	442	986	537	450	321
$60,000 to $69,999	1,760	433	164	270	556	265	291	196
$70,000 to $79,999	1,120	343	140	202	352	170	182	150
$80,000 to $89,999	631	196	84	110	227	131	96	59
$90,000 to $99,999	452	138	49	88	128	55	74	48
$100,000 or more	1,360	354	184	170	418	216	203	181
Median income of women with income	$17,389	$23,685	$22,454	$24,846	$26,386	$26,502	$26,245	$23,202
Median income of full-time workers	32,347	34,685	34,222	35,083	35,836	35,817	35,857	34,788
Percent working full-time	35.6%	50.4%	48.3%	52.3%	55.1%	55.8%	54.2%	46.1%
TOTAL NON-HISPANIC WHITE WOMEN	**100.0%**	**100.0%**	**100.0%**	**100.0%**	**100.0%**	**100.0%**	**100.0%**	**100.0%**
Without income	**8.6**	**6.3**	**6.9**	**5.7**	**5.3**	**5.0**	**5.6**	**7.8**
With income	**91.4**	**93.7**	**93.1**	**94.3**	**94.7**	**95.0**	**94.4**	**92.2**
Under $10,000	28.6	22.7	24.5	21.1	19.1	18.9	19.3	23.6
$10,000 to $19,999	21.2	16.7	16.5	16.9	16.3	16.7	15.9	17.2
$20,000 to $29,999	14.7	17.2	16.1	18.3	17.2	17.1	17.3	15.8
$30,000 to $39,999	10.3	13.1	13.5	12.8	14.2	14.5	13.9	12.0
$40,000 to $49,999	6.4	9.1	8.8	9.3	10.2	10.5	9.9	7.9
$50,000 to $59,999	3.7	5.2	4.9	5.5	6.5	6.8	6.3	5.2
$60,000 to $69,999	2.2	2.9	2.3	3.3	3.7	3.3	4.1	3.2
$70,000 to $79,999	1.4	2.3	2.0	2.5	2.3	2.1	2.5	2.4
$80,000 to $89,999	0.8	1.3	1.2	1.4	1.5	1.7	1.3	1.0
$90,000 to $99,999	0.6	0.9	0.7	1.1	0.8	0.7	1.0	0.8
$100,000 or more	1.7	2.3	2.6	2.1	2.8	2.7	2.8	2.9

Note: Non-Hispanic whites include only those who identified themselves as white alone and non-Hispanic.
Source: Bureau of the Census, data from the 2003 Current Population Survey Annual Social and Economic Supplement, Internet site http://ferret.bls.census.gov/macro/032003/perinc/toc.htm; calculations by New Strategist

Earnings Rise with Education

The highest earners are men with professional degrees.

A college degree has been well worth its cost for the Baby-Boom generation. The higher their educational level, the greater their earnings. Among men aged 35 to 64 in 2002 (Boomers were aged 38 to 56 in that year), those with professional degrees (such as physicians and lawyers) who worked full-time had median earnings of $100,000 or more. Among women aged 35 to 54 who work full-time, median earnings were highest for those with doctorates, ranging from $66,000 to $71,000 in 2002.

Among men aged 35 to 64 who dropped out of high school, the earnings of those working full-time range from just $26,000 to $29,000. For their male counterparts with at least a college degree, earnings range from $67,000 to $70,000. The pattern is the same for women. Among women aged 35 to 64 working full-time who dropped out of high school, earnings range from $18,000 to $21,000. Among college graduates, earnings are a higher $45,000 to $47,000.

■ The steeply rising cost of a college degree combined with competition from well-educated but lower-paid workers in other countries may reduce the financial return of a college education in the years ahead.

The college bonus is still big

(median earnings of men aged 45 to 54 who work full-time, by education, 2002)

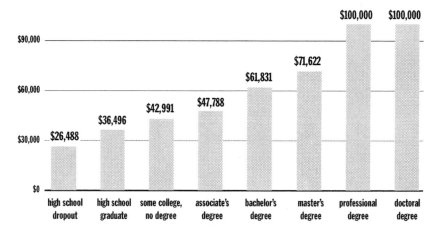

Table 4.26 Earnings of Men by Education, 2002: Aged 35 to 44

(number and percent distribution of men aged 35 to 44 by earnings and education, 2002; men in thousands as of 2003)

	total	less than 9th grade	9th to 12th grade, no degree	high school graduate, including GED	some college, no degree	associate's degree	bachelor's degree or more				
							total	bachelor's degree	master's degree	professional degree	doctoral degree
TOTAL MEN AGED 35 TO 44	21,733	1,013	1,906	7,066	3,665	1,768	6,314	4,228	1,385	402	299
Without earnings	1,795	163	333	710	270	78	240	167	60	9	4
With earnings	19,938	850	1,573	6,356	3,395	1,690	6,074	4,061	1,325	393	295
Under $10,000	1,268	117	216	504	199	89	142	105	27	6	5
$10,000 to $19,999	2,329	325	387	919	282	123	292	220	62	2	9
$20,000 to $29,999	3,235	232	428	1,421	524	248	380	300	64	9	7
$30,000 to $39,999	3,340	100	282	1,351	647	320	640	488	113	20	20
$40,000 to $49,999	2,436	31	121	808	563	306	607	433	123	22	30
$50,000 to $59,999	1,984	21	69	575	399	215	707	514	148	20	26
$60,000 to $69,999	1,314	12	34	318	260	137	553	378	142	18	16
$70,000 to $79,999	1,145	2	17	193	167	86	678	432	174	31	39
$80,000 to $89,999	612	–	4	86	109	50	363	245	78	14	25
$90,000 to $99,999	442	2	–	48	59	34	299	181	82	19	18
$100,000 or more	1,833	8	17	130	185	83	1,410	767	311	229	103
Median earnings of men with earnings	$38,947	$19,568	$23,025	$31,477	$40,477	$41,296	$62,353	$58,764	$67,443	$100,000	$77,364
Median earnings of full-time workers	42,211	21,335	26,451	34,204	42,401	44,277	66,836	61,324	70,809	100,000	79,280
Percent working full-time	76.6%	62.8%	60.5%	73.5%	76.2%	82.5%	85.7%	85.6%	83.8%	92.0%	86.6%

TOTAL MEN AGED 35 TO 44	total	less than 9th grade	9th to 12th grade, no degree	high school graduate, including GED	some college, no degree	associate's degree	bachelor's degree or more				
							total	bachelor's degree	master's degree	professional degree	doctoral degree
	100.0%	100.0%	100.0%	100.0%	100.0%	100.0%	100.0%	100.0%	100.0%	100.0%	100.0%
Without earnings	8.3	16.1	17.5	10.1	7.4	4.4	3.8	3.9	4.3	2.2	1.3
With earnings	91.7	83.9	82.5	90.0	92.6	95.6	96.2	96.1	95.7	97.8	98.7
Under $10,000	5.8	11.5	11.3	7.1	5.4	5.0	2.2	2.5	1.9	1.5	1.7
$10,000 to $19,999	10.7	32.1	20.3	1.3	7.7	7.0	4.6	5.2	4.5	0.5	3.0
$20,000 to $29,999	14.9	22.9	22.5	20.1	14.3	14.0	6.0	7.1	4.6	2.2	2.3
$30,000 to $39,999	15.4	9.9	14.8	19.1	17.7	18.1	10.1	11.5	8.2	5.0	6.7
$40,000 to $49,999	11.2	3.1	6.3	11.4	15.4	17.3	9.6	10.2	8.9	5.5	10.0
$50,000 to $59,999	9.1	2.1	3.6	8.1	10.9	12.2	11.2	12.2	10.7	5.0	8.7
$60,000 to $69,999	6.1	1.2	1.8	4.5	7.1	7.7	8.8	8.9	10.3	4.5	5.4
$70,000 to $79,999	5.3	0.2	0.9	2.7	4.6	4.9	10.7	10.2	12.6	7.7	13.0
$80,000 to $89,999	2.8	–	0.2	1.2	3.0	2.8	5.7	5.8	5.6	3.5	8.4
$90,000 to $99,999	2.0	0.2	–	0.7	1.6	1.9	4.7	4.3	5.9	4.7	6.0
$100,000 or more	8.4	0.8	0.9	1.8	5.1	4.7	22.3	18.1	22.5	57.0	34.4

Note: (–) means number is less than 500 or sample is too small to make a reliable estimate.
Source: Bureau of the Census, data from the 2003 Current Population Survey Annual Social and Economic Supplement, Internet site http://ferret.bls.census.gov/macro/032003/perinc/new03_000.htm; calculations by New Strategist

Table 4.27 Earnings of Men by Education, 2002: Aged 45 to 54

(number and percent distribution of men aged 45 to 54 by earnings and education, 2002; men in thousands as of 2003)

	total	less than 9th grade	9th to 12th grade, no degree	high school graduate, including GED	some college, no degree	associate's degree	bachelor's degree or more				
							total	bachelor's degree	master's degree	professional degree	doctoral degree
TOTAL MEN AGED 45 TO 54	19,606	896	1,376	5,837	3,602	1,587	6,308	3,846	1,557	484	422
Without earnings	2,177	282	308	783	351	181	272	195	66	4	7
With earnings	17,429	614	1,068	5,054	3,251	1,406	6,036	3,651	1,491	480	415
Under $10,000	1,041	65	148	389	193	70	174	134	26	9	4
$10,000 to $19,999	1,806	237	257	640	330	96	245	189	37	10	9
$20,000 to $29,999	2,473	166	295	1,022	450	174	367	265	80	6	15
$30,000 to $39,999	2,761	79	207	1,063	583	225	604	407	150	21	26
$40,000 to $49,999	2,197	29	73	733	471	246	645	448	147	27	26
$50,000 to $59,999	1,824	15	37	514	427	214	615	374	183	29	29
$60,000 to $69,999	1,274	9	15	271	246	129	604	391	165	27	19
$70,000 to $79,999	1,082	12	17	189	201	102	561	358	127	43	32
$80,000 to $89,999	670	–	5	86	117	64	398	213	125	19	42
$90,000 to $99,999	410	–	–	31	56	22	299	158	99	26	17
$100,000 or more	1,894	3	11	113	177	65	1,525	715	354	260	196
Median earnings of men with earnings	$41,633	$20,158	$23,801	$33,178	$40,772	$45,080	$65,193	$60,122	$66,562	$100,000	$92,358
Median earnings of full-time workers	46,300	21,430	26,488	36,496	42,991	47,788	69,616	61,831	71,622	100,000	100,000
Percent working full-time	74.5%	51.6%	56.1%	71.2%	74.3%	74.7%	84.9%	84.3%	83.8%	89.7%	88.9%

TOTAL MEN AGED 45 TO 54	total	less than 9th grade	9th to 12th grade, no degree	high school graduate, including GED	some college, no degree	associate's degree	bachelor's degree or more				
							total	bachelor's degree	master's degree	professional degree	doctoral degree
	100.0%	100.0%	100.0%	100.0%	100.0%	100.0%	100.0%	100.0%	100.0%	100.0%	100.0%
Without earnings	11.1	31.5	22.4	13.4	9.7	11.4	4.3	5.1	4.2	0.8	1.7
With earnings	88.9	68.5	77.6	86.6	90.3	88.6	95.7	94.9	95.8	99.2	98.3
Under $10,000	5.3	7.3	10.8	6.7	5.4	4.4	2.8	3.5	1.7	1.9	0.9
$10,000 to $19,999	9.2	26.5	18.7	11.0	9.2	6.1	3.9	4.9	2.4	2.1	2.1
$20,000 to $29,999	12.6	18.5	21.4	17.5	12.5	11.0	5.8	6.9	5.1	1.2	3.6
$30,000 to $39,999	14.1	8.8	15.0	18.2	16.2	14.2	9.6	10.6	9.6	4.3	6.2
$40,000 to $49,999	11.2	3.2	5.3	12.6	13.1	15.5	10.2	11.6	9.4	5.6	6.2
$50,000 to $59,999	9.3	1.7	2.7	8.8	11.9	13.5	9.7	9.7	11.8	6.0	6.9
$60,000 to $69,999	6.5	1.0	1.1	4.6	6.8	8.1	9.6	10.2	10.6	5.6	4.5
$70,000 to $79,999	5.5	1.3	1.2	3.2	5.6	6.4	8.9	9.3	8.2	8.9	7.6
$80,000 to $89,999	3.4	–	0.4	1.5	3.2	4.0	6.3	5.5	8.0	3.9	10.0
$90,000 to $99,999	2.1	–	–	0.5	1.6	1.4	4.7	4.1	6.4	5.4	4.0
$100,000 or more	9.7	0.3	0.8	1.9	4.9	4.1	24.2	18.6	22.7	53.7	46.4

Note: (–) means number is less than 500 or sample is too small to make a reliable estimate.
Source: Bureau of the Census, data from the 2003 Current Population Survey Annual Social and Economic Supplement, Internet site http://ferret.bls.census.gov/macro/032003/perinc/new03_000.htm; calculations by New Strategist

Table 4.28 Earnings of Men by Education, 2002: Aged 55 to 64

(number and percent distribution of men aged 55 to 64 by earnings and education, 2002; men in thousands as of 2003)

	total	less than 9th grade	9th to 12th grade, no degree	high school graduate, including GED	some college, no degree	associate's degree	bachelor's degree or more				
							total	bachelor's degree	master's degree	professional degree	doctoral degree
TOTAL MEN AGED 55 TO 64	13,166	866	1,120	3,872	2,182	932	4,193	2,287	1,194	331	381
Without earnings	3,478	407	443	1,150	516	212	749	456	204	41	48
With earnings	9,688	459	677	2,722	1,666	720	3,444	1,831	990	290	333
Under $10,000	973	93	86	325	153	97	218	107	71	14	27
$10,000 to $19,999	1,225	117	161	420	179	78	268	159	76	15	19
$20,000 to $29,999	1,301	122	159	467	205	116	232	163	45	15	11
$30,000 to $39,999	1,340	59	120	474	264	93	333	222	80	13	18
$40,000 to $49,999	1,094	34	61	362	238	110	290	169	91	7	23
$50,000 to $59,999	919	12	29	279	199	65	336	165	137	4	28
$60,000 to $69,999	603	5	9	127	146	60	254	140	65	16	33
$70,000 to $79,999	639	3	23	105	121	37	351	193	112	26	19
$80,000 to $89,999	319	4	14	60	50	12	178	92	45	21	19
$90,000 to $99,999	202	2	4	22	19	19	137	78	21	8	28
$100,000 or more	1,074	6	10	83	94	35	846	343	245	152	107
Median earnings of men with earnings	$40,017	$20,805	$25,832	$31,917	$40,989	$36,517	$60,832	$52,306	$58,725	$100,000	$76,019
Median earnings of full-time workers	45,995	25,029	29,061	36,651	46,121	44,020	70,353	61,312	70,536	100,000	82,644
Percent working full-time	55.8%	36.8%	42.9%	51.9%	58.2%	56.5%	65.4%	64.7%	64.6%	71.0%	67.5%

TOTAL MEN AGED 55 TO 64	total	less than 9th grade	9th to 12th grade, no degree	high school graduate, including GED	some college, no degree	associate's degree	bachelor's degree or more				
							total	bachelor's degree	master's degree	professional degree	doctoral degree
	100.0%	100.0%	100.0%	100.0%	100.0%	100.0%	100.0%	100.0%	100.0%	100.0%	100.0%
Without earnings	26.4	47.0	39.6	29.7	23.6	22.7	17.9	19.9	17.1	12.4	12.6
With earnings	73.6	53.0	60.4	70.3	76.4	77.3	82.1	80.1	82.9	87.6	87.4
Under $10,000	7.4	10.7	7.7	8.4	7.0	10.4	5.2	4.7	5.9	4.2	7.1
$10,000 to $19,999	9.3	13.5	14.4	10.8	8.2	8.4	6.4	7.0	6.4	4.5	5.0
$20,000 to $29,999	9.9	14.1	14.2	12.1	9.4	12.4	5.5	7.1	3.8	4.5	2.9
$30,000 to $39,999	10.2	6.8	10.7	12.2	12.1	10.0	7.9	9.7	6.7	3.9	4.7
$40,000 to $49,999	8.3	3.9	5.4	9.3	10.9	11.8	6.9	7.4	7.6	2.1	6.0
$50,000 to $59,999	7.0	1.4	2.6	7.2	9.1	7.0	8.0	7.2	11.5	1.2	7.3
$60,000 to $69,999	4.6	0.6	0.8	3.3	6.7	6.4	6.1	6.1	5.4	4.8	8.7
$70,000 to $79,999	4.9	0.3	2.1	2.7	5.5	4.0	8.4	8.4	9.4	7.9	5.0
$80,000 to $89,999	2.4	0.5	1.2	1.5	2.3	1.3	4.2	4.0	3.8	6.3	5.0
$90,000 to $99,999	1.5	0.2	0.4	0.6	0.9	2.0	3.3	3.4	1.8	2.4	7.3
$100,000 or more	8.2	0.7	0.9	2.1	4.3	3.8	20.2	15.0	20.5	45.9	28.1

Source: Bureau of the Census, data from the 2003 Current Population Survey Annual Social and Economic Supplement, Internet site http://ferret.bls.census.gov/macro/032003/perinc/new03_000.htm; calculations by New Strategist

Table 4.29 Earnings of Women by Education, 2002: Aged 35 to 44

(number and percent distribution of women aged 35 to 44 by earnings and education, 2002; women in thousands as of 2003)

	total	less than 9th grade	9th to 12th grade, no degree	high school graduate, including GED	some college, no degree	associate's degree	bachelor's degree or more				
							total	bachelor's degree	master's degree	professional degree	doctoral degree
TOTAL WOMEN AGED 35 TO 44	22,341	814	1,548	6,828	3,996	2,496	6,658	4,687	1,498	284	189
Without earnings	4,838	387	547	1,531	793	375	1,204	934	213	34	23
With earnings	17,502	427	1,001	5,297	3,203	2,121	5,454	3,753	1,285	250	166
Under $10,000	2,863	132	292	1,015	527	289	609	484	108	8	8
$10,000 to $19,999	3,773	213	406	1,492	701	382	579	451	103	14	12
$20,000 to $29,999	3,766	70	218	1,456	834	498	691	581	86	13	11
$30,000 to $39,999	2,726	11	56	713	549	439	957	666	239	37	14
$40,000 to $49,999	1,705	1	15	332	275	264	817	514	253	36	12
$50,000 to $59,999	969	1	5	137	147	135	544	325	169	24	26
$60,000 to $69,999	533	–	3	64	62	52	351	231	93	11	17
$70,000 to $79,999	396	–	–	48	49	34	264	164	75	10	17
$80,000 to $89,999	241	–	4	10	27	12	187	110	46	20	10
$90,000 to $99,999	142	–	–	8	3	4	127	72	36	11	9
$100,000 or more	389	–	–	22	28	12	327	155	77	64	32
Median earnings of women with earnings	$25,110	$13,663	$14,733	$20,642	$23,942	$27,022	$38,401	$35,368	$42,109	$55,599	$60,041
Median earnings of full-time workers	31,039	16,403	18,483	24,568	29,418	32,223	45,312	41,737	50,125	61,296	65,528
Percent working full-time	51.6%	30.7%	37.5%	52.2%	53.2%	56.4%	53.9%	52.6%	54.5%	65.5%	64.6%

TOTAL WOMEN AGED 35 TO 44	total	less than 9th grade	9th to 12th grade, no degree	high school graduate, including GED	some college, no degree	associate's degree	bachelor's degree or more				
							total	bachelor's degree	master's degree	professional degree	doctoral degree
	100.0%	100.0%	100.0%	100.0%	100.0%	100.0%	100.0%	100.0%	100.0%	100.0%	100.0%
Without earnings	21.7	47.5	35.3	22.4	19.8	15.0	18.1	19.9	14.2	12.0	12.2
With earnings	78.3	52.5	64.7	77.6	80.2	85.0	81.9	80.1	85.8	88.0	87.8
Under $10,000	12.8	16.2	18.9	14.9	13.2	11.6	9.1	10.3	7.2	2.8	4.2
$10,000 to $19,999	16.9	26.2	26.2	21.9	17.5	15.3	8.7	9.6	6.9	4.9	6.3
$20,000 to $29,999	16.9	8.6	14.1	21.3	20.9	20.0	10.4	12.4	5.7	4.6	5.8
$30,000 to $39,999	12.2	1.4	3.6	10.4	13.7	17.6	14.4	14.2	16.0	13.0	7.4
$40,000 to $49,999	7.6	0.1	1.0	4.9	6.9	10.6	12.3	11.0	16.9	12.7	6.3
$50,000 to $59,999	4.3	0.1	0.3	2.0	3.7	5.4	8.2	6.9	11.3	8.5	13.8
$60,000 to $69,999	2.4	–	0.2	0.9	1.6	2.1	5.3	4.9	6.2	3.9	9.0
$70,000 to $79,999	1.8	–	–	0.7	1.2	1.4	4.0	3.5	5.0	3.5	9.0
$80,000 to $89,999	1.1	–	0.3	0.1	0.7	0.5	2.8	2.3	3.1	7.0	5.3
$90,000 to $99,999	0.6	–	–	0.1	0.1	0.2	1.9	1.5	2.4	3.9	4.8
$100,000 or more	1.7	–	–	0.3	0.7	0.5	4.9	3.3	5.1	22.5	16.9

Note: (–) means number is less than 500 or sample is too small to make a reliable estimate.
Source: Bureau of the Census, data from the 2003 Current Population Survey Annual Social and Economic Supplement, Internet site http://ferret.bls.census.gov/macro/032003/perinc/new03_000.htm; calculations by New Strategist

Table 4.30 Earnings of Women by Education, 2002: Aged 45 to 54

(number and percent distribution of women aged 45 to 54 by earnings and education, 2002; women in thousands as of 2003)

	total	less than 9th grade	9th to 12th grade, no degree	high school graduate, including GED	some college, no degree	associate's degree	bachelor's degree or more				
							total	bachelor's degree	master's degree	professional degree	doctoral degree
TOTAL WOMEN AGED 45 TO 54	**20,627**	**854**	**1,282**	**6,614**	**3,700**	**2,224**	**5,953**	**3,730**	**1,797**	**232**	**194**
Without earnings	**4,427**	**428**	**539**	**1,534**	**732**	**344**	**849**	**604**	**184**	**39**	**22**
With earnings	**16,201**	**426**	**743**	**5,080**	**2,968**	**1,880**	**5,104**	**3,126**	**1,613**	**193**	**172**
Under $10,000	2,169	122	178	784	421	211	452	323	110	15	3
$10,000 to $19,999	3,201	192	261	1,374	540	338	495	367	99	14	14
$20,000 to $29,999	3,426	81	216	1,386	718	421	606	466	114	10	14
$30,000 to $39,999	2,683	16	55	802	567	390	855	588	218	38	10
$40,000 to $49,999	1,833	8	20	382	333	232	858	518	293	29	17
$50,000 to $59,999	1,154	2	8	147	184	161	653	302	306	19	27
$60,000 to $69,999	632	3	5	105	84	56	380	181	164	19	14
$70,000 to $79,999	388	–	1	58	45	26	258	114	113	9	23
$80,000 to $89,999	213	–	–	15	23	12	162	78	68	8	8
$90,000 to $99,999	123	–	–	5	7	23	89	41	34	5	8
$100,000 or more	382	–	1	25	45	11	300	143	95	28	34
Median earnings of women with earnings	$27,112	$12,750	$16,987	$21,879	$26,700	$28,901	$41,057	$36,244	$48,969	$45,366	$60,324
Median earnings of full-time workers	32,106	16,419	20,621	26,069	31,664	32,871	46,941	41,858	51,345	53,156	70,793
Percent working full-time	54.3%	28.8%	34.7%	53.3%	56.3%	59.2%	60.3%	57.6%	64.9%	61.2%	67.5%

	total	less than 9th grade	9th to 12th grade, no degree	high school graduate, including GED	some college, no degree	associate's degree	bachelor's degree or more				
							total	bachelor's degree	master's degree	professional degree	doctoral degree
TOTAL WOMEN AGED 45 TO 54	100.0%	100.0%	100.0%	100.0%	100.0%	100.0%	100.0%	100.0%	100.0%	100.0%	100.0%
Without earnings	**21.5**	**50.1**	**42.0**	**23.2**	**19.8**	**15.5**	**14.3**	**16.2**	**10.2**	**16.8**	**11.3**
With earnings	**78.5**	**49.9**	**58.0**	**76.8**	**80.2**	**84.5**	**85.7**	**83.8**	**89.8**	**83.2**	**88.7**
Under $10,000	10.5	14.3	13.9	11.9	11.4	9.5	7.6	8.7	6.1	6.5	1.5
$10,000 to $19,999	15.5	22.5	20.4	20.8	14.6	15.2	8.3	9.8	5.5	6.0	7.2
$20,000 to $29,999	16.6	9.5	16.8	21.0	19.4	18.9	10.2	12.5	6.3	4.3	7.2
$30,000 to $39,999	13.0	1.9	4.3	12.1	15.3	17.5	14.4	15.8	12.1	16.4	5.2
$40,000 to $49,999	8.9	0.9	1.6	5.8	9.0	10.4	14.4	13.9	16.3	12.5	8.8
$50,000 to $59,999	5.6	0.2	0.6	2.2	5.0	7.2	11.0	8.1	17.0	8.2	13.9
$60,000 to $69,999	3.1	0.4	0.4	1.6	2.3	2.5	6.4	4.9	9.1	8.2	7.2
$70,000 to $79,999	1.9	–	0.1	0.9	1.2	1.2	4.3	3.1	6.3	3.9	11.9
$80,000 to $89,999	1.0	–	–	0.2	0.6	0.5	2.7	2.1	3.8	3.4	4.1
$90,000 to $99,999	0.6	–	–	0.1	0.2	1.0	1.5	1.1	1.9	2.2	4.1
$100,000 or more	1.9	–	0.1	0.4	1.2	0.5	5.0	3.8	5.3	12.1	17.5

Note: (–) means number is less than 500 or sample is too small to make a reliable estimate.
Source: Bureau of the Census, data from the 2003 Current Population Survey Annual Social and Economic Supplement, Internet site http://ferret.bls.census.gov/macro/ 032003/perinc/new03_000.htm; calculations by New Strategist

Table 4.31 Earnings of Women by Education, 2002: Aged 55 to 64

(number and percent distribution of women aged 55 to 64 by earnings and education, 2002; women in thousands as of 2003)

	total	less than 9th grade	9th to 12th grade, no degree	high school graduate, including GED	some college, no degree	associate's degree	bachelor's degree or more				
							total	bachelor's degree	master's degree	professional degree	doctoral degree
TOTAL WOMEN AGED 55 TO 64	**14,233**	**835**	**1,239**	**5,295**	**2,470**	**1,173**	**3,222**	**1,966**	**1,036**	**104**	**115**
Without earnings	**5,613**	**558**	**723**	**2,228**	**883**	**385**	**838**	**592**	**203**	**17**	**25**
With earnings	**8,620**	**277**	**516**	**3,067**	**1,587**	**788**	**2,384**	**1,374**	**833**	**87**	**90**
Under $10,000	1,610	94	149	639	282	125	318	229	83	3	2
$10,000 to $19,999	1,832	112	178	817	335	129	262	159	81	9	12
$20,000 to $29,999	1,728	46	100	771	338	181	291	206	74	7	3
$30,000 to $39,999	1,244	16	40	447	220	169	353	212	117	13	12
$40,000 to $49,999	857	5	29	234	169	85	336	181	148	2	4
$50,000 to $59,999	494	–	10	50	125	63	245	127	95	13	10
$60,000 to $69,999	323	3	3	47	37	15	218	93	106	9	10
$70,000 to $79,999	201	2	5	27	31	10	128	59	47	11	10
$80,000 to $89,999	66	–	–	7	7	–	52	24	21	4	2
$90,000 to $99,999	44	–	1	–	15	–	27	10	10	3	2
$100,000 or more	219	–	–	28	26	12	154	73	48	13	20
Median earnings of women with earnings	$24,801	$12,786	$15,453	$20,828	$25,227	$27,266	$38,615	$33,250	$42,472	$54,394	$56,121
Median earnings of full-time workers	31,294	16,844	20,742	26,194	31,294	32,991	47,413	42,181	49,166	–	–
Percent working full-time	38.0%	18.3%	24.5%	35.9%	43.6%	42.1%	46.0%	41.4%	51.4%	63.5%	60.0%

TOTAL WOMEN AGED 55 TO 64	total	less than 9th grade	9th to 12th grade, no degree	high school graduate, including GED	some college, no degree	associate's degree	bachelor's degree or more				
							total	bachelor's degree	master's degree	professional degree	doctoral degree
	100.0%	100.0%	100.0%	100.0%	100.0%	100.0%	100.0%	100.0%	100.0%	100.0%	100.0%
Without earnings	39.4	66.8	58.4	42.1	35.7	32.8	26.0	30.1	19.6	16.3	21.7
With earnings	60.6	33.2	41.6	57.9	64.3	67.2	74.0	69.9	80.4	83.7	78.3
Under $10,000	11.3	11.3	12.0	12.1	11.4	10.7	9.9	11.6	8.0	2.9	1.7
$10,000 to $19,999	12.9	13.4	14.4	15.4	13.6	11.0	8.1	8.1	7.8	8.7	10.4
$20,000 to $29,999	12.1	5.5	8.1	14.6	13.7	15.4	9.0	10.5	7.1	6.7	2.6
$30,000 to $39,999	8.7	1.9	3.2	8.4	8.9	14.4	11.0	10.8	11.3	12.5	10.4
$40,000 to $49,999	6.0	0.6	2.3	4.4	6.8	7.2	10.4	9.2	14.3	1.9	3.5
$50,000 to $59,999	3.5	–	0.8	0.9	5.1	5.4	7.6	6.5	9.2	12.5	8.7
$60,000 to $69,999	2.3	0.4	0.2	0.9	1.5	1.3	6.8	4.7	10.2	8.7	8.7
$70,000 to $79,999	1.4	0.2	0.4	0.5	1.3	0.9	4.0	3.0	4.5	10.6	8.7
$80,000 to $89,999	0.5	–	–	0.1	0.3	–	1.6	1.2	2.0	3.8	1.7
$90,000 to $99,999	0.3	–	0.1	–	0.6	–	0.8	0.5	1.0	2.9	1.7
$100,000 or more	1.5	–	–	0.5	1.1	1.0	4.8	3.7	4.6	12.5	17.4

Note: (–) means number is less than 500 or sample is too small to make a reliable estimate.
Source: Bureau of the Census, data from the 2003 Current Population Survey Annual Social and Economic Supplement, Internet site http://ferret.bls.census.gov/macro/ 032003/perinc/new03_000.htm; calculations by New Strategist

Most Boomer Men and Women Have Wage or Salary Income

Among people aged 55 to 64, a substantial share receive retirement income.

Earnings are the most common source of income for people ranging in age from 35 to 64 (Boomers were aged 38 to 56 in 2002). More than 90 percent of men and 85 percent of women aged 35 to 54 received earnings in 2002. Among those aged 55 to 64, the proportion falls to 76 percent for men and 67 percent for women. The largest share of people receive wage or salary earnings from an employer, while a much smaller share earns money through self-employment.

The second most common source of income for middle-aged adults is interest, received by 49 to 59 percent of men and women aged 35 to 64. Few can afford to live on interest income, however, since the median amount received in 2002 ranged from just $1,323 to $1,519. Since many 55-to-64-year-olds are early retirees, it's no surprise that 20 percent of men and 13 percent of women in the age group received retirement income in 2002. The median was $8,988 for women and $19,116 for men.

■ The proportion of 55-to-64-year-olds who receive retirement income is likely to decline as Boomers enter the age group and postpone retirement.

Wage and salary earnings are the biggest source of income

(percent of people aged 35 to 64 who receive wage or salary earnings, by age and sex, 2002)

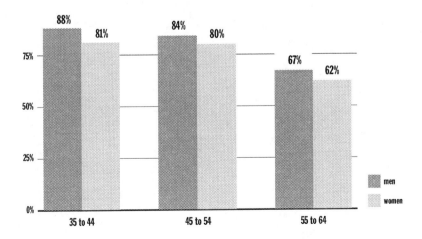

Table 4.32 Sources of Income for Men Aged 35 to 44, 2002

(number and percent distribution of men aged 35 to 44 with income and median income for those with income, by selected sources of income, 2002; men in thousands as of 2003)

	number	percent with income	median income
Total men aged 35 to 44 with income	**20,979**	**100.0%**	**$37,892**
Earnings	19,938	95.0	38,947
Wages and salary	18,511	88.2	39,649
Nonfarm self-employment	1,976	9.4	21,468
Farm self-employment	306	1.5	2,268
Social Security	568	2.7	7,989
SSI (Supplemental Security Income)	388	1.8	5,611
Public assistance	90	0.4	1,983
Veterans' benefits	202	1.0	5,461
Survivor benefits	53	0.3	–
Disability benefits	114	0.5	8,148
Unemployment compensation	1,423	6.8	3,732
Workers' compensation	295	1.4	4,128
Property income	10,909	52.0	1,421
Interest	10,336	49.3	1,331
Dividends	3,579	17.1	1,385
Rents, royalties, estates or trusts	1,127	5.4	1,950
Retirement income	320	1.5	10,478
Pension income	206	1.0	12,190
Alimony	5	0.0	–
Child support	134	0.6	2,354
Educational assistance	349	1.7	2,415
Financial assistance from other household	111	0.5	3,629
Other income	92	0.4	1,931

Note: (–) means sample is too small to make a reliable estimate.
Source: Bureau of the Census, data from the 2003 Current Population Survey Annual Social and Economic Supplement, Internet site http://ferret.bls.census.gov/macro/032003/perinc/new08_000.htm; calculations by New Strategist

Table 4.33 Sources of Income for Men Aged 45 to 54, 2002

(number and percent distribution of men aged 45 to 54 with income and median income for those with income, by selected sources of income, 2002; men in thousands as of 2003)

	number	percent with income	median income
Total men aged 45 to 54 with income	**18,971**	**100.0%**	**$40,969**
Earnings	17,429	91.9	41,633
Wages and salary	15,892	83.8	42,363
Nonfarm self-employment	2,059	10.9	20,119
Farm self-employment	367	1.9	2,256
Social Security	858	4.5	9,638
SSI (Supplemental Security Income)	348	1.8	5,898
Public assistance	77	0.4	1,865
Veterans' benefits	401	2.1	8,187
Survivor benefits	98	0.5	10,902
Disability benefits	245	1.3	9,045
Unemployment compensation	1,160	6.1	3,845
Workers' compensation	340	1.8	4,729
Property income	11,121	58.6	1,546
Interest	10,499	55.3	1,414
Dividends	3,814	20.1	1,442
Rents, royalties, estates or trusts	1,413	7.4	2,016
Retirement income	876	4.6	14,093
Pension income	599	3.2	16,361
Alimony	–	–	–
Child support	40	0.2	–
Educational assistance	164	0.9	1,996
Financial assistance from other household	90	0.5	4,252
Other income	63	0.3	–

Note: (–) means sample is too small to make a reliable estimate.
Source: Bureau of the Census, data from the 2003 Current Population Survey Annual Social and Economic Supplement, Internet site http://ferret.bls.census.gov/macro/032003/perinc/new08_000.htm; calculations by New Strategist

Table 4.34 Sources of Income for Men Aged 55 to 64, 2002

(number and percent distribution of men aged 55 to 64 with income and median income for those with income, by selected sources of income, 2002; men in thousands as of 2003)

	number	percent with income	median income
Total men aged 55 to 64 with income	**12,750**	**100.0%**	**$36,277**
Earnings	9,688	76.0	40,017
Wages and salary	8,591	67.4	40,846
Nonfarm self-employment	1,420	11.1	20,366
Farm self-employment	259	2.0	2,237
Social Security	2,178	17.1	11,521
SSI (Supplemental Security Income)	350	2.7	6,388
Public assistance	43	0.3	–
Veterans' benefits	504	4.0	6,254
Survivor benefits	64	0.5	–
Disability benefits	288	2.3	9,960
Unemployment compensation	694	5.4	4,199
Workers' compensation	227	1.8	3,985
Property income	7,835	61.5	1,730
Interest	7,387	57.9	1,519
Dividends	2,975	23.3	1,555
Rents, royalties, estates or trusts	1,236	9.7	2,271
Retirement income	2,560	20.1	19,116
Pension income	2,296	1.8	19,927
Alimony	3	0.0	–
Child support	10	0.1	–
Educational assistance	43	0.3	–
Financial assistance from other household	54	0.4	–
Other income	78	0.6	1,500

Note: (–) means sample is too small to make a reliable estimate.
Source: Bureau of the Census, data from the 2003 Current Population Survey Annual Social and Economic Supplement, Internet site http://ferret.bls.census.gov/macro/032003/perinc/new08_000.htm; calculations by New Strategist

Table 4.35 Sources of Income for Women Aged 35 to 44, 2002

(number and percent distribution of women aged 35 to 44 with income and median income for those with income, by selected sources of income, 2002; women in thousands as of 2003)

	number	percent with income	median income
Total women aged 35 to 44 with income	**20,487**	**100.0%**	**$22,322**
Earnings	17,502	85.4	25,110
Wages and salary	16,587	81.0	25,484
Nonfarm self-employment	1,311	6.4	9,963
Farm self-employment	172	0.8	1,561
Social Security	681	3.3	7,052
SSI (Supplemental Security Income)	515	2.5	5,837
Public assistance	399	1.9	2,950
Veterans' benefits	63	0.3	–
Survivor benefits	98	0.5	10,276
Disability benefits	156	0.8	5,983
Unemployment compensation	953	4.7	3,095
Workers' compensation	245	1.2	2,861
Property income	11,363	55.5	1,396
Interest	10,849	53.0	1,323
Dividends	3,270	16.0	1,375
Rents, royalties, estates or trusts	1,021	5.0	1,764
Retirement income	307	1.5	5,647
Pension income	112	0.5	6,146
Alimony	108	0.5	4,839
Child support	2,007	9.8	3,936
Educational assistance	509	2.5	2,142
Financial assistance from other household	182	0.9	3,770
Other income	152	0.7	1,950

Note: (–) means sample is too small to make a reliable estimate.
Source: Bureau of the Census, data from the 2003 Current Population Survey Annual Social and Economic Supplement, Internet site http://ferret.bls.census.gov/macro/032003/perinc/new08_000.htm; calculations by New Strategist

Table 4.36 Sources of Income for Women Aged 45 to 54, 2002

(number and percent distribution of women aged 45 to 54 with income and median income for those with income, by selected sources of income, 2002; women in thousands as of 2003)

	number	percent with income	median income
Total women aged 45 to 54 with income	**19,094**	**100.0%**	**$25,165**
Earnings	16,201	84.8	27,112
Wages and salary	15,313	80.2	27,410
Nonfarm self-employment	1,294	6.8	9,043
Farm self-employment	187	1.0	1,920
Social Security	916	4.8	7,380
SSI (Supplemental Security Income)	551	2.9	5,726
Public assistance	196	1.0	2,391
Veterans' benefits	66	0.3	–
Survivor benefits	160	0.8	8,105
Disability benefits	252	1.3	6,936
Unemployment compensation	883	4.6	3,329
Workers' compensation	264	1.4	2,282
Property income	11,296	59.2	1,495
Interest	10,747	56.3	1,378
Dividends	3,568	18.7	1,431
Rents, royalties, estates or trusts	1,385	7.3	1,881
Retirement income	632	3.3	9,397
Pension income	313	1.6	12,419
Alimony	107	–	11,841
Child support	762	4.0	4,138
Educational assistance	297	1.6	2,215
Financial assistance from other household	132	0.7	4,453
Other income	120	0.6	1,807

Note: (–) means sample is too small to make a reliable estimate.
Source: Bureau of the Census, data from the 2003 Current Population Survey Annual Social and Economic Supplement, Internet site http://ferret.bls.census.gov/macro/032003/perinc/new08_000.htm; calculations by New Strategist

Table 4.37 Sources of Income for Women Aged 55 to 64, 2002

(number and percent distribution of women aged 55 to 64 with income and median income for those with income, by selected sources of income, 2002; women in thousands as of 2003)

	number	percent with income	median income
Total women aged 55 to 64 with income	**12,926**	**100.0%**	**$19,165**
Earnings	8,620	66.7	24,801
Wages and salary	8,005	61.9	25,556
Nonfarm self-employment	795	6.2	7,965
Farm self-employment	118	0.9	1,709
Social Security	2,724	21.1	7,061
SSI (Supplemental Security Income)	542	4.2	5,282
Public assistance	84	0.6	2,007
Veterans' benefits	59	0.5	–
Survivor benefits	364	2.8	6,911
Disability benefits	208	1.6	6,115
Unemployment compensation	371	2.9	3,656
Workers' compensation	114	0.9	2,400
Property income	8,094	62.6	1,657
Interest	7,645	59.1	1,487
Dividends	2,855	22.1	1,534
Rents, royalties, estates or trusts	1,266	9.8	2,085
Retirement income	1,722	13.3	8,988
Pension income	1,240	9.6	10,504
Alimony	99	0.8	5,565
Child support	86	0.7	3,062
Educational assistance	50	0.4	–
Financial assistance from other household	97	0.8	4,325
Other income	94	0.7	2,111

Note: (–) means sample is too small to make a reliable estimate.
Source: Bureau of the Census, data from the 2003 Current Population Survey Annual Social and Economic Supplement, Internet site http://ferret.bls.census.gov/macro/032003/perinc/new08_000.htm; calculations by New Strategist

The Poverty Rate of Boomers Is below Average

But poverty among black and Hispanic Boomers is three times the level among non-Hispanic whites.

While 12 percent of all Americans were poor in 2002, the poverty rate among the Baby-Boom generation, aged 38 to 56, was a smaller 8 percent. Boomers account for only 18 percent of the nation's poor, although 28 percent of the nation's population is in the age group.

The poverty rate for non-Hispanic white Boomers was just 5 percent in 2002, only one-third of the rate among their black and Hispanic counterparts. Sixteen percent of Hispanics and 17 percent of blacks aged 38 to 56 are poor. Although much higher than the rate for non-Hispanic whites, these figures are well below the 22 percent poverty rate for Hispanics and the 24 percent rate for blacks. Overall, non-Hispanic whites account for just 49 percent of poor Boomers, while blacks account for 26 percent and Hispanics for 20 percent.

■ The poverty rate bottoms out in the 45-to-54 age group, now entirely filled with the Baby-Boom generation. As Boomers age, the poverty rate may rise.

Black Boomers are most likely to be poor

(percent of people aged 38 to 56 below poverty level, by race and Hispanic origin, 2002)

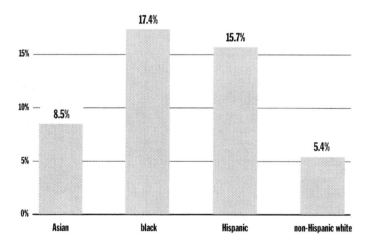

Table 4.38 People below Poverty Level by Age, Race and Hispanic Origin, 2002

(number, percent, and percent distribution of people below poverty level, by age, race and Hispanic origin, 2002; people in thousands as of 2003)

	total	Asian	black	Hispanic	non-Hispanic white
NUMBER IN POVERTY					
TOTAL PEOPLE	34,570	1,243	8,884	8,555	15,567
Boomers (aged 38 to 56)	6,361	283	1,632	1,283	3,097
Under age 35	21,343	771	5,954	6,206	8,235
Aged 35 to 54	7,086	315	1,791	1,575	3,339
Aged 35 to 44	4,087	212	968	1,016	1,854
Aged 45 to 54	2,999	103	823	559	1,485
Aged 55 to 59	1,302	41	239	169	829
Aged 60 or older	4,839	115	901	604	3,165
PERCENT IN POVERTY					
TOTAL PEOPLE	12.1%	10.0%	23.9%	21.8%	8.0%
Boomers (aged 38 to 56)	8.0	8.5	17.4	15.7	5.4
Under age 35	15.3	11.3	27.9	24.4	9.7
Aged 35 to 54	8.4	8.5	17.5	16.4	5.6
Aged 35 to 44	9.3	10.2	17.4	17.2	6.1
Aged 45 to 54	7.5	6.3	17.6	15.2	5.0
Aged 55 to 59	8.4	7.6	15.7	14.2	6.9
Aged 60 or older	10.5	8.1	22.0	20.4	8.5
PERCENT DISTRIBUTION OF POOR BY AGE					
TOTAL PEOPLE	100.0%	100.0%	100.0%	100.0%	100.0%
Boomers (aged 38 to 56)	18.4	22.8	18.4	15.0	19.9
Under age 35	61.7	62.0	67.0	72.5	52.9
Aged 35 to 54	20.5	25.3	20.2	18.4	21.4
Aged 35 to 44	11.8	17.1	10.9	11.9	11.9
Aged 45 to 54	8.7	8.3	9.3	6.5	9.5
Aged 55 to 59	3.8	3.3	2.7	2.0	5.3
Aged 60 or older	14.0	9.3	10.1	7.1	20.3
PERCENT DISTRIBUTION OF POOR BY RACE AND HISPANIC ORIGIN					
TOTAL PEOPLE	100.0%	3.6%	25.7%	24.7%	45.0%
Boomers (aged 38 to 56)	100.0	4.4	25.7	20.2	48.7
Under age 35	100.0	3.6	27.9	29.1	38.6
Aged 35 to 54	100.0	4.4	25.3	22.2	47.1
Aged 35 to 44	100.0	5.2	23.7	24.9	45.4
Aged 45 to 54	100.0	3.4	27.4	18.6	49.5
Aged 55 to 59	100.0	3.1	18.4	13.0	63.7
Aged 60 or older	100.0	2.4	18.6	12.5	65.4

Note: Numbers will not add to total because each racial category includes those who identified themselves as being of the race alone and those who identified themselves as being of the race in combination with one or more other races, because Hispanics may be of any race, and because not all races are shown. Non-Hispanic whites include only those who identified themselves as "white alone" and non-Hispanic.
Source: Bureau of the Census, data from the 2003 Current Population Survey Annual Social and Economic Supplement, Internet site http://ferret.bls.census.gov/macro/032003/pov/new34_100.htm and http://ferret.bls.census.gov/macro/032003/pov/new01_000.htm; calculations by New Strategist

5

Labor Force

■ The labor force participation rate of men aged 55 to 59 grew by 0.6 percentage points between 2000 and 2003. Behind the rise is the end of early retirement for millions of older workers.

■ Among the nation's 147 million workers in 2003, 64 million were aged 40 to 59 (Boomers were aged 39 to 57 in that year). The 40-to-59 age group accounts for 43 percent of the labor force.

■ Seventy-one percent of couples aged 35 to 54 are dual earners, while the husband is the only one in the labor force in another 23 percent.

■ Middle-aged workers are at the peak of their career. They account for 65 percent of chief executives, 62 percent of human resources managers, and 61 percent of registered nurses.

■ The percentage of men aged 35 to 59 who have been with their current employer for ten or more years fell sharply between 1991 and 2002.

■ Between 2003 and 2012, the oldest members of the Baby-Boom generation will enter their sixties. The labor force participation rate of people aged 60 or older is projected to rise as many postpone retirement.

Fewer Men in Their Forties Are at Work

Men aged 55 to 59 are increasingly likely to work, however.

Trends in the labor force participation rates of middle-aged men and women are complicated by job losses, the entry of career-oriented Baby-Boom women into the older age groups, and the end of early retirement.

Among men in their forties and fifties, the labor force participation rate has declined since 1990. This continues a long-term trend of falling participation among men as more women have gone to work. Between 2000 and 2003, however, the labor force participation rate of men aged 55 to 59 grew by 0.6 percentage points. Behind this rise is a reversal of the trend toward ever-earlier retirement as the stock market declined and nest eggs vanished.

Among women aged 45 to 59, labor force participation has surged since 1990 as Boomers entered the age group (the oldest Boomers turned 57 in 2003). But the participation rate has fallen since 2000 for women in their forties because of the recession and the rise in the number of discouraged workers.

The gap between the labor force participation rates of men and women aged 55 to 59 was 25 percentage points in 1990. By 2003, it had shrunk to just 12 percentage points.

■ In contrast to older generations, the lifestyles of Baby-Boom men and women are similar—a fact that has changed families and workplaces.

A growing share of 55-to-59-year-olds are in the labor force

(percent of people aged 55 to 59 in the labor force, by sex, 2000 and 2003)

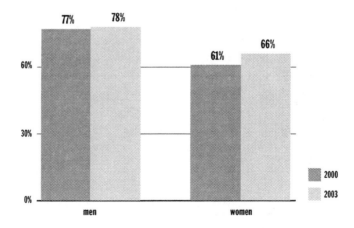

Table 5.1 Labor Force Participation Rate of People Aged 40 to 59 by Sex, 1990 to 2003

(civilian labor force participation rate of people aged 16 or older and aged 40 to 59, by sex, 1990 to 2003; percentage point change, 2000–2003 and 1990–2003)

				percentage point change	
	2003	2000	1990	2000–03	1990–03
Men aged 16 or older	**73.5%**	**74.8%**	**76.4%**	**–1.3**	**–2.9**
Aged 40 to 44	91.4	92.1	93.9	–0.7	–2.5
Aged 45 to 49	89.2	90.2	92.2	–1.0	–3.0
Aged 50 to 54	86.0	86.8	88.8	–0.8	–2.8
Aged 55 to 59	77.6	77.0	79.9	0.6	–2.3
Women aged 16 or older	**59.5**	**59.9**	**57.5**	**–0.4**	**2.0**
Aged 40 to 44	77.4	78.7	77.5	–1.3	–0.1
Aged 45 to 49	78.6	79.1	74.7	–0.5	3.9
Aged 50 to 54	74.7	74.1	66.9	0.6	7.8
Aged 55 to 59	65.5	61.4	55.3	4.1	10.2

Source: Bureau of Labor Statistics, Public Query Data Tool, Internet site http://www.bls.gov/data; calculations by New Strategist

Boomers Are a Large Share of the Nation's Workers

Nearly half of Boomer workers are women.

Among the nation's 147 million workers in 2003, 64 million were aged 40 to 59 (Boomers were aged 39 to 57 in that year), accounting for 43 percent of the labor force. Among workers in the 40-to-59 age group, fully 30 million—or 47 percent—are women.

Eighty-seven percent of men and 75 percent of women aged 40 to 59 are in the labor force. For both men and women, the labor force participation rate falls within the age group. Among men aged 40 to 44, fully 91 percent are in the labor force. The figure drops to just 78 percent among men aged 55 to 59 as some opt for early retirement. Among women, the labor force participation rate declines from a high of 78 percent among those in their late forties to 66 percent among those aged 55 to 59.

Because unemployment is less common among the middle-aged than young adults, people aged 40 to 59 account for a smaller share of the unemployed (31 percent) than they do of the labor force as a whole. Boomer women are slightly less likely to be unemployed than their male counterparts.

■ The oldest Boomers are entering the ages of early retirement, but few will be able to retire before reaching the age of eligibility for Social Security and Medicare benefits.

Labor force participation rate is lowest among the oldest Boomer men

(percent of men aged 40 to 59 in the labor force, by age, 2003)

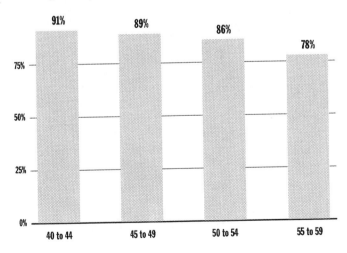

Table 5.2 Employment Status by Sex and Age, 2003

(number and percent of people aged 16 or older in the civilian labor force by sex, age, and employment status, 2003; numbers in thousands)

| | civilian noninstitutional population | civilian labor force | | | unemployed | |
		total	percent of population	employed	number	percent of labor force
Total aged 16 or older	**221,168**	**146,510**	**66.2%**	**137,736**	**8,774**	**6.0%**
Under age 40	95,969	72,011	75.0	66,398	5,613	7.8
Aged 40 to 59	78,843	63,537	80.6	60,817	2,721	4.3
Aged 40 to 44	22,696	19,125	84.3	18,218	907	4.7
Aged 45 to 49	21,581	18,081	83.8	17,325	756	4.2
Aged 50 to 54	18,941	15,189	80.2	14,589	601	4.0
Aged 55 to 59	15,625	11,142	71.3	10,685	457	4.1
Aged 60 to 64	12,103	6,170	51.0	5,913	257	4.2
Aged 65 or older	34,253	4,792	14.0	4,608	183	3.8
Men aged 16 or older	**106,435**	**78,238**	**73.5**	**73,332**	**4,906**	**6.3**
Under age 40	47,727	38,884	81.5	35,767	3,115	8.0
Aged 40 to 59	38,435	33,360	86.8	31,831	1,530	4.6
Aged 40 to 44	11,123	10,167	91.4	9,659	508	5.0
Aged 45 to 49	10,563	9,424	89.2	8,998	427	4.5
Aged 50 to 54	9,221	7,927	86.0	7,590	337	4.3
Aged 55 to 59	7,528	5,842	77.6	5,584	258	4.4
Aged 60 to 64	5,777	3,302	57.2	3,149	154	4.7
Aged 65 or older	14,496	2,692	18.6	2,585	107	4.0
Women aged 16 or older	**114,733**	**68,272**	**59.5**	**64,404**	**3,868**	**5.7**
Under age 40	48,241	33,128	68.7	30,630	2,499	7.5
Aged 40 to 59	40,408	30,177	74.7	28,986	1,190	3.9
Aged 40 to 44	11,572	8,958	77.4	8,559	399	4.5
Aged 45 to 49	11,019	8,657	78.6	8,327	329	3.8
Aged 50 to 54	9,720	7,262	74.7	6,999	263	3.6
Aged 55 to 59	8,097	5,300	65.5	5,101	199	3.8
Aged 60 to 64	6,326	2,868	45.3	2,765	103	3.6
Aged 65 or older	19,758	2,099	10.6	2,023	76	3.6

Source: Bureau of Labor Statistics, 2003 Current Population Survey, Internet site http://www.bls.gov/cps/home.htm; calculations by New Strategist

Among Boomer Men, Blacks Have the Lowest Labor Force Rate

Only 78 percent of black men aged 40 to 59 are in the labor force.

Among men aged 40 to 59, from 87 to 91 percent of Asians, Hispanics, and whites were in the labor force in 2003 (when Boomers were aged 39 to 57). The labor force includes both the employed and the unemployed. The labor force participation rate is lowest among black men. Only 78 percent of those aged 40 to 59 were in the labor force in 2003, and the rate dips as low as 68 percent among black men aged 55 to 59.

The unemployment rate was significantly higher in 2003 for black men than for Asian, Hispanic, or white men. Only 4.1 percent of white men aged 40 to 59 were unemployed versus 7.8 percent of black, 6.1 percent of Asian, and 5.7 percent of Hispanic men in the age group.

■ Black men have a more difficult time findings jobs than white men, some of them becoming so discouraged that they give up looking for a job and drop out of the labor force altogether.

Labor force participation rates vary by race and Hispanic origin

(percent of men aged 40 to 59 in the labor force by race and Hispanic origin, 2003)

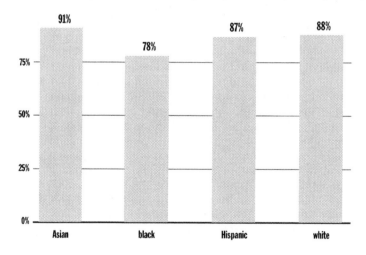

Table 5.3 Employment Status of Men by Race, Hispanic Origin, and Age, 2003

(number and percent of men aged 16 or older in the civilian labor force by race, Hispanic origin, age, and employment status, 2003; numbers in thousands)

	civilian noninstitutional population	civilian labor force			unemployed	
		total	percent of population	employed	number	percent of labor force
ASIAN MEN						
Total aged 16 or older	**4,338**	**3,277**	**75.6%**	**3,073**	**204**	**6.2%**
Under age 40	2,253	1,716	76.2	1,607	110	6.4
Aged 40 to 59	1,479	1,339	90.5	1,257	81	6.1
Aged 40 to 44	470	435	92.7	411	24	5.6
Aged 45 to 49	411	380	92.5	353	27	7.1
Aged 50 to 54	338	307	90.9	289	18	5.8
Aged 55 to 59	260	217	83.2	204	12	5.6
Aged 60 to 64	197	139	70.4	130	9	6.3
Aged 65 or older	409	83	20.3	79	4	4.5
BLACK MEN						
Total aged 16 or older	**11,454**	**7,711**	**67.3**	**6,820**	**891**	**11.6**
Under age 40	5,842	4,182	71.6	3,555	626	15.0
Aged 40 to 59	3,955	3,079	77.9	2,841	239	7.8
Aged 40 to 44	1,236	1,031	83.4	932	99	9.6
Aged 45 to 49	1,147	904	78.8	838	67	7.4
Aged 50 to 54	947	723	76.3	681	42	5.8
Aged 55 to 59	625	421	67.5	390	31	7.4
Aged 60 to 64	564	264	46.7	248	16	5.9
Aged 65 or older	1,093	186	17.0	176	10	5.6
HISPANIC MEN						
Total aged 16 or older	**14,098**	**11,288**	**80.1**	**10,479**	**809**	**7.2**
Under age 40	8,926	7,526	84.3	6,930	596	7.9
Aged 40 to 59	3,894	3,373	86.6	3,182	192	5.7
Aged 40 to 44	1,411	1,302	92.3	1,232	70	5.4
Aged 45 to 49	1,096	952	86.9	893	59	6.2
Aged 50 to 54	814	678	83.3	640	38	5.7
Aged 55 to 59	573	441	77.1	417	25	5.6
Aged 60 to 64	416	239	57.5	223	16	6.8
Aged 65 or older	862	150	17.4	144	5	3.6
WHITE MEN						
Total aged 16 or older	**88,249**	**65,509**	**74.2**	**61,866**	**3,643**	**5.6**
Under age 40	38,246	31,937	83.5	29,677	2,260	7.1
Aged 40 to 59	32,256	28,330	87.8	27,165	1,165	4.1
Aged 40 to 44	9,188	8,505	92.6	8,137	368	4.3
Aged 45 to 49	8,797	7,959	90.5	7,638	321	4.0
Aged 50 to 54	7,758	6,749	87.0	6,479	270	4.0
Aged 55 to 59	6,513	5,117	78.6	4,911	206	4.0
Aged 60 to 64	4,929	2,856	57.9	2,729	127	4.4
Aged 65 or older	12,818	2,386	18.6	2,295	91	3.8

Note: Race is shown only for those selecting that race group only. People who selected more than one race are not included. Hispanics may be of any race.
Source: Bureau of Labor Statistics, 2003 Current Population Survey, Internet site http://www.bls.gov/cps/home.htm; calculations by New Strategist

Hispanic Women Have the Lowest Participation Rate

But the majority are in the labor force.

Among Asian, black, and white women aged 40 to 59, from 73 to 75 percent are in the labor force. The participation rate is a smaller 65 percent for their Hispanic counterparts. Labor force participation varies within the 40 to 59 age group. While 70 percent of Hispanic women aged 40 to 44 are in the labor force, only 56 percent of those aged 55 to 59 are working or looking for work. Rates also fall within the age group for Asian, black, and white women as some opt for early retirement when their typically older husbands reach retirement age.

Within the 40-to-59 age group, unemployment rates are higher for black and Hispanic women than for Asian or white women. While 3.5 percent of white women in the age group were unemployed in 2003, the figure was more than 6 percent among black and Hispanic women.

■ Hispanic women aged 40 to 59 are less likely to work than black or white women because their families are larger and more of them are busy raising children.

Hispanic women are least likely to work

(percent of women aged 40 to 59 in the labor force by race and Hispanic origin, 2003)

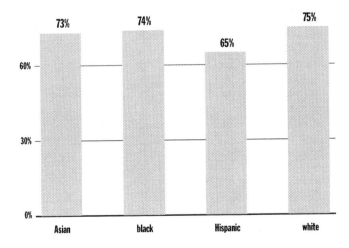

Table 5.4 Employment Status of Women by Race, Hispanic Origin, and Age, 2003

(number and percent of women aged 16 or older in the civilian labor force by race, Hispanic origin, age, and employment status, 2003; numbers in thousands)

	civilian noninstitutional population	civilian labor force total	civilian labor force percent of population	civilian labor force employed	unemployed number	unemployed percent of labor force
ASIAN WOMEN						
Total aged 16 or older	**4,882**	**2,845**	**58.3%**	**2,683**	**162**	**5.7%**
Under age 40	2,432	1,488	61.2	1,391	97	6.5
Aged 40 to 59	1,676	1,218	72.7	1,158	60	4.9
Aged 40 to 44	494	359	72.8	343	16	4.5
Aged 45 to 49	467	356	76.2	337	19	5.4
Aged 50 to 54	406	305	75.2	291	14	4.6
Aged 55 to 59	309	198	64.0	187	11	5.3
Aged 60 to 64	219	91	41.5	87	4	4.6
Aged 65 or older	555	48	8.7	47	1	3.1
BLACK WOMEN						
Total aged 16 or older	**14,232**	**8,815**	**61.9**	**7,919**	**895**	**10.2**
Under age 40	6,923	4,749	68.6	4,109	637	13.4
Aged 40 to 59	4,897	3,610	73.7	3,379	232	6.4
Aged 40 to 44	1,519	1,226	80.7	1,134	93	7.5
Aged 45 to 49	1,382	1,061	76.8	1,000	61	5.7
Aged 50 to 54	1,151	818	71.1	770	48	5.9
Aged 55 to 59	845	505	59.8	475	30	5.9
Aged 60 to 64	659	276	41.8	260	16	5.8
Aged 65 or older	1,753	180	10.3	171	10	5.3
HISPANIC WOMEN						
Total aged 16 or older	**13,452**	**7,525**	**55.9**	**6,894**	**631**	**8.4**
Under age 40	7,890	4,684	59.4	4,229	455	9.7
Aged 40 to 59	3,921	2,563	65.4	2,401	162	6.3
Aged 40 to 44	1,355	948	70.0	890	58	6.1
Aged 45 to 49	1,089	750	68.9	706	44	5.8
Aged 50 to 54	847	514	60.7	472	42	8.2
Aged 55 to 59	630	351	55.8	333	18	5.1
Aged 60 to 64	475	169	35.6	159	10	5.7
Aged 65 or older	1,166	109	9.4	105	4	4.4
WHITE WOMEN						
Total aged 16 or older	**93,043**	**55,037**	**59.2**	**52,369**	**2,668**	**4.8**
Under age 40	37,481	25,969	69.3	24,308	1,661	6.4
Aged 40 to 59	33,005	24,762	75.0	23,900	862	3.5
Aged 40 to 44	9,287	7,168	77.2	6,894	274	3.8
Aged 45 to 49	8,939	7,067	79.1	6,829	238	3.4
Aged 50 to 54	7,972	6,011	75.4	5,815	196	3.3
Aged 55 to 59	6,807	4,516	66.3	4,362	154	3.4
Aged 60 to 64	5,341	2,454	46.0	2,373	81	3.3
Aged 65 or older	17,216	1,852	10.8	1,788	64	3.5

Note: Race is shown only for those selecting that race group only. People who selected more than one race are not included. Hispanics may be of any race.
Source: Bureau of Labor Statistics, 2003 Current Population Survey, Internet site http://www.bls.gov/cps/home.htm; calculations by New Strategist

More than 70 Percent of Boomer Couples Are Dual Earners

In fewer than one-fourth only the husband is in the labor force.

Dual incomes are by far the norm among married couples. Both husband and wife are in the labor force in 56 percent of married couples. In another 22 percent, the husband is the only worker. Not far behind are the 17 percent of couples in which neither spouse is in the labor force. The wife is the sole worker among 6 percent of couples.

Seventy-one percent of couples aged 35 to 54 are dual earners, while the husband is the only one in the labor force in another 23 percent. This dual-earner lifestyle accounts for a much smaller 46 percent of couples aged 55 to 64. The wife is the only one employed in a substantial 12 percent of couples in this older age group. In these homes, typically, the older husband is retired while the younger wife is still at work. For 72 percent of couples aged 65 or older, neither husband nor wife is working.

■ As Boomers fill the 55-to-64 age group, the dual-income couple share will rise because fewer Boomers will have the opportunity to retire before age 65.

Dual earners are most common among Boomer couples

(percent of married couples in which both husband and wife are in the labor force, by age, 2002)

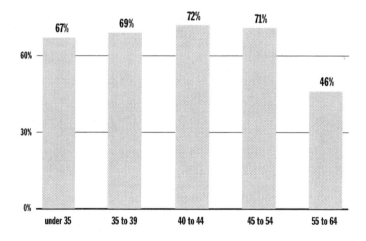

Table 5.5 Labor Force Status of Married-Couple Family Groups by Age of Reference Person, 2002

(number and percent distribution of married-couple family groups by age of reference person and labor force status of husband and wife, 2002; numbers in thousands)

	total	husband and/or wife in labor force			neither husband nor wife in labor force
		husband and wife	husband only	wife only	
Total married-couple family groups	**57,919**	**32,194**	**12,672**	**3,470**	**9,583**
Under age 35	11,363	7,568	3,308	287	200
Aged 35 to 54	27,793	19,620	6,317	1,151	703
Aged 35 to 39	6,919	4,739	1,857	207	115
Aged 40 to 44	7,499	5,424	1,686	261	128
Aged 45 to 54	13,375	9,457	2,774	683	460
Aged 55 to 64	9,062	4,206	2,003	1,127	1,726
Aged 65 or older	9,702	797	1,045	905	6,953
PERCENT DISTRIBUTION					
Total married-couple family groups	**100.0%**	**55.6%**	**21.9%**	**6.0%**	**16.5%**
Under age 35	100.0	66.6	29.1	2.5	1.8
Aged 35 to 54	100.0	70.6	22.7	4.1	2.5
Aged 35 to 39	100.0	68.5	26.8	3.0	1.7
Aged 40 to 44	100.0	72.3	22.5	3.5	1.7
Aged 45 to 54	100.0	70.7	20.7	5.1	3.4
Aged 55 to 64	100.0	46.4	22.1	12.4	19.1
Aged 65 or older	100.0	8.2	10.8	9.3	71.7

Note: Number of married-couple family groups exceeds number of married-couple householders because some households contain more than one married couple.
Source: Bureau of the Census, 2002 Current Population Survey Annual Demographic Supplement, Internet site http://www.census.gov/population/www/socdemo/hh-fam/cps2002.html; calculations by New Strategist

Workers Aged 35 to 54 Dominate Many Occupations

They account for the majority of managers and professionals.

Among the 138 million employed Americans in 2003, 67 million (or 48 percent) were aged 35 to 54 (Boomers were aged 39 to 57 in that year). In many occupations, well over 50 percent of workers are aged 35 to 54. Middle-aged workers account for 65 percent of chief executives. They are also 65 percent of computer and information systems managers, 64 percent of aircraft pilots, 64 percent of electrical engineers, 62 percent of human resources managers, and 61 percent of registered nurses. Behind this dominance is the fact that people aged 35 to 54 are usually at the height of their career. While only 35 percent of all workers are in management or professional occupations, the figure is 40 percent among those aged 45 to 54.

Middle-aged workers are least likely to be found in the lowest-paid occupations. They account for only 21 percent of waiters and waitresses and 24 percent of cashiers. These occupations tend to attract young adults who are just starting out in the labor force.

■ Because Boomers are at the height of their career, they are also in their peak earning years.

People aged 35 to 54 account for the majority of workers in some occupations

(percent of workers aged 35 to 54, by occupation, 2003)

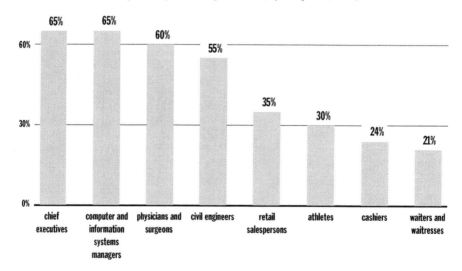

Table 5.6 Occupations of Workers Aged 35 to 64, 2003

(number of employed workers aged 16 or older, median age of workers, and number of workers aged 35 to 64, by occupation, 2003; numbers in thousands)

	total	median age	aged 35 to 54 total	35 to 44	45 to 54	55 to 64
TOTAL WORKERS	**137,736**	**40.4**	**66,795**	**34,881**	**31,914**	**16,598**
Management and professional occupations	**47,929**	**42.6**	**25,895**	**13,006**	**12,889**	**6,561**
Management, business, and financial operations	19,934	44.0	11,325	5,673	5,652	3,055
Management	14,468	44.7	8,445	4,171	4,274	2,307
Business and financial operations	5,465	42.1	2,879	1,502	1,377	749
Professional and related occupations	27,995	41.5	14,570	7,333	7,237	3,506
Computer and mathematical	3,122	38.6	1,583	932	651	239
Architecture and engineering	2,727	41.5	1,521	812	709	322
Life, physical, and social science	1,375	41.2	669	335	334	170
Community and social services	2,184	43.1	1,102	492	610	321
Legal	1,508	43.1	781	395	386	232
Education, training, and library	7,768	42.6	3,907	1,791	2,116	1,177
Arts, design, entertainment, sports, and media	2,663	40.0	1,280	689	591	278
Health care practitioner and technical	6,648	41.9	3,726	1,886	1,840	766
Service occupations	**22,086**	**36.3**	**8,760**	**4,865**	**3,895**	**2,122**
Health care support	2,926	38.1	1,341	729	612	294
Protective service	2,727	39.9	1,330	750	580	272
Food preparation and serving	7,254	28.6	2,027	1,192	835	440
Building and grounds cleaning and maintenance	4,947	40.8	2,341	1,244	1,097	651
Personal care and service	4,232	37.9	1,721	951	770	465
Sales and office occupations	**35,496**	**39.7**	**16,015**	**8,289**	**7,726**	**4,421**
Sales and related	15,960	38.8	6,697	3,629	3,068	1,940
Office and administrative support	19,536	40.5	9,318	4,660	4,658	2,482
Natural resources, construction, and maintenance occupations	**14,205**	**38.9**	**7,006**	**3,895**	**3,111**	**1,342**
Farming, fishing, and forestry	1,050	36.7	416	242	174	103
Construction and extraction	8,114	38.2	3,923	2,240	1,683	683
Installation, maintenance, and repair	5,041	40.4	2,668	1,413	1,255	556
Production, transportation, and material moving occupations	**18,020**	**40.7**	**9,118**	**4,825**	**4,293**	**2,152**
Production	9,700	41.1	5,147	2,712	2,435	1,176
Transportion and material moving	8,320	40.1	3,972	2,114	1,858	976

Source: Bureau of Labor Statistics, unpublished data from the 2003 Current Population Survey; calculations by New Strategist

Table 5.7 Distribution of Workers Aged 35 to 64 by Occupation, 2003

(percent distribution of employed people aged 16 or older and aged 35 to 64 by occupation, 2003)

	total	aged 35 to 54 total	35 to 44	45 to 54	55 to 64
TOTAL WORKERS	**100.0%**	**100.0%**	**100.0%**	**100.0%**	**100.0%**
Management and professional occupations	**34.8**	**38.8**	**37.3**	**40.4**	**39.5**
Management, business, and financial operations	14.5	17.0	16.3	17.7	18.4
Management	10.5	12.6	12.0	13.4	13.9
Business and financial operations	4.0	4.3	4.3	4.3	4.5
Professional and related occupations	20.3	21.8	21.0	22.7	21.1
Computer and mathematical	2.3	2.4	2.7	2.0	1.4
Architecture and engineering	2.0	2.3	2.3	2.2	1.9
Life, physical, and social science	1.0	0.1	1.0	1.1	1.0
Community and social services	1.6	1.6	1.4	1.9	1.9
Legal	1.1	1.2	1.1	1.2	1.4
Education, training, and library	5.6	5.8	5.1	6.6	7.1
Arts, design, entertainment, sports, and media	1.9	1.9	2.0	1.9	1.7
Health care practitioner and technical	4.8	5.6	5.4	5.8	4.6
Service occupations	**16.0**	**13.1**	**13.9**	**12.2**	**12.8**
Health care support	2.1	2.0	2.1	1.9	1.8
Protective service	2.0	2.0	2.2	1.8	1.6
Food preparation and serving	5.3	3.0	3.4	2.6	2.7
Building and grounds cleaning and maintenance	3.6	3.5	3.6	3.4	3.9
Personal care and service	3.1	2.6	2.7	2.4	2.8
Sales and office occupations	**25.8**	**24.0**	**23.8**	**24.2**	**26.6**
Sales and related	11.6	10.0	10.4	9.6	11.7
Office and administrative support	14.2	14.0	13.4	14.6	15.0
Natural resources, construction, and maintenance occupations	**10.3**	**10.5**	**11.2**	**9.7**	**8.1**
Farming, fishing, and forestry	0.8	0.6	0.7	0.5	0.6
Construction and extraction	5.9	5.9	6.4	5.3	4.1
Installation, maintenance, and repair	3.7	4.0	4.1	3.9	3.3
Production, transportation, and material moving occupations	**13.1**	**13.7**	**13.8**	**13.5**	**13.0**
Production	7.0	7.7	7.8	7.6	7.1
Transportion and material moving	6.0	5.9	6.1	5.8	5.9

Source: Calculations by New Strategist based on Bureau of Labor Statistics unpublished 2003 Current Population Survey data

Table 5.8 Share of Workers Aged 35 to 64 by Occupation, 2003

(employed people aged 35 to 64 as a percent of total employed people aged 16 or older by occupation, 2003)

	total	aged 35 to 54 total	35 to 44	45 to 54	55 to 64
TOTAL WORKERS	100.0%	48.5%	25.3%	23.2%	12.1%
Management and professional occupations	**100.0**	**54.0**	**27.1**	**26.9**	**13.7**
Management, business, and financial operations	100.0	56.8	28.5	28.4	15.3
Management	100.0	58.4	28.8	29.5	15.9
Business and financial operations	100.0	52.7	27.5	25.2	13.7
Professional and related occupations	100.0	52.1	26.2	25.9	12.5
Computer and mathematical	100.0	50.7	29.9	20.9	7.7
Architecture and engineering	100.0	55.8	29.8	26.0	11.8
Life, physical, and social science	100.0	48.7	24.4	24.3	12.4
Community and social services	100.0	50.5	22.5	27.9	14.7
Legal	100.0	51.8	26.2	25.6	15.4
Education, training, and library	100.0	50.3	23.1	27.2	15.2
Arts, design, entertainment, sports, and media	100.0	48.1	25.9	22.2	10.4
Health care practitioner and technical	100.0	56.1	28.4	27.7	11.5
Service occupations	**100.0**	**39.7**	**22.0**	**17.6**	**9.6**
Health care support	100.0	45.8	24.9	20.9	10.1
Protective service	100.0	48.8	27.5	21.3	10.0
Food preparation and serving	100.0	27.9	16.4	11.5	6.1
Building and grounds cleaning and maintenance	100.0	47.3	25.1	22.2	13.2
Personal care and service	100.0	40.7	22.5	18.2	11.0
Sales and office occupations	**100.0**	**45.1**	**23.4**	**21.8**	**12.5**
Sales and related	100.0	42.0	22.7	19.2	12.2
Office and administrative support	100.0	47.7	23.9	23.8	12.7
Natural resources, construction, and maintenance occupations	**100.0**	**49.3**	**27.4**	**21.9**	**9.4**
Farming, fishing, and forestry	100.0	39.6	23.1	16.6	9.8
Construction and extraction	100.0	48.3	27.6	20.7	8.4
Installation, maintenance, and repair	100.0	52.9	28.0	24.9	11.0
Production, transportation, and material moving occupations	**100.0**	**50.6**	**26.8**	**23.8**	**11.9**
Production	100.0	53.1	28.0	25.1	12.1
Transportion and material moving	100.0	47.7	25.4	22.3	11.7

Source: Calculations by New Strategist based on Bureau of Labor Statistics unpublished 2003 Current Population Survey data

Table 5.9 Workers Aged 35 to 64 by Detailed Occupation, 2003

(number of employed workers aged 16 or older, median age, and number and percent aged 35 to 64, by selected detailed occupation; 2003; numbers in thousands)

	total workers	median age	total aged 35 to 54		aged 35 to 44		aged 45 to 54		aged 55 to 64	
			number	percent of total	number	percent of total	number	percent of total	number	percent of total
Total workers	**137,736**	**40.4**	**66,795**	**48.5%**	**34,881**	**25.3%**	**31,914**	**23.2%**	**16,598**	**12.1%**
Chief executives	1,617	48.2	1,046	64.7	461	28.5	585	36.2	328	20.3
Legislators	14	53.2	6	42.9	4	28.6	2	14.3	4	28.6
Marketing, sales mgrs.	888	41.6	506	57.0	288	32.4	218	24.5	103	11.6
Computer and information systems managers	347	41.7	226	65.1	119	34.3	107	30.8	29	8.4
Financial managers	1,041	42.1	611	58.7	334	32.1	277	26.6	140	13.4
Human resources mgrs.	263	45.1	164	62.4	80	30.4	84	31.9	46	17.5
Farmers and ranchers	825	54.0	325	39.4	144	17.5	181	21.9	201	24.4
Education admins.	748	48.9	437	58.4	168	22.5	269	36.0	170	22.7
Food service managers	875	39.5	434	49.6	232	26.5	202	23.1	88	10.1
Medical and health services managers	480	46.1	316	65.8	126	26.2	190	39.6	71	14.8
Accountants, auditors	1,639	41.1	858	52.3	467	28.5	391	23.9	195	11.9
Computer scientists and systems analysts	722	40.4	396	54.8	213	29.5	183	25.3	72	10.0
Computer programmers	563	38.7	294	52.2	183	32.5	111	19.7	46	8.2
Computer software engineers	758	38.3	384	50.7	237	31.3	147	19.4	49	6.5
Architects	180	42.0	94	52.2	50	27.8	44	24.4	23	12.8
Civil engineers	278	42.9	153	55.0	75	27.0	78	28.1	38	13.7
Electrical engineers	363	42.7	231	63.6	122	33.6	109	30.0	42	11.6
Mechanical engineers	285	41.0	156	54.7	87	30.5	69	24.2	33	11.6
Medical scientists	101	39.9	53	52.5	30	29.7	23	22.8	10	9.9
Psychologists	185	50.2	94	50.8	33	17.8	61	33.0	44	23.8
Social workers	673	41.4	345	51.3	167	24.8	178	26.4	87	12.9
Clergy	410	49.9	212	51.7	83	20.2	129	31.5	84	20.5
Lawyers	952	44.4	506	53.2	251	26.4	255	26.8	160	16.8
Postsecondary teachers	1,121	43.8	501	44.7	245	21.9	256	22.8	213	19.0
Preschool and kindergarten teachers	665	38.9	300	45.1	149	22.4	151	22.7	73	11.0
Elementary and middle school teachers	2,557	42.7	1,331	52.1	616	24.1	715	28.0	371	14.5
Secondary school teachers	1,124	43.7	598	53.2	250	22.2	348	31.0	176	15.7
Librarians	194	49.6	101	52.1	27	13.9	74	38.1	49	25.3
Teacher assistants	932	41.8	513	55.0	247	26.5	266	28.5	116	12.4
Artists	212	43.8	108	50.9	54	25.5	54	25.5	36	17.0
Actors	30	36.6	11	36.7	6	20.0	5	16.7	3	10.0
Athletes	215	30.1	65	30.2	40	18.6	25	11.6	12	5.6
Editors	163	40.8	73	44.8	35	21.5	38	23.3	21	12.9
Writers and authors	190	44.8	97	51.1	50	26.3	47	24.7	31	16.3
Dentists	188	46.0	108	57.4	55	29.3	53	28.2	37	19.7
Pharmacists	232	42.1	103	44.4	59	25.4	44	19.0	37	15.9
Physicians, surgeons	819	44.2	488	59.6	248	30.3	240	29.3	110	13.4
Registered nurses	2,449	43.1	1,482	60.5	716	29.2	766	31.3	305	12.5
Physical therapists	182	37.6	85	46.7	43	23.6	42	23.1	12	6.6
Licensed practical nurses	531	43.3	316	59.5	154	29.0	162	30.5	70	13.2
Nursing, psychiatric, home health aides	1,811	39.2	836	46.2	448	24.7	388	21.4	211	11.7

	total workers	median age	total aged 35 to 54		aged 35 to 44		aged 45 to 54		aged 55 to 64	
			number	percent of total	number	percent of total	number	percent of total	number	percent of total
Firefighters	258	38.3	136	52.7%	89	34.5%	47	18.2%	11	4.3%
Police and sheriff's patrol officers	612	38.7	329	53.8	216	35.3	113	18.5	30	4.9
Security guards, gaming surveillance officers	781	40.7	276	35.3	135	17.3	141	18.1	124	15.9
Chefs and head cooks	281	37.8	131	46.6	73	26.0	58	20.6	21	7.5
Cooks	1,814	32.1	608	33.5	370	20.4	238	13.1	130	7.2
Food prep. workers	612	29.4	177	28.9	98	16.0	79	12.9	43	7.0
Waiters and waitresses	1,842	24.6	384	20.8	234	12.7	150	8.1	59	3.2
Janitors, bldg. cleaners	1,973	43.2	956	48.5	480	24.3	476	24.1	320	16.2
Maids, housekeeping cleaners	1,370	42.2	704	51.4	377	27.5	327	23.9	193	14.1
Grounds maintenance workers	1,135	34.1	436	38.4	257	22.6	179	15.8	82	7.2
Hairdressers, hairstylists, and cosmetologists	718	39.0	331	46.1	198	27.6	133	18.5	84	11.7
Child care workers	1,284	35.4	467	36.4	244	19.0	223	17.4	123	9.6
Cashiers	2,903	26.1	706	24.3	384	13.2	322	11.1	186	6.4
Retail salespersons	3,113	35.9	1,074	34.5	576	18.5	498	16.0	360	11.6
Insurance sales agents	552	44.1	286	51.8	147	26.6	139	25.2	88	15.9
Securities, commodities, financial services sales agents	389	39.8	182	46.8	110	28.3	72	18.5	41	10.5
Sales reps., wholesale, manufacturing	1,399	41.7	762	54.5	426	30.5	336	24.0	186	13.3
Real estate brokers and sales agents	850	48.6	396	46.6	181	21.3	215	25.3	200	23.5
Bookkeeping, accounting, and auditing clerks	1,545	44.5	805	52.1	396	25.6	409	26.5	257	16.6
Customer service reps.	1,747	36.0	708	40.5	393	22.5	315	18.0	163	9.3
Receptionists and information clerks	1,376	36.9	485	35.2	229	16.6	256	18.6	168	12.2
Stock clerks, order fillers	1,360	33.6	496	36.5	255	18.8	241	17.7	114	8.4
Secretaries, admin. assistants	3,632	43.7	1,981	54.5	941	25.9	1,040	28.6	592	16.3
Misc. agric. workers	741	33.8	256	34.5	161	21.7	95	12.8	54	7.3
Carpenters	1,595	37.4	749	47.0	440	27.6	309	19.4	119	7.5
Construction laborers	1,151	34.8	462	40.1	284	24.7	178	15.5	84	7.3
Automotive service techs. and mechanics	884	37.6	411	46.5	230	26.0	181	20.5	76	8.6
Misc. assemblers and fabricators	1,080	39.9	536	49.6	290	26.9	246	22.8	115	10.6
Machinists	454	42.3	256	56.4	126	27.8	130	28.6	67	14.8
Aircraft pilots and flight engineers	116	44.2	74	63.8	36	31.0	38	32.8	18	15.5
Driver/sales workers and truck drivers	3,214	42.1	1,662	51.7	889	27.7	773	24.1	437	13.6
Laborers and freight, stock and material movers, hand	1,748	33.4	657	37.6	377	21.6	280	16.0	112	6.4

Source: Bureau of Labor Statistics, unpublished tables from the 2003 Current Population Survey; calculations by New Strategist

Few Boomers Work Part-time

Men and women aged 35 to 54 are less likely than the average worker to hold part-time jobs.

Among men aged 35 to 54 in the civilian labor force in 2003 (Boomers were aged 39 to 57 in that year), only 4 percent have part-time jobs, well below the 11 percent share among all working men. Among women aged 35 to 54 in the civilian labor force, only 20 percent work part-time—less than the 26 percent share among all working women.

The 6 million women aged 35 to 54 who work part-time account for a significant 38 percent of the 16 million women who work part-time. Men aged 35 to 54 account for only 19 percent of all men who work part-time. The majority of full-time workers, both men and women, are in the 35-to-54 age group.

■ Most men and women aged 35 to 54 are in the labor force, and most of those with jobs work full-time. Workplaces, schools, and community organizations must adapt to the busy schedules of Boomers.

Most Boomer men and women work full-time

(percent of workers aged 35 to 54 who work full-time, by sex, 2003)

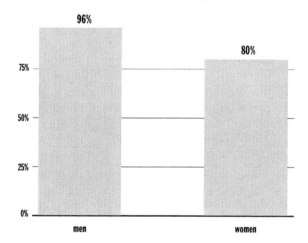

Table 5.10 Full- and Part-time Workers by Age and Sex, 2003

(number and percent distribution of employed people aged 16 or older in the civilian labor force by full- and part-time employment status, by age and sex, 2003; numbers in thousands)

	men			women		
	total	full-time	part-time	total	full-time	part-time
Total employed	**73,332**	**65,379**	**7,953**	**64,405**	**47,946**	**16,459**
Under age 35	26,652	22,143	4,509	23,084	15,918	7,166
Aged 35 to 54	35,362	33,868	1,494	31,432	25,124	6,308
Aged 35 to 44	18,774	18,039	735	16,106	12,667	3,439
Aged 45 to 54	16,588	15,829	759	15,326	12,457	2,869
Aged 55 to 64	8,733	7,824	909	7,866	5,984	1,882
Aged 65 or older	2,585	1,544	1,041	2,023	920	1,103
PERCENT DISTRIBUTION BY AGE						
Total employed	**100.0%**	**100.0%**	**100.0%**	**100.0%**	**100.0%**	**100.0%**
Under age 35	36.3	33.9	56.7	35.8	33.2	43.5
Aged 35 to 54	48.2	51.8	18.8	48.8	52.4	38.3
Aged 35 to 44	25.6	27.6	9.2	25.0	26.4	20.9
Aged 45 to 54	22.6	24.2	9.5	23.8	26.0	17.4
Aged 55 to 64	11.9	12.0	11.4	12.2	12.5	11.4
Aged 65 or older	3.5	2.4	13.1	3.1	1.9	6.7
PERCENT DISTRIBUTION BY EMPLOYMENT STATUS						
Total employed	**100.0%**	**89.2%**	**10.8%**	**100.0%**	**74.4%**	**25.6%**
Under age 35	100.0	83.1	16.9	100.0	69.0	31.0
Aged 35 to 54	100.0	95.8	4.2	100.0	79.9	20.1
Aged 35 to 44	100.0	96.1	3.9	100.0	78.6	21.4
Aged 45 to 54	100.0	95.4	4.6	100.0	81.3	18.7
Aged 55 to 64	100.0	89.6	10.4	100.0	76.1	23.9
Aged 65 or older	100.0	59.7	40.3	100.0	45.5	54.5

Source: Unpublished data from the Bureau of Labor Statistics; calculations by New Strategist

Few Boomers Are Self-Employed

But 35-to-54-year-olds are more likely to be self-employed than the average worker.

Despite plenty of media hype about entrepreneurs, few Americans are self-employed. Only 7 percent of the nation's workers were self-employed in 2003. Among 35-to-54-year-olds, a slightly larger 8 percent were self-employed. The middle aged account for 54 percent of all those who work for themselves.

Men are more likely to be self-employed than women. Among 35-to-54-year-old workers in 2003, 10 percent of men and 7 percent of women were self-employed. Self-employment rises with age, to nearly one in five workers aged 65 or older.

■ If health insurance was more readily available, many more Americans probably would opt for self-employment.

Self-employment rises with age

(percent of workers who are self-employed, by age, 2003)

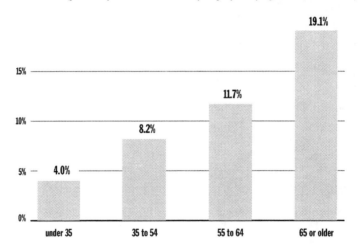

Table 5.11 Self-Employed Workers by Sex and Age, 2003

(number of employed workers aged 16 or older, number and percent who are self-employed, and percent distribution of self-employed, by sex and age, 2003; numbers in thousands)

	total	self-employed number	self-employed percent	percent distribution of self-employed by age
Total workers	**137,736**	**10,295**	**7.5%**	**100.0%**
Under age 35	49,735	1,969	4.0	19.1
Aged 35 to 54	66,795	5,508	8.2	53.5
Aged 35 to 44	34,881	2,717	7.8	26.4
Aged 45 to 54	31,914	2,791	8.7	27.1
Aged 55 to 64	16,598	1,938	11.7	18.8
Aged 65 or older	4,608	880	19.1	8.5
Total men	**73,331**	**6,430**	**8.8**	**100.0**
Under age 35	26,651	1,227	4.6	19.1
Aged 35 to 54	35,362	3,382	9.6	52.6
Aged 35 to 44	18,775	1,635	8.7	25.4
Aged 45 to 54	16,587	1,747	10.5	27.2
Aged 55 to 64	8,733	1,231	14.1	19.1
Aged 65 or older	2,585	590	22.8	9.2
Total women	**64,404**	**3,866**	**6.0**	**100.0**
Under age 35	23,084	743	3.2	19.2
Aged 35 to 54	31,432	2,125	6.8	55.0
Aged 35 to 44	16,106	1,082	6.7	28.0
Aged 45 to 54	15,326	1,043	6.8	27.0
Aged 55 to 64	7,865	707	9.0	18.3
Aged 65 or older	2,023	291	14.4	7.5

Source: Bureau of Labor Statistics, 2003 Current Population Survey, Internet site http://www.bls.gov/cps/home.htm; calculations by New Strategist

Men's Job Tenure Has Declined

Long-term employment is less common among middle-aged men.

Job tenure (the number of years a worker has been with his current employer) has been declining for more than a decade because of changes in the economy, the recession of 2001, and continuing lay-offs in many industrial sectors. Middle-aged men have been particularly hard-hit. Among men aged 35 to 64, job tenure declined by one to three years between 1991 and 2002. The biggest decline occurred among men aged 55 to 64, the age group now filling with Boomers. Among middle-aged women, job tenure fell slightly during the 1991 to 2002 period.

As job tenure declines, so does long-term employment. The percentage of men aged 35 to 59 who have been with their current employer for ten or more years fell sharply between 1991 and 2002, although long-term employment has increased among men aged 50 to 59 since 2000. Among women, long-term employment fell for most in the 35-to-59 age group.

■ Among men in their fifties, long-term employment rose between 2000 and 2002 as fewer opted for early retirement.

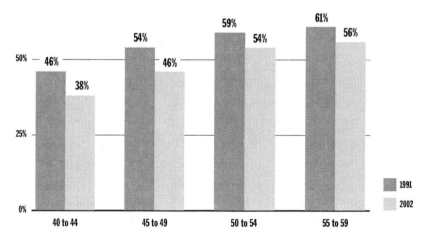

Fewer men have long-term jobs

(percent of men aged 40 to 59 who have worked for their current employer for ten or more years, 1991 and 2002)

Table 5.12 Job Tenure by Sex and Age, 1991 to 2002

(median number of years that employed wage and salary workers aged 25 or older have been with their current employer, by sex and age, 1991 to 2002; change in years, 2000–2002 and 1991–2002)

				change in years	
	2002	2000	1991	2000–02	1991–02
Total workers aged 25 or older	**4.7**	**4.7**	**4.8**	**0.0**	**–0.1**
Aged 25 to 34	2.7	2.6	2.9	0.1	–0.2
Aged 35 to 44	4.6	4.8	5.4	–0.2	–0.8
Aged 45 to 54	7.6	8.2	8.9	–0.6	–1.3
Aged 55 to 64	9.9	10.0	11.1	–0.1	–1.2
Aged 65 or older	8.7	9.5	8.1	–0.8	0.6
Total men aged 25 or older	**4.9**	**5.0**	**5.4**	**–0.1**	**–0.5**
Aged 25 to 34	2.9	2.7	3.1	0.2	–0.2
Aged 35 to 44	5.1	5.4	6.5	–0.3	–1.4
Aged 45 to 54	9.1	9.5	11.2	–0.4	–2.1
Aged 55 to 64	10.2	10.2	13.4	0.0	–3.2
Aged 65 or older	8.1	9.1	7.0	–1.0	1.1
Total women aged 25 or older	**4.4**	**4.4**	**4.3**	**0.0**	**0.1**
Aged 25 to 34	2.5	2.5	2.7	0.0	–0.2
Aged 35 to 44	4.3	4.3	4.5	0.0	–0.2
Aged 45 to 54	6.5	7.3	6.7	–0.8	–0.2
Aged 55 to 64	9.6	9.9	9.9	–0.3	–0.3
Aged 65 or older	9.5	9.7	9.5	–0.2	0.0

Source: Bureau of Labor Statistics, Employee Tenure in 2002, *Internet site http://www.bls.gov/news.release/tenure.t01.htm; calculations by New Strategist*

Table 5.13 Long-Term Employment of People Aged 35 to 59 by Sex, 1991 to 2002

(percent of employed wage and salary workers aged 25 or older and aged 35 to 59 who have been with their current employer for ten or more years, by sex and age, 1991 to 2002; percentage point change in share, 2000–2002 and 1991–2002)

	2002	2000	1991	percentage point change 2000–02	1991–02
Total workers aged 25 or older	**31.0%**	**31.7%**	**32.2%**	**–0.7**	**–1.2**
Aged 35 to 39	25.3	26.2	31.1	–0.9	–5.8
Aged 40 to 44	34.1	35.9	39.3	–1.8	–5.2
Aged 45 to 49	41.4	45.3	46.5	–3.9	–5.1
Aged 50 to 54	49.2	48.6	51.4	0.6	–2.2
Aged 55 to 59	53.2	53.1	56.7	0.1	–3.5
Men aged 25 or older	**33.0**	**33.6**	**35.9**	**–0.6**	**–2.9**
Aged 35 to 39	27.3	29.5	35.6	–2.2	–8.3
Aged 40 to 44	37.7	40.4	46.3	–2.7	–8.6
Aged 45 to 49	45.7	49.0	53.5	–3.3	–7.8
Aged 50 to 54	53.8	51.6	58.5	2.2	–4.7
Aged 55 to 59	56.4	53.7	61.0	2.7	–4.6
Women aged 25 or older	**28.8**	**29.5**	**28.2**	**–0.7**	**0.6**
Aged 35 to 39	23.0	22.4	26.1	0.6	–3.1
Aged 40 to 44	30.2	31.4	32.0	–1.2	–1.8
Aged 45 to 49	37.1	41.5	39.3	–4.4	–2.2
Aged 50 to 54	44.6	45.6	43.4	–1.0	1.2
Aged 55 to 59	49.9	52.5	51.4	–2.6	–1.5

Source: Bureau of Labor Statistics, Employee Tenure in 2002, *Internet site http://www.bls.gov/news.release/tenure.t02.htm; calculations by New Strategist*

Independent Contracting Appeals to Older Workers

More than one in ten workers aged 45 or older has an alternative work arrangement.

Among the nation's 12 million alternative workers, more than 6 million (53 percent) are aged 35 to 54. The Bureau of Labor Statistics defines alternative workers as independent contractors, on-call workers (such as substitute teachers), temporary-help agency workers, and people who work for contract firms (such as lawn or janitorial service companies).

The most popular alternative work arrangement is independent contracting—which includes most of the self-employed. Among the 12.5 million alternative workers, 8.6 million are independent contractors—or 69 percent. Among alternative workers aged 35 to 54, a larger 74 percent are independent contractors. Few people aged 35 to 54 choose other types of alternative work, such as temporary or on-call work.

The percentage of workers with alternative work arrangements surges in the 65-or-older age group. Fully one in five workers aged 65 or older has an alternative work arrangement, 17 percent being independent contractors.

■ Many older workers opt for self-employment because it gives them more control over their work schedule and their government-provided health insurance coverage allows them the freedom to strike out on their own.

Older workers are more likely to be independent contractors

(percent of employed workers who are independent contractors, by age, 2001)

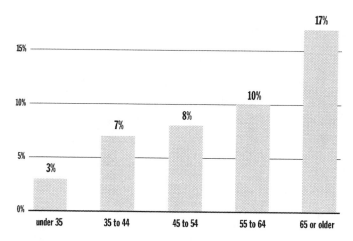

Table 5.14 Alternative Work Arrangements by Age, 2001

(number and percent distribution of employed people aged 16 or older with alternative work arrangements by age and type of alternative work, 2001; numbers in thousands)

	employed	with traditional work arrangements	with alternative work arrangements total	independent contractors	on-call workers	temporary help agency workers	workers provided by contract firms
Total people	**134,605**	**121,917**	**12,476**	**8,585**	**2,089**	**1,169**	**633**
Under age 35	49,935	46,478	3,314	1,653	866	571	224
Aged 35 to 44	36,740	33,194	3,498	2,486	538	291	183
Aged 45 to 54	29,946	26,824	3,100	2,410	374	165	151
Aged 55 to 64	13,955	12,227	1,720	1,357	191	124	48
Aged 65 or older	4,029	3,193	844	679	119	18	28

PERCENT DISTRIBUTION BY ALTERNATIVE WORK STATUS

Total people	**100.0%**	**90.6%**	**9.3%**	**6.4%**	**1.6%**	**0.9%**	**0.5%**
Under age 35	100.0	93.1	6.6	3.3	1.7	1.1	0.4
Aged 35 to 44	100.0	90.3	9.5	6.8	1.5	0.8	0.5
Aged 45 to 54	100.0	89.6	10.4	8.1	1.2	0.6	0.5
Aged 55 to 64	100.0	87.6	12.3	9.7	1.4	0.9	0.3
Aged 65 or older	100.0	79.3	20.9	16.9	3.0	0.4	0.7

PERCENT DISTRIBUTION BY AGE

Total people	**100.0%**	**100.0%**	**100.0%**	**100.0%**	**100.0%**	**100.0%**	**100.0%**
Under age 35	37.1	38.1	26.6	19.3	41.5	48.8	35.4
Aged 35 to 44	27.3	27.2	28.0	29.0	25.8	24.9	28.9
Aged 45 to 54	22.2	22.0	24.8	28.1	17.9	14.1	23.9
Aged 55 to 64	10.4	10.0	13.8	15.8	9.1	10.6	7.6
Aged 65 or older	3.0	2.6	6.8	7.9	5.7	1.5	4.4

Note: Numbers may not add to total because the total employed includes day laborers, an alternative arrangement not shown separately, and a small number of workers who were both on call and provided by contract firms. Independent contractors are self-employed (except incorporated) or wage and salary workers who obtain customers on their own to provide a product or service. On-call workers are in a pool of workers who are called to work only as needed, such as substitute teachers and construction workers supplied by a union hiring hall. Temporary help agency workers are those who said they are paid by a temporary help agency. Workers provided by contract firms are those employed by a company that provides employees or their services to others under contract, such as security, landscaping, and computer programming.
Source: Bureau of Labor Statistics, Contingent and Alternative Employment Arrangements, February 2001, USDL 01-153, Internet site http://www.bls.gov/news.release/conemp.toc.htm; calculations by New Strategist

Many Workers Have Flexible Schedules

Men are more likely than women to have flexible schedules.

Twenty-nine percent of the nation's wage and salary workers have flexible schedules— meaning they may vary the time they begin or end work, according to the Bureau of Labor Statistics. Men are more likely than women to have flexible schedules—30 versus 27 percent in 2001.

The percentage of workers with flexible schedules varies little by age. Among men, those aged 65 or older are most likely to have flexible schedules (37 percent). Among women, those under age 45 (many with young children at home) are most likely to have flexible schedules (28 percent).

Fifteen percent of wage and salary workers do not work a regular daytime schedule. The youngest workers are most likely to work shifts—23 percent of those aged 16 to 24 work the evening, night, or other shift. Among the middle-aged, only 13 percent do not work a regular daytime schedule.

■ Younger workers are less likely to work a regular daytime shift because many are in school during the day.

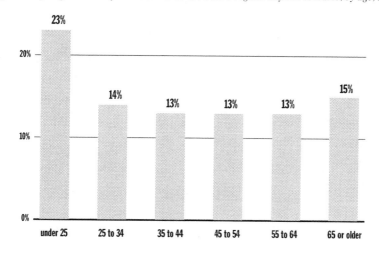

The middle aged are least likely to be shift workers

(percent of wage and salary workers who do not work a regular daytime schedule, by age, 2001)

Table 5.15 Workers with Flexible Work Schedules by Age, 2001

(number and percent distribution of full-time wage and salary workers aged 16 or older with flexible work schedules, by sex and age, 2001; numbers in thousands)

	total	with flexible schedules	
		number	percent
Full-time wage and salary workers	**99,631**	**28,724**	**28.8%**
Under age 35	35,656	10,100	28.3
Aged 35 to 44	28,702	8,578	29.9
Aged 45 to 54	23,946	6,990	29.2
Aged 55 to 64	9,971	2,633	26.4
Aged 65 or older	1,357	423	31.2
Men	**56,066**	**16,792**	**30.0**
Under age 35	20,265	5,740	28.3
Aged 35 to 44	16,522	5,120	31.0
Aged 45 to 54	12,902	4,032	31.3
Aged 55 to 64	5,531	1,590	28.7
Aged 65 or older	847	311	36.7
Women	**43,566**	**11,931**	**27.4**
Under age 35	15,391	4,359	28.3
Aged 35 to 44	12,180	3,458	28.4
Aged 45 to 54	11,044	2,958	26.8
Aged 55 to 64	4,440	1,043	23.5
Aged 65 or older	510	112	22.0

Note: Flexible schedules are those that allow workers to vary the time they begin or end work.
Source: Bureau of Labor Statistics, Workers on Flexible and Shift Schedules in 2001, USDL 02-225, 2002, Internet site http://www.bls.gov/news.release/flex.toc.htm

Table 5.16 Workers by Shift Usually Worked and Age, 2001

(number of full-time wage and salary workers aged 16 or older and percent distribution by shift usually worked and age, 2001; numbers in thousands)

	total	16 to 24	25 to 34	35 to 44	45 to 54	55 to 64	65 or older
Total full-time wage and salary workers, number	**99,631**	**11,104**	**24,552**	**28,702**	**23,946**	**9,971**	**1,357**
Total full-time wage and salary workers, percent	**100.0%**	**100.0%**	**100.0%**	**100.0%**	**100.0%**	**100.0%**	**100.0%**
Regular daytime schedule	84.8	76.6	84.9	86.2	86.3	86.3	84.9
Shift workers	14.5	22.5	14.4	13.2	13.1	13.2	15.0
Evening shift	4.8	9.4	4.9	3.7	4.1	4.5	3.9
Night shift	3.3	4.8	3.3	3.3	2.9	3.1	2.1
Rotating shift	2.3	3.3	2.3	2.3	2.3	1.7	1.7
Split shift	0.4	0.3	0.6	0.4	0.3	0.4	1.3
Employer-arranged irregular schedule	2.8	3.8	2.4	2.8	2.6	2.8	5.5
Other	0.7	0.8	0.8	0.6	0.8	0.6	0.5

Source: Bureau of Labor Statistics, Workers on Flexible and Shift Schedules in 2001, *USDL 02-225, 2002, Internet site http://www.bls.gov/news.release/flex.toc.htm*

Most Minimum-Wage Workers Are Young Adults

Fewer than one in four are middle-aged.

Among the nation's 73 million workers who are paid hourly rates, only 2 million (3 percent) make minimum wage or less, according to the Bureau of Labor Statistics. Fully 71 percent of minimum-wage workers are under age 35. Only 22 percent are between the ages of 35 and 59. Among hourly workers in the 35-to-59 age group, only 1 percent make minimum wage or less.

The percentage of workers who make minimum wage or less rises in the 60-or-older age group to 3 percent. Many are retirees working part-time jobs to supplement their retirement income.

■ Younger workers are most likely to earn minimum wage or less because many are entry-level and/or part-time workers.

Few middle-aged workers make minimum wage or less

(percent distribution of workers making minimum wage or less, by age, 2002)

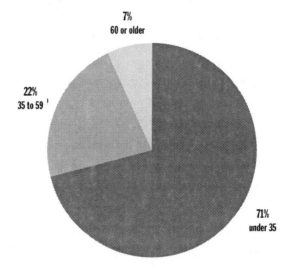

7%
60 or older

22%
35 to 59

71%
under 35

Table 5.17 Workers Earning Minimum Wage by Age, 2002

(number and percent distribution of workers paid hourly rates at or below minimum wage, by age, 2002; numbers in thousands)

	total paid hourly rates	at or below minimum wage		
		total	at $5.15/hour	below $5.15/hour
Total aged 16 or older	**72,720**	**2,168**	**570**	**1,598**
Under age 35	32,548	1,533	421	1,112
Aged 35 to 59	35,755	487	102	385
Aged 35 to 39	8,408	139	33	106
Aged 40 to 44	8,744	125	26	99
Aged 45 to 49	7,888	97	18	79
Aged 50 to 54	6,302	69	13	56
Aged 55 to 59	4,413	57	12	45
Aged 60 or older	4,419	148	47	101
PERCENT DISTRIBUTION BY AGE				
Total aged 16 or older	**100.0%**	**100.0%**	**100.0%**	**100.0%**
Under age 35	44.8	70.7	73.9	69.6
Aged 35 to 59	49.2	22.5	17.9	24.1
Aged 35 to 39	11.6	6.4	5.8	6.6
Aged 40 to 44	12.0	5.8	4.6	6.2
Aged 45 to 49	10.8	4.5	3.2	4.9
Aged 50 to 54	8.7	3.2	2.3	3.5
Aged 55 to 59	6.1	2.6	2.1	2.8
Aged 60 or older	6.1	6.8	8.2	6.3
PERCENT DISTRIBUTION BY WAGE STATUS				
Total aged 16 or older	**100.0%**	**3.0%**	**0.8%**	**2.2%**
Under age 35	100.0	4.7	1.3	3.4
Aged 35 to 59	100.0	1.4	0.3	1.1
Aged 35 to 39	100.0	1.7	0.4	1.3
Aged 40 to 44	100.0	1.4	0.3	1.1
Aged 45 to 49	100.0	1.2	0.2	1.0
Aged 50 to 54	100.0	1.1	0.2	0.9
Aged 55 to 59	100.0	1.3	0.3	1.0
Aged 60 or older	100.0	3.3	1.1	2.3

Source: Bureau of Labor Statistics, Characteristics of Minimum Wage Workers, 2002, Internet site http://www.bls.gov/cps/minwage2002.htm; calculations by New Strategist

Union Membership Peaks among Workers Aged 45 to 54

Men are more likely than women to be union members.

Union membership has fallen sharply over the past few decades. In 1970, 30 percent of nonagricultural workers were members of labor unions. In 2003, only 13 percent were union members. A slightly larger 14 percent of workers are represented by unions.

The percentage of workers who belong to a union peaks in the 45-to-54 age group at 20 percent of men and 16 percent of women. A larger percentage of men are union members because they are more likely to work in jobs that are traditional strongholds of labor unions. In fact, the decline of labor unions is partly the result of the shift in jobs from manufacturing to services.

■ Union membership will continue to decline because the increasingly cut-throat economy rewards companies with more flexible workforces.

Few workers belong to unions

(percent of employed wage and salary workers who are members of unions, by age, 2003)

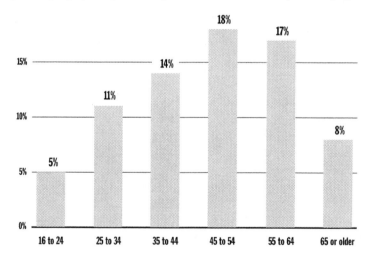

Table 5.18 Union Membership by Sex and Age, 2003

(number and percent of employed wage and salary workers aged 16 or older by union affiliation, sex, and age, 2003; numbers in thousands)

	total employed	represented by unions		members of unions	
		number	percent	number	percent
Total aged 16+	**122,358**	**17,448**	**14.3%**	**15,776**	**12.9%**
Aged 16 to 24	18,904	1,124	5.9	966	5.1
Aged 25 to 34	28,179	3,455	12.3	3,097	11.0
Aged 35 to 44	30,714	4,717	15.4	4,308	14.0
Aged 45 to 54	27,567	5,307	19.3	4,848	17.6
Aged 55 to 64	13,633	2,547	18.7	2,300	16.9
Aged 65 or older	3,361	297	8.8	258	7.7
Men aged 16+	**63,236**	**9,848**	**15.6**	**9,044**	**14.3**
Aged 16 to 24	9,683	685	7.1	595	6.1
Aged 25 to 34	15,263	2,005	13.1	1,826	12.0
Aged 35 to 44	16,080	2,735	17.0	2,535	15.8
Aged 45 to 54	13,723	2,891	21.1	2,684	19.6
Aged 55 to 64	6,776	1,377	20.3	1,271	18.8
Aged 65 or older	1,710	155	9.0	133	7.8
Women aged 16+	**59,122**	**7,601**	**12.9**	**6,732**	**11.4**
Aged 16 to 24	9,221	439	4.8	371	4.0
Aged 25 to 34	12,916	1,451	11.2	1,270	9.8
Aged 35 to 44	14,634	1,982	13.5	1,773	12.1
Aged 45 to 54	13,844	2,416	17.5	2,163	15.6
Aged 55 to 64	6,857	1,170	17.1	1,029	15.0
Aged 65 or older	1,651	142	8.6	125	7.6

Source: Bureau of Labor Statistics, 2003 Current Population Survey, Internet site http://www.bls.gov/cps/home.htm

Many More People in Their Sixties Will Be in the Labor Force

The labor force participation rate of older workers is projected to rise.

During the next ten years, the oldest members of the Baby-Boom generation will enter their sixties. Because early retirement will be uncommon among Boomers, the labor force participation rate of people aged 60 or older is projected to rise. Among men aged 60 to 61, labor force participation is projected to rise by 1.5 percentage points between 2003 and 2012 (when the oldest Boomers turn 66), to 69 percent. The increase will be an even larger 3.9 percentage points for men aged 62 to 64. Rates are also projected to rise for women in the age group.

The number of older workers will soar during the coming decade. The Bureau of Labor Statistics projects a 56 percent increase in the number of workers aged 60 to 64—a gain of more than 3 million.

According to a survey by AARP, most older workers see retirement as a chance to spend more time with family and friends, an opportunity to relax, and a time to have more fun. With fully 68 percent planning to work for pay in "retirement," however, many Boomers may be disappointed in their so-called leisure years.

■ Millions of Baby Boomers will work well into their sixties, longing for more free time to relax and have fun.

More men in their sixties will be working in 2012

(labor force participation rate of men aged 60 to 69, by age, 2003 and 2012)

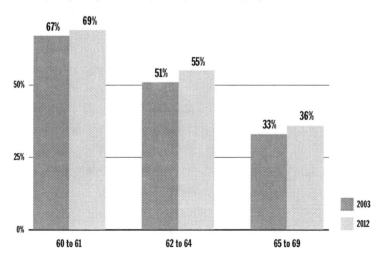

Table 5.19 Projections of the Labor Force by Sex and Age, 2003 to 2012

(number and percent of people aged 16 or older in the civilian labor force by sex and age, 2003 and 2012; percent change in number and percentage point change in participation rate, 2003–12; numbers in thousands)

	number			participation rate		
	2003	2012	percent change 2003–12	2003	2012	percentage point change 2003–12
Total labor force	**147,003**	**162,269**	**10.4%**	**67.1%**	**67.2%**	**0.1**
Total men in labor force	**78,560**	**85,252**	**8.5**	**74.4**	**73.1**	**–1.3**
Under age 35	29,486	31,530	6.9	79.9	79.6	–0.3
Aged 35 to 44	19,734	18,244	–7.6	92.3	92.3	0.0
Aged 35 to 39	9,529	8,817	–7.5	93.1	93.0	–0.1
Aged 40 to 44	10,205	9,428	–7.6	91.6	91.6	0.0
Aged 45 to 54	17,511	19,122	9.2	88.3	88.6	0.3
Aged 45 to 49	9,530	9,575	0.5	90.0	90.1	0.1
Aged 50 to 54	7,981	9,546	19.6	86.3	87.1	0.8
Aged 55 to 64	9,232	12,714	37.7	69.3	69.9	0.6
Aged 55 to 59	5,907	7,684	30.1	77.8	77.9	0.1
Aged 60 to 64	3,325	5,031	51.3	58.0	60.4	2.4
Aged 60 to 61	1,708	2,374	39.0	67.2	68.7	1.5
Aged 62 to 64	1,617	2,656	64.3	50.7	54.6	3.9
Aged 65 or older	2,598	3,641	40.1	18.3	20.8	2.5
Aged 65 to 69	1,461	2,269	55.3	32.6	36.3	3.7
Aged 70 or older	1,137	1,372	20.7	11.7	12.2	0.5
Total women in labor force	**68,443**	**77,017**	**12.5**	**60.4**	**61.6**	**1.2**
Under age 35	25,640	28,253	10.2	68.7	71.1	2.4
Aged 35 to 44	17,002	16,189	–4.8	76.8	79.9	3.1
Aged 35 to 39	8,029	7,674	–4.4	75.8	79.1	3.3
Aged 40 to 44	8,973	8,515	–5.1	77.7	80.6	2.9
Aged 45 to 54	15,824	17,905	13.2	76.3	79.8	3.5
Aged 45 to 49	8,595	8,931	3.9	78.2	81.4	3.2
Aged 50 to 54	7,229	8,974	24.1	74.3	78.2	3.9
Aged 55 to 64	8,043	11,902	48.0	55.8	60.6	4.8
Aged 55 to 59	5,211	7,355	41.1	64.5	70.0	5.5
Aged 60 to 64	2,831	4,547	60.6	44.7	49.7	5.0
Aged 60 to 61	1,487	2,303	54.9	53.4	61.1	7.7
Aged 62 to 64	1,345	2,244	66.8	37.8	41.8	4.0
Aged 65 or older	1,934	2,769	43.2	10.3	12.1	1.8
Aged 65 to 69	1,080	1,619	49.9	20.9	22.8	1.9
Aged 70 or older	854	1,149	34.5	6.3	7.3	1.0

Source: Bureau of Labor Statistics, Internet site http://www.bls.gov/emp/emplab1.htm; calculations by New Strategist

Table 5.20 Retirement Definitions and Plans, 2003

(percent of working people aged 50 to 70 who "very much" or "somewhat" agree that the statement fits their personal definition of retirement, and percent distribution by plans for retirement, 2003)

	percent who agree very much or somewhat
RETIREMENT MEANS	
Spending more time with family and friends	78%
A chance to relax	73
A chance to have more fun	73
Receiving retirement benefits from Social Security or pension payments	72
A chance to do things you never had time for	72
A chance to travel	67
Doing volunteer or charity work	57
Slowing down and working fewer hours/part-time	56
Working for enjoyment, not money	53
A chance to stop working for pay completely	48
Having to do some kind of work to help pay the bills	42
A chance to leave your main career to try a different type of work	28
Feeling less useful or less productive	20

	percent distribution
PLANS FOR RETIREMENT	
Total	**100%**
Not work for pay at all	29
Work for pay	68
Work part-time, doing the same type of work you do now	24
Work part-time, doing something different	22
Start your own business/work for yourself, doing the same type of work you do now	5
Start your own business/work for yourself, doing something different	5
Work full-time, doing the same type of work you do now	5
Work full-time, doing something different	2
Never expect to retire	5
Don't know	3

Source: © 2003, AARP, Staying Ahead of the Curve 2003: The AARP Working in Retirement Study

Living Arrangements

■ Most Boomers are married. In 2003, 58 to 60 percent of households headed by people aged 35 to 59 (Boomers were aged 39 to 57 in that year) were headed by married couples.

■ Household size peaks among householders aged 35 to 39. As householders age into their forties, the nest empties.

■ Householders aged 35 to 44 are most likely to have children under age 18 at home. In 2002, 63 percent of householders in the age group had dependent children in their household.

■ Among householders aged 45 to 54, only 32 percent have school-aged children at home. But 17 percent have adult children (aged 18 or older) living with them.

■ Most men and women aged 35 to 54 are married and living with their spouse—65 percent of women and 67 percent of men.

■ The proportion of people who are currently divorced peaks in mid-life. Twenty-one percent of women aged 45 to 54 are currently divorced or separated—the highest proportion among all age groups.

Most Boomer Households Are Headed by Married Couples

Households vary little by type among the middle aged.

In middle age, the lifestyles of the Baby-Boom generation are similar—despite the nearly 20-year span between the youngest and oldest Boomers. Fifty-eight to 60 percent of households headed by people aged 35 to 59 (Boomers were aged 39 to 57 in 2003) are headed by married couples. There is more variation in the female-headed family share of Boomer households, which ranges from 16 percent in the 35-to-39 age group to just 8 percent in the 55-to-59 age group.

People living alone account for a substantial share of households among those in their fifties. While there is little variation within the age group in the percentage of households headed by men living alone, the share headed by women living alone more than doubles, rising from 7 percent among 35-to-44-year-olds to 15 percent among 55-to-59-year-olds. Behind the rise is a wife's growing chance of becoming widowed as her husband ages.

■ Among people who live alone, women begin to outnumber men in the 55-to-59 age group.

As householders age into their fifties, a growing share are women who live alone

(single-person households headed by women as a share of total households, by age of householder, 2003)

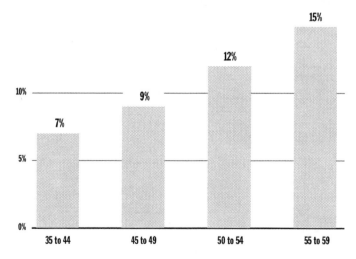

Table 6.1 Households Headed by People Aged 35 to 59 by Household Type, 2003: Total Households

(number and percent distribution of total households and households headed by people aged 35 to 59, by household type, 2003; numbers in thousands)

	total	35 to 39	40 to 44	45 to 49	50 to 54	55 to 59
Total households	**111,278**	**11,486**	**12,583**	**11,957**	**10,666**	**9,192**
Family households	75,596	8,965	9,776	9,119	7,744	6,511
Married couples	57,320	6,640	7,361	7,085	6,212	5,513
Female householder,						
no spouse present	13,620	1,826	1,826	1,505	1,139	753
Male householder,						
no spouse present	4,656	498	589	529	393	245
Nonfamily households	35,682	2,521	2,807	2,838	2,922	2,680
Female householder	19,662	943	1,108	1,295	1,494	1,552
Living alone	16,919	771	867	1,054	1,249	1,406
Male householder	16,020	1,578	1,700	1,543	1,428	1,128
Living alone	12,511	1,178	1,395	1,292	1,224	980
PERCENT DISTRIBUTION BY TYPE						
Total households	**100.0%**	**100.0%**	**100.0%**	**100.0%**	**100.0%**	**100.0%**
Family households	67.9	78.1	77.7	76.3	72.6	70.8
Married couples	51.5	57.8	58.5	59.3	58.2	60.0
Female householder,						
no spouse present	12.2	15.9	14.5	12.6	10.7	8.2
Male householder,						
no spouse present	4.2	4.3	4.7	4.4	3.7	2.7
Nonfamily households	32.1	21.9	22.3	23.7	27.4	29.2
Female householder	17.7	8.2	8.8	10.8	14.0	16.9
Living alone	15.2	6.7	6.9	8.8	11.7	15.3
Male householder	14.4	13.7	13.5	12.9	13.4	12.3
Living alone	11.2	10.3	11.1	10.8	11.5	10.7
PERCENT DISTRIBUTION BY AGE						
Total households	**100.0%**	**10.3%**	**11.3%**	**10.7%**	**9.6%**	**8.3%**
Family households	100.0	11.9	12.9	12.1	10.2	8.6
Married couples	100.0	11.6	12.8	12.4	10.8	9.6
Female householder,						
no spouse present	100.0	13.4	13.4	11.1	8.4	5.5
Male householder,						
no spouse present	100.0	10.7	12.7	11.4	8.4	5.3
Nonfamily households	100.0	7.1	7.9	8.0	8.2	7.5
Female householder	100.0	4.8	5.6	6.6	7.6	7.9
Living alone	100.0	4.6	5.1	6.2	7.4	8.3
Male householder	100.0	9.9	10.6	9.6	8.9	7.0
Living alone	100.0	9.4	11.2	10.3	9.8	7.8

Source: Bureau of the Census, 2003 Current Population Survey, Annual Social and Economic Supplement, Internet site http:// ferret.bls.census.gov/macro/032003/hhinc/new02_000.htm; calculations by New Strategist

Few Black Households Are Headed by Married Couples

Couples dominate Asian, Hispanic, and non-Hispanic white households.

In 2003, married couples accounted for the majority of Asian, Hispanic, and non-Hispanic white households headed by people aged 35 to 59 (the Baby-Boom generation was aged 39 to 57 in 2003). The married-couple share of households ranged from a low of 57 percent (among Hispanic householders aged 45 to 54) to a high of 71 percent (among Asian householders aged 40 to 49). In contrast, married couples head only 35 to 37 percent of black households in the 35-to-59 age group. Female-headed families are a large share (20 to 36 percent) of black households headed by the middle aged, even outnumbering married couples among householders aged 35 to 39. Among non-Hispanic whites, female-headed families account for just 6 to 12 percent of households in the 35-to-59 age group.

Among middle-aged householders, the percentage of households headed by women who live alone rises with age regardless of race or Hispanic origin. Hispanic and Asian women are least likely to live alone. In the 55-to-59 age group, only 11 percent of Asian or Hispanic households are headed by women living alone. The figures are 15 percent for non-Hispanic whites and 23 percent for blacks.

■ The household incomes of blacks are lower than those of non-Hispanic whites in part because married couples—the most affluent household type—are a much smaller share of black households.

Married couples head a minority of households among blacks

(married couples as a percent of households headed by people aged 35 to 59, by race and Hispanic origin, 2003)

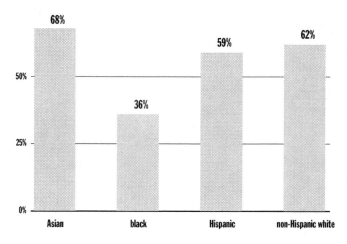

Table 6.2 Households Headed by People Aged 35 to 59 by Household Type, 2003: Asian Households

(number and percent distribution of total households headed by Asians and households headed by Asians aged 35 to 59, by household type, 2003; numbers in thousands)

	total	35 to 39	40 to 44	45 to 49	50 to 54	55 to 59
Total Asian households	**4,079**	**546**	**483**	**444**	**368**	**284**
Family households	2,939	434	410	376	292	225
Married couples	2,344	359	343	317	241	182
Female householder, no spouse present	354	45	32	42	43	36
Male householder, no spouse present	241	30	35	17	7	7
Nonfamily households	1,140	112	73	68	76	59
Female householder	567	48	22	29	41	34
Living alone	435	44	17	21	36	30
Male householder	573	64	51	39	35	25
Living alone	411	45	40	35	23	23
PERCENT DISTRIBUTION BY TYPE						
Total Asian households	**100.0%**	**100.0%**	**100.0%**	**100.0%**	**100.0%**	**100.0%**
Family households	72.1	79.5	84.9	84.7	79.3	79.2
Married couples	57.5	65.8	71.0	71.4	65.5	64.1
Female householder, no spouse present	8.7	8.2	6.6	9.5	11.7	12.7
Male householder, no spouse present	5.9	5.5	7.2	3.8	1.9	2.5
Nonfamily households	27.9	20.5	15.1	15.3	20.7	20.8
Female householder	13.9	8.8	4.6	6.5	11.1	12.0
Living alone	10.7	8.1	3.5	4.7	9.8	10.6
Male householder	14.1	11.7	10.6	8.8	9.5	8.8
Living alone	10.1	8.2	8.3	7.9	6.2	8.1
PERCENT DISTRIBUTION BY AGE						
Total Asian households	**100.0%**	**13.4%**	**11.8%**	**10.9%**	**9.0%**	**7.0%**
Family households	100.0	14.8	14.0	12.8	9.9	7.7
Married couples	100.0	15.3	14.6	13.5	10.3	7.8
Female householder, no spouse present	100.0	12.7	9.0	11.9	12.1	10.2
Male householder, no spouse present	100.0	12.4	14.5	7.1	2.9	2.9
Nonfamily households	100.0	9.8	6.4	6.0	6.7	5.2
Female householder	100.0	8.5	3.9	5.1	7.2	6.0
Living alone	100.0	10.1	3.9	4.8	8.3	6.9
Male householder	100.0	11.2	8.9	6.8	6.1	4.4
Living alone	100.0	10.9	9.7	8.5	5.6	5.6

Note: Number of Asian households includes both those identifying themselves as Asian alone and those identifying themselves as Asian in combination with other races.
Source: Bureau of the Census, 2003 Current Population Survey, Annual Social and Economic Supplement, Internet site http:// ferret.bls.census.gov/macro/032003/hhinc/new02_000.htm; calculations by New Strategist

Table 6.3 Households Headed by People Aged 35 to 59 by Household Type, 2003: Black Households

(number and percent distribution of total households headed by blacks and households headed by blacks aged 35 to 59, by household type, 2003; numbers in thousands)

	total	35 to 39	40 to 44	45 to 49	50 to 54	55 to 59
Total black households	**13,778**	**1,524**	**1,663**	**1,541**	**1,295**	**1,022**
Family households	9,128	1,154	1,246	1,086	825	612
Married couples	4,268	527	598	581	471	372
Female householder, no spouse present	4,069	550	555	427	289	203
Male householder, no spouse present	791	77	92	78	65	37
Nonfamily households	4,650	371	417	454	470	410
Female householder	2,550	145	173	224	278	251
Living alone	2,318	126	160	196	248	239
Male householder	2,100	226	244	231	193	159
Living alone	1,753	183	210	204	167	144
PERCENT DISTRIBUTION BY TYPE						
Total black households	**100.0%**	**100.0%**	**100.0%**	**100.0%**	**100.0%**	**100.0%**
Family households	66.3	75.7	74.9	70.5	63.7	59.9
Married couples	31.0	34.6	36.0	37.7	36.4	36.4
Female householder, no spouse present	29.5	36.1	33.4	27.7	22.3	19.9
Male householder, no spouse present	5.7	5.1	5.5	5.1	5.0	3.6
Nonfamily households	33.7	24.3	25.1	29.5	36.3	40.1
Female householder	18.5	9.5	10.4	14.5	21.5	24.6
Living alone	16.8	8.3	9.6	12.7	19.2	23.4
Male householder	15.2	14.8	14.7	15.0	14.9	15.6
Living alone	12.7	12.0	12.6	13.2	12.9	14.1
PERCENT DISTRIBUTION BY AGE						
Total black households	**100.0%**	**11.1%**	**12.1%**	**11.2%**	**9.4%**	**7.4%**
Family households	100.0	12.6	13.7	11.9	9.0	6.7
Married couples	100.0	12.3	14.0	13.6	11.0	8.7
Female householder, no spouse present	100.0	13.5	13.6	10.5	7.1	5.0
Male householder, no spouse present	100.0	9.7	11.6	9.9	8.2	4.7
Nonfamily households	100.0	8.0	9.0	9.8	10.1	8.8
Female householder	100.0	5.7	6.8	8.8	10.9	9.8
Living alone	100.0	5.4	6.9	8.5	10.7	10.3
Male householder	100.0	10.8	11.6	11.0	9.2	7.6
Living alone	100.0	10.4	12.0	11.6	9.5	8.2

Note: Number of black households includes both those identifying themselves as black alone and those identifying themselves as black in combination with other races.
Source: Bureau of the Census, 2003 Current Population Survey, Annual Social and Economic Supplement, Internet site http:// ferret.bls.census.gov/macro/032003/hhinc/new02_000.htm; calculations by New Strategist

Table 6.4 Households Headed by People Aged 35 to 59 by Household Type, 2003: Hispanic Households

(number and percent distribution of total households headed by Hispanics and households headed by Hispanics aged 35 to 59, by household type, 2003; numbers in thousands)

	total	35 to 39	40 to 44	45 to 49	50 to 54	55 to 59
Total Hispanic households	**11,339**	**1,625**	**1,478**	**1,092**	**822**	**654**
Family households	9,090	1,409	1,256	900	657	504
Married couples	6,189	994	867	627	472	405
Female householder, no spouse present	2,029	304	289	202	137	76
Male householder, no spouse present	872	111	100	70	48	22
Nonfamily households	2,249	216	222	192	165	150
Female householder	1,021	60	81	80	87	86
Living alone	791	48	55	63	61	74
Male householder	1,228	156	141	112	78	64
Living alone	809	110	103	81	57	58
PERCENT DISTRIBUTION BY TYPE						
Total Hispanic households	**100.0%**	**100.0%**	**100.0%**	**100.0%**	**100.0%**	**100.0%**
Family households	80.2	86.7	85.0	82.4	79.9	77.1
Married couples	54.6	61.2	58.7	57.4	57.4	61.9
Female householder, no spouse present	17.9	18.7	19.6	18.5	16.7	11.6
Male householder, no spouse present	7.7	6.8	6.8	6.4	5.8	3.4
Nonfamily households	19.8	13.3	15.0	17.6	20.1	22.9
Female householder	9.0	3.7	5.5	7.3	10.6	13.1
Living alone	7.0	3.0	3.7	5.8	7.4	11.3
Male householder	10.8	9.6	9.5	10.3	9.5	9.8
Living alone	7.1	6.8	7.0	7.4	6.9	8.9
PERCENT DISTRIBUTION BY AGE						
Total Hispanic households	**100.0%**	**14.3%**	**13.0%**	**9.6%**	**7.2%**	**5.8%**
Family households	100.0	15.5	13.8	9.9	7.2	5.5
Married couples	100.0	16.1	14.0	10.1	7.6	6.5
Female householder, no spouse present	100.0	15.0	14.2	10.0	6.8	3.7
Male householder, no spouse present	100.0	12.7	11.5	8.0	5.5	2.5
Nonfamily households	100.0	9.6	9.9	8.5	7.3	6.7
Female householder	100.0	5.9	7.9	7.8	8.5	8.4
Living alone	100.0	6.1	7.0	8.0	7.7	9.4
Male householder	100.0	12.7	11.5	9.1	6.4	5.2
Living alone	100.0	13.6	12.7	10.0	7.1	7.2

Source: Bureau of the Census, 2003 Current Population Survey, Annual Social and Economic Supplement. Internet site http://ferret.bls.census.gov/macro/032003/hhinc/new02_000.htm; calculations by New Strategist

Table 6.5 Households Headed by People Aged 35 to 59 by Household Type, 2003: Non-Hispanic White Households

(number and percent distribution of total households headed by non-Hispanic whites and households headed by non-Hispanic whites aged 35 to 59, by household type, 2003; numbers in thousands)

	total	35 to 39	40 to 44	45 to 49	50 to 54	55 to 59
Total non-Hispanic white households	**81,166**	**7,702**	**8,851**	**8,795**	**8,080**	**7,130**
Family households	53,845	5,892	6,784	6,692	5,899	5,111
Married couples	44,101	4,718	5,479	5,512	4,966	4,509
Female householder, no spouse present	7,070	908	952	826	660	431
Male householder, no spouse present	2,674	266	353	353	273	171
Nonfamily households	27,321	1,810	2,067	2,104	2,181	2,018
Female householder	15,353	682	817	955	1,072	1,159
Living alone	13,233	549	625	763	889	1,042
Male householder	11,968	1,128	1,250	1,149	1,109	860
Living alone	9,421	838	1,034	961	966	736
PERCENT DISTRIBUTION BY TYPE						
Total non-Hispanic white households	**100.0%**	**100.0%**	**100.0%**	**100.0%**	**100.0%**	**100.0%**
Family households	66.3	76.5	76.6	76.1	73.0	71.7
Married couples	54.3	61.3	61.9	62.7	61.5	63.2
Female householder, no spouse present	8.7	11.8	10.8	9.4	8.2	6.0
Male householder, no spouse present	3.3	3.5	4.0	4.0	3.4	2.4
Nonfamily households	33.7	23.5	23.4	23.9	27.0	28.3
Female householder	18.9	8.9	9.2	10.9	13.3	16.3
Living alone	16.3	7.1	7.1	8.7	11.0	14.6
Male householder	14.7	14.6	14.1	13.1	13.7	12.1
Living alone	11.6	10.9	11.7	10.9	12.0	10.3
PERCENT DISTRIBUTION BY AGE						
Total non-Hispanic white households	**100.0%**	**9.5%**	**10.9%**	**10.8%**	**10.0%**	**8.8%**
Family households	100.0	10.9	12.6	12.4	11.0	9.5
Married couples	100.0	10.7	12.4	12.5	11.3	10.2
Female householder, no spouse present	100.0	12.8	13.5	11.7	9.3	6.1
Male householder, no spouse present	100.0	9.9	13.2	13.2	10.2	6.4
Nonfamily households	100.0	6.6	7.6	7.7	8.0	7.4
Female householder	100.0	4.4	5.3	6.2	7.0	7.5
Living alone	100.0	4.1	4.7	5.8	6.7	7.9
Male householder	100.0	9.4	10.4	9.6	9.3	7.2
Living alone	100.0	8.9	11.0	10.2	10.3	7.8

Note: Number of non-Hispanic white households includes only those identifying themselves as white alone and non-Hispanic.
Source: Bureau of the Census, 2003 Current Population Survey, Annual Social and Economic Supplement, Internet site http://ferret.bls.census.gov/macro/032003/hhinc/new02_000.htm; calculations by New Strategist

Boomer Households Are Shrinking

Household size peaks in the 35-to-39 age group.

The average American household was home to 2.58 people in 2002. Household size peaks among householders aged 35 to 39, who are most likely to have more than one child at home. As householders age into their forties, the nest empties. The average number of children per household falls below one in the 45-to-49 age group.

Boomer households are shrinking as a growing proportion become empty nesters. The youngest Boomers (aged 38 in 2002) are about to exit the most crowded nest stage, with an average of 3.29 people per household in the 35-to-39 age group. The oldest Boomers (aged 56 in 2002) have only 2.27 people, on average, in their home.

■ As their children grow up and leave home, Boomers will have more free time and discretionary income.

The nest is emptying for householders in their forties

(average household size by age of householder, 2002)

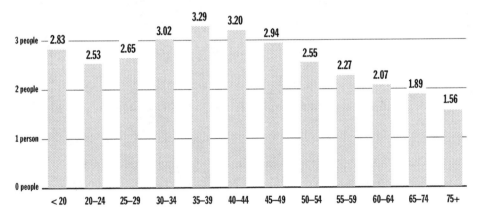

Table 6.6 Average Size of Household by Age of Householder, 2002

(number of households, average number of people per household, and average number of people under age 18 per household. by age of householder, 2002; numbers in thousands)

	number	average number of people	average number of people under age 18
Total households	**109,297**	**2.58**	**0.66**
Under age 20	907	2.83	0.80
Aged 20 to 24	5,484	2.53	0.58
Aged 25 to 29	8,412	2.65	0.86
Aged 30 to 34	10,576	3.02	1.22
Aged 35 to 39	11,599	3.29	1.42
Aged 40 to 44	12,432	3.20	1.20
Aged 45 to 49	11,754	2.94	0.78
Aged 50 to 54	10,455	2.55	0.39
Aged 55 to 59	8,611	2.27	0.20
Aged 60 to 64	6,592	2.07	0.14
Aged 65 to 74	11,472	1.89	0.09
Aged 75 or older	11,004	1.56	0.03

Source: Bureau of the Census, 2002 Current Population Survey Annual Demographic Supplement, http://www.census.gov/population/www/socdemo/hh-fam/cps2002.html

Most Middle-Aged Households include Children under Age 18

The proportion falls sharply in the 45 to 54 age group, however.

Householders aged 35 to 44 are most likely to have children under age 18 at home. In 2002, 63 percent of householders in the age group had dependent children in their household. The proportion falls to just 33 percent in the 45-to-54 age group. But 51 percent of households aged 45 to 54 have children of any age at home—meaning many have children aged 18 or older living with them or in college dormitories (the Census Bureau classifies college students in dormitories as living at home).

Hispanic householders aged 35 to 44 are most likely to have children under age 18 at home (72 percent). Among Asian householders in the age group, 67 percent live with dependent children. The figures are 62 percent for non-Hispanic whites and 60 percent for blacks.

Married couples and female-headed families are more likely to have children under age 18 at home than are male-headed families (many families include older children or other relatives). The percentage of households that include children under age 18 peaks at more than 90 percent among families headed by black, Hispanic, or non-Hispanic white women aged 35 to 39.

■ Although a shrinking share of Boomer households include dependent children, many Boomers live with adult children who have not yet established their own households.

Only one-third of households headed by older Boomers include children under age 18

(percent of households with children under age 18, by age of householder, 2002)

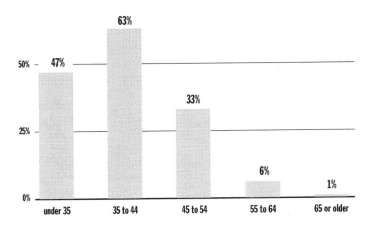

Table 6.7 Households by Type, Age of Householder, and Presence of Children, 2002: Total Households

(total number of households and number and percent with own children under age 18 at home, by household type and age of householder, 2002; numbers in thousands)

	total	with own children under age 18 number	with own children under age 18 percent
Total households	**109,297**	**35,705**	**32.7%**
Under age 35	25,379	12,016	47.3
Aged 35 to 54	46,239	22,587	48.8
Aged 35 to 44	24,031	15,149	63.0
Aged 35 to 39	11,599	7,716	66.5
Aged 40 to 44	12,432	7,433	59.8
Aged 45 to 54	22,208	7,438	33.5
Aged 55 to 64	15,203	923	6.1
Aged 65 or older	22,476	180	0.8
Married couples	**56,747**	**25,792**	**45.5**
Under age 35	10,919	7,682	70.4
Aged 35 to 54	27,315	17,224	63.1
Aged 35 to 44	14,178	11,385	80.3
Aged 35 to 39	6,804	5,707	83.9
Aged 40 to 44	7,374	5,678	77.0
Aged 45 to 54	13,137	5,839	44.4
Aged 55 to 64	8,922	744	8.3
Aged 65 or older	9,591	141	1.5
Female householder, no spouse present	**13,143**	**8,010**	**60.9**
Under age 35	4,213	3,591	85.2
Aged 35 to 54	6,126	4,285	69.9
Aged 35 to 44	3,596	3,067	85.3
Aged 35 to 39	1,828	1,666	91.1
Aged 40 to 44	1,768	1,401	79.2
Aged 45 to 54	2,530	1,218	48.1
Aged 55 to 64	1,188	105	8.8
Aged 65 or older	1,616	29	1.8
Male householder, no spouse present	**4,438**	**1,903**	**42.9**
Under age 35	1,700	744	43.8
Aged 35 to 54	1,918	1,077	56.2
Aged 35 to 44	1,045	696	66.6
Aged 35 to 39	492	342	69.5
Aged 40 to 44	553	354	64.0
Aged 45 to 54	873	381	43.6
Aged 55 to 64	389	74	19.0
Aged 65 or older	431	10	2.3

Source: Bureau of the Census, Children's Living Arrangements and Characteristics: March 2002, Detailed Tables, *Internet site http://www.census.gov/population/www/socdemo/hh-fam/cps2002.html; calculations by New Strategist*

Table 6.8 Households by Type, Age of Householder, and Presence of Children, 2002: Asian Households

(total number of Asian households and number and percent with own children under age 18 at home, by household type and age of householder, 2002: numbers in thousands)

	total	with own children under age 18	
		number	percent
Total Asian households	**4,071**	**1,582**	**38.9%**
Under age 35	1,326	406	30.6
Aged 35 to 54	1,890	1,118	59.2
Aged 35 to 44	1,011	674	66.7
Aged 35 to 39	513	349	68.0
Aged 40 to 44	498	325	65.3
Aged 45 to 54	879	444	50.5
Aged 55 to 64	436	45	10.3
Aged 65 or older	419	14	3.3
Married couples	**2,378**	**1,362**	**57.3**
Under age 35	551	343	62.3
Aged 35 to 54	1,312	967	73.7
Aged 35 to 44	685	575	83.9
Aged 35 to 39	351	287	81.8
Aged 40 to 44	334	288	86.2
Aged 45 to 54	627	392	62.5
Aged 55 to 64	301	40	13.3
Aged 65 or older	214	13	6.1
Female householder, no spouse present	**415**	**190**	**45.8**
Under age 35	131	54	41.2
Aged 35 to 54	193	130	67.4
Aged 35 to 44	112	87	77.7
Aged 35 to 39	65	55	84.6
Aged 40 to 44	47	32	68.1
Aged 45 to 54	81	43	53.1
Aged 55 to 64	43	4	9.3
Aged 65 or older	49	–	–
Male householder, no spouse present	**187**	**30**	**16.0**
Under age 35	102	10	9.8
Aged 35 to 54	64	20	31.2
Aged 35 to 44	37	11	29.7
Aged 35 to 39	16	7	43.8
Aged 40 to 44	21	4	19.1
Aged 45 to 54	27	9	33.3
Aged 55 to 64	11	1	9.1
Aged 65 or older	11	–	–

Note: (–) means number is less than 500 or sample is too small to make a reliable estimate.
Source: Bureau of the Census, Children's Living Arrangements and Characteristics: March 2002, Detailed Tables, Internet site http://www.census.gov/population/www/socdemo/hh-fam/cps2002.html; calculations by New Strategist

Table 6.9 Households by Type, Age of Householder, and Presence of Children, 2002: Black Households

(total number of black households and number and percent with own children under age 18 at home, by household type and age of householder, 2002; numbers in thousands)

	total	with own children under age 18 number	with own children under age 18 percent
Total black households	**13,315**	**5,065**	**38.0%**
Under age 35	3,764	2,214	58.8
Aged 35 to 54	5,925	2,705	45.7
Aged 35 to 44	3,186	1,918	60.2
Aged 35 to 39	1,583	1,016	64.2
Aged 40 to 44	1,603	902	56.3
Aged 45 to 54	2,739	787	28.7
Aged 55 to 64	1,648	113	6.9
Aged 65 or older	1,976	33	1.7
Married couples	**4,233**	**2,148**	**50.7**
Under age 35	910	701	77.0
Aged 35 to 54	2,141	1,361	63.6
Aged 35 to 44	1,171	942	80.4
Aged 35 to 39	572	471	82.3
Aged 40 to 44	599	471	78.6
Aged 45 to 54	970	419	43.2
Aged 55 to 64	577	64	11.1
Aged 65 or older	606	22	3.6
Female householder, no spouse present	**3,838**	**2,593**	**67.6**
Under age 35	1527	1,379	90.3
Aged 35 to 54	1,690	1,171	69.3
Aged 35 to 44	1,040	864	83.1
Aged 35 to 39	545	494	90.6
Aged 40 to 44	495	370	74.7
Aged 45 to 54	650	307	47.2
Aged 55 to 64	315	33	10.5
Aged 65 or older	307	10	3.3
Male householder, no spouse present	**773**	**324**	**41.9**
Under age 35	287	134	46.7
Aged 35 to 54	338	173	51.2
Aged 35 to 44	191	112	58.6
Aged 35 to 39	88	52	59.1
Aged 40 to 44	103	60	58.3
Aged 45 to 54	147	61	41.5
Aged 55 to 64	75	16	21.3
Aged 65 or older	73	1	1.4

Source: Bureau of the Census, Children's Living Arrangements and Characteristics: March 2002, Detailed Tables, *Internet site http://www.census.gov/population/www/socdemo/hh-fam/cps2002.html; calculations by New Strategist*

Table 6.10 Households by Type, Age of Householder, and Presence of Children, 2002:
Hispanic Households

*(total number of Hispanic households and number and percent with own children under age 18 at home, by
household type and age of householder, 2002; numbers in thousands)*

| | total | with own children under age 18 | |
		number	percent
Total Hispanic			
households	**10,499**	**5,343**	**50.9%**
Under age 35	3,993	2,514	63.0
Aged 35 to 54	4,423	2,688	60.8
Aged 35 to 44	2,675	1,932	72.2
Aged 35 to 39	1,410	1,076	76.3
Aged 40 to 44	1,265	856	67.7
Aged 45 to 54	1,748	756	43.2
Aged 55 to 64	1,020	108	10.6
Aged 65 or older	1,062	32	3.0
Married couples	**5,778**	**3,754**	**65.0**
Under age 35	2,015	1,690	83.9
Aged 35 to 54	2,676	1,958	73.2
Aged 35 to 44	1,630	1,392	85.4
Aged 35 to 39	887	789	89.0
Aged 40 to 44	743	603	81.2
Aged 45 to 54	1,046	566	54.1
Aged 55 to 64	590	85	14.4
Aged 65 or older	497	21	4.2
Female householder,			
no spouse present	**1,922**	**1,259**	**65.5**
Under age 35	757	632	83.5
Aged 35 to 54	861	603	70.0
Aged 35 to 44	539	453	84.0
Aged 35 to 39	269	243	90.3
Aged 40 to 44	270	210	77.8
Aged 45 to 54	322	150	46.6
Aged 55 to 64	161	17	10.6
Aged 65 or older	143	6	4.2
Male householder,			
no spouse present	**817**	**330**	**40.4**
Under age 35	490	192	39.2
Aged 35 to 54	257	127	49.4
Aged 35 to 44	166	87	52.4
Aged 35 to 39	90	44	48.9
Aged 40 to 44	76	43	56.6
Aged 45 to 54	91	40	44.0
Aged 55 to 64	39	5	12.8
Aged 65 or older	31	4	12.9

*Source: Bureau of the Census, Children's Living Arrangements and Characteristics: March 2002, Detailed Tables, Internet site
http://www.census.gov/population/www/socdemo/hh-fam/cps2002.html; calculations by New Strategist*

Table 6.11 Households by Type, Age of Householder, and Presence of Children, 2002: Non-Hispanic White Households

(total number of non-Hispanic white households and number and percent with own children under age 18 at home, by household type and age of householder, 2002; numbers in thousands)

	total	with own children under age 18	
		number	percent
Total non-Hispanic white households	**80,818**	**23,532**	**29.1%**
Under age 35	16,206	6,843	42.2
Aged 35 to 54	33,677	15,940	47.3
Aged 35 to 44	17,001	10,545	62.0
Aged 35 to 39	8,006	5,226	65.3
Aged 40 to 44	8,995	5,319	59.1
Aged 45 to 54	16,676	5,395	32.4
Aged 55 to 64	12,010	652	5.4
Aged 65 or older	18,925	99	0.5
Married couples	**44,117**	**18,415**	**41.7**
Under age 35	7,409	4,925	66.5
Aged 35 to 54	21,042	12,856	61.1
Aged 35 to 44	10,622	8,427	79.3
Aged 35 to 39	4,962	4,135	83.3
Aged 40 to 44	5,660	4,292	75.8
Aged 45 to 54	10,420	4,429	42.5
Aged 55 to 64	7,414	552	7.4
Aged 65 or older	8,252	83	0.1
Female householder, no spouse present	**6,884**	**3,927**	**57.1**
Under age 35	1,799	1,523	84.7
Aged 35 to 54	3,333	2,344	70.3
Aged 35 to 44	1,878	1,640	87.3
Aged 35 to 39	932	859	92.2
Aged 40 to 44	946	781	82.6
Aged 45 to 54	1,455	704	48.4
Aged 55 to 64	658	49	7.4
Aged 65 or older	1,094	12	1.1
Male householder, no spouse present	**2,618**	**1,190**	**45.5**
Under age 35	814	393	48.3
Aged 35 to 54	1,234	740	60.0
Aged 35 to 44	640	478	74.7
Aged 35 to 39	292	232	79.5
Aged 40 to 44	348	246	70.7
Aged 45 to 54	594	262	44.1
Aged 55 to 64	253	52	20.6
Aged 65 or older	315	4	1.3

Source: Bureau of the Census, Children's Living Arrangements and Characteristics: March 2002, Detailed Tables, *Internet site http://www.census.gov/population/www/socdemo/hh-fam/cps2002.html; calculations by New Strategist*

Many Boomers Have School-Aged Children at Home

The proportion with adult children at home rises sharply in the 45-to-54 age group.

Among householders aged 35 to 44, the 55 percent majority had school-aged children at home in 2002 (the Baby-Boom generation was aged 38 to 56 in that year). In the 45-to-54 age group, the proportion living with school-aged children falls to 32 percent. But 17 percent of householders in the 45-to-54 age group have adult children (aged 18 or older) living with them.

Among married couples aged 35 to 54, 63 percent have children under age 18 at home, with most having one or two children living with them. The proportion of couples having children under age 18 at home falls from 84 percent among those aged 35 to 39 to 44 percent in the 45-to-54 age group. Female-headed families are more likely than married couples to have just one child under age 18 at home.

■ Many Boomers are raising teenagers and fretting about the soaring cost of college.

A large share of households headed by older Boomers include adult children

(percent of households with children aged 18 or older, by age of householder, 2002)

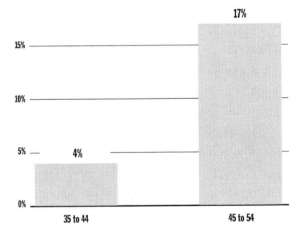

Table 6.12 Households by Presence and Age of Children and Age of Householder, 2002

(number and percent distribution of total households and households with children at home, by age of children and age of householder, 2002; numbers in thousands)

	total	under 35	aged 35 to 54 total	35 to 39	40 to 44	45 to 54	55 to 64	65 or older
Total households	**109,297**	**25,379**	**46,239**	**11,599**	**12,432**	**22,208**	**15,203**	**22,476**
With children of any age	45,812	12,095	27,329	7,883	8,212	11,234	3,630	2,757
Under age 25	40,967	12,076	26,490	7,873	8,163	10,454	2,076	325
Under age 18	35,705	12,016	22,587	7,716	7,433	7,438	923	180
Under age 12	26,376	11,625	14,373	6,343	4,885	3,145	290	90
Under age 6	15,376	9,100	6,141	3,493	1,820	828	101	33
Under age 3	8,909	6,021	2,835	1,789	750	296	36	17
Under age 1	2,958	2,136	808	505	220	83	9	3
Aged 6 to 17	27,438	6,230	20,191	6,355	6,779	7,057	864	155

PERCENT DISTRIBUTION BY AGE OF CHILD

Total households	**100.0%**	**100.0%**	**100.0%**	**100.0%**	**100.0%**	**100.0%**	**100.0%**	**100.0%**
With children of any age	41.9	47.7	59.1	68.0	66.1	50.6	23.9	12.3
Under age 25	37.5	47.6	57.3	67.9	65.7	47.1	13.7	1.4
Under age 18	32.7	47.3	48.8	66.5	59.8	33.5	6.1	0.8
Under age 12	24.1	45.8	31.1	54.7	39.3	14.2	1.9	0.4
Under age 6	14.1	35.9	13.3	30.1	14.6	3.7	0.7	0.1
Under age 3	8.2	23.7	6.1	15.4	6.0	1.3	0.2	0.1
Under age 1	2.7	8.4	1.7	4.4	1.8	0.4	0.1	0.0
Aged 6 to 17	25.1	24.5	43.7	54.8	54.5	31.8	5.7	0.7

PERCENT DISTRIBUTION BY AGE OF HOUSEHOLDER

Total households	**100.0%**	**23.2%**	**42.3%**	**10.6%**	**11.4%**	**20.3%**	**13.9%**	**20.6%**
With children of any age	100.0	26.4	59.7	17.2	17.9	24.5	7.9	6.0
Under age 25	100.0	29.5	64.7	19.2	19.9	25.5	5.1	0.8
Under age 18	100.0	33.7	63.3	21.6	20.8	20.8	2.6	0.5
Under age 12	100.0	44.1	54.5	24.1	18.5	11.9	1.1	0.3
Under age 6	100.0	59.2	39.9	22.7	11.8	5.4	0.7	0.2
Under age 3	100.0	67.6	31.8	20.1	8.4	3.3	0.4	0.2
Under age 1	100.0	72.2	27.3	17.1	7.4	2.8	0.3	0.1
Aged 6 to 17	100.0	22.7	73.6	23.2	24.7	25.7	3.1	0.6

Source: Bureau of the Census, Children's Living Arrangements and Characteristics: March 2002, Detailed Tables, *Internet site http://www.census.gov/population/www/socdemo/hh-fam/cps2002.html; calculations by New Strategist*

Table 6.13 Married Couples by Presence and Number of Children and Age of Householder, 2002

(number and percent distribution of married couples by presence and number of own children under age 18 at home, by age of householder, 2002; numbers in thousands)

	total	under 35	aged 35 to 54 total	35 to 39	40 to 44	45 to 54	55 to 64	65 or older
Total married couples	**56,747**	**10,920**	**27,315**	**6,804**	**7,374**	**13,137**	**8,922**	**9,591**
Without children under 18	30,955	3,238	10,089	1,096	1,695	7,298	8,178	9,449
With children under 18	25,792	7,682	17,224	5,707	5,678	5,839	744	141
One	9,832	2,917	6,290	1,401	1,767	3,122	529	95
Two	10,440	3,069	7,174	2,613	2,592	1,969	166	31
Three	4,058	1,257	2,756	1,216	958	582	34	12
Four or more	1,461	439	1,004	477	361	166	15	4

PERCENT DISTRIBUTION BY NUMBER OF CHILDREN

Total married couples	**100.0%**	**100.0%**	**100.0%**	**100.0%**	**100.0%**	**100.0%**	**100.0%**	**100.0%**
Without children under 18	54.5	29.7	36.9	16.1	23.0	55.6	91.7	98.5
With children under 18	45.5	70.3	63.1	83.9	77.0	44.4	8.3	1.5
One	17.3	26.7	23.0	20.6	24.0	23.8	5.9	1.0
Two	18.4	28.1	26.3	38.4	35.2	15.0	1.9	0.3
Three	7.2	11.5	10.1	17.9	13.0	4.4	0.4	0.1
Four or more	2.6	4.0	3.7	7.0	4.9	1.3	0.2	0.0

Source: Bureau of the Census, Children's Living Arrangements and Characteristics: March 2002, Detailed Tables, Internet site http://www.census.gov/population/www/socdemo/hh-fam/cps2002.html; calculations by New Strategist

Table 6.14 Female-Headed Families by Presence and Number of Children and Age of Householder, 2002

(number and percent distribution of female-headed families by presence and number of own children under age 18 at home, by age of householder, 2002; numbers in thousands)

	total	under 35	aged 35 to 54 total	35 to 39	40 to 44	45 to 54	55 to 64	65 or older
Total female-headed families	**13,143**	**4,213**	**6,126**	**1,828**	**1,768**	**2,530**	**1,188**	**1,617**
Without children under 18	5,133	622	1,841	162	367	1,312	1,083	1,588
With children under 18	8,010	3,591	4,285	1,666	1,401	1,218	105	29
One	3,967	1,609	2,249	695	751	803	84	25
Two	2,580	1,172	1,391	598	467	326	13	4
Three	1,085	582	497	275	144	78	7	–
Four or more	378	228	150	99	39	12	2	–

PERCENT DISTRIBUTION BY NUMBER OF CHILDREN

	total	under 35	aged 35 to 54 total	35 to 39	40 to 44	45 to 54	55 to 64	65 or older
Total female-headed families	**100.0%**	**100.0%**	**100.0%**	**100.0%**	**100.0%**	**100.0%**	**100.0%**	**100.0%**
Without children under 18	39.1	14.8	30.1	8.9	20.8	51.9	91.2	98.2
With children under 18	60.9	85.2	69.9	91.1	79.2	48.1	8.8	1.8
One	30.2	38.2	36.7	38.0	42.5	31.7	7.1	1.5
Two	19.6	27.8	22.7	32.7	26.4	12.9	1.1	0.2
Three	8.3	13.8	8.1	15.0	8.1	3.1	0.6	–
Four or more	2.9	5.4	2.4	5.4	2.2	0.5	0.2	–

Note: (–) means number is less than 500 or sample is too small to make a reliable estimate.
Source: Bureau of the Census, Children's Living Arrangements and Characteristics: March 2002, Detailed Tables, *Internet site http://www.census.gov/population/www/socdemo/hh-fam/cps2002.html; calculations by New Strategist*

Table 6.15 Male-Headed Families by Presence and Number of Children and Age of Householder, 2002

(number and percent distribution of male-headed families by presence and number of own children under age 18 at home, by age of householder, 2002; numbers in thousands)

	total	under 35	aged 35 to 54				55 or older
			total	35 to 39	40 to 44	45 to 54	
Total male-headed families	**4,438**	**1,700**	**1,918**	**492**	**553**	**873**	**820**
Without children under 18	2,535	955	842	150	199	493	738
With children under 18	1,903	744	1,077	342	354	381	84
One	1,162	475	627	159	197	271	61
Two	538	204	319	123	105	91	15
Three	157	54	95	44	38	13	8
Four or more	45	11	34	16	13	5	–
PERCENT DISTRIBUTION BY NUMBER OF CHILDREN							
Total male-headed families	**100.0%**	**100.0%**	**100.0%**	**100.0%**	**100.0%**	**100.0%**	**100.0%**
Without children under 18	57.1	56.2	43.9	30.5	36.0	56.5	90.0
With children under 18	42.9	43.8	56.2	69.5	64.0	43.6	10.2
One	26.2	27.9	32.7	32.3	35.6	31.0	7.4
Two	12.1	12.0	16.6	25.0	19.0	10.4	1.8
Three	3.5	3.2	5.0	8.9	6.9	1.5	1.0
Four or more	1.0	0.6	1.8	3.3	2.4	0.6	–

Note: (–) means number is less than 500 or sample is too small to make a reliable estimate.
Source: Bureau of the Census, Children's Living Arrangements and Characteristics: March 2002, Detailed Tables, *Internet site http://www.census.gov/population/www/socdemo/hh-fam/cps2002.html; calculations by New Strategist*

Most Middle-Aged Men and Women Live with a Spouse

The percentage of women who live alone rises substantially in the fiftysomething age group, however.

Most Boomer men and women are married and living with their spouse. Among women aged 35 to 54 in 2002 (Boomers were aged 38 to 56 in that year), 65 percent of women and 67 percent of men were living with a spouse. Among men, the proportion living with a spouse rises to 74 percent among 55-to-64-year-olds, the age group now filling with Boomers. Among women, the proportion drops slightly, to 62 percent, in the 55-to-64 age group.

Fourteen percent of women aged 35 to 54 are heading their own family household, the second-most common living arrangement among Boomer women. As women age into their fifties, however, they are less likely to head family households and more likely to live alone. Among women aged 55 to 59, nearly 18 percent live by themselves.

Among Boomer men, living alone ranks second as a living arrangement, accounting for 12 percent of men aged 35 to 54. The percentage of middle-aged men who live alone does not vary much by age.

■ The wants and needs of Boomer men and women will diverge as they age and lifestyle differences grow.

Women are increasingly likely to live alone as they age through their fifties

(percent of women aged 35 to 59 who live alone, by age, 2003)

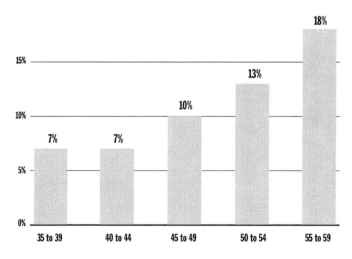

Table 6.16 Living Arrangements of Men Aged 35 to 64, 2002

(number and percent distribution of total men and men aged 35 to 64 by living arrangement, 2002; numbers in thousands)

	total	aged 35 to 54				55 to 64
		total	35 to 39	40 to 44	45 to 54	
Total men	**106,819**	**41,104**	**10,693**	**11,109**	**19,302**	**12,363**
In family household	84,724	32,968	8,433	8,845	15,690	10,162
Living with spouse	56,747	27,387	6,808	7,337	13,242	9,111
Other family householder	4,439	1,917	491	553	873	389
Living with parents	18,077	2,131	770	601	760	203
Other family member	5,461	1,533	364	354	815	459
In nonfamily household	22,096	8,135	2,261	2,264	3,610	2,200
Living alone	12,004	4,968	1,231	1,382	2,355	1,549
Living with nonrelatives	10,092	3,167	1,030	882	1,255	651

PERCENT DISTRIBUTION BY LIVING ARRANGEMENT

	total	aged 35 to 54				55 to 64
		total	35 to 39	40 to 44	45 to 54	
Total men	**100.0%**	**100.0%**	**100.0%**	**100.0%**	**100.0%**	**100.0%**
In family household	79.3	80.2	78.9	79.6	81.3	82.2
Living with spouse	53.1	66.6	63.7	66.1	68.6	73.7
Other family householder	4.2	4.7	4.6	5.0	4.5	3.1
Living with parents	16.9	5.2	7.2	5.4	3.9	1.6
Other family member	5.1	3.7	3.4	3.2	4.2	3.7
In nonfamily household	20.7	19.8	21.1	20.4	18.7	17.8
Living alone	11.2	12.1	11.5	12.4	12.2	12.5
Living with nonrelatives	9.4	7.7	9.6	7.9	6.5	5.3

PERCENT DISTRIBUTION BY AGE

	total	aged 35 to 54				55 to 64
		total	35 to 39	40 to 44	45 to 54	
Total men	**100.0%**	**38.5%**	**10.0%**	**10.4%**	**18.1%**	**11.6%**
In family household	100.0	38.9	10.0	10.4	18.5	12.0
Living with spouse	100.0	48.3	12.0	12.9	23.3	16.1
Other family householder	100.0	43.2	11.1	12.5	19.7	8.8
Living with parents	100.0	11.8	4.3	3.3	4.2	1.1
Other family member	100.0	28.1	6.7	6.5	14.9	8.4
In nonfamily household	100.0	36.8	10.2	10.2	16.3	10.0
Living alone	100.0	41.4	10.3	11.5	19.6	12.9
Living with nonrelatives	100.0	31.4	10.2	8.7	12.4	6.5

Source: Bureau of the Census, 2002 Current Population Survey Annual Demographic Supplement, Internet site http://www.census.gov/population/www/socdemo/hh-fam/cps2002.html; calculations by New Strategist

Table 6.17 Living Arrangements of Women aged 35 to 64, 2002

(number and percent distribution of total women and women aged 35 to 64 by living arrangement, 2002; numbers in thousands)

	total	total	35 to 39	40 to 44	45 to 54	55 to 64
		aged 35 to 54				
Total women	**114,639**	**42,662**	**10,947**	**11,506**	**20,209**	**13,497**
In family household	90,451	36,597	9,674	10,093	16,830	10,330
Living with spouse	56,747	27,761	7,104	7,636	13,021	8,397
Other family householder	13,143	6,126	1,828	1,768	2,530	1,188
Living with parents	14,475	1,171	391	313	467	131
Other family member	6,086	1,539	351	376	812	614
In nonfamily household	24,188	6,066	1,274	1,413	3,379	3,167
Living alone	16,771	3,878	652	838	2,388	2,699
Living with nonrelatives	7,417	2,188	622	575	991	468

PERCENT DISTRIBUTION BY LIVING ARRANGEMENT

Total women	**100.0%**	**100.0%**	**100.0%**	**100.0%**	**100.0%**	**100.0%**
In family household	78.9	85.8	88.4	87.7	83.3	76.5
Living with spouse	49.5	65.1	64.9	66.4	64.4	62.2
Other family householder	11.5	14.4	16.7	15.4	12.5	8.8
Living with parents	12.6	2.7	3.6	2.7	2.3	1.0
Other family member	5.3	3.6	3.2	3.3	4.0	4.5
In nonfamily household	21.1	14.2	11.6	12.3	16.7	23.5
Living alone	14.6	9.1	6.0	7.3	11.8	20.0
Living with nonrelatives	6.5	5.1	5.7	5.0	4.9	3.5

PERCENT DISTRIBUTION BY AGE

Total women	**100.0%**	**37.2%**	**9.5%**	**10.0%**	**17.6%**	**11.8%**
In family household	100.0	40.5	10.7	11.2	18.6	11.4
Living with spouse	100.0	48.9	12.5	13.5	22.9	14.8
Other family householder	100.0	46.6	13.9	13.5	19.2	9.0
Living with parents	100.0	8.1	2.7	2.2	3.2	0.9
Other family member	100.0	25.3	5.8	6.2	13.3	10.1
In nonfamily household	100.0	25.1	5.3	5.8	14.0	13.1
Living alone	100.0	23.1	3.9	5.0	14.2	16.1
Living with nonrelatives	100.0	29.5	8.4	7.8	13.4	6.3

Source: Bureau of the Census, 2002 Current Population Survey Annual Demographic Supplement, Internet site http:// www.census.gov/population/www/socdemo/hh-fam/cps2002.html; calculations by New Strategist

Table 6.18 People Who Live Alone by Age, 2003

(number of people aged 15 or older and number and percent who live alone by sex and age, 2003; numbers in thousands)

	total	living alone	
		number	percent
Total people	**225,250**	**29,430**	**13.1%**
Under age 35	79,309	5,348	6.7
Aged 35 to 54	84,308	9,030	10.7
Aged 35 to 44	44,074	4,211	9.6
Aged 35 to 39	21,284	1,949	9.2
Aged 40 to 44	22,790	2,262	9.9
Aged 45 to 54	40,234	4,819	12.0
Aged 45 to 49	21,420	2,346	11.0
Aged 50 to 54	18,814	2,473	13.1
Aged 55 to 59	15,470	2,386	15.4
Aged 60 or older	46,164	12,666	27.4
Total men	**108,814**	**12,511**	**11.5**
Under age 35	39,780	2,934	7.4
Aged 35 to 54	41,339	5,089	12.3
Aged 35 to 44	21,733	2,573	11.8
Aged 35 to 39	10,510	1,178	11.2
Aged 40 to 44	11,223	1,395	12.4
Aged 45 to 54	19,606	2,516	12.8
Aged 45 to 49	10,449	1,292	12.4
Aged 50 to 54	9,157	1,224	13.4
Aged 55 to 59	7,493	980	13.1
Aged 60 or older	20,201	3,508	17.4
Total women	**116,436**	**16,919**	**14.5**
Under age 35	39,529	2,414	6.1
Aged 35 to 54	42,969	3,941	9.2
Aged 35 to 44	22,341	1,638	7.3
Aged 35 to 39	10,774	771	7.2
Aged 40 to 44	11,567	867	7.5
Aged 45 to 54	20,628	2,303	11.2
Aged 45 to 49	10,971	1,054	9.6
Aged 50 to 54	9,657	1,249	12.9
Aged 55 to 59	7,977	1,406	17.6
Aged 60 or older	25,963	9,158	35.3

Source: Bureau of the Census, 2003 Current Population Survey, Annual Social and Economic Supplement, Internet sites http://ferret.bls.census.gov/macro/032003/perinc/new01_019.htm and http://ferret.bls.census.gov/macro/032003/hhinc/new02_000.html; calculations by New Strategist

The Divorced Population Peaks in Middle Age

But the solid majority of Boomers are married.

The proportion of people who are currently divorced peaks in mid-life. Eighteen percent of women aged 45 to 54 are divorced. Adding the currently separated to this figure brings the total to 21 percent—the highest proportion among all age groups. Among men aged 45 to 54, 16 percent are either divorced (14 percent) or separated (2 percent). The percentage of Boomers who have ever been divorced is much higher than these figures, of course, since many of the divorced have remarried. Despite their high rates of divorce, the 67 percent majority of people aged 35 to 54 are currently married. Only 13 percent have never married.

Older Americans are much less likely than the middle-aged to be currently divorced, but they are far more likely to be widowed. Among women age 65 or older, 46 percent are widows.

■ The lifestyles of Baby-Boom men and women will diverge as they enter their sixties and a growing proportion of women become widows and live alone.

Most Boomers are married

(percent distribution of people aged 35 to 54 by marital status, 2002)

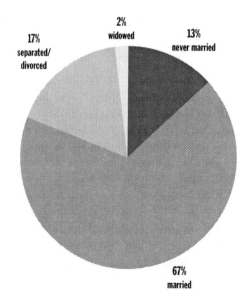

Table 6.19 Marital Status by Sex and Age, 2002: Total People

(number and percent distribution of people aged 15 or older by sex, age, and current marital status, 2002; numbers in thousands)

	total	never married	married, spouse present	married, spouse absent	separated	divorced	widowed
Total people	**221,459**	**63,090**	**115,838**	**2,926**	**4,606**	**20,955**	**14,044**
Under age 35	78,083	49,381	23,597	901	1,301	2,752	150
Aged 35 to 54	83,767	10,952	56,077	1,208	2,452	11,776	1,302
Aged 35 to 39	21,640	3,868	14,121	323	699	2,496	134
Aged 40 to 44	22,616	3,171	15,207	317	678	2,960	281
Aged 45 to 54	39,511	3,913	26,749	568	1,075	6,320	887
Aged 55 to 64	25,859	1,533	17,796	343	542	3,921	1,725
Aged 65 or older	33,750	1,224	18,368	474	311	2,506	10,867
Total women	**114,639**	**28,861**	**57,919**	**1,376**	**2,808**	**12,268**	**11,408**
Under age 35	38,957	22,721	13,180	442	810	1,680	122
Aged 35 to 54	42,662	4,732	28,245	527	1,526	6,645	989
Aged 35 to 39	10,947	1,613	7,215	147	469	1,402	102
Aged 40 to 44	11,506	1,320	7,769	123	403	1,677	215
Aged 45 to 54	20,209	1,799	13,261	257	654	3,566	672
Aged 55 to 64	13,497	715	8,530	157	305	2,384	1,407
Aged 65 or older	19,523	693	7,964	250	167	1,559	8,890
Total men	**106,819**	**34,229**	**57,919**	**1,551**	**1,798**	**8,686**	**2,636**
Under age 35	39,125	26,659	10,417	462	490	1,068	28
Aged 35 to 54	41,104	6,220	27,833	680	927	5,133	313
Aged 35 to 39	10,693	2,255	6,906	176	230	1,094	32
Aged 40 to 44	11,109	1,852	7,439	194	276	1,284	66
Aged 45 to 54	19,302	2,113	13,488	310	421	2,755	215
Aged 55 to 64	12,363	818	9,265	186	237	1,538	318
Aged 65 or older	14,227	532	10,404	223	144	947	1,977

	total	never married	married, spouse present	married, spouse absent	separated	divorced	widowed
PERCENT DISTRIBUTION							
Total people	**100.0%**	**28.5%**	**52.3%**	**1.3%**	**2.1%**	**9.5%**	**6.3%**
Under age 35	100.0	63.2	30.2	1.2	1.7	3.5	0.2
Aged 35 to 54	100.0	13.1	66.9	1.4	2.9	14.1	1.6
Aged 35 to 39	100.0	17.9	65.3	1.5	3.2	11.5	0.6
Aged 40 to 44	100.0	14.0	67.2	1.4	3.0	13.1	1.2
Aged 45 to 54	100.0	9.9	67.7	1.4	2.7	16.0	2.2
Aged 55 to 64	100.0	5.9	68.8	1.3	2.1	15.2	6.7
Aged 65 or older	100.0	3.6	54.4	1.4	0.9	7.4	32.2
Total women	**100.0**	**25.2**	**50.5**	**1.2**	**2.4**	**10.7**	**10.0**
Under age 35	100.0	58.3	33.8	1.1	2.1	4.3	0.3
Aged 35 to 54	100.0	11.1	66.2	1.2	3.6	15.6	2.3
Aged 35 to 39	100.0	14.7	65.9	1.3	4.3	12.8	0.9
Aged 40 to 44	100.0	11.5	67.5	1.1	3.5	14.6	1.9
Aged 45 to 54	100.0	8.9	65.6	1.3	3.2	17.6	3.3
Aged 55 to 64	100.0	5.3	63.2	1.2	2.3	17.7	10.4
Aged 65 or older	100.0	3.5	40.8	1.3	0.9	8.0	45.5
Total men	**100.0**	**32.0**	**54.2**	**1.5**	**1.7**	**8.1**	**2.5**
Under age 35	100.0	68.1	26.6	1.2	1.3	2.7	0.1
Aged 35 to 54	100.0	15.1	67.7	1.7	2.3	12.5	0.8
Aged 35 to 39	100.0	21.1	64.6	1.6	2.2	10.2	0.3
Aged 40 to 44	100.0	16.7	67.0	1.7	2.5	11.6	0.6
Aged 45 to 54	100.0	10.9	69.9	1.6	2.2	14.3	1.1
Aged 55 to 64	100.0	6.6	74.9	1.5	1.9	12.4	2.6
Aged 65 or older	100.0	3.7	73.1	1.6	1.0	6.7	13.9

Source: Bureau of the Census, 2002 Current Population Survey Annual Demographic Supplement, Internet site http:// www.census.gov/population/www/socdemo/hh-fam/cps2002.html

Regardless of Race, the Middle Aged Are Most Likely to Be Married

At every age, black men and women are least likely to be married.

In the first half of the 20th century, blacks and whites were about equally likely to be married. But as the marriage rate fell, it dropped faster for blacks. Consequently, blacks today are far less likely to be married than Asians, Hispanics, or non-Hispanic whites.

Among black women aged 35 to 54, only 39 percent are currently married. The figure is a much higher 64 percent among Hispanics, 71 percent among non-Hispanic whites, and peaks at 76 percent among Asian women in the age group.

Half of black men aged 35 to 54 are currently married. This is far below the 64 percent of Hispanic men, 70 percent of non-Hispanic white men, and 75 percent of Asian men in the age group who are currently married.

■ The differences in marital status by age, race, and Hispanic origin are a major reason for the diversity of lifestyles in America today.

Middle-aged blacks are less likely to be married

(percent of people aged 35 to 54 who are currently married, by race, Hispanic Origin, and sex, 2002)

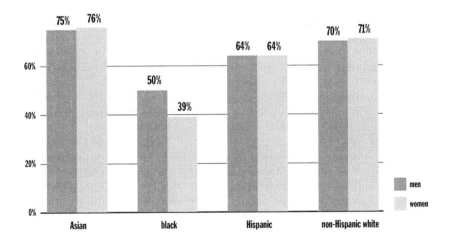

Table 6.20 Marital Status by Sex and Age, 2002: Asians

(number and percent distribution of Asians aged 15 or older by sex, age, and current marital status, 2002; numbers in thousands)

	total	never married	married, spouse present	married, spouse absent	separated	divorced	widowed
Total Asians	**9,837**	**3,229**	**5,246**	**318**	**137**	**488**	**418**
Under age 35	4,206	2,758	1,243	89	36	79	3
Aged 35 to 54	3,794	391	2,859	144	71	274	53
Aged 35 to 39	1,081	157	795	36	22	66	4
Aged 40 to 44	990	110	743	35	23	69	9
Aged 45 to 54	1,723	124	1,321	73	26	139	40
Aged 55 to 64	938	53	664	41	18	77	85
Aged 65 or older	899	27	480	44	12	58	277
Asian women	**5,079**	**1,363**	**2,822**	**139**	**93**	**316**	**346**
Under age 35	2,091	1,170	794	46	24	54	3
Aged 35 to 54	1,971	146	1,498	54	48	180	44
Aged 35 to 39	543	54	409	12	18	46	4
Aged 40 to 44	520	44	397	16	12	45	6
Aged 45 to 54	908	48	692	26	18	89	34
Aged 55 to 64	510	27	324	22	13	52	73
Aged 65 or older	507	20	206	17	8	30	226
Asian men	**4,758**	**1,866**	**2,423**	**180**	**44**	**172**	**72**
Under age 35	2,115	1,585	447	43	12	27	–
Aged 35 to 54	1,823	245	1,362	91	22	94	9
Aged 35 to 39	538	103	387	24	4	20	–
Aged 40 to 44	470	66	346	20	11	24	3
Aged 45 to 54	815	76	629	47	7	50	6
Aged 55 to 64	428	27	340	19	5	25	12
Aged 65 or older	392	9	274	27	5	26	51

PERCENT DISTRIBUTION	total	never married	married, spouse present	married, spouse absent	separated	divorced	widowed
Total Asians	**100.0%**	**32.8%**	**53.3%**	**3.2%**	**1.4%**	**5.0%**	**4.2%**
Under age 35	100.0	65.6	29.6	2.1	0.9	1.9	0.1
Aged 35 to 54	100.0	10.3	75.4	3.8	1.9	7.2	1.4
Aged 35 to 39	100.0	14.5	73.5	3.3	2.0	6.1	0.4
Aged 40 to 44	100.0	11.1	75.1	3.5	2.3	7.0	0.9
Aged 45 to 54	100.0	7.2	76.7	4.2	1.5	8.1	2.3
Aged 55 to 64	100.0	5.7	70.8	4.4	1.9	8.2	9.1
Aged 65 or older	100.0	3.0	53.4	4.9	1.3	6.5	30.8
Asian women	**100.0**	**26.8**	**55.6**	**2.7**	**1.8**	**6.2**	**6.8**
Under age 35	100.0	56.0	38.0	2.2	1.1	2.6	0.1
Aged 35 to 54	100.0	7.4	76.0	2.7	2.4	9.1	2.2
Aged 35 to 39	100.0	9.9	75.3	2.2	3.3	8.5	0.7
Aged 40 to 44	100.0	8.5	76.3	3.1	2.3	8.7	1.2
Aged 45 to 54	100.0	5.3	76.2	2.9	2.0	9.8	3.7
Aged 55 to 64	100.0	5.3	63.5	4.3	2.5	10.2	14.3
Aged 65 or older	100.0	3.9	40.6	3.4	1.6	5.9	44.6
Asian men	**100.0**	**39.2**	**50.9**	**3.8**	**0.9**	**3.6**	**1.5**
Under age 35	100.0	74.9	21.1	2.0	0.6	1.3	–
Aged 35 to 54	100.0	13.4	74.7	5.0	1.2	5.2	0.5
Aged 35 to 39	100.0	19.1	71.9	4.5	0.7	3.7	–
Aged 40 to 44	100.0	14.0	73.6	4.3	2.3	5.1	0.6
Aged 45 to 54	100.0	9.3	77.2	5.8	0.9	6.1	0.7
Aged 55 to 64	100.0	6.3	79.4	4.4	1.2	5.8	2.8
Aged 65 or older	100.0	2.3	69.9	6.9	1.3	6.6	13.0

Note: (–) means number is less than 500 or sample is too small to make a reliable estimate.
Source: Bureau of the Census, 2002 Current Population Survey Annual Demographic Supplement, Internet site http://www.census.gov/population/www/socdemo/hh-fam/cps2002.html

Table 6.21 Marital Status by Sex and Age, 2002: Blacks

(number and percent distribution of blacks aged 15 or older by sex, age, and current marital status, 2002; numbers in thousands)

	total	never married	married, spouse present	married, spouse absent	separated	divorced	widowed
Total blacks	**26,137**	**11,334**	**8,640**	**522**	**1,241**	**2,727**	**1,673**
Under age 35	10,837	8,130	1,959	168	272	294	17
Aged 35 to 54	9,953	2,738	4,392	256	684	1,610	271
Aged 35 to 39	2,730	977	1,200	63	159	310	20
Aged 40 to 44	2,761	804	1,261	73	184	386	52
Aged 45 to 54	4,462	957	1,931	120	341	914	199
Aged 55 to 64	2,495	305	1,137	59	182	504	308
Aged 65 or older	2,852	161	1,152	39	103	319	1,077
Black women	**14,442**	**6,068**	**4,216**	**272**	**772**	**1,758**	**1,354**
Under age 35	5,816	4,255	1,073	105	188	177	17
Aged 35 to 54	5,475	1,528	2,150	116	425	1,050	205
Aged 35 to 39	1,514	538	607	32	117	204	15
Aged 40 to 44	1,513	443	621	28	112	270	39
Aged 45 to 54	2,448	547	922	56	196	576	151
Aged 55 to 64	1,421	188	536	26	99	324	248
Aged 65 or older	1,730	97	457	25	60	207	884
Black men	**11,695**	**5,266**	**4,423**	**249**	**469**	**968**	**319**
Under age 35	5,025	3,876	887	63	83	115	1
Aged 35 to 54	4,476	1,209	2,242	140	259	561	66
Aged 35 to 39	1,216	439	593	31	42	106	5
Aged 40 to 44	1,247	361	640	45	72	117	13
Aged 45 to 54	2,013	409	1,009	64	145	338	48
Aged 55 to 64	1,074	118	600	33	83	180	59
Aged 65 or older	1,120	63	694	13	44	112	193

	total	never married	married, spouse present	married, spouse absent	separated	divorced	widowed
PERCENT DISTRIBUTION							
Total blacks	100.0%	43.4%	33.1%	2.0%	4.7%	10.4%	6.4%
Under age 35	100.0	75.0	18.1	1.6	2.5	2.7	0.2
Aged 35 to 54	100.0	27.5	44.1	2.6	6.9	16.2	2.7
Aged 35 to 39	100.0	35.8	44.0	2.3	5.8	11.4	0.7
Aged 40 to 44	100.0	29.1	45.7	2.6	6.7	14.0	1.9
Aged 45 to 54	100.0	21.4	43.3	2.7	7.6	20.5	4.5
Aged 55 to 64	100.0	12.2	45.6	2.4	7.3	20.2	12.3
Aged 65 or older	100.0	5.6	40.4	1.4	3.6	11.2	37.8
Black women	100.0	42.0	29.2	1.9	5.3	12.2	9.4
Under age 35	100.0	73.2	18.4	1.8	3.2	3.0	0.3
Aged 35 to 54	100.0	27.9	39.3	2.1	7.8	19.2	3.7
Aged 35 to 39	100.0	35.5	40.1	2.1	7.7	13.5	1.0
Aged 40 to 44	100.0	29.3	41.0	1.9	7.4	17.8	2.6
Aged 45 to 54	100.0	22.3	37.7	2.3	0.8	23.5	6.2
Aged 55 to 64	100.0	13.2	37.7	1.8	7.0	22.8	17.5
Aged 65 or older	100.0	5.6	26.4	1.4	3.5	12.0	51.1
Black men	100.0	45.0	37.8	2.1	4.0	8.3	2.7
Under age 35	100.0	77.1	17.7	1.3	1.7	2.3	0.0
Aged 35 to 54	100.0	27.0	50.1	3.1	5.8	12.5	1.5
Aged 35 to 39	100.0	36.1	48.8	2.5	3.5	8.7	0.4
Aged 40 to 44	100.0	28.9	51.3	3.6	5.8	9.4	1.0
Aged 45 to 54	100.0	20.3	50.1	3.2	7.2	16.8	2.4
Aged 55 to 64	100.0	11.0	55.9	3.1	7.7	16.8	5.5
Aged 65 or older	100.0	5.6	62.0	1.2	3.9	10.0	17.2

Source: Bureau of the Census, 2002 Current Population Survey Annual Demographic Supplement, Internet site http://www.census.gov/population/www/socdemo/hh-fam/cps2002.html

Table 6.22 Marital Status by Sex and Age, 2002: Hispanics

(number and percent distribution of Hispanics aged 15 or older by sex, age, and current marital status, 2002; numbers in thousands)

	total	never married	married, spouse present	married, spouse absent	separated	divorced	widowed
Total Hispanics	**26,332**	**9,557**	**12,432**	**846**	**889**	**1,734**	**875**
Under age 35	13,671	8,014	4,571	378	308	372	28
Aged 35 to 54	8,825	1,271	5,636	347	426	992	154
Aged 35 to 39	2,952	490	1,901	126	132	279	23
Aged 40 to 44	2,480	410	1,556	91	117	270	37
Aged 45 to 54	3,393	371	2,179	130	177	443	94
Aged 55 to 64	1,939	176	1,245	73	89	228	128
Aged 65 or older	1,897	96	980	48	66	142	565
Hispanic women	**12,900**	**3,936**	**6,316**	**289**	**604**	**1,026**	**727**
Under age 35	6,414	3,311	2,529	129	205	217	23
Aged 35 to 54	4,374	491	2,779	107	300	572	124
Aged 35 to 39	1,394	186	923	34	97	132	21
Aged 40 to 44	1,206	144	754	27	82	170	28
Aged 45 to 54	1,774	161	1,102	46	121	270	75
Aged 55 to 64	1,024	80	606	29	56	143	111
Aged 65 or older	1,088	54	402	24	43	94	469
Hispanic men	**13,432**	**5,621**	**6,116**	**556**	**284**	**707**	**147**
Under age 35	7,259	4,704	2,043	250	102	155	5
Aged 35 to 54	4,449	779	2,856	240	126	420	28
Aged 35 to 39	1,557	304	978	92	36	147	1
Aged 40 to 44	1,273	265	802	63	34	100	9
Aged 45 to 54	1,619	210	1,076	85	56	173	18
Aged 55 to 64	915	96	639	44	34	85	17
Aged 65 or older	809	42	578	22	22	47	97

PERCENT DISTRIBUTION	total	never married	married, spouse present	married, spouse absent	separated	divorced	widowed
Total Hispanics	**100.0%**	**36.3%**	**47.2%**	**3.2%**	**3.4%**	**6.6%**	**3.3%**
Under age 35	100.0	58.6	33.4	2.8	2.3	2.7	0.2
Aged 35 to 54	100.0	14.4	63.9	3.9	4.8	11.2	1.7
Aged 35 to 39	100.0	16.6	64.4	4.3	4.5	9.5	0.8
Aged 40 to 44	100.0	16.5	62.7	3.7	4.7	10.9	1.5
Aged 45 to 54	100.0	10.9	64.2	3.8	5.2	13.1	2.8
Aged 55 to 64	100.0	9.1	64.2	3.8	4.6	11.8	6.6
Aged 65 or older	100.0	5.1	51.7	2.5	3.5	7.5	29.8
Hispanic women	**100.0**	**30.5**	**49.0**	**2.2**	**4.7**	**8.0**	**5.6**
Under age 35	100.0	51.6	39.4	2.0	3.2	3.4	0.4
Aged 35 to 54	100.0	11.2	63.5	2.4	6.9	13.1	2.8
Aged 35 to 39	100.0	13.3	66.2	2.4	7.0	9.5	1.5
Aged 40 to 44	100.0	11.9	62.5	2.2	6.8	14.1	2.3
Aged 45 to 54	100.0	9.1	62.1	2.6	6.8	15.2	4.2
Aged 55 to 64	100.0	7.8	59.2	2.8	5.5	14.0	10.8
Aged 65 or older	100.0	5.0	36.9	2.2	4.0	8.6	43.1
Hispanic men	**100.0**	**41.8**	**45.5**	**4.1**	**2.1**	**5.3**	**1.1**
Under age 35	100.0	64.8	28.1	3.4	1.4	2.1	0.1
Aged 35 to 54	100.0	17.5	64.2	5.4	2.8	9.4	0.6
Aged 35 to 39	100.0	19.5	62.8	5.9	2.3	9.4	0.1
Aged 40 to 44	100.0	20.8	63.0	4.9	2.7	7.9	0.7
Aged 45 to 54	100.0	13.0	66.5	5.3	3.5	10.7	1.1
Aged 55 to 64	100.0	10.5	69.8	4.8	3.7	9.3	1.9
Aged 65 or older	100.0	5.2	71.4	2.7	2.7	5.8	12.0

Source: Bureau of the Census, 2002 Current Population Survey Annual Demographic Supplement. Internet site http:// www.census.gov/population/www/socdemo/hh-fam/cps2002.html

Table 6.23 Marital Status by Sex and Age, 2002: Non-Hispanic Whites

(number and percent distribution of non-Hispanic whites aged 15 or older by sex, age, and current marital status, 2002; numbers in thousands)

	total	never married	married, spouse present	married, spouse absent	separated	divorced	widowed
Total non-Hispanic whites	**158,188**	**38,770**	**89,082**	**1,250**	**2,327**	**15,778**	**10,981**
Under age 35	49,145	30,325	15,781	270	691	1,975	100
Aged 35 to 54	60,734	6,513	42,935	465	1,248	8,771	803
Aged 35 to 39	14,757	2,224	10,170	100	368	1,809	87
Aged 40 to 44	16,258	1,828	11,578	123	348	2,202	178
Aged 45 to 54	29,719	2,461	21,187	242	532	4,760	538
Aged 55 to 64	20,353	994	14,676	171	259	3,070	1,184
Aged 65 or older	27,956	938	15,690	344	129	1,962	8,894
Non-Hispanic white women	**81,625**	**17,373**	**44,303**	**667**	**1,332**	**9,045**	**8,904**
Under age 35	24,492	13,890	8,751	161	397	1,213	81
Aged 35 to 54	30,572	2,543	21,673	242	740	4,775	599
Aged 35 to 39	7,422	827	5,244	68	225	997	62
Aged 40 to 44	8,186	681	5,944	54	197	1,171	139
Aged 45 to 54	14,964	1,035	10,485	120	318	2,607	398
Aged 55 to 64	10,465	420	7,025	79	140	1,842	959
Aged 65 or older	16,096	520	6,854	185	55	1,215	7,265
Non-Hispanic white men	**76,564**	**21,397**	**44,779**	**583**	**995**	**6,733**	**2,077**
Under age 35	24,654	16,437	7,032	109	297	764	19
Aged 35 to 54	30,162	3,969	21,262	223	507	3,995	204
Aged 35 to 39	7,335	1,396	4,926	32	143	812	25
Aged 40 to 44	8,072	1,147	5,634	69	151	1,031	39
Aged 45 to 54	14,755	1,426	10,702	122	213	2,152	140
Aged 55 to 64	9,888	573	7,651	92	119	1,228	225
Aged 65 or older	11,860	418	8,834	159	72	746	1,629

	total	never married	married, spouse present	married, spouse absent	separated	divorced	widowed
PERCENT DISTRIBUTION							
Total non-Hispanic							
whites	**100.0%**	**24.5%**	**56.3%**	**0.8%**	**1.5%**	**10.0%**	**6.9%**
Under age 35	100.0	61.7	32.1	0.5	1.4	4.0	0.2
Aged 35 to 54	100.0	10.7	70.7	0.8	2.1	14.4	1.3
Aged 35 to 39	100.0	15.1	68.9	0.7	2.5	12.3	0.6
Aged 40 to 44	100.0	11.2	71.2	0.8	2.1	13.5	1.1
Aged 45 to 54	100.0	8.3	71.3	0.8	1.8	16.0	1.8
Aged 55 to 64	100.0	4.9	72.1	0.8	1.3	15.1	5.8
Aged 65 or older	100.0	3.4	56.1	1.2	0.5	7.0	31.8
Non-Hispanic							
white women	**100.0**	**21.3**	**54.3**	**0.8**	**1.6**	**11.1**	**10.9**
Under age 35	100.0	56.7	35.7	0.7	1.6	5.0	0.3
Aged 35 to 54	100.0	8.3	70.9	0.8	2.4	15.6	2.0
Aged 35 to 39	100.0	11.1	70.7	0.9	3.0	13.4	0.8
Aged 40 to 44	100.0	8.3	72.6	0.7	2.4	14.3	1.7
Aged 45 to 54	100.0	6.9	70.1	0.8	2.1	17.4	2.7
Aged 55 to 64	100.0	4.0	67.1	0.8	1.3	17.6	9.2
Aged 65 or older	100.0	3.2	42.6	1.1	0.3	7.5	45.1
Non-Hispanic							
white men	**100.0**	**27.9**	**58.5**	**0.8**	**1.3**	**8.8**	**2.7**
Under age 35	100.0	66.7	28.5	0.4	1.2	3.1	0.1
Aged 35 to 54	100.0	13.2	70.5	0.7	1.7	13.2	0.7
Aged 35 to 39	100.0	19.0	67.2	0.4	1.9	11.1	0.3
Aged 40 to 44	100.0	14.2	69.8	0.9	1.9	12.8	0.5
Aged 45 to 54	100.0	9.7	72.5	0.8	1.4	14.6	0.9
Aged 55 to 64	100.0	5.8	77.4	0.9	1.2	12.4	2.3
Aged 65 or older	100.0	3.5	74.5	1.3	0.6	6.3	13.7

Source: Bureau of the Census, 2002 Current Population Survey Annual Demographic Supplement, Internet site http://www.census.gov/population/www/socdemo/hh-fam/cps2002.html

Population

■ The nation's 78 million Baby Boomers (born between 1946 and 1964) account for 28 percent of the U.S. population. They are the largest generation of Americans.

■ In the ten years between 2000 and 2010, Boomers will entirely fill the 45-to-64 age group. The number of 45-to-64-year-olds will expand by 30 percent during those years.

■ Seventy-three percent of the Baby-Boom generation is non-Hispanic white. This figure is far greater than the 58 percent among children under age 5, but less than the 84 percent among people aged 65 or older.

■ The 35-to-54 age group accounted for 29 percent of the total population in 2002, but represented a larger 37 percent of the foreign born.

■ The number of legal immigrants admitted to the United States surpassed 1 million in 2002. More than 283,000 were aged 35 to 54, accounting for 27 percent of the total.

■ In most states, younger Boomers are more diverse than their older counterparts—sometimes strikingly so. In California, non-Hispanic whites account for just 47 percent of the population aged 35 to 39 but for a much larger 60 percent of people aged 50 to 54.

Boomers Are the Largest Generation

But Millennials are not far behind.

The 2000 census counted 78 million Baby Boomers in the United States, a figure that includes everyone born between 1946 and 1964. Boomers account for 28 percent of the total population, making them the largest generation—but not by much. Millennials, most of them children of Boomers, are in second place. They numbered 73 million in 2000 and accounted for 26 percent of the population.

Between 2000 and 2002, Boomers began to enter the 55-to-59 age group. During those two years, the number of 55-to-59-year-olds grew 11 percent, much faster than the 2.5 percent gain for the overall population. In contrast, as Boomers moved out of the 35-to-39 age group, it shrank by 3 percent.

In the ten years between 2000 and 2010, Boomers will entirely fill the 45-to-64 age group. The number of 45-to-64-year-olds will expand by 30 percent during those years. In the following decade, the number of 65-to-84-year-olds will increase by 39 percent, faster than any other age group, as Boomers become the nation's elders.

■ Boomers are entering an age of transition, from crowded to empty nest, and from work to retirement. These changes will affect many businesses and reshape American society.

The number of people aged 45 to 64 will grow 30 percent during this decade

(percent change in number of people by age, 2000–10)

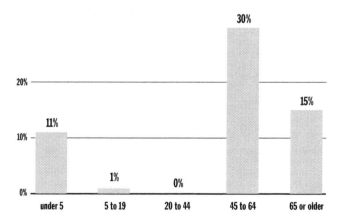

Table 7.1 Population by Age and Generation, 2000 Census

(number and percent distribution of people by age and generation, 2000; numbers in thousands)

	number	percent distribution
TOTAL PEOPLE	281,422	100.0%
Under age 5	19,176	6.8
Aged 5 to 9	20,550	7.3
Aged 10 to 14	20,528	7.3
Aged 15 to 19	20,220	7.2
Aged 20 to 24	18,964	6.7
Aged 25 to 29	19,381	6.9
Aged 30 to 34	20,510	7.3
Aged 35 to 44	45,149	16.0
Aged 35 to 39	22,707	8.1
Aged 40 to 44	22,442	8.0
Aged 45 to 54	37,678	13.4
Aged 45 to 49	20,092	7.1
Aged 50 to 54	17,586	6.2
Aged 55 to 59	13,469	4.8
Aged 60 to 64	10,805	3.8
Aged 65 to 69	9,534	3.4
Aged 70 to 74	8,857	3.1
Aged 75 to 79	7,416	2.6
Aged 80 to 84	4,945	1.8
Aged 85 or older	4,240	1.5
TOTAL PEOPLE	281,422	100.0
Post-Millennial (under age 6)	23,141	8.2
Millennial (aged 6 to 23)	72,655	25.8
Generation X (aged 24 to 35)	48,049	17.1
Baby Boom (aged 36 to 54)	**78,310**	**27.8**
Swing (aged 55 to 67)	30,061	10.7
World War II (aged 68 or older)	29,205	10.4

Source: Bureau of the Census, Census 2000 Summary File 1, Internet site http://factfinder.census.gov/servlet/BasicFactsServlet; calculations by New Strategist

Table 7.2 Population by Age and Sex, 2000 Census

(number of people by age and sex, and sex ratio by age, 2000; numbers in thousands)

	total	female	male	sex ratio
Total people	**281,422**	**143,368**	**138,054**	**96**
Under age 5	19,176	9,365	9,811	105
Aged 5 to 9	20,550	10,026	10,523	105
Aged 10 to 14	20,528	10,008	10,520	105
Aged 15 to 19	20,220	9,829	10,391	106
Aged 20 to 24	18,964	9,276	9,688	104
Aged 25 to 29	19,381	9,583	9,799	102
Aged 30 to 34	20,510	10,189	10,322	101
Aged 35 to 54	82,827	41,882	40,945	98
Aged 35 to 44	45,149	22,701	22,448	99
Aged 35 to 39	22,707	11,388	11,319	99
Aged 40 to 44	22,442	11,313	11,129	98
Aged 45 to 54	37,678	19,181	18,497	96
Aged 45 to 49	20,092	10,203	9,890	97
Aged 50 to 54	17,586	8,978	8,608	96
Aged 55 to 59	13,469	6,961	6,509	94
Aged 60 to 64	10,805	5,669	5,137	91
Aged 65 to 69	9,534	5,133	4,400	86
Aged 70 to 74	8,857	4,955	3,903	79
Aged 75 to 79	7,416	4,371	3,044	70
Aged 80 to 84	4,945	3,110	1,835	59
Aged 85 or older	4,240	3,013	1,227	41

Note: The sex ratio is the number of men per 100 women.
Source: Bureau of the Census, Census 2000 Summary File 1, Internet site http://factfinder.census.gov/servlet/BasicFactsServlet; calculations by New Strategist

Table 7.3 Population by Age, 2000 and 2002

(number of people by age, April 1, 2000, and July 1, 2002; percent change 2000–02; numbers in thousands)

	2000	2002	percent change 2000–02
Total people	**281,422**	**288,369**	**2.5%**
Under age 5	19,176	19,609	2.3
Aged 5 to 9	20,550	19,901	−3.2
Aged 10 to 14	20,528	21,136	3.0
Aged 15 to 19	20,220	20,376	0.8
Aged 20 to 24	18,964	20,214	6.6
Aged 25 to 29	19,381	18,972	−2.1
Aged 30 to 34	20,510	20,956	2.2
Aged 35 to 54	37,678	40,084	6.4
Aged 35 to 44	45,149	44,917	−0.5
Aged 35 to 39	22,707	21,915	−3.5
Aged 40 to 44	22,442	23,002	2.5
Aged 45 to 54	37,678	40,084	6.4
Aged 45 to 49	20,092	21,302	6.0
Aged 50 to 54	17,586	18,782	6.8
Aged 55 to 59	13,469	14,991	11.3
Aged 60 to 64	10,805	11,611	7.5
Aged 65 to 69	9,534	9,581	0.5
Aged 70 to 74	8,857	8,693	−1.9
Aged 75 to 79	7,416	7,420	0.1
Aged 80 to 84	4,945	5,314	7.5
Aged 85 to 89	2,790	2,943	5.5
Aged 90 to 94	1,113	1,250	12.4
Aged 95 to 99	287	342	19.2
Aged 100 or older	50	59	16.3

Source: Bureau of the Census, National Population Estimates, Internet site http://eire.census.gov/popest/data/national/tables/ asro/NA-EST2002-ASRO-01.php; calculations by New Strategist

Table 8.4 Population by Age, 2000 to 2020

(number and percent distribution of people by age, 2000 to 2020; percent and percentage point change, 2000–2010 and 2010–20; numbers in thousands)

	2000	2010	2020	percent change 2000–10	percent change 2010–20
Total people	**282,125**	**308,936**	**335,805**	**9.5%**	**8.7%**
Under age 5	19,218	21,426	22,932	11.5	7.0
Aged 5 to 19	61,331	61,810	65,955	0.8	6.7
Aged 20 to 44	104,075	104,444	108,632	0.4	4.0
Aged 45 to 64	62,440	81,012	83,653	29.7	3.3
Aged 65 to 84	30,794	34,120	47,363	10.8	38.8
Aged 85 or older	4,267	6,123	7,269	43.5	18.7

	2000	2010	2020	percentage point change 2000–10	percentage point change 2010–20
Percent distribution by age					
Total people	**100.0%**	**100.0%**	**100.0%**	–	–
Under age 5	6.8	6.9	6.8	0.1	–0.1
Aged 5 to 19	21.7	20.0	19.6	–1.7	–0.4
Aged 20 to 44	36.9	33.8	32.3	–3.1	–1.5
Aged 45 to 64	22.1	26.2	24.9	4.1	–1.3
Aged 65 to 84	10.9	11.0	14.1	0.1	3.1
Aged 85 or older	1.5	2.0	2.2	0.5	0.2

Source: Bureau of the Census. U.S. Interim Projections by Age, Sex, Race, and Hispanic Origin, 2004. Internet site http://www.census.gov/ipc/www/usinterimproj/; calculations by New Strategist

Boomers Are Less Diverse than Younger Americans

They are more diverse than their parents, however.

Seventy-three percent of the Baby-Boom generation is non-Hispanic white, according to the 2000 census. This figure is greater than the 69 percent for the population as a whole, and far surpasses the share among the youngest Americans—only 58 percent of children under age 5 are non-Hispanic white. The Baby-Boom generation is more diverse than older generations of Americans, however. Among people aged 65 or older, 84 percent are non-Hispanic white.

Twenty-nine percent of the nation's non-Hispanic whites are Baby Boomers versus just 22 percent of the nation's Hispanics. In fact, the number of Hispanics in Generation X surpasses the number of Hispanics in the Baby-Boom generation.

Among the 7 million multiracial Americans, only 20 percent are members of the Baby-Boom generation. A much larger 36 percent are members of the Millennial generation. Fewer than 2 percent of Baby Boomers claimed to be multiracial on the 2000 census.

■ The contrast in the racial and ethnic makeup of Boomers versus younger generations of Americans will create political tension in the years ahead.

Nearly three out of four Baby Boomers are non-Hispanic white

(non-Hispanic white share of population by generation, 2000)

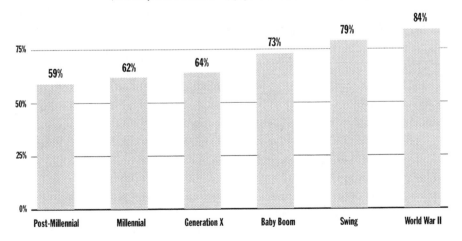

Table 7.5 Population by Age, Race, and Hispanic Origin, 2000 Census

(number and percent distribution of people by age, race, and Hispanic origin, 2000; numbers in thousands)

	total	American Indian	Asian	black	Native Hawaiian	white total	white non-Hispanic	other race	multiracial	Hispanic
Total people	**281,422**	**4,119**	**11,899**	**36,419**	**874**	**216,931**	**194,553**	**18,521**	**6,826**	**35,306**
Under age 5	19,176	359	919	3,167	88	13,656	11,194	2,017	948	3,718
Aged 5 to 14	41,078	791	1,771	6,823	175	29,533	25,186	3,648	1,533	6,787
Aged 15 to 24	39,184	697	1,878	5,853	168	28,164	24,355	3,690	1,174	6,581
Aged 25 to 34	39,892	588	2,179	5,374	140	29,096	25,356	3,578	997	6,510
Aged 35 to 44	45,149	644	1,953	5,699	126	34,984	31,801	2,693	891	5,129
Aged 45 to 54	37,678	501	1,499	4,194	86	30,494	28,387	1,553	607	3,136
Aged 55 to 64	24,275	281	839	2,429	47	20,316	19,028	718	332	1,710
Aged 65 or older	34,992	260	862	2,881	44	30,688	29,245	625	344	1,734

PERCENT DISTRIBUTION BY RACE AND HISPANIC ORIGIN

	total	American Indian	Asian	black	Native Hawaiian	white total	white non-Hispanic	other race	multiracial	Hispanic
Total people	**100.0%**	**1.5%**	**4.2%**	**12.9%**	**0.3%**	**77.1%**	**69.1%**	**6.6%**	**2.4%**	**12.5%**
Under age 5	100.0	1.9	4.8	16.5	0.5	71.2	58.4	10.5	4.9	19.4
Aged 5 to 14	100.0	1.9	4.3	16.6	0.4	71.9	61.3	8.9	3.7	16.5
Aged 15 to 24	100.0	1.8	4.8	14.9	0.4	71.9	62.2	9.4	3.0	16.8
Aged 25 to 34	100.0	1.5	5.5	13.5	0.4	72.9	63.6	9.0	2.5	16.3
Aged 35 to 44	100.0	1.4	4.3	12.6	0.3	77.5	70.4	6.0	2.0	11.4
Aged 45 to 54	100.0	1.3	4.0	11.1	0.2	80.9	75.3	4.1	1.6	8.3
Aged 55 to 64	100.0	1.2	3.5	10.0	0.2	83.7	78.4	3.0	1.4	7.1
Aged 65 or older	100.0	0.7	2.5	8.2	0.1	87.7	83.6	1.8	1.0	5.0

Note: Numbers will not add to total because each racial category includes those who identified themselves as being of the race alone and those who identified themselves as being of the race in combination with one or more other races, because the multiracial are shown, and because Hispanics may be of any race. Non-Hispanic whites include only those who identified themselves as "white alone" and non-Hispanic.
Source: Bureau of the Census, Census 2000 Summary File 1; Internet site http://factfinder.census.gov/servlet/BasicFactsServlet; calculations by New Strategist

Table 7.6 Population by Generation, Race, and Hispanic Origin, 2000 Census

(number and percent distribution of people by generation, race, and Hispanic origin, 2000; numbers in thousands)

	total	American Indian	Asian	black	Native Hawaiian	white total	white non-Hispanic	other race	Hispanic
TOTAL PEOPLE	281,422	4,119	11,899	36,419	874	216,931	194,553	18,521	35,306
Post-Millennial (under age 6)	23,141	432	1,100	3,833	106	16,475	13,539	2,414	4,451
Millennial (aged 6 to 23)	72,655	1,356	3,266	11,498	311	52,303	45,002	6,551	11,948
Generation X (24 to 35)	48,049	711	2,592	6,486	169	35,076	30,585	4,295	7,812
Baby Boom (aged 36 to 54)	78,310	1,080	3,240	9,293	198	62,074	57,154	3,919	7,652
Swing (aged 55 to 67)	30,061	337	1,024	2,999	57	25,214	23,629	859	2,085
World War II (aged 68+)	29,205	203	676	2,310	34	25,790	24,644	484	1,360

PERCENT DISTRIBUTION BY RACE AND HISPANIC ORIGIN

	total	American Indian	Asian	black	Native Hawaiian	white total	white non-Hispanic	other race	Hispanic
TOTAL PEOPLE	100.0%	100.0%	100.0%	100.0%	100.0%	100.0%	100.0%	100.0%	100.0%
Post-Millennial (under age 6)	8.2	10.5	9.2	10.5	12.2	7.6	7.0	13.0	12.6
Millennial (aged 6 to 23)	25.8	32.9	27.5	31.6	35.5	24.1	23.1	35.4	33.8
Generation X (aged 24 to 35)	17.1	17.3	21.8	17.8	19.3	16.2	15.7	23.2	22.1
Baby Boom (aged 36 to 54)	27.8	26.2	27.2	25.5	22.6	28.6	29.4	21.2	21.7
Swing (aged 55 to 67)	10.7	8.2	8.6	8.2	6.5	11.6	12.1	4.6	5.9
World War II (aged 68+)	10.4	4.9	5.7	6.3	3.9	11.9	12.7	2.6	3.9

PERCENT DISTRIBUTION BY GENERATION

	total	American Indian	Asian	black	Native Hawaiian	white total	white non-Hispanic	other race	Hispanic
TOTAL PEOPLE	100.0%	1.5%	4.2%	12.9%	0.3%	77.1%	69.1%	6.6%	12.5%
Post-Millennial (under age 6)	100.0	1.9	4.8	16.6	0.5	71.2	58.5	10.4	19.2
Millennial (aged 6 to 23)	100.0	1.9	4.5	15.8	0.4	72.0	61.9	9.0	16.4
Generation X (aged 24 to 35)	100.0	1.5	5.4	13.5	0.4	73.0	63.7	8.9	16.3
Baby Boom (aged 36 to 54)	100.0	1.4	4.1	11.9	0.3	79.3	73.0	5.0	9.8
Swing (aged 55 to 67)	100.0	1.1	3.4	10.0	0.2	83.9	78.6	2.9	6.9
World War II (aged 68+)	100.0	0.7	2.3	7.9	0.1	88.3	84.4	1.7	4.7

Note: Numbers will not add to total because each racial category includes those who identified themselves as being of the race alone and those who identified themselves as being of the race in combination with one or more other races, and because Hispanics may be of any race. Non-Hispanic whites include only those who identified themselves as "white alone" and non-Hispanic.
Source: Bureau of the Census, Census 2000 Summary File 2, Internet site http://factfinder.census.gov/servlet/BasicFactsServlet; calculations by New Strategist

Table 7.7 Multiracial Population by Age and Generation, 2000 Census

(number of total people and number and percent distribution of the multiracial population, by age and generation, 2000; numbers in thousands)

	total	multiracial number	multiracial percent distribution	multiracial share of total
TOTAL PEOPLE	**281,422**	**6,826**	**100.0%**	**2.4%**
Under age 5	19,176	948	13.9	4.9
Aged 5 to 9	20,550	830	12.2	4.0
Aged 10 to 14	20,528	703	10.3	3.4
Aged 15 to 19	20,220	622	9.1	3.1
Aged 20 to 24	18,964	552	8.1	2.9
Aged 25 to 29	19,381	512	7.5	2.6
Aged 30 to 34	20,510	484	7.1	2.4
Aged 35 to 39	22,707	471	6.9	2.1
Aged 40 to 44	22,442	421	6.2	1.9
Aged 45 to 49	20,092	338	5.0	1.7
Aged 50 to 54	17,586	269	3.9	1.5
Aged 55 to 59	13,469	189	2.8	1.4
Aged 60 to 64	10,805	143	2.1	1.3
Aged 65 to 69	9,534	112	1.6	1.2
Aged 70 to 74	8,857	91	1.3	1.0
Aged 75 to 79	7,416	67	1.0	0.9
Aged 80 to 84	4,945	41	0.6	0.8
Aged 85 or older	4,240	34	0.5	0.8
TOTAL PEOPLE	**281,422**	**6,826**	**100.0**	**2.4**
Post-Millennial (under 6)	23,141	1,122	16.4	4.8
Millennial (aged 6 to 23)	72,655	2,429	35.6	3.3
Generation X (24 to 35)	48,049	1,200	17.6	2.5
Baby Boom (aged 36 to 54)	**78,310**	**1,399**	**20.5**	**1.8**
Swing (aged 55 to 67)	30,061	402	5.9	1.3
World War II (68+)	29,205	274	4.0	0.9

Source: Bureau of the Census, Census 2000 Summary File 2, Internet site http://factfinder.census.gov/servlet/BasicFactsServlet; calculations by New Strategist

Many People Aged 35 to 54 Are Foreign Born

One in seven middle-aged Americans was born in another country.

A substantial 12 percent of all Americans were born abroad, and the proportion is a higher 14 percent among 35-to-54-year-olds. Among the 11.9 million 35-to-54-year-olds who were born in a foreign country, 43 percent are naturalized citizens. The 35-to-54 age group accounted for 29 percent of the total population in 2002, but it represented a larger 37 percent of the foreign born.

Among the foreign born in the 35-to-54 age group, 33 percent were born in Central America (a region that includes Mexico in these statistics). Twenty-nine percent were born in Asia, and only 13 percent in Europe. Within the 35-to-54 age group, the figures vary—45-to-54-year-olds are more likely to be from Europe and less likely to be from Central America than 35-to-44-year-olds.

■ The foreign-born population adds to the multicultural mix which is becoming a significant factor in American business and politics.

One-third of foreign-born 35-to-54-year-olds are from Central America

(percent distribution of foreign-born people aged 35 to 54 by region of birth, 2002)

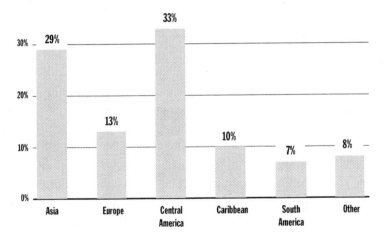

Table 7.8 Population Aged 35 to 54 by Citizenship Status, 2002

(number and percent distribution of total people and people aged 35 to 54 by citizenship status, 2002; numbers in thousands)

			foreign born		
	total	native born	total	naturalized citizen	not a citizen
TOTAL PEOPLE	**282,082**	**249,629**	**32,453**	**11,962**	**20,491**
Total aged 35 to 54	**83,829**	**71,893**	**11,937**	**5,152**	**6,785**
Aged 35 to 44	44,284	37,279	7,005	2,628	4,377
Aged 45 to 54	39,545	34,614	4,932	2,524	2,408
PERCENT DISTRIBUTION BY CITIZENSHIP STATUS					
TOTAL PEOPLE	**100.0%**	**88.5%**	**11.5%**	**4.2%**	**7.3%**
Total aged 35 to 54	**100.0**	**85.8**	**14.2**	**6.1**	**8.1**
Aged 35 to 44	100.0	84.2	15.8	5.9	9.9
Aged 45 to 54	100.0	87.5	12.5	6.4	6.1
PERCENT DISTRIBUTION BY AGE					
TOTAL PEOPLE	**100.0%**	**100.0%**	**100.0%**	**100.0%**	**100.0%**
Total aged 35 to 54	**29.7**	**28.8**	**36.8**	**43.1**	**33.1**
Aged 35 to 44	15.7	14.9	21.6	22.0	21.4
Aged 45 to 54	14.0	13.9	15.2	21.1	11.8

Source: Bureau of the Census, Foreign-Born Population of the United States, Current Population Survey, March 2002, *Internet site http://www.census.gov/population/www/socdemo/foreign/ppl-162.html; calculations by New Strategist*

Table 7.9 Foreign-Born Population Aged 35 to 54, 2002

(number and percent distribution of total people and people aged 35 to 54 by foreign-born status and region of birth, 2002; numbers in thousands)

| | | foreign born | | | | | | | |
| | | | | | Latin America | | | | |
	total	total	Asia	Europe	total	Caribbean	Central America	South America	other
TOTAL PEOPLE	282,082	32,453	8,281	4,548	16,943	3,102	11,819	2,022	2,680
Total aged 35 to 54	83,829	11,936	3,451	1,525	5,979	1,176	3,959	845	980
Aged 35 to 44	44,284	7,005	1,888	764	3,773	671	2,580	523	579
Aged 45 to 54	39,545	4,931	1,563	761	2,206	505	1,379	322	401
PERCENT DISTRIBUTION OF FOREIGN-BORN BY REGION OF BIRTH									
TOTAL PEOPLE	–	100.0%	25.5%	14.0%	52.2%	9.6%	36.4%	6.2%	8.3%
Total aged 35 to 54	–	100.0	28.9	12.8	50.1	9.9	33.2	7.1	8.2
Aged 35 to 44	–	100.0	27.0	10.9	53.9	9.6	36.8	7.5	8.3
Aged 45 to 54	–	100.0	31.7	15.4	44.7	10.2	28.0	6.5	8.1
PERCENT DISTRIBUTION BY AGE									
TOTAL PEOPLE	100.0%	100.0%	100.0%	100.0%	100.0%	100.0%	100.0%	100.0%	100.0%
Total aged 35 to 54	29.7	36.8	41.7	33.5	35.3	37.9	33.5	41.8	36.6
Aged 35 to 44	15.7	21.6	22.8	16.8	22.3	21.6	21.8	25.9	21.6
Aged 45 to 54	14.0	15.2	18.9	16.7	13.0	16.3	11.7	15.9	15.0

Note: Central America includes Mexico in these statistics; (–) means not applicable.
Source: Bureau of the Census, Foreign-Born Population of the United States, Current Population Survey, March 2002, Internet site http://www.census.gov/population/www/socdemo/foreign/ppl-162.html; calculations by New Strategist

The Middle Aged Are a Substantial Share of Immigrants

More than one in four immigrants is aged 35 to 54.

The number of immigrants admitted to the United States was over 1 million in 2002. More than 283,000 were aged 35 to 54, accounting for 27 percent of the total. Although a larger share of immigrants are young adults (38 percent were aged 20 to 34) many middle-aged workers and their families arrive in the United States every year.

Within the 35-to-54 age group, the immigrant share declines steadily with age. Eleven percent of immigrants admitted to the U.S. in 2002 were aged 35 to 39, placing the age group third in importance after 30-to-34 (15 percent) and 25-to-29 (14 percent) cohorts. But immigrants aged 45 to 49 accounted for fewer than 4 percent of the total.

■ Because most immigrants are children and young adults, immigration has a much greater impact on the diversity of younger Americans than on the middle-aged or older population.

Immigrants aged 35 to 54 account for 27 percent of the total

(percent distribution of immigrants by age, 2002)

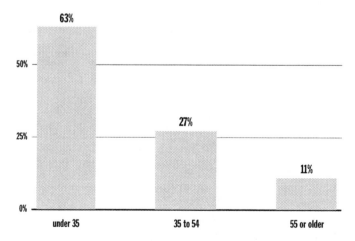

Table 7.10 **Immigrants by Age, 2002**

(number and percent distribution of immigrants by age, 2002)

	number	percent distribution
Total immigrants	**1,063,732**	**100.0%**
Under age 1	11,673	1.1
Aged 1 to 4	31,791	3.0
Aged 5 to 9	54,493	5.1
Aged 10 to 14	70,860	6.7
Aged 15 to 19	92,566	8.7
Aged 20 to 24	93,132	8.8
Aged 25 to 29	152,476	14.3
Aged 30 to 34	160,962	15.1
Aged 35 to 54	**283,120**	**26.6**
Aged 35 to 44	187,990	17.7
Aged 35 to 39	112,247	10.6
Aged 40 to 44	75,743	7.1
Aged 45 to 54	95,130	8.9
Aged 45 to 49	54,811	5.2
Aged 50 to 54	40,319	3.8
Aged 55 to 59	31,694	3.0
Aged 60 to 64	29,201	2.7
Aged 65 to 74	39,014	3.7
Aged 75 or older	12,541	1.2

Source: U.S. Citizenship and Immigration Services, 2002 Yearbook of Immigration Statistics, *Internet site http://uscis.gov/graphics/shared/aboutus/statistics/IMM02yrbk/IMM2002list.htm*

The Largest Share of Baby Boomers Lives in the South

Boomers account for only 24 percent of the population of Utah but 33 percent of the population of Alaska.

The South is home to the largest share of the population, and consequently to the largest share of the Baby-Boom generation. The 2000 census found 35 percent of Boomers living in the South, where they accounted for 28 percent of the population.

By state, the smallest proportion of Boomers is found in Utah, where only 24 percent of the population was aged 35 to 54 in 2000. Behind this low figure is Utah's high fertility rate, boosting its child and young-adult population. In Alaska, Boomers account for 33 percent of the population, the highest share among the states.

Only in Hawaii are non-Hispanic whites a minority among 35-to-54-year-olds. In the nation's most populous state, California, just 47 percent of all its residents are non-Hispanic white. Among Californian's 35-to-54-year-olds, however, the 53 percent majority are non-Hispanic white. In New Mexico, non-Hispanic whites account for the 45 percent minority of the total population but for 50 percent of Boomers.

In most states, younger Boomers are more diverse than their older counterparts—sometimes strikingly so. In California, non-Hispanic whites account for just 47 percent of the population aged 35 to 39 but for a much larger 60 percent of people aged 50 to 54.

■ As younger generations enter the 35-to-54 age group, the diversity of the middle-aged will grow in every state and region.

The smallest share of Boomers lives in the Northeast

(percent distribtion of the Baby-Boom generation by region, 2000)

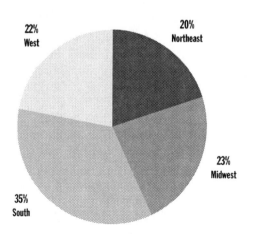

22%
West

20%
Northeast

23%
Midwest

35%
South

Table 7.11 Population Aged 35 to 54 by Region, 2000 Census

(number and percent distribution of total people and people aged 35 to 54 by age and region, 2000; numbers in thousands)

	total	Northeast	Midwest	South	West
TOTAL PEOPLE	**281,422**	**53,594**	**64,393**	**100,237**	**63,198**
Total, aged 35 to 54	**82,827**	**16,191**	**18,953**	**29,242**	**18,440**
Aged 35 to 39	22,707	4,425	5,096	8,065	5,120
Aged 40 to 44	22,442	4,383	5,182	7,882	4,995
Aged 45 to 49	20,092	3,901	4,668	7,046	4,477
Aged 50 to 54	17,586	3,482	4,007	6,249	3,848
PERCENT DISTRIBUTION BY AGE					
TOTAL PEOPLE	**100.0%**	**100.0%**	**100.0%**	**100.0%**	**100.0%**
Total, aged 35 to 54	**29.4**	**30.2**	**29.4**	**29.1**	**29.2**
Aged 35 to 39	8.1	8.3	7.9	8.0	8.1
Aged 40 to 44	8.0	8.2	8.1	7.9	7.9
Aged 45 to 49	7.1	7.3	7.2	7.0	7.1
Aged 50 to 54	6.2	6.5	6.2	6.2	6.1
PERCENT DISTRIBUTION BY REGION					
TOTAL PEOPLE	**100.0%**	**19.0%**	**22.9%**	**35.6%**	**22.5%**
Total, aged 35 to 54	**100.0**	**19.5**	**22.9**	**35.3**	**22.3**
Aged 35 to 39	100.0	19.5	22.4	35.5	22.5
Aged 40 to 44	100.0	19.5	23.1	35.1	22.3
Aged 45 to 49	100.0	19.4	23.2	35.1	22.3
Aged 50 to 54	100.0	19.8	22.8	35.5	21.9

Source: Bureau of the Census, Census 2000 Summary File 2, Internet site http://factfinder.census.gov/servlet/BasicFactsServlet; calculations by New Strategist

Table 7.12 Regional Populations by Generation, 2000 Census

(number and percent distribution of people by generation and region, 2000; numbers in thousands)

	total	Northeast	Midwest	South	West
TOTAL PEOPLE	**281,422**	**53,594**	**64,393**	**100,237**	**63,198**
Post-Millennial (under age 6)	23,141	4,115	5,255	8,238	5,532
Millennial (aged 6 to 23)	72,655	13,059	16,826	25,834	16,936
Generation X (aged 24 to 35)	48,049	8,938	10,547	17,248	11,315
Baby Boom (aged 36 to 54)	**78,310**	**15,303**	**17,958**	**27,635**	**17,415**
Swing (aged 55 to 67)	30,061	5,957	6,863	10,995	6,246
World War II (aged 68 or older)	29,205	6,222	6,944	10,286	5,753
PERCENT DISTRIBUTION BY GENERATION					
TOTAL PEOPLE	**100.0%**	**100.0%**	**100.0%**	**100.0%**	**100.0%**
Post-Millennial (under age 6)	8.2	7.7	8.2	8.2	8.8
Millennial (aged 6 to 23)	25.8	24.4	26.1	25.8	26.8
Generation X (aged 24 to 35)	17.1	16.7	16.4	17.2	17.9
Baby Boom (aged 36 to 54)	**27.8**	**28.6**	**27.9**	**27.6**	**27.6**
Swing (aged 55 to 67)	10.7	11.1	10.7	11.0	9.9
World War II (aged 68 or older)	10.4	11.6	10.8	10.3	9.1
PERCENT DISTRIBUTION BY REGION					
TOTAL PEOPLE	**100.0%**	**19.0%**	**22.9%**	**35.6%**	**22.5%**
Post-Millennial (under age 6)	100.0	17.8	22.7	35.6	23.9
Millennial (aged 6 to 23)	100.0	18.0	23.2	35.6	23.3
Generation X (aged 24 to 35)	100.0	18.6	22.0	35.9	23.5
Baby Boom (aged 36 to 54)	**100.0**	**19.5**	**22.9**	**35.3**	**22.2**
Swing (aged 55 to 67)	100.0	19.8	22.8	36.6	20.8
World War II (aged 68 or older)	100.0	21.3	23.8	35.2	19.7

Source: Bureau of the Census, Census 2000 Summary File 2, Internet site http://factfinder.census.gov/servlet/BasicFactsServlet; calculations by New Strategist

Table 7.13 Population Aged 35 to 54 by State, 2000 Census

(number and percent of people aged 35 to 54 by state, 2000; numbers in thousands)

	number				percent distribution			
	total population	aged 35 to 54			total population	aged 35 to 54		
		total	35–44	45–54		total	35–44	45–54
United States	**281,422**	**82,827**	**45,149**	**37,678**	**100.0%**	**29.4%**	**16.0%**	**13.4%**
Alabama	4,447	1,286	686	600	100.0	28.9	15.4	13.5
Alaska	627	209	114	95	100.0	33.3	18.2	15.1
Arizona	5,131	1,397	769	628	100.0	27.2	15.0	12.2
Arkansas	2,673	748	398	350	100.0	28.0	14.9	13.1
California	33,872	9,817	5,485	4,332	100.0	29.0	16.2	12.8
Colorado	4,301	1,351	737	614	100.0	31.4	17.1	14.3
Connecticut	3,406	1,062	581	481	100.0	31.2	17.1	14.1
Delaware	784	232	128	104	100.0	29.6	16.3	13.3
District of Columbia	572	163	88	75	100.0	28.5	15.3	13.2
Florida	15,982	4,555	2,485	2,070	100.0	28.5	15.5	12.9
Georgia	8,186	2,434	1,354	1,080	100.0	29.7	16.5	13.2
Hawaii	1,212	362	191	171	100.0	29.9	15.8	14.1
Idaho	1,294	363	193	170	100.0	28.1	14.9	13.2
Illinois	12,419	3,611	1,984	1,627	100.0	29.1	16.0	13.1
Indiana	6,080	1,778	961	817	100.0	29.2	15.8	13.4
Iowa	2,926	838	445	393	100.0	28.6	15.2	13.4
Kansas	2,688	775	420	354	100.0	28.8	15.6	13.2
Kentucky	4,042	1,200	643	557	100.0	29.7	15.9	13.8
Louisiana	4,469	1,278	692	586	100.0	28.6	15.5	13.1
Maine	1,275	406	213	193	100.0	31.8	16.7	15.1
Maryland	5,296	1,671	916	755	100.0	31.6	17.3	14.3
Massachusetts	6,349	1,936	1,063	873	100.0	30.5	16.7	13.8
Michigan	9,938	2,966	1,598	1,368	100.0	29.8	16.1	13.8
Minnesota	4,919	1,490	824	666	100.0	30.3	16.8	13.5
Mississippi	2,845	787	425	362	100.0	27.7	15.0	12.7
Missouri	5,595	1,630	888	743	100.0	29.1	15.9	13.3
Montana	902	277	142	135	100.0	30.7	15.7	15.0
Nebraska	1,711	490	264	226	100.0	28.6	15.4	13.2
Nevada	1,998	591	322	269	100.0	29.6	16.1	13.5
New Hampshire	1,236	405	221	184	100.0	32.8	17.9	14.9
New Jersey	8,414	2,594	1,435	1,159	100.0	30.8	17.1	13.8
New Mexico	1,819	528	282	246	100.0	29.0	15.5	13.5
New York	18,976	5,627	3,074	2,553	100.0	29.7	16.2	13.5
North Carolina	8,049	2,372	1,287	1,085	100.0	29.5	16.0	13.5
North Dakota	642	183	98	85	100.0	28.6	15.3	13.3
Ohio	11,353	3,372	1,805	1,566	100.0	29.7	15.9	13.8
Oklahoma	3,451	977	524	454	100.0	28.3	15.2	13.1
Oregon	3,421	1,034	527	507	100.0	30.2	15.4	14.8
Pennsylvania	12,281	3,653	1,948	1,705	100.0	29.7	15.9	13.9

	number				percent distribution			
	total population	aged 35 to 54			total population	aged 35 to 54		
		total	35–44	45–54		total	35–44	45–54
Rhode Island	1,048	312	170	142	100.0%	29.8%	16.2%	13.5%
South Carolina	4,012	1,175	625	550	100.0	29.3	15.6	13.7
South Dakota	755	213	115	98	100.0	28.2	15.3	12.9
Tennessee	5,689	1,689	903	787	100.0	29.7	15.9	13.8
Texas	20,852	5,933	3,322	2,611	100.0	28.5	15.9	12.5
Utah	2,233	537	300	238	100.0	24.1	13.4	10.6
Vermont	609	196	102	94	100.0	32.1	16.7	15.4
Virginia	7,079	2,200	1,201	999	100.0	31.1	17.0	14.1
Washington	5,894	1,821	975	846	100.0	30.9	16.5	14.4
West Virginia	1,808	543	272	271	100.0	30.0	15.1	15.0
Wisconsin	5,364	1,608	876	732	100.0	30.0	16.3	13.7
Wyoming	494	153	79	74	100.0	31.0	16.0	15.0

Source: Bureau of the Census, Census 2000 Summary File 2, Internet site http://factfinder.census.gov/servlet/BasicFactsServlet

Table 7.14 Population Aged 35 to 54 by State, Race, and Hispanic Origin, 2000 Census

(total number of people, number aged 35 to 54, and percent distribution by race and Hispanic origin, by state, 2000)

	total number	total percent	American Indian	Asian	black	Native Hawaiian	white total	white non-Hispanic	other	Hispanic
ALABAMA										
State total	4,447,100	100.0%	1.0%	0.9%	26.3%	0.1%	72.0%	70.3%	0.9%	1.7%
Total 35 to 54	1,285,721	100.0	1.1	0.9	24.5	0.1	73.8	72.5	0.6	1.2
Aged 35 to 39	340,300	100.0	1.1	1.0	25.3	0.1	72.6	71.1	0.8	1.7
Aged 40 to 44	345,212	100.0	1.2	0.9	25.8	0.1	72.4	71.0	0.6	1.3
Aged 45 to 49	315,173	100.0	1.1	0.8	24.9	0.1	73.5	72.2	0.4	1.0
Aged 50 to 54	285,036	100.0	1.1	0.8	21.3	0.1	77.3	76.1	0.3	0.8
ALASKA										
State total	626,932	100.0	19.0	5.2	4.3	0.9	74.0	67.6	2.4	4.1
Total 35 to 54	209,001	100.0	14.2	4.8	3.3	0.6	78.6	74.5	2.0	3.1
Aged 35 to 39	55,723	100.0	16.4	4.9	4.1	0.7	75.4	70.5	2.3	3.9
Aged 40 to 44	58,326	100.0	14.4	4.8	3.4	0.6	78.2	73.9	2.1	3.3
Aged 45 to 49	53,515	100.0	13.0	4.6	2.9	0.5	80.2	76.6	1.8	2.6
Aged 50 to 54	41,437	100.0	12.4	4.6	2.3	0.5	81.3	77.9	1.7	2.4
ARIZONA										
State total	5,130,632	100.0	5.7	2.3	3.6	0.3	77.9	63.8	13.2	25.3
Total 35 to 54	1,396,708	100.0	4.9	2.3	3.4	0.2	80.8	69.7	10.4	20.0
Aged 35 to 39	392,687	100.0	5.5	2.6	3.8	0.2	77.0	63.9	13.2	24.6
Aged 40 to 44	376,117	100.0	5.1	2.4	3.7	0.2	79.9	68.6	10.9	20.7
Aged 45 to 49	331,903	100.0	4.7	2.2	3.2	0.2	82.4	72.0	9.2	18.1
Aged 50 to 54	296,001	100.0	4.2	2.0	2.6	0.2	85.3	76.0	7.4	15.3
ARKANSAS										
State total	2,673,400	100.0	1.4	1.0	16.0	0.1	81.2	78.6	1.8	3.2
Total 35 to 54	747,646	100.0	1.5	0.9	14.6	0.1	82.8	80.8	1.2	2.3
Aged 35 to 39	200,340	100.0	1.5	1.0	15.4	0.1	81.4	79.0	1.7	3.2
Aged 40 to 44	197,787	100.0	1.5	1.0	15.7	0.1	81.6	79.4	1.3	2.5
Aged 45 to 49	181,913	100.0	1.5	0.9	14.9	0.1	82.7	80.9	1.0	1.9
Aged 50 to 54	167,606	100.0	1.6	0.8	11.9	0.1	86.1	84.4	0.8	1.5
CALIFORNIA										
State total	33,871,648	100.0	1.9	12.3	7.4	0.7	63.4	46.7	19.4	32.4
Total 35 to 54	9,816,976	100.0	1.8	12.6	7.1	0.6	66.4	53.1	15.3	25.5
Aged 35 to 39	2,814,743	100.0	1.8	12.4	7.6	0.6	63.1	47.3	18.8	31.1
Aged 40 to 44	2,670,598	100.0	1.9	12.6	7.4	0.6	65.5	51.8	16.1	26.5
Aged 45 to 49	2,331,792	100.0	1.8	12.9	6.9	0.5	67.7	55.5	13.7	22.9
Aged 50 to 54	1,999,843	100.0	1.8	12.4	6.4	0.5	70.9	59.9	11.2	19.5
COLORADO										
State total	4,301,261	100.0	1.9	2.8	4.4	0.2	85.2	74.5	8.5	17.1
Total 35 to 54	1,350,948	100.0	1.7	2.4	3.9	0.2	87.6	79.8	6.2	12.6
Aged 35 to 39	366,092	100.0	1.8	2.8	4.5	0.2	85.1	75.9	7.8	15.4
Aged 40 to 44	370,731	100.0	1.8	2.4	4.1	0.2	87.1	79.4	6.4	12.7
Aged 45 to 49	334,855	100.0	1.7	2.2	3.6	0.2	88.8	81.7	5.3	11.2
Aged 50 to 54	279,270	100.0	1.6	2.0	3.1	0.2	90.1	83.0	4.7	10.6

	total		American Indian	Asian	black	Native Hawaiian	white		other	Hispanic
	number	percent					total	non-Hispanic		
CONNECTICUT										
State total	3,405,565	100.0%	0.7%	2.8%	10.0%	0.1%	83.3%	77.5%	5.5%	9.4%
Total 35 to 54	1,061,856	100.0	0.7	2.6	8.5	0.1	85.8	81.2	4.1	7.2
Aged 35 to 39	290,866	100.0	0.7	3.1	9.7	0.1	82.9	77.4	5.4	9.2
Aged 40 to 44	290,183	100.0	0.7	2.5	8.6	0.1	85.6	80.9	4.2	7.4
Aged 45 to 49	252,754	100.0	0.7	2.4	7.8	0.1	87.2	83.0	3.4	6.2
Aged 50 to 54	228,053	100.0	0.6	2.1	7.6	0.1	88.0	84.2	3.0	5.6
DELAWARE										
State total	783,600	100.0	0.8	2.4	20.1	0.1	75.9	72.5	2.6	4.8
Total 35 to 54	231,600	100.0	0.8	2.4	18.9	0.1	77.2	74.9	1.8	3.3
Aged 35 to 39	64,654	100.0	0.8	2.8	20.5	0.1	74.8	71.9	2.3	4.4
Aged 40 to 44	62,947	100.0	0.8	2.3	19.5	0.1	76.7	74.4	1.8	3.2
Aged 45 to 49	54,775	100.0	0.8	2.2	18.5	0.1	78.0	76.0	1.5	2.8
Aged 50 to 54	49,224	100.0	0.8	2.2	16.5	0.1	80.3	78.4	1.3	2.4
DISTRICT OF COLUMBIA										
District total	572,059	100.0	0.8	3.1	61.3	0.1	32.2	27.8	5.0	7.9
Total 35 to 54	162,987	100.0	1.0	2.7	61.8	0.1	32.5	28.4	4.4	7.0
Aged 35 to 39	45,949	100.0	0.9	3.0	58.5	0.1	34.5	29.3	5.8	9.1
Aged 40 to 44	41,728	100.0	0.9	2.6	64.5	0.1	29.8	25.8	4.7	7.2
Aged 45 to 49	39,397	100.0	1.1	2.7	64.3	0.1	30.4	26.8	3.8	6.2
Aged 50 to 54	35,913	100.0	1.1	2.6	60.2	0.1	35.3	32.1	3.0	5.1
FLORIDA										
State total	15,982,378	100.0	0.7	2.1	15.5	0.2	79.7	65.4	4.4	16.8
Total 35 to 54	4,554,726	100.0	0.8	2.2	14.4	0.1	80.7	66.7	3.9	16.2
Aged 35 to 39	1,261,040	100.0	0.8	2.3	15.7	0.2	78.7	62.4	4.8	19.3
Aged 40 to 44	1,224,207	100.0	0.9	2.3	15.4	0.2	79.5	65.7	4.1	16.3
Aged 45 to 49	1,085,400	100.0	0.9	2.3	14.2	0.1	81.1	68.1	3.5	15.0
Aged 50 to 54	984,079	100.0	0.8	2.1	12.0	0.1	84.1	71.9	2.8	13.7
GEORGIA										
State total	8,186,453	100.0	0.6	2.4	29.2	0.1	66.1	62.6	2.9	5.3
Total 35 to 54	2,433,500	100.0	0.7	2.4	27.4	0.1	68.6	66.1	1.9	3.5
Aged 35 to 39	698,735	100.0	0.7	2.6	29.4	0.1	65.7	62.5	2.7	5.0
Aged 40 to 44	654,773	100.0	0.7	2.5	28.6	0.1	67.3	64.8	2.0	3.7
Aged 45 to 49	573,017	100.0	0.7	2.3	27.2	0.1	69.2	67.1	1.4	2.8
Aged 50 to 54	506,975	100.0	0.7	2.1	23.5	0.1	73.5	71.8	1.0	2.1
HAWAII										
State total	1,211,537	100.0	2.1	58.0	2.8	23.3	39.3	22.9	3.9	7.2
Total 35 to 54	362,156	100.0	1.8	55.3	2.0	18.6	39.7	27.7	3.2	5.3
Aged 35 to 39	95,935	100.0	2.0	54.7	2.9	21.4	39.6	25.6	3.8	6.6
Aged 40 to 44	95,242	100.0	1.9	56.3	2.1	19.3	38.7	26.2	3.4	5.8
Aged 45 to 49	90,404	100.0	1.8	55.4	1.5	17.5	40.0	28.9	2.9	4.6
Aged 50 to 54	80,575	100.0	1.6	54.8	1.2	15.7	40.6	30.7	2.6	3.9

	total		American Indian	Asian	black	Native Hawaiian	white		other	Hispanic
	number	percent					total	non-Hispanic		
IDAHO										
State total	1,293,953	100.0%	2.1%	1.3%	0.6%	0.2%	92.8%	88.1%	5.0%	7.9%
Total 35 to 54	363,216	100.0	2.0	1.2	0.4	0.2	94.0	90.6	3.6	5.6
Aged 35 to 39	94,913	100.0	2.3	1.4	0.6	0.2	92.2	88.0	5.0	7.7
Aged 40 to 44	98,055	100.0	2.0	1.2	0.4	0.2	94.0	90.3	3.8	5.9
Aged 45 to 49	92,172	100.0	2.0	1.2	0.4	0.1	94.7	91.7	3.1	4.7
Aged 50 to 54	78,076	100.0	1.9	1.0	0.3	0.1	95.6	92.9	2.4	3.9
ILLINOIS										
State total	12,419,293	100.0	0.6	3.8	15.6	0.1	75.1	67.8	6.8	12.3
Total 35 to 54	3,610,612	100.0	0.6	3.7	14.2	0.1	77.7	72.2	5.2	9.3
Aged 35 to 39	996,886	100.0	0.6	3.9	14.8	0.1	75.8	69.1	6.4	11.8
Aged 40 to 44	986,984	100.0	0.6	3.6	14.6	0.1	77.2	71.7	5.3	9.6
Aged 45 to 49	873,812	100.0	0.6	3.7	13.9	0.1	78.5	73.7	4.6	8.1
Aged 50 to 54	752,930	100.0	0.6	3.8	13.1	0.1	79.8	75.5	3.9	7.0
INDIANA										
State total	6,080,485	100.0	0.6	1.2	8.8	0.1	88.6	85.8	2.0	3.5
Total 35 to 54	1,777,568	100.0	0.7	1.1	7.8	0.1	89.9	88.0	1.3	2.5
Aged 35 to 39	478,207	100.0	0.7	1.3	8.3	0.1	88.8	86.6	1.8	3.2
Aged 40 to 44	482,496	100.0	0.7	1.0	8.2	0.1	89.4	87.4	1.4	2.6
Aged 45 to 49	437,122	100.0	0.7	0.9	7.6	0.1	90.3	88.6	1.1	2.2
Aged 50 to 54	379,743	100.0	0.7	0.9	6.8	0.1	91.4	89.7	0.9	1.9
IOWA										
State total	2,926,324	100.0	0.6	1.5	2.5	0.1	94.9	92.6	1.6	2.8
Total 35 to 54	837,993	100.0	0.6	1.1	1.9	0.1	95.9	94.5	1.1	1.9
Aged 35 to 39	217,897	100.0	0.6	1.5	2.2	0.1	94.8	92.9	1.6	2.7
Aged 40 to 44	227,302	100.0	0.6	1.1	1.9	0.1	95.9	94.4	1.1	2.0
Aged 45 to 49	212,663	100.0	0.5	1.0	1.7	0.0	96.4	95.2	0.8	1.5
Aged 50 to 54	180,131	100.0	0.5	1.0	1.5	0.0	96.8	95.7	0.7	1.3
KANSAS										
State total	2,688,418	100.0	1.8	2.1	6.3	0.1	87.9	83.1	4.0	7.0
Total 35 to 54	774,498	100.0	1.7	1.8	5.6	0.1	89.4	86.2	2.8	4.9
Aged 35 to 39	207,549	100.0	1.7	2.2	6.4	0.1	87.4	83.4	3.8	6.5
Aged 40 to 44	212,802	100.0	1.7	1.8	6.0	0.1	89.0	85.7	2.9	5.0
Aged 45 to 49	192,679	100.0	1.6	1.7	5.0	0.1	90.5	87.7	2.3	4.1
Aged 50 to 54	161,468	100.0	1.6	1.7	4.6	0.1	91.4	88.7	1.9	3.5
KENTUCKY										
State total	4,041,769	100.0	0.6	0.9	7.7	0.1	91.0	89.3	0.8	1.5
Total 35 to 54	1,199,597	100.0	0.7	0.8	6.9	0.1	91.7	90.5	0.5	1.1
Aged 35 to 39	321,931	100.0	0.6	1.1	7.5	0.1	90.8	89.4	0.7	1.5
Aged 40 to 44	320,734	100.0	0.7	0.8	7.5	0.1	91.2	90.0	0.5	1.1
Aged 45 to 49	293,976	100.0	0.7	0.7	6.8	0.1	92.1	90.9	0.4	0.9
Aged 50 to 54	262,956	100.0	0.7	0.7	5.8	0.1	93.2	92.1	0.3	0.7

| | total | | American | | | Native | white | | | |
	number	percent	Indian	Asian	black	Hawaiian	total	non-Hispanic	other	Hispanic
LOUISIANA										
State total	**4,468,976**	**100.0%**	**1.0%**	**1.4%**	**32.9%**	**0.1%**	**64.8%**	**62.5%**	**1.1%**	**2.4%**
Total 35 to 54	**1,278,237**	**100.0**	**1.0**	**1.4**	**30.0**	**0.1**	**67.6**	**65.5**	**0.9**	**2.3**
Aged 35 to 39	343,128	100.0	1.0	1.5	31.3	0.1	66.0	63.8	1.1	2.6
Aged 40 to 44	348,838	100.0	0.9	1.4	30.7	0.1	66.8	64.8	1.0	2.3
Aged 45 to 49	315,768	100.0	0.9	1.4	30.1	0.1	67.6	65.6	0.8	2.1
Aged 50 to 54	270,503	100.0	1.0	1.3	27.4	0.1	70.4	68.5	0.8	2.0
MAINE										
State total	**1,274,923**	**100.0**	**1.0**	**0.9**	**0.7**	**0.1**	**97.9**	**96.5**	**0.4**	**0.7**
Total 35 to 54	**405,576**	**100.0**	**1.0**	**0.8**	**0.5**	**0.1**	**98.2**	**97.2**	**0.3**	**0.5**
Aged 35 to 39	104,149	100.0	1.1	0.9	0.6	0.1	97.8	96.7	0.4	0.7
Aged 40 to 44	108,831	100.0	1.1	0.8	0.5	0.1	98.1	97.0	0.3	0.6
Aged 45 to 49	101,921	100.0	0.9	0.7	0.4	0.1	98.4	97.5	0.3	0.5
Aged 50 to 54	90,675	100.0	0.8	0.6	0.3	0.1	98.6	97.7	0.2	0.4
MARYLAND										
State total	**5,296,486**	**100.0**	**0.7**	**4.5**	**28.8**	**0.1**	**65.4**	**62.1**	**2.5**	**4.3**
Total 35 to 54	**1,671,188**	**100.0**	**0.8**	**4.4**	**27.6**	**0.1**	**66.7**	**64.1**	**2.0**	**3.5**
Aged 35 to 39	464,788	100.0	0.8	4.7	29.6	0.1	64.0	60.8	2.6	4.5
Aged 40 to 44	451,368	100.0	0.8	4.4	28.2	0.1	66.0	63.3	2.1	3.7
Aged 45 to 49	399,390	100.0	0.8	4.3	26.7	0.1	67.8	65.5	1.8	3.0
Aged 50 to 54	355,642	100.0	0.8	4.1	25.2	0.1	69.9	67.8	1.3	2.4
MASSACHUSETTS										
State total	**6,349,097**	**100.0**	**0.6**	**4.2**	**6.3**	**0.1**	**86.2**	**81.9**	**5.1**	**6.8**
Total 35 to 54	**1,936,348**	**100.0**	**0.6**	**3.5**	**5.5**	**0.1**	**88.2**	**84.9**	**3.8**	**5.1**
Aged 35 to 39	540,593	100.0	0.6	4.2	6.2	0.1	86.1	82.0	4.9	6.6
Aged 40 to 44	522,402	100.0	0.6	3.6	5.7	0.1	87.8	84.5	4.0	5.2
Aged 45 to 49	461,945	100.0	0.6	3.3	5.1	0.1	89.1	86.3	3.3	4.4
Aged 50 to 54	411,408	100.0	0.5	2.8	4.6	0.1	90.5	87.9	2.8	3.8
MICHIGAN										
State total	**9,938,444**	**100.0**	**1.3**	**2.1**	**14.8**	**0.1**	**81.8**	**78.6**	**2.0**	**3.3**
Total 35 to 54	**2,966,312**	**100.0**	**1.2**	**1.8**	**13.1**	**0.1**	**83.8**	**81.5**	**1.4**	**2.3**
Aged 35 to 39	787,367	100.0	1.3	2.3	13.4	0.1	82.7	80.0	1.8	2.9
Aged 40 to 44	811,006	100.0	1.2	1.7	13.3	0.1	83.6	81.4	1.4	2.4
Aged 45 to 49	734,905	100.0	1.2	1.6	13.1	0.1	84.1	82.1	1.3	2.1
Aged 50 to 54	633,034	100.0	1.1	1.6	12.6	0.1	84.8	82.9	1.1	1.8
MINNESOTA										
State total	**4,919,479**	**100.0**	**1.6**	**3.3**	**4.1**	**0.1**	**90.8**	**88.2**	**1.8**	**2.9**
Total 35 to 54	**1,489,878**	**100.0**	**1.4**	**2.2**	**3.1**	**0.1**	**93.1**	**91.5**	**1.1**	**1.8**
Aged 35 to 39	412,490	100.0	1.5	2.8	3.9	0.1	91.3	89.3	1.6	2.6
Aged 40 to 44	411,692	100.0	1.4	2.1	3.3	0.1	92.8	91.2	1.1	1.9
Aged 45 to 49	364,247	100.0	1.3	2.0	2.7	0.1	93.8	92.5	0.9	1.5
Aged 50 to 54	301,449	100.0	1.2	1.9	2.1	0.1	94.8	93.6	0.7	1.2

	total		American			Native	white			
	number	percent	Indian	Asian	black	Hawaiian	total	non-Hispanic	other	Hispanic
MISSISSIPPI										
State total	2,844,658	100.0%	0.7%	0.8%	36.6%	0.1%	61.9%	60.7%	0.7%	1.4%
Total 35 to 54	787,353	100.0	0.7	0.8	33.6	0.1	65.0	63.9	0.5	1.2
Aged 35 to 39	212,309	100.0	0.7	0.9	35.3	0.1	63.0	61.8	0.7	1.5
Aged 40 to 44	213,063	100.0	0.7	0.8	35.5	0.1	63.0	61.9	0.5	1.2
Aged 45 to 49	192,111	100.0	0.7	0.8	33.8	0.1	64.9	63.9	0.4	1.1
Aged 50 to 54	169,870	100.0	0.7	0.7	28.8	0.1	70.0	69.1	0.3	0.9
MISSOURI										
State total	5,595,211	100.0	1.1	1.4	11.7	0.1	86.1	83.8	1.2	2.1
Total 35 to 54	1,630,031	100.0	1.2	1.2	10.5	0.1	87.3	85.5	0.8	1.6
Aged 35 to 39	443,250	100.0	1.1	1.4	11.4	0.1	86.1	84.1	1.1	2.0
Aged 40 to 44	444,319	100.0	1.2	1.2	11.1	0.1	86.7	84.9	0.9	1.7
Aged 45 to 49	395,616	100.0	1.2	1.1	10.2	0.1	87.8	86.1	0.7	1.4
Aged 50 to 54	346,846	100.0	1.1	1.1	9.2	0.1	88.9	87.4	0.5	1.2
MONTANA										
State total	902,195	100.0	7.4	0.8	0.5	0.1	92.2	89.5	0.9	2.0
Total 35 to 54	277,029	100.0	6.0	0.6	0.3	0.1	93.6	91.6	0.7	1.5
Aged 35 to 39	66,580	100.0	7.5	0.7	0.4	0.1	91.9	89.5	0.9	1.9
Aged 40 to 44	75,361	100.0	6.4	0.6	0.3	0.1	93.2	91.1	0.8	1.6
Aged 45 to 49	73,398	100.0	5.3	0.6	0.2	0.1	94.3	92.6	0.6	1.3
Aged 50 to 54	61,690	100.0	4.9	0.5	0.2	0.1	94.8	93.2	0.6	1.2
NEBRASKA										
State total	1,711,263	100.0	1.3	1.6	4.4	0.1	90.8	87.3	3.3	5.5
Total 35 to 54	489,588	100.0	1.1	1.3	3.7	0.1	92.4	90.2	2.2	3.8
Aged 35 to 39	130,027	100.0	1.2	1.5	4.3	0.1	90.7	87.9	3.1	5.2
Aged 40 to 44	133,807	100.0	1.1	1.2	3.9	0.1	92.2	89.8	2.4	4.0
Aged 45 to 49	122,714	100.0	1.0	1.1	3.4	0.1	93.3	91.4	1.8	3.1
Aged 50 to 54	103,040	100.0	0.9	1.2	3.1	0.1	93.9	92.1	1.4	2.6
NEVADA										
State total	1,998,257	100.0	2.1	5.6	7.5	0.8	78.4	65.2	9.7	19.7
Total 35 to 54	591,011	100.0	2.1	5.9	6.8	0.7	80.3	70.7	7.2	14.5
Aged 35 to 39	165,910	100.0	2.2	5.8	7.6	0.8	77.4	65.2	9.6	19.2
Aged 40 to 44	156,051	100.0	2.1	5.9	7.2	0.7	79.4	69.5	7.7	15.1
Aged 45 to 49	140,214	100.0	2.0	6.1	6.5	0.6	81.3	72.8	6.2	12.4
Aged 50 to 54	128,836	100.0	1.9	5.8	5.6	0.6	84.0	76.7	4.6	9.8
NEW HAMPSHIRE										
State total	1,235,786	100.0	0.6	1.6	1.0	0.1	97.0	95.1	0.9	1.7
Total 35 to 54	405,165	100.0	0.7	1.3	0.7	0.1	97.4	96.0	0.6	1.2
Aged 35 to 39	109,654	100.0	0.7	1.6	1.0	0.1	96.8	95.1	0.8	1.6
Aged 40 to 44	111,525	100.0	0.7	1.3	0.7	0.1	97.5	96.1	0.6	1.2
Aged 45 to 49	98,117	100.0	0.7	1.2	0.6	0.1	97.6	96.3	0.5	1.1
Aged 50 to 54	85,869	100.0	0.7	1.0	0.5	0.0	98.0	96.8	0.5	0.8

	total		American Indian	Asian	black	Native Hawaiian	white		other	Hispanic
	number	percent					total	non-Hispanic		
NEW JERSEY										
State total	8,414,350	100.0%	0.6%	6.2%	14.4%	0.1%	74.4%	66.0%	6.9%	13.3%
Total 35 to 54	2,594,004	100.0	0.6	6.4	13.0	0.1	76.1	68.7	6.0	11.6
Aged 35 to 39	727,924	100.0	0.6	7.0	14.3	0.1	73.3	64.5	7.3	14.0
Aged 40 to 44	707,182	100.0	0.6	6.6	13.2	0.1	75.7	68.2	6.2	11.7
Aged 45 to 49	611,357	100.0	0.6	6.2	12.4	0.1	77.5	70.8	5.4	10.4
Aged 50 to 54	547,541	100.0	0.5	5.7	11.9	0.1	79.0	72.7	4.6	9.4
NEW MEXICO										
State total	1,819,046	100.0	10.5	1.5	2.3	0.2	69.9	44.7	19.4	42.1
Total 35 to 54	527,828	100.0	9.0	1.4	2.0	0.2	72.9	50.5	17.5	37.8
Aged 35 to 39	140,378	100.0	10.4	1.6	2.3	0.2	68.0	43.8	20.7	42.7
Aged 40 to 44	141,631	100.0	9.4	1.4	2.1	0.2	71.4	49.1	18.6	38.8
Aged 45 to 49	131,000	100.0	8.2	1.4	2.0	0.2	75.0	53.7	16.0	35.2
Aged 50 to 54	114,819	100.0	7.6	1.3	1.6	0.1	78.1	56.6	14.1	33.4
NEW YORK										
State total	18,976,457	100.0	0.9	6.2	17.0	0.2	70.0	62.0	9.1	15.1
Total 35 to 54	5,627,234	100.0	0.9	6.5	15.9	0.1	71.5	64.4	8.0	13.3
Aged 35 to 39	1,566,083	100.0	0.9	6.9	17.3	0.2	68.5	60.4	9.5	15.6
Aged 40 to 44	1,508,215	100.0	0.9	6.7	16.3	0.1	70.8	63.7	8.2	13.5
Aged 45 to 49	1,341,138	100.0	0.9	6.3	15.2	0.1	72.8	66.3	7.4	12.2
Aged 50 to 54	1,211,798	100.0	0.8	5.9	14.4	0.1	74.8	68.4	6.5	11.3
NORTH CAROLINA										
State total	8,049,313	100.0	1.6	1.7	22.1	0.1	73.1	70.2	2.8	4.7
Total 35 to 54	2,372,270	100.0	1.6	1.5	20.9	0.1	75.1	73.2	1.6	2.9
Aged 35 to 39	655,440	100.0	1.6	1.8	21.8	0.1	73.2	70.6	2.5	4.4
Aged 40 to 44	631,680	100.0	1.6	1.6	21.7	0.1	74.2	72.2	1.8	3.1
Aged 45 to 49	570,411	100.0	1.6	1.4	21.2	0.1	75.3	73.7	1.2	2.1
Aged 50 to 54	514,739	100.0	1.5	1.2	18.6	0.1	78.5	77.2	0.9	1.6
NORTH DAKOTA										
State total	642,200	100.0	5.5	0.8	0.8	0.1	93.4	91.7	0.6	1.2
Total 35 to 54	183,435	100.0	4.3	0.6	0.5	0.1	94.8	93.7	0.4	0.8
Aged 35 to 39	46,991	100.0	5.6	0.9	0.7	0.1	93.0	91.7	0.5	1.1
Aged 40 to 44	51,013	100.0	4.3	0.5	0.6	0.1	94.7	93.7	0.4	0.8
Aged 45 to 49	47,436	100.0	3.6	0.5	0.4	0.1	95.7	94.8	0.4	0.6
Aged 50 to 54	37,995	100.0	3.5	0.7	0.2	0.0	95.8	94.9	0.4	0.7
OHIO										
State total	11,353,140	100.0	0.7	1.4	12.1	0.1	86.1	84.0	1.1	1.9
Total 35 to 54	3,371,700	100.0	0.7	1.3	10.7	0.1	87.3	85.9	0.8	1.5
Aged 35 to 39	883,771	100.0	0.7	1.5	11.5	0.1	86.2	84.5	1.0	1.8
Aged 40 to 44	921,545	100.0	0.7	1.2	11.2	0.1	86.9	85.4	0.9	1.5
Aged 45 to 49	834,831	100.0	0.7	1.2	10.5	0.0	87.7	86.3	0.7	1.3
Aged 50 to 54	731,553	100.0	0.7	1.2	9.5	0.0	88.9	87.6	0.6	1.1

	total		American			Native	white			
	number	percent	Indian	Asian	black	Hawaiian	total	non-Hispanic	other	Hispanic
OKLAHOMA										
State total	3,450,654	100.0%	11.4%	1.7%	8.3%	0.1%	80.3%	74.1%	3.0%	5.2%
Total 35 to 54	977,283	100.0	10.1	1.6	7.3	0.1	82.4	77.6	2.1	3.7
Aged 35 to 39	259,131	100.0	10.7	1.8	8.3	0.1	80.0	74.6	2.9	5.0
Aged 40 to 44	264,391	100.0	10.2	1.5	7.9	0.1	81.7	76.8	2.3	3.9
Aged 45 to 49	240,805	100.0	9.8	1.5	7.0	0.1	83.4	78.9	1.8	3.1
Aged 50 to 54	212,956	100.0	9.5	1.4	6.0	0.1	85.0	80.8	1.4	2.5
OREGON										
State total	3,421,399	100.0	2.5	3.7	2.1	0.5	89.3	83.5	5.2	8.1
Total 35 to 54	1,033,729	100.0	2.4	3.3	1.7	0.3	91.2	87.3	3.3	5.1
Aged 35 to 39	255,751	100.0	2.6	4.1	2.0	0.4	88.5	83.5	5.0	7.6
Aged 40 to 44	270,823	100.0	2.5	3.4	1.9	0.4	90.6	86.5	3.6	5.5
Aged 45 to 49	271,315	100.0	2.3	3.0	1.6	0.3	92.4	89.0	2.6	4.0
Aged 50 to 54	235,840	100.0	2.2	2.6	1.4	0.3	93.5	90.4	2.0	3.2
PENNSYLVANIA										
State total	12,281,054	100.0	0.4	2.0	10.5	0.1	86.3	84.1	1.9	3.2
Total 35 to 54	3,653,108	100.0	0.4	1.8	9.4	0.1	87.7	86.0	1.4	2.5
Aged 35 to 39	951,400	100.0	0.4	2.1	10.4	0.1	86.0	84.0	1.9	3.2
Aged 40 to 44	996,676	100.0	0.4	1.8	9.6	0.1	87.4	85.8	1.5	2.5
Aged 45 to 49	908,650	100.0	0.4	1.7	8.9	0.1	88.4	86.9	1.2	2.1
Aged 50 to 54	796,382	100.0	0.4	1.7	8.3	0.1	89.1	87.8	1.1	1.9
RHODE ISLAND										
State total	1,048,319	100.0	1.0	2.7	5.5	0.2	86.9	81.9	6.6	8.7
Total 35 to 54	312,173	100.0	0.9	2.2	4.5	0.1	89.4	85.7	5.0	6.5
Aged 35 to 39	85,364	100.0	0.9	2.5	5.1	0.2	87.3	82.7	6.4	8.6
Aged 40 to 44	84,946	100.0	0.9	2.3	4.8	0.1	88.8	85.1	5.2	6.6
Aged 45 to 49	75,429	100.0	0.9	2.1	4.5	0.1	90.0	86.7	4.4	5.6
Aged 50 to 54	66,434	100.0	0.8	1.7	3.5	0.1	92.1	89.2	3.5	4.6
SOUTH CAROLINA										
State total	4,012,012	100.0	0.7	1.1	29.9	0.1	68.0	66.1	1.3	2.4
Total 35 to 54	1,175,445	100.0	0.7	1.1	28.3	0.1	69.7	68.4	0.8	1.7
Aged 35 to 39	314,558	100.0	0.7	1.2	29.1	0.1	68.4	66.7	1.2	2.4
Aged 40 to 44	310,566	100.0	0.8	1.1	29.4	0.1	68.6	67.1	0.9	1.8
Aged 45 to 49	287,778	100.0	0.7	1.1	28.8	0.1	69.4	68.3	0.7	1.3
Aged 50 to 54	262,543	100.0	0.7	1.0	25.5	0.1	73.0	72.0	0.5	1.1
SOUTH DAKOTA										
State total	754,844	100.0	9.1	0.8	0.9	0.1	89.9	88.0	0.7	1.4
Total 35 to 54	213,068	100.0	6.7	0.6	0.6	0.1	92.3	91.1	0.5	1.0
Aged 35 to 39	56,587	100.0	8.1	0.8	0.8	0.1	90.4	89.0	0.7	1.4
Aged 40 to 44	58,799	100.0	6.9	0.7	0.6	0.1	92.2	90.9	0.5	1.1
Aged 45 to 49	53,865	100.0	5.8	0.6	0.4	0.0	93.4	92.4	0.4	0.8
Aged 50 to 54	43,817	100.0	5.8	0.5	0.3	0.1	93.7	92.7	0.3	0.7

	total		American Indian	Asian	black	Native Hawaiian	white		other	Hispanic
	number	percent					total	non-Hispanic		
TENNESSEE										
State total	5,689,283	100.0%	0.7%	1.2%	16.8%	0.1%	81.2%	79.2%	1.3%	2.2%
Total 35 to 54	1,689,443	100.0	0.8	1.1	15.3	0.1	82.7	81.3	0.8	1.5
Aged 35 to 39	453,327	100.0	0.7	1.3	16.5	0.1	81.1	79.4	1.2	2.1
Aged 40 to 44	449,200	100.0	0.8	1.2	16.3	0.1	81.6	80.2	0.9	1.6
Aged 45 to 49	412,704	100.0	0.8	1.1	15.4	0.1	82.8	81.5	0.7	1.2
Aged 50 to 54	374,212	100.0	0.8	0.9	12.8	0.1	85.7	84.6	0.5	1.0
TEXAS										
State total	20,851,820	100.0	1.0	3.1	12.0	0.1	73.1	52.4	13.3	32.0
Total 35 to 54	5,933,375	100.0	1.1	3.2	11.7	0.1	75.3	58.0	10.6	26.3
Aged 35 to 39	1,688,883	100.0	1.1	3.4	12.4	0.1	72.3	53.0	12.9	30.5
Aged 40 to 44	1,633,355	100.0	1.1	3.2	12.1	0.1	74.6	57.2	10.9	26.7
Aged 45 to 49	1,416,178	100.0	1.1	3.2	11.5	0.1	76.6	60.2	9.4	24.2
Aged 50 to 54	1,194,959	100.0	1.1	3.0	10.2	0.1	79.2	63.5	8.1	22.4
UTAH										
State total	2,233,169	100.0	1.8	2.2	1.1	1.0	91.1	85.3	5.1	9.0
Total 35 to 54	537,246	100.0	1.7	2.1	0.9	0.7	91.8	87.4	4.2	7.3
Aged 35 to 39	150,695	100.0	2.0	2.3	1.1	0.8	89.9	84.5	5.6	9.6
Aged 40 to 44	148,841	100.0	1.7	2.1	1.0	0.7	91.6	87.2	4.3	7.4
Aged 45 to 49	131,665	100.0	1.5	2.1	0.8	0.6	92.6	89.0	3.6	6.2
Aged 50 to 54	106,045	100.0	1.4	2.0	0.7	0.6	93.6	90.0	2.9	5.4
VERMONT										
State total	608,827	100.0	1.1	1.1	0.7	0.1	97.9	96.2	0.4	0.9
Total 35 to 54	195,721	100.0	1.1	0.8	0.5	0.0	98.3	96.9	0.3	0.7
Aged 35 to 39	49,376	100.0	1.1	0.9	0.6	0.1	98.0	96.5	0.4	0.7
Aged 40 to 44	52,513	100.0	1.1	0.8	0.5	0.0	98.2	96.8	0.4	0.7
Aged 45 to 49	50,107	100.0	1.2	0.7	0.5	0.0	98.3	96.9	0.3	0.7
Aged 50 to 54	43,725	100.0	1.1	0.6	0.3	0.1	98.6	97.3	0.3	0.6
VIRGINIA										
State total	7,078,515	100.0	0.7	4.3	20.4	0.1	73.9	70.2	2.7	4.7
Total 35 to 54	2,199,946	100.0	0.8	4.1	18.9	0.1	75.5	72.6	2.0	3.6
Aged 35 to 39	610,810	100.0	0.8	4.5	20.4	0.1	73.2	69.6	2.8	4.9
Aged 40 to 44	589,880	100.0	0.8	4.2	20.0	0.1	74.2	71.2	2.2	3.9
Aged 45 to 49	526,221	100.0	0.8	4.0	18.7	0.1	76.1	73.6	1.6	3.0
Aged 50 to 54	473,035	100.0	0.7	3.7	15.9	0.1	79.5	77.3	1.2	2.4
WASHINGTON										
State total	5,894,121	100.0	2.7	6.7	4.0	0.7	84.9	78.9	4.9	7.5
Total 35 to 54	1,821,059	100.0	2.4	6.1	3.4	0.6	86.6	82.8	3.2	4.9
Aged 35 to 39	483,950	100.0	2.6	6.8	4.1	0.7	84.3	79.5	4.4	6.7
Aged 40 to 44	491,137	100.0	2.5	6.3	3.7	0.6	86.1	82.0	3.4	5.2
Aged 45 to 49	454,223	100.0	2.4	5.9	3.1	0.5	87.7	84.3	2.7	4.0
Aged 50 to 54	391,749	100.0	2.2	5.5	2.6	0.4	89.1	86.1	2.1	3.3

	total		American			Native	white			
	number	percent	Indian	Asian	black	Hawaiian	total	non-Hispanic	other	Hispanic
WEST VIRGINIA										
State total	1,808,344	100.0%	0.6%	0.7%	3.5%	0.1%	95.9%	94.6%	0.3%	0.7%
Total 35 to 54	542,715	100.0	0.6	0.6	3.1	0.0	96.1	95.1	0.2	0.6
Aged 35 to 39	129,816	100.0	0.6	0.7	3.3	0.1	95.8	94.8	0.2	0.6
Aged 40 to 44	142,433	100.0	0.7	0.5	3.3	0.0	95.9	94.9	0.2	0.6
Aged 45 to 49	141,229	100.0	0.7	0.5	3.3	0.0	96.0	95.0	0.2	0.5
Aged 50 to 54	129,237	100.0	0.7	0.6	2.6	0.0	96.6	95.7	0.2	0.4
WISCONSIN										
State total	5,363,675	100.0	1.3	1.9	6.1	0.1	90.0	87.3	2.0	3.6
Total 35 to 54	1,607,828	100.0	1.1	1.3	4.8	0.1	92.2	90.5	1.2	2.4
Aged 35 to 39	435,255	100.0	1.3	1.6	5.4	0.1	90.8	88.7	1.7	3.1
Aged 40 to 44	440,267	100.0	1.2	1.2	5.0	0.1	92.0	90.2	1.3	2.5
Aged 45 to 49	397,693	100.0	1.1	1.1	4.6	0.1	92.8	91.3	1.1	2.0
Aged 50 to 54	334,613	100.0	1.0	1.0	4.1	0.1	93.6	92.3	0.9	1.7
WYOMING										
State total	493,782	100.0	3.0	0.8	1.0	0.1	93.7	88.9	3.2	6.4
Total 35 to 54	152,844	100.0	2.6	0.7	0.7	0.1	94.8	91.0	2.5	5.0
Aged 35 to 39	36,482	100.0	3.0	0.8	0.9	0.1	93.5	89.3	3.2	6.1
Aged 40 to 44	42,283	100.0	2.7	0.7	0.7	0.1	94.5	90.8	2.7	5.2
Aged 45 to 49	40,701	100.0	2.4	0.7	0.6	0.1	95.3	91.9	2.2	4.4
Aged 50 to 54	33,378	100.0	2.3	0.6	0.5	0.1	95.8	92.2	2.0	4.3

Note: Percentages will not add to 100 because each race includes those who identified themselves as the race alone and those who identified themselves as the race in combination with one or more other races, and because Hispanics may be of any race. Non-Hispanic whites include only those who identified themselves as "white alone" and non-Hispanic. American Indians include Alaska natives. Native Hawaiians include other Pacific Islanders.
Source: Bureau of the Census, Census 2000 Summary File 2, Internet site http://factfinder.census.gov/servlet/BasicFactsServlet; calculations by New Strategist

Spending

■ While most households spent more in 2002 than in 1997, for many—especially older Boomers—the spending increase was devoted to necessities such as health care, property taxes, and insurance.

■ Between 1997 and 2002, householders aged 35 to 44 boosted their spending by 7 percent, after adjusting for inflation. In contrast, those aged 45 to 54 spent 4 percent less.

■ Households headed by people aged 35 to 44 spend 19 percent more than the average household. Spending by householders in the age group is particularly high for items commonly purchased by parents with children under age 18.

■ The 45-to-54 age group spent, on average, only $418 more than the 35-to-44 age group in 2002. The spending gap between the two age groups has been shrinking as the younger age group spends more and the older age group cuts back.

■ As older Boomers filled the 45-to-54 age group during the past few years, they proved themselves to be cautious spenders. Their belt tightening is likely to continue as their financial worries grow with approaching retirement.

The Nation's Biggest Spenders Are Spending Less

Younger Boomers are spending more, but older Boomers are cutting back.

The Baby-Boom generation is at the ages of peak spending. Householders aged 45 to 54 are the biggest spenders, followed by those aged 35 to 44. In 2002, the older age group spent an average of $48,748, 20 percent more than the average household. The younger age group spent a slightly smaller $48,330 in 2002.

Between 1997 and 2002, householders aged 35 to 44 boosted their spending by 7 percent, after adjusting for inflation. In contrast, those aged 45 to 54 spent 4 percent less. While most age groups spent more in 2002 than in 1997, in many cases the spending increase was devoted to necessities such as health care, property taxes, and insurance.

The spending pattern of younger Boomers differed from that of older Boomers on many items between 1997 and 2002. Spending on alcoholic beverages fell 6 percent among householders aged 35 to 44, but rose 16 percent for householders aged 45 to 54. Spending on food away from home (mostly restaurant and carry-out meals) fell 7 percent for the older age group and rose 6 percent for the younger one. Entertainment spending rose 13 percent for householders aged 35 to 44 and fell 5 percent for those aged 45 to 54.

Both age groups spent less on apparel, while health care spending soared. Out-of-pocket costs for health insurance were up 22 percent for 35-to-44-year-olds and an even larger 25 percent for 45-to-54-year-olds, after adjusting for inflation. Spending on gifts for non-household members fell sharply in both age groups. Younger and older Boomers spent more on mortgage interest as homeownership increased, and they spent more on telephone service as cell phones became commonplace.

■ With nondiscretionary items such as health care demanding a larger share of the household budget, economic recovery has been slow for businesses that sell discretionary items.

Older Boomers are spending less

(percent change in average household spending by age of householder, 1997–2002; in 2002 dollars)

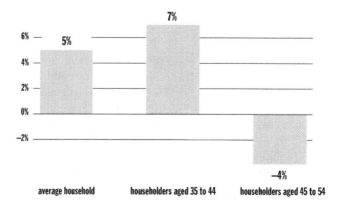

Table 8.1 Average Spending of Householders Aged 35 to 54, 1997 and 2002

(average annual spending of total consumer units and consumer units headed by people aged 35 to 54, 1997 and 2002; percent change, 1997–2002; in 2002 dollars)

	total consumer units			aged 35 to 44			aged 45 to 54		
	2002	1997	percent change 1997–02	2002	1997	percent change 1997–02	2002	1997	percent change 1997–02
Number of consumer units (in 000s)	112,108	105,576	6.2%	24,394	24,560	–0.7%	22,691	19,343	17.3%
Average before-tax income	$49,430	$44,610	10.8	$61,532	$54,512	12.9	$64,974	$61,743	5.2
Average annual spending	40,677	38,904	4.6	48,330	45,154	7.0	48,748	50,546	–3.6
FOOD	**$5,375**	**$5,364**	**0.2%**	**$6,314**	**$6,331**	**–0.3%**	**$6,228**	**$6,735**	**–7.5%**
FOOD AT HOME	3,099	3,218	–3.7	3,601	3,779	–4.7	3,528	3,844	–8.2
Cereals and bakery products	450	506	–11.1	542	603	–10.2	500	612	–18.3
Cereals and cereal products	154	180	–14.4	191	220	–13.2	169	211	–20.0
Bakery products	296	326	–9.3	351	384	–8.7	332	401	–17.2
Meats, poultry, fish, and eggs	798	830	–3.9	918	967	–5.0	929	1,022	–9.1
Beef	231	250	–7.7	271	295	–8.1	273	317	–14.0
Pork	167	175	–4.8	198	194	1.8	188	216	–12.8
Other meats	101	107	–5.8	122	134	–0.9	117	124	–5.7
Poultry	144	162	–11.1	164	194	–15.6	168	192	–12.6
Fish and seafood	121	99	21.7	126	108	16.3	146	131	11.7
Eggs	34	37	–7.8	38	39	–2.8	37	43	–12.9
Dairy products	328	351	–6.5	392	432	–9.3	367	401	–8.5
Fresh milk and cream	127	143	–11.2	153	183	–16.5	136	154	–11.8
Other dairy products	201	208	–3.3	238	250	–4.9	232	247	–6.1
Fruits and vegetables	552	532	3.8	597	587	1.8	627	624	0.6
Fresh fruits	178	168	6.2	191	180	6.2	204	194	4.9
Fresh vegetables	175	160	9.5	185	169	9.7	205	194	5.4
Processed fruits	116	114	1.8	128	131	–2.1	127	131	–2.9
Processed vegetables	83	89	–7.1	93	106	–12.4	91	104	–12.4
Other food at home	970	1,000	–3.0	1,153	1,191	–3.2	1,106	1,184	–6.6
Sugar and other sweets	117	127	–8.1	139	145	–4.3	130	155	–16.3
Fats and oils	85	91	–6.1	93	98	–5.4	99	105	–5.7
Miscellaneous foods	472	450	4.8	572	560	2.2	531	516	2.9
Nonalcoholic beverages	254	274	–7.2	303	329	–7.8	296	326	–9.3
Food prepared by household on trips	41	58	–29.4	46	58	–20.8	49	82	–39.9
Food away from home	2,276	2,146	6.0	2,712	2,551	6.3	2,700	2,892	–6.6
ALCOHOLIC BEVERAGES	**376**	**345**	**8.9**	**367**	**389**	**–5.6**	**465**	**400**	**16.2**
HOUSING	**13,283**	**12,594**	**5.5**	**16,350**	**14,989**	**9.1**	**15,476**	**15,522**	**–0.3**
Shelter	**7,829**	**7,088**	**10.4**	**9,902**	**8,787**	**12.7**	**9,223**	**8,748**	**5.4**
Owned dwellings	5,165	4,397	17.5	7,105	5,859	21.3	6,787	6,241	8.7
Mortgage interest, charges	2,962	2,486	19.1	4,608	3,853	19.6	4,061	3,794	7.0
Property taxes	1,242	1,085	14.5	1,473	1,178	25.1	1,557	1,456	6.9

	total consumer units			aged 35 to 44			aged 45 to 54		
	2002	1997	percent change 1997–02	2002	1997	percent change 1997–02	2002	1997	percent change 1997–02
Maintenance, repairs, insurance, other expenses	$960	$825	16.4%	$1,024	$830	23.3%	$1,169	$991	18.0%
Rented dwellings	2,160	2,216	–2.5	2,351	2,496	–5.8	1,733	1,693	2.4
Other lodging	505	476	6.1	446	431	3.4	704	815	–13.6
Utilities, fuels, and public services	**2,684**	**2,695**	**–0.4**	**3,026**	**3,010**	**0.5**	**3,106**	**3,229**	**–3.8**
Natural gas	330	336	–1.9	369	365	1.0	383	359	6.8
Electricity	981	1,016	–3.4	1,105	1,134	–2.6	1,138	1,245	–8.6
Fuel oil and other fuels	88	121	–27.1	86	121	–28.7	90	164	–45.2
Telephone services	957	904	5.9	1,096	1,029	6.5	1,109	1,064	4.3
Water, other public services	328	320	2.6	369	361	2.2	387	399	–3.0
Household services	**706**	**612**	**15.3**	**1,010**	**809**	**24.9**	**613**	**619**	**–1.0**
Personal services	331	294	12.6	580	503	15.4	165	163	1.1
Other household services	375	318	17.8	430	306	40.5	448	457	–2.0
Housekeeping supplies	**545**	**508**	**7.2**	**589**	**586**	**0.6**	**633**	**617**	**2.6**
Laundry and cleaning supplies	131	130	1.1	152	155	–2.1	147	153	–4.0
Other household products	283	235	20.6	295	278	6.0	333	288	15.5
Postage and stationery	131	144	–9.1	142	152	–6.6	153	175	–12.8
Household furnishings and equipment	**1,518**	**1,689**	**–10.1**	**1,823**	**1,798**	**1.4**	**1,900**	**2,308**	**–17.7**
Household textiles	136	88	54.1	137	89	53.3	152	130	17.3
Furniture	401	432	–7.3	524	480	9.1	453	575	–21.3
Floor coverings	40	87	–54.1	44	64	–30.9	59	78	–24.6
Major appliances	188	189	–0.4	252	202	24.6	219	216	1.6
Small appliances, misc. housewares	100	103	–2.7	88	108	–18.8	124	146	–15.3
Misc. household equipment	652	790	–17.5	776	854	–9.1	893	1,163	–23.2
APPAREL, SERVICES	**1,749**	**1,932**	**–9.5**	**2,101**	**2,304**	**–8.8**	**2,029**	**2,354**	**–13.8**
Men and boys	**409**	**455**	**–10.1**	**562**	**554**	**1.4**	**477**	**615**	**–22.4**
Men, aged 16 or older	319	361	–11.6	383	372	2.9	391	511	–23.4
Boys, aged 2 to 15	90	94	–4.1	179	182	–1.7	85	104	–18.2
Women and girls	**704**	**760**	**–7.3**	**787**	**886**	**–11.2**	**850**	**932**	**–8.8**
Women, aged 16 or older	587	641	–8.5	540	646	–16.4	732	803	–8.9
Girls, aged 2 to 15	117	118	–1.2	247	240	2.8	118	129	–8.2
Children under age 2	**83**	**86**	**–3.5**	**97**	**101**	**–3.5**	**51**	**57**	**–10.5**
Footwear	313	352	–11.1	382	436	–12.3	365	388	–5.9
Other apparel products and services	240	279	–14.1	273	327	–16.6	286	363	–21.2
TRANSPORTATION	**7,759**	**7,215**	**7.5**	**9,400**	**8,105**	**16.0**	**9,173**	**9,759**	**–0.6**
Vehicle purchases	**3,665**	**3,057**	**19.9**	**4,592**	**3,394**	**35.3**	**4,203**	**4,139**	**1.6**
Cars and trucks, new	1,753	1,373	27.7	2,394	1,540	55.5	1,966	2,020	–2.7
Cars and trucks, used	1,842	1,636	12.6	2,115	1,781	18.8	2,109	2,066	2.1
Gasoline and motor oil	**1,235**	**1,227**	**0.7**	**1,473**	**1,446**	**1.9**	**1,495**	**1,598**	**–6.4**

	total consumer units			aged 35 to 44			aged 45 to 54		
	2002	1997	percent change 1997–02	2002	1997	percent change 1997–02	2002	1997	percent change 1997–02
Other vehicle expenses	$2,471	$2,492	-0.8%	$2,935	$2,856	2.8%	$3,055	$3,440	-11.2%
Vehicle finance charges	397	327	21.3	529	390	35.7	479	434	10.5
Maintenance and repairs	697	762	-8.5	843	880	-4.3	848	1,053	-19.4
Vehicle insurance	894	844	6.0	987	935	5.5	1,125	1,111	1.3
Vehicle rental, leases, licenses, other charges	483	560	-13.7	576	650	-11.4	603	844	-28.5
Public transportation	389	439	-11.4	400	408	-1.9	421	583	-27.8
HEALTH CARE	2,350	2,057	14.2	1,980	1,793	10.4	2,550	2,173	17.3
Health insurance	1,168	984	18.7	1,023	836	22.4	1,180	944	25.0
Medical services	590	593	-0.6	556	611	-9.0	768	735	4.5
Drugs	487	358	36.2	303	235	29.1	490	339	44.7
Medical supplies	105	121	-13.0	99	112	-11.4	112	155	-27.9
ENTERTAINMENT	2,079	2,026	2.6	2,685	2,379	12.9	2,565	2,699	-5.0
Fees and admissions	542	526	3.0	743	641	15.9	662	759	-12.7
Television, radio, sound equipment	692	645	7.3	817	750	9.0	806	763	5.6
Pets, toys, and playground equipment	369	365	1.0	463	450	2.8	466	441	5.6
Other entertainment supplies, services	476	491	-3.0	662	537	23.2	631	736	-14.3
PERSONAL CARE PRODUCTS, SERVICES	526	590	-10.8	615	655	-6.1	588	712	-17.4
READING	139	183	-24.1	135	179	-24.5	167	229	-27.1
EDUCATION	752	638	17.9	738	675	9.4	1,208	1,193	1.2
TOBACCO PRODUCTS, SMOKING SUPPLIES	320	295	8.5	376	368	2.3	415	349	19.1
MISCELLANEOUS	792	946	-16.3	841	1,105	-23.9	989	1,236	-20.0
CASH CONTRIBUTIONS	1,277	1,118	14.2	1,247	1,056	18.1	1,571	1,599	-1.7
PERSONAL INSURANCE AND PENSIONS	3,899	3,601	8.3	5,183	4,829	7.3	5,323	5,584	-4.7
Life, other personal insurance	406	424	-4.1	409	428	-4.4	559	675	-17.2
Pensions and Social Security	3,493	3,178	9.9	4,774	4,401	8.5	4,764	4,910	-3.0
PERSONAL TAXES	2,496	3,621	-31.1	3,075	4,780	-35.7	4,051	5,434	-25.4
Federal income taxes	1,843	2,758	-33.2	2,258	3,625	-37.7	3,052	4,198	-27.3
State and local income taxes	506	721	-29.8	680	1,002	-32.2	798	1,051	-24.1
Other taxes	147	144	2.0	136	153	-11.2	201	183	9.7
GIFTS FOR NON-HOUSEHOLD MEMBERS	1,036	1,183	-12.4	868	1,017	-14.6	1,604	1,999	-19.8
Food	82	76	7.9	60	83	-27.4	153	145	5.3
Alcoholic beverages	13	–	–	16	14	–	–	–	–
Housing	259	305	-15.1	231	275	-16.0	387	476	-18.7
Housekeeping supplies	42	41	1.6	41	51	-20.2	51	44	17.0
Household textiles	14	9	56.6	11	7	64.1	14	13	4.4

	total consumer units			aged 35 to 44			aged 45 to 54		
	2002	1997	percent change 1997–02	2002	1997	percent change 1997–02	2002	1997	percent change 1997–02
Appliances and misc. housewares	$24	$30	–20.4%	$17	$20	–15.5%	$28	$47	–40.3%
Major appliances	8	7	19.3	7	3	108.8	9	11	–19.5
Small appliances and miscellaneous housewares	16	24	–31.8	9	17	–46.3	20	35	–42.3
Misc. household equipment	65	74	–11.9	65	67	–3.0	94	117	–19.9
Other housing	114	151	–24.4	98	129	–23.7	199	256	–22.2
Apparel and services	**237**	**282**	**–15.8**	**208**	**256**	**–18.7**	**257**	**424**	**–39.3**
Males, aged 2 or older	64	68	–6.1	63	49	28.1	69	106	–35.0
Females, aged 2 or older	82	91	–9.4	56	93	–39.6	89	123	–27.6
Children under age 2	40	37	8.5	45	37	22.1	40	44	–8.2
Other apparel products and services	52	86	–39.6	44	77	–42.9	59	152	–61.2
Jewelry and watches	24	55	–56.2	20	45	–55.3	23	107	–78.6
All other apparel products and services	28	32	–13.6	23	32	–29.0	36	45	–19.5
Transportation	**44**	**64**	**–30.9**	**45**	**32**	**38.9**	**80**	**94**	**–14.8**
Health Care	**33**	**34**	**–1.6**	**21**	**21**	**–1.1**	**55**	**54**	**2.6**
Entertainment	**78**	**111**	**–29.5**	**86**	**94**	**–8.4**	**106**	**164**	**–35.5**
Toys, games, hobbies, and tricycles	30	46	–34.5	29	39	–25.8	36	49	–26.8
Other entertainment	48	65	–25.9	57	55	4.1	69	115	–40.0
Personal care products and services	**21**	–	–	**27**	–	–	**26**	–	–
Reading	**1**	–	–	**1**	–	–	**1**	–	–
Education	**184**	**173**	**6.2**	**108**	**113**	**–4.3**	**415**	**498**	**–16.7**
All other gifts	**84**	**140**	**–39.9**	**67**	**142**	**–52.8**	**112**	**144**	**–22.3**

Note: The Bureau of Labor Statistics uses consumer unit rather than household as the sampling unit in the Consumer Expenditure Survey. For the definition of consumer unit, see the glossary. Spending on gifts is included in the preceding product and service categories. (–) means sample is too small to make a reliable estimate or data are not available.
Source: Bureau of Labor Statistics, 1997 and 2002 Consumer Expenditure Surveys, Internet site http://www.bls.gov/cex/; calculations by New Strategist

Householders Aged 35 to 44 Spend More than Average

Most households in the age group include children, which accounts for their above-average spending.

Households headed by people aged 35 to 44 spend 19 percent more than the average household, $48,330 versus $40,677 in 2002. Spending by householders in the age group is particularly high for items commonly purchased by parents with children under age 18. Householders aged 35 to 44 spend 22 percent more than the average household on milk, 95 percent more on day care centers, 36 percent more on dinners at fast-food restaurants, twice the average on children's clothing, 77 percent more on video games, 44 percent more on toys, 29 percent more on computer information services, and 22 percent more on cell phone service.

The age group spends less than the average household on some surprising items. Spending on postage, for example, is 3 percent below average (reflecting their preference for e-mailing over letter writing). Householders in the age group spend 8 percent less than average on women's clothing. They spend only 13 percent more than average on new cars, but 60 percent more than average on new trucks.

■ The spending of 35-to-44-year-olds reveals not only their lifestage needs, but also the preferences of tech-savvy Boomers for computers and cell phones.

Householders aged 35 to 44 spend more than average on computers and cell phones

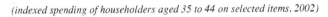

(indexed spending of householders aged 35 to 44 on selected items, 2002)

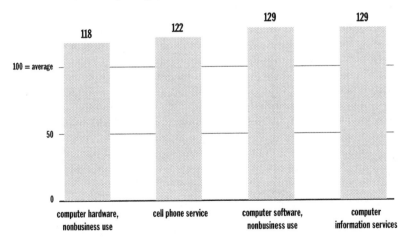

Table 8.2 Average and Indexed Spending of Householders Aged 35 to 44, 2002

(average annual spending of total consumer units (CUs) and average annual and indexed spending of consumer units headed by 35-to-44-year-olds, 2002)

	total consumer units	CUs headed by 35-to-44-year-olds average spending	CUs headed by 35-to-44-year-olds indexed spending
Number of consumer units (in 000s)	112,108	24,394	–
Average before-tax income	$49,430.00	$61,532.00	124
Average annual spending	40,676.60	48,330.48	119
FOOD	**$5,374.80**	**$6,313.58**	**117**
FOOD AT HOME	3,098.52	3,601.44	116
Cereals and bakery products	**450.13**	**542.20**	**120**
Cereals and cereal products	154.07	191.07	124
Flour	8.65	10.43	121
Prepared flour mixes	12.40	15.09	122
Ready-to-eat and cooked cereals	87.66	109.94	125
Rice	17.82	20.52	115
Pasta, cornmeal, and other cereal products	27.54	35.09	127
Bakery products	296.06	351.13	119
Bread	83.83	95.06	113
White bread	35.21	42.40	120
Bread, other than white	48.62	52.66	108
Crackers and cookies	70.67	87.55	124
Cookies	46.31	58.71	127
Crackers	24.36	28.84	118
Frozen and refrigerated bakery products	25.64	34.47	134
Other bakery products	115.92	134.05	116
Biscuits and rolls	41.04	48.87	119
Cakes and cupcakes	35.73	41.34	116
Bread and cracker products	3.50	3.51	100
Sweetrolls, coffee cakes, doughnuts	25.84	32.30	125
Pies, tarts, turnovers	9.82	8.02	82
Meats, poultry, fish, and eggs	**798.42**	**918.33**	**115**
Beef	231.17	270.97	117
Ground beef	86.29	103.14	120
Roast	40.99	48.90	119
Chuck roast	11.71	13.13	112
Round roast	10.23	13.32	130
Other roast	19.05	22.45	118
Steak	84.47	97.02	115
Round steak	13.29	14.25	107
Sirloin steak	26.62	29.50	111
Other steak	44.56	53.26	120
Pork	167.34	197.85	118
Bacon	28.45	33.69	118
Pork chops	38.43	46.04	120
Ham	37.16	41.55	112
Ham, not canned	35.66	39.58	111
Canned ham	1.50	1.96	131

	total consumer units	CUs headed by 35-to-44-year-olds	
		average spending	indexed spending
Sausage	$26.17	$32.79	125
Other pork	37.13	43.78	118
Other meats	101.08	121.81	121
Frankfurters	20.95	27.75	132
Lunch meats (cold cuts)	68.99	85.17	123
Bologna, liverwurst, salami	21.11	25.83	122
Lamb, organ meats, and others	11.14	8.90	80
Lamb and organ meats	7.99	7.51	94
Mutton, goat, and game	3.15	1.38	44
Poultry	144.13	164.14	114
Fresh and frozen chicken	113.25	131.29	116
Fresh and frozen whole chicken	32.08	34.89	109
Fresh and frozen chicken parts	81.17	96.41	119
Other poultry	30.88	32.84	106
Fish and seafood	120.97	125.71	104
Canned fish and seafood	16.13	16.69	103
Fresh fish and shellfish	69.31	66.56	96
Frozen fish and shellfish	35.53	42.46	120
Eggs	33.75	37.85	112
Dairy products	**328.34**	**391.66**	**119**
Fresh milk and cream	127.15	153.21	120
Fresh milk, all types	114.63	139.97	122
Cream	12.52	13.24	106
Other dairy products	201.19	238.45	119
Butter	18.48	20.60	111
Cheese	95.64	111.55	117
Ice cream and related products	58.74	72.27	123
Miscellaneous dairy products	28.33	34.04	120
Fruits and vegetables	**552.01**	**596.57**	**108**
Fresh fruits	178.20	190.56	107
Apples	32.59	38.01	117
Bananas	31.24	32.38	104
Oranges	20.34	21.07	104
Citrus fruits, excl. oranges	14.29	15.85	111
Other fresh fruits	79.74	83.25	104
Fresh vegetables	174.88	184.83	106
Potatoes	33.35	35.73	107
Lettuce	22.22	23.55	106
Tomatoes	33.71	35.13	104
Other fresh vegetables	85.60	90.42	106
Processed fruits	115.50	128.34	111
Frozen fruits and fruit juices	12.45	13.54	109
Frozen orange juice	6.31	7.50	119
Frozen fruits	2.79	2.19	78
Frozen fruit juices, excl. orange	3.35	3.85	115
Canned fruits	15.06	15.36	102
Dried fruits	6.06	5.19	86
Fresh fruit juice	22.20	22.74	102
Canned and bottled fruit juice	59.74	71.51	120

	total consumer units	CUs headed by 35-to-44-year-olds	
		average spending	indexed spending
Processed vegetables	$83.43	$92.84	111
Frozen vegetables	27.85	31.19	112
Canned and dried vegetables and juices	55.58	61.65	111
Canned beans	12.47	15.10	121
Canned corn	7.34	8.97	122
Canned miscellaneous vegetables	17.85	18.63	104
Dried peas	0.36	0.31	86
Dried beans	2.55	2.50	98
Dried miscellaneous vegetables	7.38	7.81	106
Dried processed vegetables	0.34	0.37	109
Frozen vegetable juices	0.06	0.13	217
Fresh and canned vegetable juices	7.23	7.83	108
Sugar and other sweets	**117.39**	**138.80**	**118**
Candy and chewing gum	75.44	90.09	119
Sugar	15.56	17.46	112
Artificial sweeteners	4.33	4.59	106
Jams, preserves, other sweets	22.06	26.66	121
Fats and oils	**85.16**	**92.79**	**109**
Margarine	9.86	9.83	100
Fats and oils	26.08	29.45	113
Salad dressings	27.01	30.53	113
Nondairy cream and imitation milk	9.33	9.33	100
Peanut butter	12.89	13.65	106
Miscellaneous foods	**471.92**	**571.58**	**121**
Frozen prepared foods	98.09	126.43	129
Frozen meals	29.88	32.02	107
Other frozen prepared foods	68.22	94.41	138
Canned and packaged soups	35.82	39.06	109
Potato chips, nuts, and other snacks	100.53	127.06	126
Potato chips and other snacks	76.37	104.44	137
Nuts	24.16	22.62	94
Condiments and seasonings	86.81	100.70	116
Salt, spices, and other seasonings	21.14	25.15	119
Olives, pickles, relishes	9.70	11.28	116
Sauces and gravies	37.78	43.90	116
Baking needs and miscellaneous products	18.19	20.37	112
Other canned/packaged prepared foods	150.67	178.33	118
Prepared salads	21.46	24.08	112
Prepared desserts	10.32	13.45	130
Baby food	31.57	33.87	107
Miscellaneous prepared foods	87.24	106.60	122
Nonalcoholic beverages	253.94	303.16	119
Cola	81.11	99.86	123
Other carbonated drinks	43.93	52.53	120
Coffee	41.59	43.62	105
Roasted coffee	27.38	29.89	109
Instant and freeze-dried coffee	14.21	13.73	97
Noncarbonated fruit-flavored drinks	18.95	27.30	144

	total consumer units	CUs headed by 35-to-44-year-olds	
		average spending	indexed spending
Tea	$15.86	$18.02	114
Nonalcoholic beer	0.64	0.98	153
Other nonalcoholic beverages and ice	51.85	60.85	117
Food prepared by CU on trips	41.20	46.35	113
FOOD AWAY FROM HOME	**2,276.29**	**2,712.13**	**119**
Meals at restaurants, carry-outs, other	**1,866.42**	**2,225.31**	**119**
Lunch	685.79	863.61	126
• At fast food, take-out, delivery, concession stands, buffet, and cafeteria (other than employer and school cafeteria)	377.71	505.45	134
• At full-service restaurants	224.82	212.35	94
• At vending machines, mobile vendors	5.50	9.17	167
• At employer and school cafeterias	77.76	136.64	176
Dinner	736.54	827.67	112
• At fast food, take-out, delivery, concession stands, buffet, and cafeteria (other than employer and school cafeteria)	213.33	289.37	136
• At full-service restaurants	518.02	532.04	103
• At vending machines, mobile vendors	1.87	2.95	158
• At employer and school cafeterias	3.32	3.31	100
Snacks and nonalcoholic beverages	262.67	342.30	130
• At fast food, take-out, delivery, concession stands, buffet, and cafeteria (other than employer and school cafeteria)	185.69	242.55	131
• At full-service restaurants	30.17	30.28	100
• At vending machines, mobile vendors	36.71	53.08	145
• At employer and school cafeterias	10.11	16.39	162
Breakfast and brunch	181.42	191.74	106
• At fast food, take-out, delivery, concession stands, buffet, and cafeteria (other than employer and school cafeteria)	87.83	105.75	120
• At full-service restaurants	87.08	77.98	90
• At vending machines, mobile vendors	1.40	1.08	77
• At employer and school cafeterias	5.11	6.94	136
Board (including at school)	**46.54**	**31.31**	**67**
Catered affairs	**69.00**	**56.73**	**82**
Food on trips	**211.49**	**232.03**	**110**
School lunches	**60.00**	**142.04**	**237**
Meals as pay	**22.86**	**24.71**	**108**
ALCOHOLIC BEVERAGES	**$375.95**	**$366.91**	**98**
At home	**228.08**	**221.68**	**97**
Beer and ale	112.34	125.07	111
Whiskey	13.90	12.42	89
Wine	77.75	58.55	75
Other alcoholic beverages	24.09	25.65	106

	total consumer units	CUs headed by 35-to-44-year-olds	
		average spending	indexed spending
Away from home	**$147.87**	**$145.23**	**98**
Beer and ale	52.86	53.57	101
• At fast food, take-out, delivery, concession stands, buffet, and cafeteria	7.99	6.79	85
• At full-service restaurants	41.95	39.06	93
• At vending machines, mobile vendors	0.32	0.14	44
• At catered affairs	2.59	7.58	293
Wine	25.85	22.70	88
• At fast food, take-out, delivery, concession stands, buffet and cafeteria	4.41	4.13	94
• At full-service restaurants	20.36	17.77	87
• At catered affairs	1.09	0.80	73
Other alcoholic beverages	69.16	68.96	100
• At fast food, take-out, delivery, concession stands, buffet, and cafeteria	3.50	3.16	90
• At full-service restaurants	28.94	26.26	91
• At catered affairs	3.94	3.34	85
Alcoholic beverages purchased on trips	32.78	36.20	110
HOUSING	**$13,283.08**	**$16,349.51**	**123**
SHELTER	**7,829.41**	**9,902.03**	**126**
Owned dwellings*	**5,164.96**	**7,105.47**	**138**
Mortgage interest and charges	2,962.16	4,608.18	156
Mortgage interest	2,811.49	4,428.51	158
Interest paid, home equity loan	88.61	116.04	131
Interest paid, home equity line of credit	61.88	63.52	103
Property taxes	1,242.36	1,473.22	119
Maintenance, repairs, insurance, other expenses	960.43	1,024.08	107
Homeowner's insurance	283.30	294.53	104
Ground rent	40.96	34.19	83
Maintenance and repair services	519.60	546.76	105
Painting and papering	55.58	62.32	112
Plumbing and water heating	46.63	46.63	100
Heat, air conditioning, electrical work	86.28	78.51	91
Roofing and gutters	71.20	77.93	109
Other repair and maintenance services	214.77	240.95	112
Repair, replacement of hard-surface flooring	43.54	38.92	89
Repair of built-in appliances	1.62	1.50	93
Maintenance and repair materials	83.75	119.20	142
Paints, wallpaper, and supplies	14.71	21.82	148
Tools, equipment for painting, wallpapering	1.58	2.34	148
Plumbing supplies and equipment	5.62	6.25	111
Electrical supplies, heating, cooling equip.	3.46	2.67	77
Hard-surface flooring, repair and replacement	8.72	14.56	167
Roofing and gutters	5.29	7.32	138
Plaster, paneling, siding, windows, doors, screens, awnings	13.92	14.42	104
Patio, walk, fence, driveway, masonry, brick, and stucco materials	1.29	2.25	174

	total consumer units	CUs headed by 35-to-44-year-olds	
		average spending	indexed spending
Landscape maintenance	$4.73	$7.43	157
Miscellaneous supplies and equipment	24.43	40.15	164
Insulation, other maintenance, repair	13.15	23.35	178
Finish basement, remodel rooms, build patios, walks, etc.	11.28	16.80	149
Property management and security	27.64	25.23	91
Property management	21.94	19.45	89
Management and upkeep services for security	5.71	5.78	101
Parking	5.17	4.17	81
Rented dwellings	**2,159.89**	**2,350.84**	**109**
Rent	2,104.66	2,297.90	109
Rent as pay	27.17	28.25	104
Maintenance, insurance, and other expenses	28.06	24.69	88
Tenant's insurance	8.90	9.40	106
Maintenance and repair services	11.16	7.42	66
Repair and maintenance services	10.58	6.96	66
Repair, replacement of hard-surface flooring	0.51	0.42	82
Repair of built-in appliances	0.07	0.04	57
Maintenance and repair materials	8.00	7.87	98
Paint, wallpaper, and supplies	1.01	1.17	116
Painting and wallpapering tools	0.11	0.13	118
Plastering, paneling, roofing, gutters, etc.	0.90	1.04	116
Plumbing supplies and equipment	0.80	1.21	151
Electrical supplies, heating, cooling equip.	0.30	0.53	177
Miscellaneous supplies and equipment	3.67	3.21	87
Insulation, other maintenance and repair	1.09	0.82	75
Materials for additions, finishing basements, remodeling rooms	2.43	2.33	96
Construction materials for jobs not started	0.15	0.06	40
Hard-surface flooring	0.73	0.30	41
Landscape maintenance	0.49	0.28	57
Other lodging	**504.56**	**445.72**	**88**
Owned vacation homes	171.55	137.67	80
Mortgage interest and charges	71.98	76.82	107
Property taxes	63.76	38.58	61
Maintenance, insurance and other expenses	35.81	22.28	62
Homeowner's insurance	9.70	9.65	99
Ground rent	2.93	0.62	21
Maintenance and repair services	16.76	8.37	50
Maintenance and repair materials	2.07	2.16	104
Property management and security	3.60	1.07	30
Property management	2.50	0.95	38
Management, upkeep services for security	1.10	0.12	11
Parking	0.76	0.41	54
Housing while attending school	80.14	31.81	40
Lodging on trips	252.87	276.23	109

	total consumer units	CUs headed by 35-to-44-year-olds	
		average spending	indexed spending
UTILITIES, FUELS, PUBLIC SERVICES	$2,684.32	$3,025.84	113
Natural gas	329.75	369.38	112
Natural gas (renter)	60.32	73.95	123
Natural gas (owner)	266.79	293.73	110
Natural gas (vacation)	2.54	1.70	67
Electricity	981.09	1,105.26	113
Electricity (renter)	223.26	270.64	121
Electricity (owner)	750.48	830.36	111
Electricity (vacation)	6.32	3.00	47
Fuel oil and other fuels	88.41	86.14	97
Fuel oil	45.98	47.75	104
Fuel oil (renter)	4.64	7.80	168
Fuel oil (owner)	40.98	39.85	97
Fuel oil (vacation)	0.36	0.10	28
Coal	0.07	0.09	129
Bottled/tank gas	35.27	32.60	92
Gas (renter)	5.09	3.64	72
Gas (owner)	27.19	26.12	96
Gas (vacation)	2.98	2.84	95
Wood and other fuels	7.09	5.70	80
Wood and other fuels (renter)	1.32	1.17	89
Wood and other fuels (owner)	5.68	4.54	80
Telephone services	956.74	1,095.80	115
Residential telephone and pay phones	641.00	712.52	111
Cellular phone service	293.76	358.45	122
Pager service	1.71	1.62	95
Phone cards	20.28	23.21	114
Water and other public services	328.33	369.25	112
Water and sewerage maintenance	237.16	272.73	115
Water and sewerage maintenance (renter)	32.76	43.20	132
Water and sewerage maintenance (owner)	201.79	228.21	113
Water and sewerage maintenance (vacation)	2.36	1.33	56
Trash and garbage collection	89.05	94.56	106
Trash and garbage collection (renter)	9.89	12.28	124
Trash and garbage collection (owner)	76.61	81.45	106
Trash and garbage collection (vacation)	2.53	0.82	32
Septic tank cleaning	2.12	1.96	92
HOUSEHOLD SERVICES	705.71	1,010.38	143
Personal services	331.02	579.88	175
Babysitting, child care in your own home	35.91	82.39	229
Babysitting, child care in someone else's home	27.48	58.09	211
Care for elderly, invalids, handicapped, etc.	50.07	27.18	54
Adult day care centers	6.81	0.30	4
Day care centers, nurseries, and preschools	210.74	411.92	195
Other household services	374.70	430.50	115
Housekeeping services	79.90	96.20	120
Gardening, lawn care service	72.38	64.74	89
Water softening service	3.15	4.19	133

	total consumer units	CUs headed by 35-to-44-year-olds	
		average spending	indexed spending
Nonclothing laundry, dry cleaning, sent out	$1.72	$1.46	85
Nonclothing laundry, dry cleaning, coin-operated	4.13	4.43	107
Termite/pest control services	13.25	11.51	87
Home security system service fee	17.40	20.73	119
Other home services	15.06	11.64	77
Termite/pest control products	0.68	0.65	96
Moving, storage, and freight express	33.13	49.72	150
Appliance repair, including service center	10.86	9.79	90
Reupholstering and furniture repair	7.40	7.20	97
Repairs/rentals of lawn/garden equipment, hand/power tools, etc.	3.62	3.65	101
Appliance rental	1.07	1.77	165
Rental of office equipment, nonbusiness use	0.41	1.01	246
Repair of misc. household equip., furnishings	0.62	0.57	92
Repair of computer systems, nonbusiness use	2.53	3.09	122
Computer information services	107.29	138.15	129
HOUSEKEEPING SUPPLIES	**545.28**	**588.74**	**108**
Laundry and cleaning supplies	**130.57**	**152.11**	**116**
Soaps and detergents	72.89	86.49	119
Other laundry cleaning products	57.68	65.62	114
Other household products	**283.28**	**294.62**	**104**
Cleansing and toilet tissue, paper towels, and napkins	76.46	88.27	115
Miscellaneous household products	96.81	119.34	123
Lawn and garden supplies	110.01	87.02	79
Postage and stationery	**131.44**	**142.00**	**108**
Stationery, stationery supplies, giftwrap	60.20	74.05	123
Postage	69.12	67.05	97
Delivery services	2.12	0.90	42
HOUSEHOLD FURNISHINGS, EQUIPMENT	**1,518.36**	**1,822.52**	**120**
Household textiles	**135.52**	**137.34**	**101**
Bathroom linens	22.35	25.03	112
Bedroom linens	65.98	61.91	94
Kitchen and dining room linens	10.11	12.64	125
Curtains and draperies	16.65	20.98	126
Slipcovers and decorative pillows	7.40	2.43	33
Sewing materials for household items	11.44	12.27	107
Other linens	1.59	2.09	131
Furniture	**401.28**	**523.70**	**131**
Mattresses and springs	52.91	65.01	123
Other bedroom furniture	68.33	100.54	147
Sofas	85.33	114.43	134
Living room chairs	39.21	34.27	87
Living room tables	18.03	20.62	114
Kitchen and dining room furniture	61.28	88.11	144
Infants' furniture	6.46	9.58	148
Outdoor furniture	16.79	24.81	148
Wall units, cabinets, and other furniture	52.94	66.32	125

	total consumer units	CUs headed by 35-to-44-year-olds	
		average spending	indexed spending
Floor coverings	**$40.49**	**$44.20**	**109**
Wall-to-wall carpeting (renter)	0.65	0.94	145
Wall-to-wall carpet (replacement) (owner)	21.04	18.82	89
Floor coverings, nonpermanent	18.79	24.44	130
Major appliances	**188.47**	**252.35**	**134**
Dishwashers (built-in), garbage disposals, range hoods (renter)	1.24	2.51	202
Dishwashers (built-in), garbage disposals, range hoods (owner)	15.28	21.53	141
Refrigerators and freezers (renter)	5.58	6.72	120
Refrigerators and freezers (owner)	46.50	62.80	135
Washing machines (renter)	4.42	4.16	94
Washing machines (owner)	17.88	24.37	136
Clothes dryers (renter)	3.17	5.07	160
Clothes dryers (owner)	13.88	19.39	140
Cooking stoves, ovens (renter)	2.86	6.22	217
Cooking stoves, ovens (owner)	28.09	43.23	154
Microwave ovens (renter)	2.14	2.39	112
Microwave ovens (owner)	8.36	9.77	117
Portable dishwasher (renter)	0.25	0.08	32
Portable dishwasher (owner)	0.51	2.05	402
Window air conditioners (renter)	1.83	1.83	100
Window air conditioners (owner)	6.07	7.83	129
Electric floor-cleaning equipment	22.80	25.04	110
Sewing machines	4.79	5.52	115
Miscellaneous household appliances	**2.81**	**1.83**	**65**
Small appliances and misc. housewares	100.43	88.46	88
Housewares	77.55	63.36	82
Plastic dinnerware	1.57	1.94	124
China and other dinnerware	14.51	7.87	54
Flatware	3.79	4.30	113
Glassware	6.51	6.68	103
Silver serving pieces	4.05	5.51	136
Other serving pieces	1.44	1.29	90
Nonelectric cookware	24.25	15.54	64
Tableware, nonelectric kitchenware	21.44	20.24	94
Small appliances	22.89	25.10	110
Small electric kitchen appliances	17.18	18.21	106
Portable heating and cooling equipment	5.70	6.89	121
Miscellaneous household equipment	**652.17**	**776.47**	**119**
Window coverings	13.91	13.13	94
Infants' equipment	12.96	16.67	129
Laundry and cleaning equipment	15.15	18.50	122
Outdoor equipment	31.52	50.22	159
Clocks	5.87	11.26	192
Lamps and lighting fixtures	11.74	14.84	126
Other household decorative items	144.94	157.14	108
Telephones and accessories	32.73	27.26	83
Lawn and garden equipment	48.16	81.75	170

	total consumer units	CUs headed by 35-to-44-year-olds	
		average spending	indexed spending
Power tools	$33.27	$17.93	54
Office furniture for home use	10.57	12.41	117
Hand tools	8.05	10.23	127
Indoor plants and fresh flowers	49.78	50.36	101
Closet and storage items	9.98	16.55	166
Rental of furniture	4.60	6.89	150
Luggage	5.98	7.26	121
Computers and computer hardware, nonbusiness use	138.58	163.45	118
Computer software and accessories, nonbusiness use	17.67	22.76	129
Telephone answering devices	1.08	1.31	121
Calculators	1.44	2.00	139
Business equipment for home use	0.97	0.25	26
Other hardware	12.85	22.74	177
Smoke alarms (owner)	1.10	1.78	162
Smoke alarms (renter)	0.39	1.60	410
Other household appliances (owner)	8.00	6.18	77
Other household appliances (renter)	1.23	2.89	235
Misc. household equipment and parts	29.62	39.12	132
APPAREL AND SERVICES	**$1,749.22**	**$2,100.89**	**120**
Men's apparel	**319.48**	**382.72**	**120**
Suits	32.96	38.73	118
Sport coats and tailored jackets	10.65	10.00	94
Coats and jackets	33.86	43.02	127
Underwear	15.27	21.16	139
Hosiery	12.22	18.14	148
Nightwear	2.98	3.77	127
Accessories	22.41	24.63	110
Sweaters and vests	15.68	17.05	109
Active sportswear	15.13	16.67	110
Shirts	78.89	95.35	121
Pants	57.64	67.69	117
Shorts and shorts sets	12.22	14.77	121
Uniforms	3.21	3.77	117
Costumes	6.35	7.96	125
Boys' (aged 2 to 15) apparel	**89.98**	**179.14**	**199**
Coats and jackets	6.38	11.69	183
Sweaters	3.65	7.29	200
Shirts	19.50	41.07	211
Underwear	5.02	11.29	225
Nightwear	2.59	4.09	158
Hosiery	4.21	9.96	237
Accessories	4.12	6.57	159
Suits, sport coats, and vests	2.37	3.45	146
Pants	22.58	43.04	191
Shorts and shorts sets	8.66	17.05	197
Uniforms	3.35	7.50	224
Active sportswear	3.84	7.56	197
Costumes	3.72	8.58	231

	total consumer units	CUs headed by 35-to-44-year-olds average spending	CUs headed by 35-to-44-year-olds indexed spending
Women's apparel	**$586.91**	**$540.45**	**92**
Coats and jackets	50.06	32.35	65
Dresses	56.40	38.73	69
Sport coats and tailored jackets	6.48	6.78	105
Sweaters and vests	50.47	55.20	109
Shirts, blouses, and tops	103.24	82.74	80
Skirts	17.48	20.17	115
Pants	96.29	89.05	92
Shorts and shorts sets	16.09	17.21	107
Active sportswear	30.07	28.68	95
Nightwear	27.63	32.20	117
Undergarments	33.55	35.37	105
Hosiery	21.22	22.99	108
Suits	29.01	28.83	99
Accessories	33.37	35.11	105
Uniforms	6.12	7.03	115
Costumes	9.42	8.02	85
Girls' (aged 2 to 15) apparel	**117.21**	**246.96**	**211**
Coats and jackets	6.49	13.02	201
Dresses and suits	12.41	23.32	188
Shirts, blouses, and sweaters	29.33	65.89	225
Skirts and pants	24.07	48.25	200
Shorts and shorts sets	8.28	18.27	221
Active sportswear	9.32	18.89	203
Underwear and nightwear	7.63	14.53	190
Hosiery	4.30	9.51	221
Accessories	5.81	14.58	251
Uniforms	4.77	10.95	230
Costumes	4.80	9.74	203
Children under age 2	**82.60**	**97.16**	**118**
Coats, jackets, and snowsuits	2.43	2.88	119
Outerwear including dresses	23.71	25.32	107
Underwear	43.60	54.66	125
Nightwear and loungewear	4.07	4.12	101
Accessories	8.79	10.18	116
Footwear	**313.17**	**381.78**	**122**
Men's	102.90	108.10	105
Boys'	36.87	76.07	206
Women's	141.64	142.91	101
Girls'	31.76	54.70	172
Other apparel products and services	**239.87**	**272.68**	**114**
Material for making clothes	5.11	4.50	88
Sewing patterns and notions	8.20	6.98	85
Watches	13.62	18.63	137
Jewelry	89.65	94.74	106
Shoe repair and other shoe services	1.44	1.51	105
Coin-operated apparel laundry and dry cleaning	37.58	42.71	114
Apparel alteration, repair, and tailoring services	5.86	6.09	104
Clothing rental	2.66	2.32	87
Watch and jewelry repair	5.49	5.10	93
Professional laundry, dry cleaning	69.69	89.19	128
Clothing storage	0.55	0.92	167

	total consumer units	CUs headed by 35-to-44-year-olds	
		average spending	indexed spending
TRANSPORTATION	**$7,759.29**	**$9,399.89**	**121**
VEHICLE PURCHASES	3,664.93	4,591.97	125
Cars and trucks, new	**1,752.96**	**2,393.58**	**137**
New cars	883.08	997.89	113
New trucks	869.88	1,395.68	160
Cars and trucks, used	**1,842.29**	**2,115.23**	**115**
Used cars	1,113.46	1,189.73	107
Used trucks	728.82	925.50	127
Other vehicles	**69.68**	**83.16**	**119**
New motorcycles	36.26	35.58	98
Used motorcycles	33.42	47.58	142
GASOLINE AND MOTOR OIL	**1,235.06**	**1,472.79**	**119**
Gasoline	1,125.01	1,356.47	121
Diesel fuel	10.86	14.58	134
Gasoline on trips	88.24	89.54	101
Motor oil	10.05	11.30	112
Motor oil on trips	0.89	0.90	101
OTHER VEHICLE EXPENSES	**2,470.55**	**2,934.96**	**119**
Vehicle finance charges	**397.04**	**528.69**	**133**
Automobile finance charges	193.12	231.92	120
Truck finance charges	182.89	265.51	145
Motorcycle and plane finance charges	2.36	4.42	187
Other vehicle finance charges	18.67	26.84	144
Maintenance and repairs	**697.30**	**843.38**	**121**
Coolant, additives, brake, transmission fluids	3.82	4.82	126
Tires—purchased, replaced, installed	89.93	103.48	115
Parts, equipment, and accessories	41.70	43.94	105
Vehicle audio equipment, excl. labor	12.32	11.02	89
Vehicle products	4.92	8.66	176
Miscellaneous auto repair, servicing	43.69	63.51	145
Body work and painting	31.24	36.21	116
Clutch, transmission repair	48.68	60.61	125
Drive shaft and rear-end repair	6.51	7.73	119
Brake work	57.73	76.39	132
Repair to steering or front-end	16.91	18.15	107
Repair to engine cooling system	21.68	25.09	116
Motor tune-up	49.69	63.87	129
Lube, oil change, and oil filters	65.07	70.49	108
Front-end alignment, wheel balance, rotation	11.90	11.63	98
Shock absorber replacement	4.82	6.38	132
Gas tank repair, replacement	4.32	3.74	87
Tire repair and other repair work	39.83	47.90	120
Vehicle air conditioning repair	17.00	18.43	108
Exhaust system repair	12.56	11.25	90
Electrical system repair	28.42	33.85	119
Motor repair, replacement	76.62	106.31	139
Auto repair service policy	7.93	9.91	125

	total consumer units	CUs headed by 35-to-44-year-olds	
		average spending	indexed spending
Vehicle insurance	**$893.50**	**$986.86**	**110**
Vehicle rental, leases, licenses, other charges	**482.71**	**576.03**	**119**
Leased and rented vehicles	324.48	390.19	120
Rented vehicles	41.33	45.29	110
Auto rental	6.76	5.95	88
Auto rental on trips	28.28	31.73	112
Truck rental	2.21	2.94	133
Truck rental on trips	3.55	3.87	109
Leased vehicles	283.15	344.91	122
Car lease payments	149.63	134.16	90
Cash down payment (car lease)	11.13	8.14	73
Termination fee (car lease)	1.28	1.08	84
Truck lease payments	114.24	188.52	165
Cash down payment (truck lease)	4.92	9.17	186
Termination fee (truck lease)	1.94	3.83	197
Vehicle registration, state	72.82	84.64	116
Vehicle registration, local	7.76	10.11	130
Driver's license	6.26	5.90	94
Vehicle inspection	9.26	10.76	116
Parking fees	29.25	38.96	133
Parking fees in home city, excluding residence	24.24	32.38	134
Parking fees on trips	5.01	6.58	131
Tolls	10.59	13.72	130
Tolls on trips	3.94	4.33	110
Towing charges	5.60	5.60	100
Automobile service clubs	12.75	11.83	93
PUBLIC TRANSPORTATION	**388.75**	**400.18**	**103**
Airline fares	243.57	257.73	106
Intercity bus fares	11.48	11.77	103
Intracity mass transit fares	49.97	73.27	147
Local transportation on trips	10.91	10.57	97
Taxi fares and limousine service on trips	6.41	6.21	97
Taxi fares and limousine service	18.95	9.98	53
Intercity train fares	16.09	12.04	75
Ship fares	29.74	16.74	56
School bus	1.64	1.88	115
HEALTH CARE	**$2,350.32**	**$1,979.69**	**84**
HEALTH INSURANCE	**1,167.71**	**1,022.89**	**88**
Commercial health insurance	**217.53**	**263.07**	**121**
Traditional fee-for-service health plan (not BCBS)	68.27	51.56	76
Preferred-provider health plan (not BCBS)	149.26	211.51	142
Blue Cross, Blue Shield	**315.67**	**316.45**	**100**
Traditional fee-for-service health plan	53.76	36.50	68
Preferred-provider health plan	106.99	137.68	129
Health maintenance organization	101.53	124.15	122
Commercial Medicare supplement	47.35	13.34	28
Other BCBS health insurance	6.05	4.78	79

	total consumer units	CUs headed by 35-to-44-year-olds	
		average spending	indexed spending
Health maintenance plans (HMOs)	$280.47	$331.70	118
Medicare payments	186.87	32.57	17
Commercial Medicare supplements/ other health insurance	167.18	79.10	47
Commercial Medicare supplement (not BCBS)	106.32	35.66	34
Other health insurance (not BCBS)	60.86	43.44	71
MEDICAL SERVICES	589.87	555.71	94
Physician's services	147.53	137.83	93
Dental services	226.99	231.37	102
Eye care services	34.20	51.84	152
Service by professionals other than physician	42.76	40.17	94
Lab tests, X-rays	26.79	20.65	77
Hospital room	36.57	18.94	52
Hospital services other than room	51.51	41.30	80
Care in convalescent or nursing home	12.46	1.53	12
Other medical services	9.46	4.75	50
DRUGS	487.43	302.53	62
Nonprescription drugs	64.45	60.01	93
Nonprescription vitamins	49.15	28.79	59
Prescription drugs	373.83	213.74	57
MEDICAL SUPPLIES	105.31	98.56	94
Eyeglasses and contact lenses	52.26	56.86	109
Hearing aids	14.98	2.52	17
Topicals and dressings	27.56	30.25	110
Medical equipment for general use	2.69	2.40	89
Supportive, convalescent medical equipment	5.21	5.50	106
Rental of medical equipment	1.06	0.22	21
Rental of supportive, convalescent medical equipment	1.55	0.80	52
ENTERTAINMENT	$2,078.99	$2,685.22	129
FEES AND ADMISSIONS	541.67	742.60	137
Recreation expenses on trips	25.64	30.60	119
Social, recreation, civic club membership	107.92	131.61	122
Fees for participant sports	75.05	91.61	122
Participant sports on trips	29.50	40.57	138
Movie, theater, opera, ballet	98.30	123.41	126
Movie, other admissions on trips	45.57	60.68	133
Admission to sports events	36.18	53.00	146
Admission to sports events on trips	15.19	20.23	133
Fees for recreational lessons	82.69	160.29	194
Other entertainment services on trips	25.64	30.60	119
TELEVISION, RADIO, SOUND EQUIPMENT	691.90	817.37	118
Television	543.66	625.16	115
Cable service and community antenna	382.28	425.26	111
Black-and-white TV	0.80	1.18	148
Color TV, console	38.63	50.00	129
Color TV, portable, table model	39.14	36.58	93

	total consumer units	CUs headed by 35-to-44-year-olds	
		average spending	indexed spending
VCRs and video disc players	$23.25	$26.38	113
Video cassettes, tapes, and discs	33.13	40.34	122
Video game hardware and software	23.46	41.48	177
Repair of TV, radio, and sound equipment	2.50	3.06	122
Rental of television sets	0.46	0.89	193
Radio and sound equipment	**148.25**	**192.21**	**130**
Radios	3.98	1.96	49
Tape recorders and players	5.31	8.36	157
Sound components and component systems	20.19	23.95	119
Miscellaneous sound equipment	3.18	4.95	156
Sound equipment accessories	5.97	7.83	131
Satellite dishes	1.00	0.78	78
Compact disc, tape, record, video mail order clubs	6.53	8.11	124
Records, CDs, audio tapes, needles	36.47	45.11	124
Rental of VCR, radio, sound equipment	0.25	0.32	128
Musical instruments and accessories	24.82	30.46	123
Rental and repair of musical instruments	1.22	2.95	242
Rental of video cassettes, tapes, discs, films	39.33	57.42	146
PETS, TOYS, PLAYGROUND EQUIPMENT	**369.12**	**462.79**	**125**
Pets	**248.25**	**288.01**	**116**
Pet food	102.56	124.32	121
Pet purchase, supplies, and medicines	52.29	59.41	114
Pet services	21.95	23.74	108
Veterinarian services	71.44	80.54	113
Toys, games, hobbies, and tricycles	**117.34**	**169.49**	**144**
Playground equipment	**3.54**	**5.29**	**149**
OTHER ENTERTAINMENT SUPPLIES, EQUIPMENT, SERVICES	**476.30**	**662.46**	**139**
Unmotored recreational vehicles	**47.14**	**42.86**	**91**
Boat without motor and boat trailers	16.15	11.76	73
Trailer and other attachable campers	30.99	31.10	100
Motorized recreational vehicles	**170.19**	**251.86**	**148**
Motorized camper	40.05	93.26	233
Other vehicle	35.47	39.93	113
Motorboats	94.67	118.66	125
Rental of recreational vehicles	**1.99**	**2.96**	**149**
Outboard motors	**0.71**	**0.33**	**46**
Docking and landing fees	**6.66**	**5.32**	**80**
Sports, recreation, exercise equipment	**150.33**	**221.28**	**147**
Athletic gear, game tables, exercise equipment	60.51	79.11	131
Bicycles	13.45	25.96	193
Camping equipment	9.59	14.71	153
Hunting and fishing equipment	35.68	51.51	144
Winter sports equipment	5.45	7.32	134
Water sports equipment	8.95	11.39	127
Other sports equipment	14.62	27.13	186
Rental and repair of misc. sports equipment	2.07	4.15	200

	total consumer units	CUs headed by 35-to-44-year-olds	
		average spending	indexed spending
Photographic equipment and supplies	**$90.48**	**$121.38**	**134**
Film	17.74	23.38	132
Other photographic supplies	2.27	0.01	0
Film processing	26.60	34.48	130
Repair and rental of photographic equipment	0.12	0.13	108
Photographic equipment	23.34	30.55	131
Photographer fees	20.42	32.82	161
Fireworks	**1.52**	**1.86**	**122**
Souvenirs	**1.25**	**2.59**	**207**
Visual goods	**1.19**	**2.62**	**220**
Pinball, electronic video games	**4.84**	**9.40**	**194**
PERSONAL CARE PRODUCTS AND SERVICES	**$525.80**	**$614.64**	**117**
Personal care products	**276.65**	**344.16**	**124**
Hair care products	53.57	73.46	137
Hair accessories	6.57	8.87	135
Wigs and hairpieces	1.32	1.59	120
Oral hygiene products	27.33	33.34	122
Shaving products	15.09	17.78	118
Cosmetics, perfume, and bath products	129.13	150.78	117
Deodorants, feminine hygiene, misc. products	30.29	37.83	125
Electric personal care appliances	13.34	20.53	154
Personal care services	**249.15**	**270.47**	**109**
READING	**$138.57**	**$134.57**	**97**
Newspaper subscriptions	43.88	33.10	75
Newspaper, nonsubscription	11.30	13.39	118
Magazine subscriptions	16.59	14.30	86
Magazines, nonsubscription	9.35	11.10	119
Books purchased through book clubs	6.62	7.69	116
Books not purchased through book clubs	50.38	54.53	108
Encyclopedia and other reference book sets	0.33	0.11	33
EDUCATION	**$751.95**	**$738.35**	**98**
College tuition	444.45	282.97	64
Elementary and high school tuition	128.94	229.46	178
Other school tuition	25.53	36.22	142
Other school expenses including rentals	25.77	39.26	152
Books, supplies for college	57.93	34.97	60
Books, supplies for elementary, high school	16.14	35.19	218
Books, supplies for day care, nursery school	3.39	5.92	175
Miscellaneous school expenses and supplies	49.80	74.35	149

	total consumer units	CUs headed by 35-to-44-year-olds	
		average spending	indexed spending
TOBACCO PRODUCTS AND SMOKING SUPPLIES	$320.49	$375.83	117
Cigarettes	291.89	347.75	119
Other tobacco products	26.27	25.51	97
Smoking accessories	2.33	2.56	110
FINANCIAL PRODUCTS, SERVICES	$792.40	$841.42	105
Miscellaneous fees	2.25	2.76	123
Lottery and gambling losses	46.94	24.44	52
Legal fees	132.99	137.59	103
Funeral expenses	77.91	50.45	65
Safe deposit box rental	3.84	2.70	70
Checking accounts, other bank service charges	25.91	33.38	129
Cemetery lots, vaults, and maintenance fees	16.05	3.36	21
Accounting fees	57.85	55.67	96
Miscellaneous personal services	39.77	46.49	117
Finance charges, except mortgage and vehicles	271.37	305.62	113
Occupational expenses	38.46	59.00	153
Expenses for other properties	65.99	92.94	141
Credit card memberships	2.82	3.23	115
Shopping club membership fees	5.97	7.36	123
CASH CONTRIBUTIONS	$1,277.10	$1,247.46	98
Support for college students	75.94	44.56	59
Alimony expenditures	21.18	15.68	74
Child support expenditures	190.75	376.22	197
Gifts to non-CU members of stocks, bonds, and mutual funds	24.23	1.36	6
Cash contributions to charities and other organizations	137.62	105.76	77
Cash contributions to church, religious organizations	557.29	542.84	97
Cash contributions to educational institutions	33.42	29.31	88
Cash contributions to political organizations	10.90	4.08	37
Other cash gifts	225.76	127.66	57
PERSONAL INSURANCE, PENSIONS	$3,898.62	$ 5,182.53	133
Life and other personal insurance	406.11	408.79	101
Life, endowment, annuity, other personal insurance	391.65	396.24	101
Other nonhealth insurance	14.46	12.55	87
Pensions and Social Security	3,492.51	4,773.74	137
Deductions for government retirement	69.48	92.65	133
Deductions for railroad retirement	2.21	6.49	294
Deductions for private pensions	390.38	576.38	148
Nonpayroll deposit to retirement plans	426.12	429.68	101
Deductions for Social Security	2,604.32	3,668.54	141

	total consumer units	CUs headed by 35-to-44-year-olds	
		average spending	indexed spending
PERSONAL TAXES	**$2,496.26**	**$3,074.86**	**123**
Federal income taxes	1,842.57	2,258.45	123
State and local income taxes	506.45	679.93	134
Other taxes	147.24	136.49	93
GIFTS FOR NON-HOUSEHOLD MEMBERS**	**$1,036.24**	**$868.25**	**84**
FOOD	**82.18**	**59.93**	**73**
Cakes and cupcakes	2.41	2.14	89
Other fresh fruits (excl. apples, bananas, citrus)	2.26	2.38	105
Candy and chewing gum	11.69	8.50	73
Board (including at school)	21.90	15.68	72
Catered affairs	26.19	13.25	51
ALCOHOLIC BEVERAGES	**13.42**	**15.68**	**117**
Beer and ale	4.73	4.52	96
Wine	5.84	6.46	111
HOUSING	**258.69**	**231.02**	**89**
Housekeeping supplies	**42.48**	**41.42**	**98**
Laundry and cleaning supplies	2.93	2.90	99
Other household products	11.69	12.21	104
Miscellaneous household products	5.85	6.92	118
Lawn and garden supplies	4.20	3.64	87
Postage and stationery	27.86	26.30	94
Stationery, stationery supplies, giftwrap	21.13	20.59	97
Postage	6.14	5.45	89
Household textiles	**13.72**	**10.68**	**78**
Bathroom linens	2.59	2.93	113
Bedroom linens	6.10	3.52	58
Appliances and miscellaneous housewares	**23.98**	**16.51**	**69**
Major appliances	8.41	7.05	84
Electric floor cleaning equipment	2.77	2.37	86
Small appliances and miscellaneous housewares	15.57	9.46	61
China and other dinnerware	2.46	0.96	39
Nonelectric cookware	3.53	0.47	13
Tableware, nonelectric kitchenware	2.63	3.29	125
Small electric kitchen appliances	2.71	1.99	73
Miscellaneous household equipment	**64.70**	**64.81**	**100**
Infants' equipment	3.82	1.31	34
Outdoor equipment	2.07	2.23	108
Other household decorative items	25.76	28.88	112
Power tools	2.80	3.57	128
Indoor plants, fresh flowers	13.43	11.24	84
Computers and computer hardware	6.59	7.46	113
Miscellaneous household equipment	2.19	1.96	89
Other housing	**113.80**	**97.62**	**86**
Repair or maintenance services	4.51	0.42	9
Housing while attending school	39.93	15.55	39

	total consumer units	CUs headed by 35-to-44-year-olds	
		average spending	indexed spending
Natural gas (renter)	$3.62	$3.98	110
Electricity (renter)	14.67	20.07	137
Water, sewer maintenance (renter)	3.04	3.66	120
Daycare centers, nurseries, and preschools	23.81	32.80	138
APPAREL AND SERVICES	**237.13**	**208.27**	**88**
Men and boys, aged 2 or older	**63.74**	**63.44**	**100**
Men's coats and jackets	5.09	8.45	166
Men's accessories	4.45	2.62	59
Men's sweaters and vests	3.06	3.11	102
Men's active sportswear	2.76	2.73	99
Men's shirts	16.79	15.89	95
Men's pants	6.93	6.08	88
Boys' shirts	3.71	5.26	142
Boys' pants	3.76	3.55	94
Women and girls, aged 2 or older	**81.76**	**55.82**	**68**
Women's coats and jackets	5.62	0.63	11
Women's dresses	7.66	2.32	30
Women's vests and sweaters	8.50	3.35	39
Women's shirts, tops, blouses	9.06	3.84	42
Women's pants	6.62	2.01	30
Women's active sportswear	4.33	2.09	48
Women's sleepwear	6.45	9.05	140
Women's accessories	5.71	4.23	74
Girls' dresses and suits	2.98	1.92	64
Girls' shirts, blouses, sweaters	4.48	3.17	71
Girls' skirts and pants	3.32	3.76	113
Girls' accessories	2.38	5.86	246
Children under age 2	**39.99**	**45.31**	**113**
Infant dresses, outerwear	15.28	14.55	95
Infant underwear	16.91	23.53	139
Infant nightwear, loungewear	2.55	2.06	81
Infant accessories	3.93	3.51	89
Other apparel products and services	**51.63**	**43.70**	**85**
Jewelry and watches	24.01	20.36	85
Watches	2.16	2.18	101
Jewelry	21.85	18.19	83
Men's footwear	8.37	4.41	53
Boys' footwear	4.46	6.75	151
Women's footwear	8.82	7.98	90
Girls' footwear	3.30	2.60	79
TRANSPORTATION	**43.87**	**44.93**	**102**
New cars	7.09	19.18	271
Used cars	12.21	12.17	100
Airline fares	6.78	6.36	94
Ship fares	2.74	1.91	70

	total consumer units	CUs headed by 35-to-44-year-olds	
		average spending	indexed spending
HEALTH CARE	**$32.59**	**$20.64**	**63**
Physician's services	3.07	1.03	34
Dental services	4.03	3.85	96
Care in convalescent or nursing home	5.19	0.08	2
Nonprescription vitamins	3.93	1.50	38
Prescription drugs	2.38	1.32	55
ENTERTAINMENT	**78.24**	**85.78**	**110**
Toys, games, hobbies, and tricycles	29.98	29.00	97
Other entertainment	48.26	56.78	118
Fees for recreational lessons	7.88	10.19	129
Community antenna or cable TV	6.37	8.35	131
VCRs and videodisc players	2.26	2.14	95
Video game hardware and software	2.13	2.13	100
Athletic gear, game tables, exercise equipment	6.60	8.85	134
Hunting and fishing equipment	3.06	2.18	71
Photographer fees	3.19	1.79	56
PERSONAL CARE PRODUCTS, SERVICES	**21.15**	**27.07**	**128**
Cosmetics, perfume, bath preparation	12.53	13.53	108
Electric personal care appliances	3.31	6.17	186
EDUCATION	**183.88**	**107.53**	**58**
College tuition	127.83	56.74	44
Elementary and high school tuition	25.95	32.89	127
Other school tuition	4.44	1.85	42
Other school expenses including rentals	3.99	3.73	93
College books and supplies	11.93	4.24	36
Miscellaneous school supplies	7.38	5.02	68
ALL OTHER GIFTS	**83.76**	**66.84**	**80**
Gifts of trip expenses	44.40	32.28	73
Lottery and gambling losses	2.86	0.03	1
Legal fees	5.82	2.20	38
Funeral expenses	25.25	24.28	96
Miscellaneous personal services	2.16	2.98	138

This figure does not include the amount paid for mortgage principle, which is considered an asset.

** *Expenditures on gifts are also included in the preceding product and service categories. Food spending, for example, includes the amount spent on food gifts. Only gift categories with spending of $2.00 or more by the average consumer unit are shown.*

Note: The Bureau of Labor Statistics uses consumer unit rather than household as the sampling unit in the Consumer Expenditure Survey. For the definition of consumer unit, see the glossary. (–) means not applicable or the sample is too small to make a reliable estimate.

Source: Bureau of Labor Statistics, unpublished data from the 2002 Consumer Expenditure Survey; calculations by New Strategist

Householders Aged 45 to 54 Are the Biggest Spenders

But their spending is not far ahead of 35-to-44-year-olds.

Householders aged 45 to 54 spent $48,748 in 2002, or 20 percent more than the $40,677 spent by the average household. The 45-to-54 age group spends only slightly more than their younger counterparts aged 35 to 44. The spending gap between the two age groups has shrunk from several thousand dollars during the 1990s to just $418 in 2002 as the younger age group boosted its spending and the older age group cut back.

Householders aged 45 to 54 spend modestly on many discretionary items. They spend only 13 percent more than the average household on furniture, 16 percent more on new cars, and just 8 percent more on new trucks. They spend 15 percent more than average on lodging while on trips. On some discretionary items, however, they spend a considerable amount—44 percent more than average on wine consumed at home, for example, and 32 percent more on computer information services. They spend 58 percent more than average on fees for recreational lessons and 51 percent more than the average household on college tuition.

■ As older boomers filled the 45-to-54 age group during the past few years, they proved themselves to be cautious spenders. Their belt tightening is likely to continue as their financial worries grow with approaching retirement.

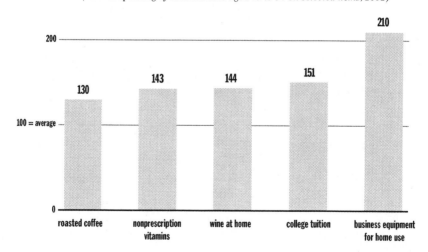

Householders aged 45 to 54 are big spenders on many items

(indexed spending of householders aged 45 to 54 on selected items, 2002)

Table 8.3 Average and Indexed Spending of Householders Aged 45 to 54, 2002

(average annual spending of total consumer units (CUs) and average annual and indexed spending of consumer units headed by 45-to-54-year-olds, 2002)

	total consumer units	CUs headed by 45-to-54-year-olds average spending	CUs headed by 45-to-54-year-olds indexed spending
Number of consumer units (in 000s)	112,108	22,691	–
Average before-tax income	$49,430.00	$64,974.00	131
Average annual spending	40,676.60	48,748.24	120
FOOD	**$5,374.80**	**$6,228.49**	**116**
FOOD AT HOME	3,098.52	3,528.31	114
Cereals and bakery products	**450.13**	**500.16**	**111**
Cereals and cereal products	154.07	168.52	109
Flour	8.65	8.82	102
Prepared flour mixes	12.40	14.27	115
Ready-to-eat and cooked cereals	87.66	92.14	105
Rice	17.82	22.16	124
Pasta, cornmeal, and other cereal products	27.54	31.13	113
Bakery products	296.06	331.65	112
Bread	83.83	90.66	108
White bread	35.21	37.01	105
Bread, other than white	48.62	53.65	110
Crackers and cookies	70.67	77.96	110
Cookies	46.31	50.16	108
Crackers	24.36	27.80	114
Frozen and refrigerated bakery products	25.64	28.86	113
Other bakery products	115.92	134.16	116
Biscuits and rolls	41.04	49.00	119
Cakes and cupcakes	35.73	42.17	118
Bread and cracker products	3.50	3.84	110
Sweetrolls, coffee cakes, doughnuts	25.84	27.58	107
Pies, tarts, turnovers	9.82	11.58	118
Meats, poultry, fish, and eggs	**798.42**	**928.61**	**116**
Beef	231.17	273.25	118
Ground beef	86.29	102.04	118
Roast	40.99	44.81	109
Chuck roast	11.71	13.50	115
Round roast	10.23	9.09	89
Other roast	19.05	22.22	117
Steak	84.47	101.81	121
Round steak	13.29	16.01	120
Sirloin steak	26.62	33.18	125
Other steak	44.56	52.61	118
Pork	167.34	188.03	112
Bacon	28.45	32.26	113
Pork chops	38.43	42.95	112
Ham	37.16	41.96	113
Ham, not canned	35.66	40.29	113
Canned ham	1.50	1.67	111

	total consumer units	CUs headed by 45-to-54-year-olds	
		average spending	indexed spending
Sausage	$26.17	$26.81	102
Other pork	37.13	44.05	119
Other meats	101.08	116.63	115
Frankfurters	20.95	22.89	109
Lunch meats (cold cuts)	68.99	78.06	113
Bologna, liverwurst, salami	21.11	23.02	109
Lamb, organ meats, and others	11.14	15.68	141
Lamb and organ meats	7.99	8.78	110
Mutton, goat, and game	3.15	6.90	219
Poultry	144.13	167.98	117
Fresh and frozen chicken	113.25	131.89	116
Fresh and frozen whole chicken	32.08	38.88	121
Fresh and frozen chicken parts	81.17	93.00	115
Other poultry	30.88	36.09	117
Fish and seafood	120.97	145.60	120
Canned fish and seafood	16.13	19.35	120
Fresh fish and shellfish	69.31	84.25	122
Frozen fish and shellfish	35.53	42.00	118
Eggs	33.75	37.12	110
Dairy products	**328.34**	**367.32**	**112**
Fresh milk and cream	127.15	135.52	107
Fresh milk, all types	114.63	121.34	106
Cream	12.52	14.18	113
Other dairy products	201.19	231.80	115
Butter	18.48	22.58	122
Cheese	95.64	111.76	117
Ice cream and related products	58.74	63.39	108
Miscellaneous dairy products	28.33	34.06	120
Fruits and vegetables	**552.01**	**626.67**	**114**
Fresh fruits	178.20	204.23	115
Apples	32.59	36.54	112
Bananas	31.24	34.89	112
Oranges	20.34	25.72	126
Citrus fruits, excl. oranges	14.29	14.33	100
Other fresh fruits	79.74	92.75	116
Fresh vegetables	174.88	204.85	117
Potatoes	33.35	35.94	108
Lettuce	22.22	26.93	121
Tomatoes	33.71	39.17	116
Other fresh vegetables	85.60	102.81	120
Processed fruits	115.50	126.53	110
Frozen fruits and fruit juices	12.45	12.08	97
Frozen orange juice	6.31	5.52	87
Frozen fruits	2.79	3.12	112
Frozen fruit juices, excl. orange	3.35	3.43	102
Canned fruits	15.06	16.06	107
Dried fruits	6.06	5.50	91
Fresh fruit juice	22.20	26.80	121
Canned and bottled fruit juice	59.74	66.09	111

	total consumer units	CUs headed by 45-to-54-year-olds	
		average spending	indexed spending
Processed vegetables	$83.43	$91.06	109
Frozen vegetables	27.85	29.99	108
Canned and dried vegetables and juices	55.58	61.07	110
Canned beans	12.47	13.92	112
Canned corn	7.34	7.34	100
Canned miscellaneous vegetables	17.85	20.96	117
Dried peas	0.36	0.32	89
Dried beans	2.55	3.19	125
Dried miscellaneous vegetables	7.38	6.83	93
Dried processed vegetables	0.34	0.59	174
Frozen vegetable juices	0.06	0.11	183
Fresh and canned vegetable juices	7.23	7.81	108
Sugar and other sweets	**117.39**	**130.49**	**111**
Candy and chewing gum	75.44	83.53	111
Sugar	15.56	17.59	113
Artificial sweeteners	4.33	4.81	111
Jams, preserves, other sweets	22.06	24.56	111
Fats and oils	**85.16**	**98.64**	**116**
Margarine	9.86	11.34	115
Fats and oils	26.08	29.32	112
Salad dressings	27.01	32.76	121
Nondairy cream and imitation milk	9.33	11.40	122
Peanut butter	12.89	13.83	107
Miscellaneous foods	**471.92**	**530.73**	**112**
Frozen prepared foods	98.09	112.12	114
Frozen meals	29.88	36.56	122
Other frozen prepared foods	68.22	75.56	111
Canned and packaged soups	35.82	42.54	119
Potato chips, nuts, and other snacks	100.53	124.25	124
Potato chips and other snacks	76.37	93.79	123
Nuts	24.16	30.46	126
Condiments and seasonings	86.81	101.88	117
Salt, spices, and other seasonings	21.14	24.34	115
Olives, pickles, relishes	9.70	11.28	116
Sauces and gravies	37.78	47.10	125
Baking needs and miscellaneous products	18.19	19.17	105
Other canned/packaged prepared foods	150.67	149.94	100
Prepared salads	21.46	25.28	118
Prepared desserts	10.32	10.41	101
Baby food	31.57	17.59	56
Miscellaneous prepared foods	87.24	96.62	111
Nonalcoholic beverages	253.94	296.27	117
Cola	81.11	93.51	115
Other carbonated drinks	43.93	50.06	114
Coffee	41.59	53.42	128
Roasted coffee	27.38	35.72	130
Instant and freeze-dried coffee	14.21	17.70	125
Noncarbonated fruit-flavored drinks	18.95	20.04	106

	total consumer units	CUs headed by 45-to-54-year-olds	
		average spending	indexed spending
Tea	$15.86	$17.28	109
Nonalcoholic beer	0.64	1.00	156
Other nonalcoholic beverages and ice	51.85	60.96	118
Food prepared by CU on trips	41.20	49.41	120
FOOD AWAY FROM HOME	**2,276.29**	**2,700.17**	**119**
Meals at restaurants, carry-outs, other	**1,866.42**	**2,179.95**	**117**
Lunch	685.79	812.62	118
• At fast food, take-out, delivery, concession stands, buffet, and cafeteria (other than employer and school cafeteria)	377.71	424.62	112
• At full-service restaurants	224.82	272.37	121
• At vending machines, mobile vendors	5.50	5.06	92
• At employer and school cafeterias	77.76	110.57	142
Dinner	736.54	837.82	114
• At fast food, take-out, delivery, concession stands, buffet, and cafeteria (other than employer and school cafeteria)	213.33	227.49	107
• At full-service restaurants	518.02	607.76	117
• At vending machines, mobile vendors	1.87	0.34	18
• At employer and school cafeterias	3.32	2.23	67
Snacks and nonalcoholic beverages	262.67	312.97	119
• At fast food, take-out, delivery, concession stands, buffet, and cafeteria (other than employer and school cafeteria)	185.69	226.78	122
• At full-service restaurants	30.17	37.08	123
• At vending machines, mobile vendors	36.71	36.68	100
• At employer and school cafeterias	10.11	12.43	123
Breakfast and brunch	181.42	216.55	119
• At fast food, take-out, delivery, concession stands, buffet, and cafeteria (other than employer and school cafeteria)	87.83	102.52	117
• At full-service restaurants	87.08	105.51	121
• At vending machines, mobile vendors	1.40	1.66	119
• At employer and school cafeterias	5.11	6.85	134
Board (including at school)	**46.54**	**99.42**	**214**
Catered affairs	**69.00**	**61.92**	**90**
Food on trips	**211.49**	**250.52**	**118**
School lunches	**60.00**	**83.11**	**139**
Meals as pay	**22.86**	**25.24**	**110**
ALCOHOLIC BEVERAGES	**$375.95**	**$465.38**	**124**
At home	**228.08**	**287.17**	**126**
Beer and ale	112.34	137.00	122
Whiskey	13.90	16.35	118
Wine	77.75	111.92	144
Other alcoholic beverages	24.09	21.89	91

	total consumer units	CUs headed by 45-to-54-year-olds	
		average spending	indexed spending
Away from home	**$147.87**	**$178.21**	**121**
Beer and ale	52.86	62.33	118
• At fast food, take-out, delivery, concession stands, buffet, and cafeteria	7.99	7.70	96
• At full-service restaurants	41.95	49.95	119
• At vending machines, mobile vendors	0.32	0.85	266
• At catered affairs	2.59	3.84	148
Wine	25.85	30.51	118
• At fast food, take-out, delivery, concession stands, buffet and cafeteria	4.41	5.94	135
• At full-service restaurants	20.36	20.20	99
• At catered affairs	1.09	4.37	401
Other alcoholic beverages	69.16	85.37	123
• At fast food, take-out, delivery, concession stands, buffet, and cafeteria	3.50	3.49	100
• At full-service restaurants	28.94	32.76	113
• At catered affairs	3.94	15.54	394
Alcoholic beverages purchased on trips	32.78	33.58	102
HOUSING	**$13,283.08**	**$15,475.55**	**117**
SHELTER	**7,829.41**	**9,223.01**	**118**
Owned dwellings*	**5,164.96**	**6,786.54**	**131**
Mortgage interest and charges	2,962.16	4,061.06	137
Mortgage interest	2,811.49	3,828.96	136
Interest paid, home equity loan	88.61	122.42	138
Interest paid, home equity line of credit	61.88	109.67	177
Property taxes	1,242.36	1,556.57	125
Maintenance, repairs, insurance, other expenses	960.43	1,168.90	122
Homeowner's insurance	283.30	352.13	124
Ground rent	40.96	39.20	96
Maintenance and repair services	519.60	632.32	122
Painting and papering	55.58	59.08	106
Plumbing and water heating	46.63	47.59	102
Heat, air conditioning, electrical work	86.28	126.76	147
Roofing and gutters	71.20	86.86	122
Other repair and maintenance services	214.77	249.76	116
Repair, replacement of hard-surface flooring	43.54	60.60	139
Repair of built-in appliances	1.62	1.69	104
Maintenance and repair materials	83.75	107.31	128
Paints, wallpaper, and supplies	14.71	19.25	131
Tools, equipment for painting, wallpapering	1.58	2.07	131
Plumbing supplies and equipment	5.62	6.43	114
Electrical supplies, heating, cooling equip.	3.46	4.24	123
Hard-surface flooring, repair and replacement	8.72	8.96	103
Roofing and gutters	5.29	8.76	166
Plaster, paneling, siding, windows, doors, screens, awnings	13.92	20.01	144
Patio, walk, fence, driveway, masonry, brick, and stucco materials	1.29	1.60	124

	total consumer units	CUs headed by 45-to-54-year-olds average spending	CUs headed by 45-to-54-year-olds indexed spending
Landscape maintenance	$4.73	$7.14	151
Miscellaneous supplies and equipment	24.43	28.86	118
Insulation, other maintenance, repair	13.15	11.37	86
Finish basement, remodel rooms, build patios, walks, etc.	11.28	17.49	155
Property management and security	27.64	33.28	120
Property management	21.94	27.33	125
Management and upkeep services for security	5.71	5.96	104
Parking	5.17	4.65	90
Rented dwellings	**2,159.89**	**1,732.87**	**80**
Rent	2,104.66	1,678.66	80
Rent as pay	27.17	25.28	93
Maintenance, insurance, and other expenses	28.06	28.93	103
Tenant's insurance	8.90	8.93	100
Maintenance and repair services	11.16	14.09	126
Repair and maintenance services	10.58	13.85	131
Repair, replacement of hard-surface flooring	0.51	0.24	47
Repair of built-in appliances	0.07	–	–
Maintenance and repair materials	8.00	5.91	74
Paint, wallpaper, and supplies	1.01	0.83	82
Painting and wallpapering tools	0.11	0.09	82
Plastering, paneling, roofing, gutters, etc.	0.90	1.14	127
Plumbing supplies and equipment	0.80	0.62	78
Electrical supplies, heating, cooling equip.	0.30	0.20	67
Miscellaneous supplies and equipment	3.67	2.67	73
Insulation, other maintenance and repair	1.09	0.83	76
Materials for additions, finishing basements, remodeling rooms	2.43	1.84	76
Construction materials for jobs not started	0.15	–	–
Hard-surface flooring	0.73	0.26	36
Landscape maintenance	0.49	0.08	16
Other lodging	**504.56**	**703.60**	**139**
Owned vacation homes	171.55	237.53	138
Mortgage interest and charges	71.98	105.10	146
Property taxes	63.76	85.18	134
Maintenance, insurance and other expenses	35.81	47.25	132
Homeowner's insurance	9.70	11.38	117
Ground rent	2.93	0.34	12
Maintenance and repair services	16.76	29.53	176
Maintenance and repair materials	2.07	0.33	16
Property management and security	3.60	4.36	121
Property management	2.50	2.91	116
Management, upkeep services for security	1.10	1.45	132
Parking	0.76	1.31	172
Housing while attending school	80.14	174.86	218
Lodging on trips	252.87	291.21	115

	total consumer units	CUs headed by 45-to-54-year-olds average spending	indexed spending
UTILITIES, FUELS, PUBLIC SERVICES	$2,684.32	$3,106.18	116
Natural gas	329.75	382.69	116
Natural gas (renter)	60.32	53.74	89
Natural gas (owner)	266.79	325.88	122
Natural gas (vacation)	2.54	3.05	120
Electricity	981.09	1,137.50	116
Electricity (renter)	223.26	190.80	85
Electricity (owner)	750.48	938.13	125
Electricity (vacation)	6.32	7.28	115
Fuel oil and other fuels	88.41	89.90	102
Fuel oil	45.98	47.08	102
Fuel oil (renter)	4.64	3.38	73
Fuel oil (owner)	40.98	43.56	106
Fuel oil (vacation)	0.36	0.13	36
Coal	0.07	0.08	114
Bottled/tank gas	35.27	36.03	102
Gas (renter)	5.09	5.80	114
Gas (owner)	27.19	26.73	98
Gas (vacation)	2.98	3.50	117
Wood and other fuels	7.09	6.72	95
Wood and other fuels (renter)	1.32	1.21	92
Wood and other fuels (owner)	5.68	5.09	90
Telephone services	956.74	1,108.93	116
Residential telephone and pay phones	641.00	722.88	113
Cellular phone service	293.76	364.57	124
Pager service	1.71	2.44	143
Phone cards	20.28	19.04	94
Water and other public services	328.33	387.16	118
Water and sewerage maintenance	237.16	282.76	119
Water and sewerage maintenance (renter)	32.76	30.65	94
Water and sewerage maintenance (owner)	201.79	248.95	123
Water and sewerage maintenance (vacation)	2.36	2.38	101
Trash and garbage collection	89.05	101.12	114
Trash and garbage collection (renter)	9.89	10.20	103
Trash and garbage collection (owner)	76.61	88.18	115
Trash and garbage collection (vacation)	2.53	2.69	106
Septic tank cleaning	2.12	3.28	155
HOUSEHOLD SERVICES	705.71	612.82	87
Personal services	331.02	165.23	50
Babysitting, child care in your own home	35.91	18.21	51
Babysitting, child care in someone else's home	27.48	9.68	35
Care for elderly, invalids, handicapped, etc.	50.07	1.21	2
Adult day care centers	6.81	5.41	79
Day care centers, nurseries, and preschools	210.74	130.72	62
Other household services	374.70	447.59	119
Housekeeping services	79.90	100.65	126
Gardening, lawn care service	72.38	76.39	106
Water softening service	3.15	3.77	120

	total consumer units	CUs headed by 45-to-54-year-olds average spending	CUs headed by 45-to-54-year-olds indexed spending
Nonclothing laundry, dry cleaning, sent out	$1.72	$1.81	105
Nonclothing laundry, dry cleaning, coin-operated	4.13	3.68	89
Termite/pest control services	13.25	14.11	106
Home security system service fee	17.40	20.94	120
Other home services	15.06	17.98	119
Termite/pest control products	0.68	0.59	87
Moving, storage, and freight express	33.13	35.06	106
Appliance repair, including service center	10.86	13.54	125
Reupholstering and furniture repair	7.40	6.25	84
Repairs/rentals of lawn/garden equipment, hand/power tools, etc.	3.62	3.72	103
Appliance rental	1.07	0.96	90
Rental of office equipment, nonbusiness use	0.41	0.22	54
Repair of misc. household equip., furnishings	0.62	1.42	229
Repair of computer systems, nonbusiness use	2.53	4.78	189
Computer information services	107.29	141.37	132
HOUSEKEEPING SUPPLIES	**545.28**	**633.42**	**116**
Laundry and cleaning supplies	**130.57**	**147.24**	**113**
Soaps and detergents	72.89	81.81	112
Other laundry cleaning products	57.68	65.43	113
Other household products	**283.28**	**333.45**	**118**
Cleansing and toilet tissue, paper towels, and napkins	76.46	86.35	113
Miscellaneous household products	96.81	137.16	142
Lawn and garden supplies	110.01	109.94	100
Postage and stationery	**131.44**	**152.73**	**116**
Stationery, stationery supplies, giftwrap	60.20	75.03	125
Postage	69.12	73.43	106
Delivery services	2.12	4.27	201
HOUSEHOLD FURNISHINGS, EQUIPMENT	**1,518.36**	**1,900.13**	**125**
Household textiles	**135.52**	**152.30**	**112**
Bathroom linens	22.35	25.67	115
Bedroom linens	65.98	77.10	117
Kitchen and dining room linens	10.11	7.99	79
Curtains and draperies	16.65	20.00	120
Slipcovers and decorative pillows	7.40	4.72	64
Sewing materials for household items	11.44	14.06	123
Other linens	1.59	2.76	174
Furniture	**401.28**	**452.57**	**113**
Mattresses and springs	52.91	54.28	103
Other bedroom furniture	68.33	82.01	120
Sofas	85.33	85.95	101
Living room chairs	39.21	49.14	125
Living room tables	18.03	22.36	124
Kitchen and dining room furniture	61.28	67.57	110
Infants' furniture	6.46	3.27	51
Outdoor furniture	16.79	20.65	123
Wall units, cabinets, and other furniture	52.94	67.35	127

	total consumer units	CUs headed by 45-to-54-year-olds	
		average spending	indexed spending
Floor coverings	**$40.49**	**$58.92**	**146**
Wall-to-wall carpeting (renter)	0.65	1.07	165
Wall-to-wall carpet (replacement) (owner)	21.04	31.54	150
Floor coverings, nonpermanent	18.79	26.31	140
Major appliances	**188.47**	**219.49**	**116**
Dishwashers (built-in), garbage disposals, range hoods (renter)	1.24	1.10	89
Dishwashers (built-in), garbage disposals, range hoods (owner)	15.28	20.98	137
Refrigerators and freezers (renter)	5.58	5.26	94
Refrigerators and freezers (owner)	46.50	46.74	101
Washing machines (renter)	4.42	2.55	58
Washing machines (owner)	17.88	16.62	93
Clothes dryers (renter)	3.17	1.65	52
Clothes dryers (owner)	13.88	14.95	108
Cooking stoves, ovens (renter)	2.86	1.37	48
Cooking stoves, ovens (owner)	28.09	34.64	123
Microwave ovens (renter)	2.14	1.55	72
Microwave ovens (owner)	8.36	9.92	119
Portable dishwasher (renter)	0.25	0.31	124
Portable dishwasher (owner)	0.51	–	–
Window air conditioners (renter)	1.83	1.75	96
Window air conditioners (owner)	6.07	10.01	165
Electric floor-cleaning equipment	22.80	42.66	187
Sewing machines	4.79	6.69	140
Miscellaneous household appliances	**2.81**	**0.72**	**26**
Small appliances and misc. housewares	100.43	123.60	123
Housewares	77.55	95.40	123
Plastic dinnerware	1.57	1.71	109
China and other dinnerware	14.51	13.72	95
Flatware	3.79	4.65	123
Glassware	6.51	10.33	159
Silver serving pieces	4.05	2.94	73
Other serving pieces	1.44	1.36	94
Nonelectric cookware	24.25	33.90	140
Tableware, nonelectric kitchenware	21.44	26.80	125
Small appliances	22.89	28.20	123
Small electric kitchen appliances	17.18	20.76	121
Portable heating and cooling equipment	5.70	7.43	130
Miscellaneous household equipment	**652.17**	**893.25**	**137**
Window coverings	13.91	18.78	135
Infants' equipment	12.96	24.01	185
Laundry and cleaning equipment	15.15	16.89	111
Outdoor equipment	31.52	71.84	228
Clocks	5.87	6.23	106
Lamps and lighting fixtures	11.74	16.02	136
Other household decorative items	144.94	186.12	128
Telephones and accessories	32.73	45.21	138
Lawn and garden equipment	48.16	47.21	98

	total consumer units	CUs headed by 45-to-54-year-olds	
		average spending	indexed spending
Power tools	$33.27	$53.50	161
Office furniture for home use	10.57	13.80	131
Hand tools	8.05	9.12	113
Indoor plants and fresh flowers	49.78	65.51	132
Closet and storage items	9.98	11.84	119
Rental of furniture	4.60	2.99	65
Luggage	5.98	7.16	120
Computers and computer hardware, nonbusiness use	138.58	196.74	142
Computer software and accessories, nonbusiness use	17.67	20.88	118
Telephone answering devices	1.08	1.37	127
Calculators	1.44	2.71	188
Business equipment for home use	0.97	2.04	210
Other hardware	12.85	17.69	138
Smoke alarms (owner)	1.10	0.78	71
Smoke alarms (renter)	0.39	–	–
Other household appliances (owner)	8.00	13.69	171
Other household appliances (renter)	1.23	0.55	45
Misc. household equipment and parts	29.62	40.55	137
APPAREL AND SERVICES	**$1,749.22**	**$2,028.73**	**116**
Men's apparel	**319.48**	**391.28**	**122**
Suits	32.96	43.59	132
Sport coats and tailored jackets	10.65	18.78	176
Coats and jackets	33.86	35.10	104
Underwear	15.27	18.49	121
Hosiery	12.22	14.48	118
Nightwear	2.98	3.25	109
Accessories	22.41	26.77	119
Sweaters and vests	15.68	20.50	131
Active sportswear	15.13	15.74	104
Shirts	78.89	100.01	127
Pants	57.64	66.83	116
Shorts and shorts sets	12.22	17.07	140
Uniforms	3.21	4.58	143
Costumes	6.35	6.09	96
Boys' (aged 2 to 15) apparel	**89.98**	**85.49**	**95**
Coats and jackets	6.38	6.73	105
Sweaters	3.65	3.38	93
Shirts	19.50	16.09	83
Underwear	5.02	3.54	71
Nightwear	2.59	2.09	81
Hosiery	4.21	2.87	68
Accessories	4.12	3.63	88
Suits, sport coats, and vests	2.37	3.32	140
Pants	22.58	23.89	106
Shorts and shorts sets	8.66	9.26	107
Uniforms	3.35	3.62	108
Active sportswear	3.84	4.29	112
Costumes	3.72	2.78	75

	total consumer units	CUs headed by 45-to-54-year-olds	
		average spending	indexed spending
Women's apparel	**$586.91**	**$731.65**	**125**
Coats and jackets	50.06	78.14	156
Dresses	56.40	54.42	96
Sport coats and tailored jackets	6.48	10.15	157
Sweaters and vests	50.47	67.02	133
Shirts, blouses, and tops	103.24	124.07	120
Skirts	17.48	18.43	105
Pants	96.29	111.24	116
Shorts and shorts sets	16.09	18.19	113
Active sportswear	30.07	44.82	149
Nightwear	27.63	32.85	119
Undergarments	33.55	39.79	119
Hosiery	21.22	26.58	125
Suits	29.01	42.29	146
Accessories	33.37	43.11	129
Uniforms	6.12	7.65	125
Costumes	9.42	12.88	137
Girls'(aged 2 to 15) apparel	**117.21**	**118.47**	**101**
Coats and jackets	6.49	6.74	104
Dresses and suits	12.41	21.02	169
Shirts, blouses, and sweaters	29.33	27.27	93
Skirts and pants	24.07	25.22	105
Shorts and shorts sets	8.28	7.31	88
Active sportswear	9.32	7.75	83
Underwear and nightwear	7.63	7.53	99
Hosiery	4.30	3.75	87
Accessories	5.81	3.36	58
Uniforms	4.77	3.86	81
Costumes	4.80	4.65	97
Children under age 2	**82.60**	**51.26**	**62**
Coats, jackets, and snowsuits	2.43	1.34	55
Outerwear including dresses	23.71	20.27	85
Underwear	43.60	22.03	51
Nightwear and loungewear	4.07	3.40	84
Accessories	8.79	4.22	48
Footwear	**313.17**	**364.79**	**116**
Men's	102.90	142.36	138
Boys'	36.87	25.50	69
Women's	141.64	161.81	114
Girls'	31.76	35.11	111
Other apparel products and services	**239.87**	**285.79**	**119**
Material for making clothes	5.11	5.23	102
Sewing patterns and notions	8.20	7.23	88
Watches	13.62	14.82	109
Jewelry	89.65	114.21	127
Shoe repair and other shoe services	1.44	2.00	139
Coin-operated apparel laundry and dry cleaning	37.58	29.58	79
Apparel alteration, repair, and tailoring services	5.86	8.13	139
Clothing rental	2.66	5.27	198
Watch and jewelry repair	5.49	5.17	94
Professional laundry, dry cleaning	69.69	93.88	135
Clothing storage	0.55	0.27	49

	total consumer units	CUs headed by 45-to-54-year-olds average spending	indexed spending
TRANSPORTATION	**$7,759.29**	**$9,173.39**	**118**
VEHICLE PURCHASES	**3,664.93**	**4,202.68**	**115**
Cars and trucks, new	**1,752.96**	**1,966.43**	**112**
New cars	883.08	1,026.46	116
New trucks	869.88	939.97	108
Cars and trucks, used	**1,842.29**	**2,108.51**	**114**
Used cars	1,113.46	1,348.44	121
Used trucks	728.82	760.07	104
Other vehicles	**69.68**	**127.74**	**183**
New motorcycles	36.26	63.62	175
Used motorcycles	33.42	64.12	192
GASOLINE AND MOTOR OIL	**1,235.06**	**1,494.67**	**121**
Gasoline	1,125.01	1,371.63	122
Diesel fuel	10.86	10.15	93
Gasoline on trips	88.24	98.99	112
Motor oil	10.05	12.91	128
Motor oil on trips	0.89	1.00	112
OTHER VEHICLE EXPENSES	**2,470.55**	**3,055.40**	**124**
Vehicle finance charges	**397.04**	**479.38**	**121**
Automobile finance charges	193.12	232.99	121
Truck finance charges	182.89	219.68	120
Motorcycle and plane finance charges	2.36	3.31	140
Other vehicle finance charges	18.67	23.40	125
Maintenance and repairs	**697.30**	**847.87**	**122**
Coolant, additives, brake, transmission fluids	3.82	4.72	124
Tires—purchased, replaced, installed	89.93	112.37	125
Parts, equipment, and accessories	41.70	53.75	129
Vehicle audio equipment, excl. labor	12.32	7.17	58
Vehicle products	4.92	3.78	77
Miscellaneous auto repair, servicing	43.69	38.11	87
Body work and painting	31.24	42.74	137
Clutch, transmission repair	48.68	68.34	140
Drive shaft and rear-end repair	6.51	7.38	113
Brake work	57.73	68.83	119
Repair to steering or front-end	16.91	18.21	108
Repair to engine cooling system	21.68	28.18	130
Motor tune-up	49.69	59.66	120
Lube, oil change, and oil filters	65.07	78.00	120
Front-end alignment, wheel balance, rotation	11.90	16.70	140
Shock absorber replacement	4.82	8.41	174
Gas tank repair, replacement	4.32	7.15	166
Tire repair and other repair work	39.83	48.81	123
Vehicle air conditioning repair	17.00	19.66	116
Exhaust system repair	12.56	15.16	121
Electrical system repair	28.42	34.81	122
Motor repair, replacement	76.62	95.66	125
Auto repair service policy	7.93	10.26	129

	total consumer units	CUs headed by 45-to-54-year-olds average spending	indexed spending
Vehicle insurance	$893.50	$1,125.08	126
Vehicle rental, leases, licenses, other charges	482.71	603.08	125
Leased and rented vehicles	324.48	416.29	128
Rented vehicles	41.33	53.27	129
Auto rental	6.76	9.75	144
Auto rental on trips	28.28	34.78	123
Truck rental	2.21	3.02	137
Truck rental on trips	3.55	4.77	134
Leased vehicles	283.15	363.02	128
Car lease payments	149.63	202.52	135
Cash down payment (car lease)	11.13	19.14	172
Termination fee (car lease)	1.28	0.84	66
Truck lease payments	114.24	133.14	117
Cash down payment (truck lease)	4.92	5.40	110
Termination fee (truck lease)	1.94	1.96	101
Vehicle registration, state	72.82	85.24	117
Vehicle registration, local	7.76	9.16	118
Driver's license	6.26	7.66	122
Vehicle inspection	9.26	10.97	118
Parking fees	29.25	34.30	117
Parking fees in home city, excluding residence	24.24	28.42	117
Parking fees on trips	5.01	5.89	118
Tolls	10.59	12.90	122
Tolls on trips	3.94	4.49	114
Towing charges	5.60	6.76	121
Automobile service clubs	12.75	15.30	120
PUBLIC TRANSPORTATION	388.75	420.64	108
Airline fares	243.57	278.73	114
Intercity bus fares	11.48	9.61	84
Intracity mass transit fares	49.97	54.05	108
Local transportation on trips	10.91	11.79	108
Taxi fares and limousine service on trips	6.41	6.92	108
Taxi fares and limousine service	18.95	16.38	86
Intercity train fares	16.09	17.26	107
Ship fares	29.74	22.76	77
School bus	1.64	3.14	191
HEALTH CARE	$2,350.32	$2,550.43	109
HEALTH INSURANCE	1,167.71	1,180.34	101
Commercial health insurance	217.53	269.41	124
Traditional fee-for-service health plan (not BCBS)	68.27	81.84	120
Preferred-provider health plan (not BCBS)	149.26	187.57	126
Blue Cross, Blue Shield	315.67	372.19	118
Traditional fee-for-service health plan	53.76	73.45	137
Preferred-provider health plan	106.99	153.87	144
Health maintenance organization	101.53	121.21	119
Commercial Medicare supplement	47.35	17.87	38
Other BCBS health insurance	6.05	5.79	96

	total consumer units	CUs headed by 45-to-54-year-olds average spending	indexed spending
Health maintenance plans (HMOs)	$280.47	$359.76	128
Medicare payments	186.87	50.98	27
Commercial Medicare supplements/ other health insurance	167.18	128.00	77
Commercial Medicare supplement (not BCBS)	106.32	64.08	60
Other health insurance (not BCBS)	60.86	63.93	105
MEDICAL SERVICES	589.87	767.62	130
Physician's services	147.53	178.25	121
Dental services	226.99	290.27	128
Eye care services	34.20	38.75	113
Service by professionals other than physician	42.76	71.71	168
Lab tests, X-rays	26.79	35.83	134
Hospital room	36.57	49.26	135
Hospital services other than room	51.51	74.36	144
Care in convalescent or nursing home	12.46	16.71	134
Other medical services	9.46	12.48	132
DRUGS	487.43	490.15	101
Nonprescription drugs	64.45	71.10	110
Nonprescription vitamins	49.15	70.38	143
Prescription drugs	373.83	348.67	93
MEDICAL SUPPLIES	105.31	112.32	107
Eyeglasses and contact lenses	52.26	70.86	136
Hearing aids	14.98	4.64	31
Topicals and dressings	27.56	28.83	105
Medical equipment for general use	2.69	3.27	122
Supportive, convalescent medical equipment	5.21	3.56	68
Rental of medical equipment	1.06	0.35	33
Rental of supportive, convalescent medical equipment	1.55	0.81	52
ENTERTAINMENT	$2,078.99	$2,565.19	123
FEES AND ADMISSIONS	541.67	662.18	122
Recreation expenses on trips	25.64	32.27	126
Social, recreation, civic club membership	107.92	124.81	116
Fees for participant sports	75.05	81.96	109
Participant sports on trips	29.50	29.97	102
Movie, theater, opera, ballet	98.30	117.75	120
Movie, other admissions on trips	45.57	51.77	114
Admission to sports events	36.18	43.20	119
Admission to sports events on trips	15.19	17.26	114
Fees for recreational lessons	82.69	130.91	158
Other entertainment services on trips	25.64	32.27	126
TELEVISION, RADIO, SOUND EQUIPMENT	691.90	806.33	117
Television	543.66	621.56	114
Cable service and community antenna	382.28	436.45	114
Black-and-white TV	0.80	1.22	153
Color TV, console	38.63	41.93	109
Color TV, portable, table model	39.14	45.57	116

	total consumer units	CUs headed by 45-to-54-year-olds	
		average spending	indexed spending
VCRs and video disc players	$23.25	$30.43	131
Video cassettes, tapes, and discs	33.13	38.13	115
Video game hardware and software	23.46	24.74	105
Repair of TV, radio, and sound equipment	2.50	2.95	118
Rental of television sets	0.46	0.14	30
Radio and sound equipment	**148.25**	**184.77**	**125**
Radios	3.98	8.88	223
Tape recorders and players	5.31	7.69	145
Sound components and component systems	20.19	26.72	132
Miscellaneous sound equipment	3.18	1.99	63
Sound equipment accessories	5.97	8.59	144
Satellite dishes	1.00	1.38	138
Compact disc, tape, record, video mail order clubs	6.53	6.86	105
Records, CDs, audio tapes, needles	36.47	47.07	129
Rental of VCR, radio, sound equipment	0.25	0.17	68
Musical instruments and accessories	24.82	28.97	117
Rental and repair of musical instruments	1.22	1.91	157
Rental of video cassettes, tapes, discs, films	39.33	44.54	113
PETS, TOYS, PLAYGROUND EQUIPMENT	**369.12**	**465.65**	**126**
Pets	**248.25**	**347.92**	**140**
Pet food	102.56	129.86	127
Pet purchase, supplies, and medicines	52.29	59.99	115
Pet services	21.95	38.88	177
Veterinarian services	71.44	119.18	167
Toys, games, hobbies, and tricycles	**117.34**	**112.26**	**96**
Playground equipment	**3.54**	**5.48**	**155**
OTHER ENTERTAINMENT SUPPLIES, EQUIPMENT, SERVICES	**476.30**	**631.04**	**132**
Unmotored recreational vehicles	**47.14**	**39.49**	**84**
Boat without motor and boat trailers	16.15	4.45	28
Trailer and other attachable campers	30.99	35.05	113
Motorized recreational vehicles	**170.19**	**277.23**	**163**
Motorized camper	40.05	51.08	128
Other vehicle	35.47	24.06	68
Motorboats	94.67	202.09	213
Rental of recreational vehicles	**1.99**	**1.53**	**77**
Outboard motors	**0.71**	**0.25**	**35**
Docking and landing fees	**6.66**	**12.65**	**190**
Sports, recreation, exercise equipment	**150.33**	**177.14**	**118**
Athletic gear, game tables, exercise equipment	60.51	81.53	135
Bicycles	13.45	14.74	110
Camping equipment	9.59	17.11	178
Hunting and fishing equipment	35.68	16.32	46
Winter sports equipment	5.45	10.66	196
Water sports equipment	8.95	16.33	182
Other sports equipment	14.62	17.27	118
Rental and repair of misc. sports equipment	2.07	3.19	154

	total consumer units	CUs headed by 45-to-54-year-olds average spending	indexed spending
Photographic equipment and supplies	**$90.48**	**$112.02**	**124**
Film	17.74	21.05	119
Other photographic supplies	2.27	6.82	300
Film processing	26.60	31.88	120
Repair and rental of photographic equipment	0.12	0.20	167
Photographic equipment	23.34	28.96	124
Photographer fees	20.42	23.11	113
Fireworks	**1.52**	**0.53**	**35**
Souvenirs	**1.25**	**1.10**	**88**
Visual goods	**1.19**	**1.02**	**86**
Pinball, electronic video games	**4.84**	**8.07**	**167**
PERSONAL CARE PRODUCTS AND SERVICES	**$525.80**	**$588.30**	**112**
Personal care products	**276.65**	**309.10**	**112**
Hair care products	53.57	62.76	117
Hair accessories	6.57	7.08	108
Wigs and hairpieces	1.32	1.49	113
Oral hygiene products	27.33	30.00	110
Shaving products	15.09	16.75	111
Cosmetics, perfume, and bath products	129.13	142.65	110
Deodorants, feminine hygiene, misc. products	30.29	29.89	99
Electric personal care appliances	13.34	18.48	139
Personal care services	**249.15**	**279.20**	**112**
READING	**$138.57**	**$166.64**	**120**
Newspaper subscriptions	43.88	48.35	110
Newspaper, nonsubscription	11.30	12.63	112
Magazine subscriptions	16.59	19.35	117
Magazines, nonsubscription	9.35	10.67	114
Books purchased through book clubs	6.62	7.49	113
Books not purchased through book clubs	50.38	66.99	133
Encyclopedia and other reference book sets	0.33	0.94	285
EDUCATION	**$751.95**	**$1,208.24**	**161**
College tuition	444.45	670.56	151
Elementary and high school tuition	128.94	296.06	230
Other school tuition	25.53	42.47	166
Other school expenses including rentals	25.77	41.84	162
Books, supplies for college	57.93	71.51	123
Books, supplies for elementary, high school	16.14	21.79	135
Books, supplies for day care, nursery school	3.39	5.29	156
Miscellaneous school expenses and supplies	49.80	58.70	118

	total consumer units	CUs headed by 45-to-54-year-olds	
		average spending	indexed spending
TOBACCO PRODUCTS AND SMOKING SUPPLIES	**$320.49**	**$415.01**	**129**
Cigarettes	291.89	383.70	131
Other tobacco products	26.27	29.21	111
Smoking accessories	2.33	2.10	90
FINANCIAL PRODUCTS, SERVICES	**$788.12**	**$985.42**	**125**
Miscellaneous fees	2.25	2.57	114
Lottery and gambling losses	46.94	87.53	186
Legal fees	132.99	175.74	132
Funeral expenses	77.91	81.06	104
Safe deposit box rental	3.84	3.55	92
Checking accounts, other bank service charges	25.91	28.96	112
Cemetery lots, vaults, and maintenance fees	16.05	15.92	99
Accounting fees	57.85	64.95	112
Miscellaneous personal services	39.77	32.79	82
Finance charges, except mortgage and vehicles	271.37	338.54	125
Occupational expenses	38.46	52.80	137
Expenses for other properties	65.99	89.09	135
Credit card memberships	2.82	3.84	136
Shopping club membership fees	5.97	8.08	135
CASH CONTRIBUTIONS	**$1,277.10**	**$1,571.36**	**123**
Support for college students	75.94	178.91	236
Alimony expenditures	21.18	34.39	162
Child support expenditures	190.75	247.34	130
Gifts to non-CU members of stocks, bonds, and mutual funds	24.23	4.18	17
Cash contributions to charities and other organizations	137.62	180.63	131
Cash contributions to church, religious organizations	557.29	699.35	125
Cash contributions to educational institutions	33.42	40.39	121
Cash contributions to political organizations	10.90	10.89	100
Other cash gifts	225.76	175.28	78
PERSONAL INSURANCE, PENSIONS	**$3,898.62**	**$5,322.82**	**137**
Life and other personal insurance	**406.11**	**559.25**	**138**
Life, endowment, annuity, other personal insurance	391.65	537.89	137
Other nonhealth insurance	14.46	21.36	148
Pensions and Social Security	**3,492.51**	**4,763.57**	**136**
Deductions for government retirement	69.48	134.23	193
Deductions for railroad retirement	2.21	2.42	110
Deductions for private pensions	390.38	621.57	159
Nonpayroll deposit to retirement plans	426.12	484.29	114
Deductions for Social Security	2,604.32	3,521.05	135

	total consumer units	CUs headed by 45-to-54-year-olds	
		average spending	indexed spending
PERSONAL TAXES	**$2,496.26**	**$4,050.63**	**162**
Federal income taxes	1,842.57	3,052.10	166
State and local income taxes	506.45	797.79	158
Other taxes	147.24	200.74	136
GIFTS FOR NON-HOUSEHOLD MEMBERS**	**$1,036.24**	**$1,604.45**	**155**
Food	**82.18**	**152.65**	**186**
Cakes and cupcakes	2.41	4.83	200
Other fresh fruits (excl. apples, bananas, citrus)	2.26	1.96	87
Candy and chewing gum	11.69	12.88	110
Board (including at school)	21.90	67.07	306
Catered affairs	26.19	40.84	156
Alcoholic Beverages	**13.42**	**13.98**	**104**
Beer and ale	4.73	4.65	98
Wine	5.84	7.46	128
Housing	**258.69**	**386.63**	**149**
Housekeeping supplies	**42.48**	**50.91**	**120**
Laundry and cleaning supplies	2.93	4.04	138
Other household products	11.69	11.81	101
Miscellaneous household products	5.85	7.22	123
Lawn and garden supplies	4.20	2.89	69
Postage and stationery	27.86	35.05	126
Stationery, stationery supplies, giftwrap	21.13	27.02	128
Postage	6.14	7.05	115
Household textiles	**13.72**	**13.89**	**101**
Bathroom linens	2.59	1.74	67
Bedroom linens	6.10	7.92	130
Appliances and miscellaneous housewares	**23.98**	**28.18**	**118**
Major appliances	8.41	8.65	103
Electric floor cleaning equipment	2.77	2.94	106
Small appliances and miscellaneous housewares	15.57	19.53	125
China and other dinnerware	2.46	2.26	92
Nonelectric cookware	3.53	5.77	163
Tableware, nonelectric kitchenware	2.63	3.82	145
Small electric kitchen appliances	2.71	3.35	124
Miscellaneous household equipment	**64.70**	**94.41**	**146**
Infants' equipment	3.82	13.93	365
Outdoor equipment	2.07	5.11	247
Other household decorative items	25.76	31.34	122
Power tools	2.80	2.06	74
Indoor plants, fresh flowers	13.43	18.12	135
Computers and computer hardware	6.59	10.31	156
Miscellaneous household equipment	2.19	2.39	109
Other housing	**113.80**	**199.24**	**175**
Repair or maintenance services	4.51	8.96	199
Housing while attending school	39.93	125.05	313

	total consumer units	CUs headed by 45-to-54-year-olds	
		average spending	indexed spending
Natural gas (renter)	$3.62	$3.69	102
Electricity (renter)	14.67	10.82	74
Water, sewer maintenance (renter)	3.04	2.56	84
Day-care centers, nurseries, and preschools	23.81	15.00	63
APPAREL AND SERVICES	**237.13**	**256.52**	**108**
Men and boys, aged 2 or older	**63.74**	**68.63**	**108**
Men's coats and jackets	5.09	7.00	138
Men's accessories	4.45	9.67	217
Men's sweaters and vests	3.06	3.30	108
Men's active sportswear	2.76	3.37	122
Men's shirts	16.79	11.93	71
Men's pants	6.93	5.41	78
Boys' shirts	3.71	3.57	96
Boys' pants	3.76	4.17	111
Women and girls, aged 2 or older	**81.76**	**88.86**	**109**
Women's coats and jackets	5.62	9.29	165
Women's dresses	7.66	7.19	94
Women's vests and sweaters	8.50	11.37	134
Women's shirts, tops, blouses	9.06	10.39	115
Women's pants	6.62	4.82	73
Women's active sportswear	4.33	4.23	98
Women's sleepwear	6.45	4.42	69
Women's accessories	5.71	3.36	59
Girls' dresses and suits	2.98	8.28	278
Girls' shirts, blouses, sweaters	4.48	6.37	142
Girls' skirts and pants	3.32	2.88	87
Girls' accessories	2.38	1.22	51
Children under age 2	**39.99**	**40.33**	**101**
Infant dresses, outerwear	15.28	18.31	120
Infant underwear	16.91	15.09	89
Infant nightwear, loungewear	2.55	2.85	112
Infant accessories	3.93	3.04	77
Other apparel products and services	**51.63**	**58.70**	**114**
Jewelry and watches	24.01	22.58	94
Watches	2.16	2.20	102
Jewelry	21.85	20.38	93
Men's footwear	8.37	10.70	128
Boys' footwear	4.46	6.39	143
Women's footwear	8.82	14.62	166
Girls' footwear	3.30	2.71	82
TRANSPORTATION	**43.87**	**80.43**	**183**
New cars	7.09	8.06	114
Used cars	12.21	27.47	225
Airline fares	6.78	12.64	186
Ship fares	2.74	2.68	98

	total consumer units	CUs headed by 45-to-54-year-olds	
		average spending	indexed spending
HEALTH CARE	**$32.59**	**$54.82**	**168**
Physician's services	3.07	6.25	204
Dental services	4.03	5.96	148
Care in convalescent or nursing home	5.19	3.31	64
Nonprescription vitamins	3.93	13.35	340
Prescription drugs	2.38	3.37	142
ENTERTAINMENT	**78.24**	**105.68**	**135**
Toys, games, hobbies, and tricycles	29.98	36.31	121
Other entertainment	48.26	69.37	144
Fees for recreational lessons	7.88	15.02	191
Community antenna or cable TV	6.37	5.13	81
VCRs and videodisc players	2.26	3.37	149
Video game hardware and software	2.13	2.45	115
Athletic gear, game tables, exercise equipment	6.60	9.12	138
Hunting and fishing equipment	3.06	0.81	26
Photographer fees	3.19	7.76	243
PERSONAL CARE PRODUCTS, SERVICES	**21.15**	**25.79**	**122**
Cosmetics, perfume, bath preparation	12.53	14.84	118
Electric personal care appliances	3.31	4.48	135
EDUCATION	**183.88**	**414.52**	**225**
College tuition	127.83	298.28	233
Elementary and high school tuition	25.95	54.39	210
Other school tuition	4.44	8.36	188
Other school expenses including rentals	3.99	11.03	276
College books and supplies	11.93	28.86	242
Miscellaneous school supplies	7.38	10.00	136
ALL OTHER GIFTS	**83.76**	**112.22**	**134**
Gifts of trip expenses	44.40	56.10	126
Lottery and gambling losses	2.86	11.23	393
Legal fees	5.82	6.05	104
Funeral expenses	25.25	32.98	131
Miscellaneous personal services	2.16	3.46	160

* This figure does not include the amount paid for mortgage principle, which is considered an asset.
** Expenditures on gifts are also included in the preceding product and service categories. Food spending, for example, includes the amount spent on food gifts. Only gift categories with spending of $2.00 or more by the average consumer unit are shown.
Note: The Bureau of Labor Statistics uses consumer unit rather than household as the sampling unit in the Consumer Expenditure Survey. For the definition of consumer unit, see the glossary. (–) means not applicable or the sample is too small to make a reliable estimate.
Source: Bureau of Labor Statistics, unpublished data from the 2002 Consumer Expenditure Survey; calculations by New Strategist

Wealth

■ The net worth of older Boomers fell 2.2 percent between 1989 and 2001, after adjusting for inflation, while the net worth of younger Boomers rose a meager 0.8 percent.

■ The median value of financial assets of householders aged 35 to 44 rose more slowly than the national average, up only 39 percent between 1989 and 2001, to $26,900 after adjusting for inflation. Those of 45-to-54-year-olds rose a faster 82 percent, to $45,700. The values are probably lower today because of the stock market decline.

■ The nonfinancial assets of householders aged 35 to 44 rose just 1.5 percent between 1989 and 2001, after adjusting for inflation. Those of householders aged 45 to 54 fell 5 percent. Behind the stagnation and decline in the nonfinancial assets of Boomers is their postponement of homeownership.

■ The debts of Boomers grew more slowly than average between 1989 and 2001—up 49 percent among householders aged 35 to 44 and up 67 percent for those aged 45 to 54, after adjusting for inflation. Nevertheless, householders aged 35 to 54 continue to be the biggest debtors.

■ Pension participation peaks among workers aged 45 to 54, at 55 percent in 2001. Because many Boomers are funding their own pensions through defined-contribution plans, they worry about having enough money to retire.

Net Worth Is Down for Boomers

More debt means less net worth.

Net worth, one of the most important measures of wealth, is what remains after a household's debts are subtracted from its assets. The net worth of householders aged 35 to 54 rose 13 to 16 percent between 1998 and 2001, a greater increase in net worth than the 10 percent for the average household. Even so, the median net worth of older Boomers (aged 45 to 54) was lower in 2001 than in 1989, while younger Boomers (aged 35 to 44) experienced only a 0.8 percent rise in net worth during those years. In contrast, the net worth of the average household rose 33 percent between 1989 and 2001, from $64,600 to $86,100.

One reason for the lackluster growth in the net worth of Boomers since 1989 is their late arrival to homeownership. Because many delayed buying homes, the home equity of middle-aged householders has declined. The widespread use of home equity loans has also eaten into net worth, as has increased credit card debt. While financial assets have grown since 1989, those gains pale in comparison to rising debt loads.

■ Because of their late arrival to homeownership, the net worth of Boomers will continue to trail that of older generations. Only a concerted effort at paying off debt will boost the net worth of the middle-aged.

The net worth of older Boomers is above the national average

(median net worth of total householders and householders aged 35 to 54, 2001)

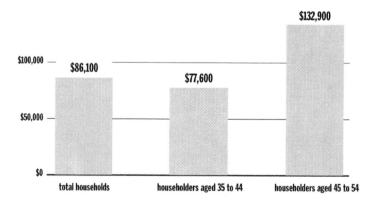

Table 9.1 Net Worth of Households by Age of Householder, 1989 to 2001

(median net worth of households by age of householder, 1989 to 2001; percent change, 1989–2001 and 1998–2001; in 2001 dollars)

	2001	1998	1995	1992	1989	percent change 1998–01	percent change 1989–01
Total households	**$86,100**	**$78,000**	**$66,400**	**$61,200**	**$64,600**	**10.4%**	**33.3%**
Under age 35	11,600	9,900	13,900	11,400	10,700	17.2	8.4
Aged 35 to 44	77,600	69,000	60,300	55,100	77,000	12.5	0.8
Aged 45 to 54	132,900	114,800	107,500	96,800	135,900	15.8	–2.2
Aged 55 to 64	181,500	139,200	133,200	141,100	134,700	30.4	34.7
Aged 65 to 74	176,300	159,500	128,000	121,700	105,000	10.5	67.9
Aged 75 or older	151,400	136,700	107,500	107,500	99,700	10.8	51.9

Source: Federal Reserve Board, results from the Survey of Consumer Finances; Internet site http://www.federalreserve.gov/pubs/oss/oss2/2001/scf2001home.html; calculations by New Strategist

Most Boomers Own Stock

But few have substantial stock portfolios.

Between 1989 and 2001, the financial assets of the average American household rose 80 percent after adjusting for inflation—to $28,000, according to the Federal Reserve Board's Survey of Consumer Finances. The financial assets of householders aged 35 to 44 rose a smaller 39 percent during those years, to $26,900. The assets of 45-to-54-year-olds rose about an average amount, up 82 percent, to $45,700.

Behind the rise in financial assets was the soaring stock market. Since the 2001 survey, the average household's financial assets probably have fallen below these figures because of the stock market decline.

Most householders aged 35 to 54 own stock, and the value of the stock they own more than doubled between 1989 and 2001. Still, Boomer stock holdings are modest at best. Among stock-owning householders aged 35 to 44, the median value of their stock holdings, both direct and indirect, stood at $27,500 in 2001. For those aged 45 to 54, the median value was $50,000. For both age groups, stocks account for more than half of their financial assets. Much of the stock owned by Boomers is in retirement accounts, which are owned by 61 to 63 percent of householders aged 35 to 54. The value of their retirement accounts stood at $28,500 for younger Boomers and $48,000 for older Boomers.

According to the Investment Company Institute and the Securities Industry Association, the Baby-Boom generation accounts for 48 percent of the nation's equity owners. Much of the stock owned by Boomers is in employer-sponsored retirement plans and mutual funds.

■ Although households own more financial assets than they once did, nonfinancial assets still account for the bulk of net worth. In particular, housing equity remains the most important asset for most Americans.

Financial assets of Boomers are modest

(median value of financial assets of total households and householders aged 35 to 54, 2001)

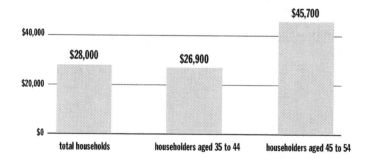

Table 9.2 Financial Assets of Households by Age of Householder, 1989 to 2001

(percentage of households owning financial assets and median value of assets for owners, by age of householder, 1989 to 2001; percentage point change in ownership and percent change in value of asset, 1989–2001 and 1998–2001; in 2001 dollars)

	2001	1998	1995	1992	1989	percentage point change 1998–01	percentage point change 1989–01
PERCENT OWNING ANY FINANCIAL ASSET							
Total households	**93.1%**	**92.9%**	**91.0%**	**90.2%**	**88.7%**	**0.2**	**4.4**
Under age 35	89.2	88.6	86.9	85.7	84.8	0.6	4.4
Aged 35 to 44	90.2	91.0	91.8	93.3	93.3	–0.8	–3.1
Aged 45 to 54	94.4	94.9	92.8	92.5	90.6	–0.5	3.8
Aged 55 to 64	94.8	95.6	90.8	92.5	87.5	–0.8	7.3
Aged 65 to 74	94.6	95.6	92.6	91.2	92.0	–1.0	2.6
Aged 75 or older	95.1	92.1	94.2	92.1	91.4	3.0	3.7

	2001	1998	1995	1992	1989	percent change 1998–01	percent change 1989–01
MEDIAN VALUE OF FINANCIAL ASSET							
Total households	**$28,000**	**$24,498**	**$17,992**	**$14,230**	**$15,554**	**14.3%**	**80.0%**
Under age 35	6,250	5,002	6,242	4,578	3,716	25.0	68.2
Aged 35 to 44	26,900	24,890	15,922	12,374	19,339	8.1	39.1
Aged 45 to 54	45,700	41,127	32,363	23,634	25,052	11.1	82.4
Aged 55 to 64	56,630	49,634	37,911	35,265	35,981	14.1	57.4
Aged 65 to 74	51,400	49,852	24,504	31,553	26,772	3.1	92.0
Aged 75 or older	40,000	39,882	26,469	26,047	40,537	0.3	–1.3

Source: Federal Reserve Board, results from the Survey of Consumer Finances; Internet site http://www.federalreserve.gov/pubs/oss/oss2/2001/scf2001home.html; calculations by New Strategist

Table 9.3 Financial Assets of Households by Type of Asset and Age of Householder, 2001

(percent of household owning selected financial assets, and median value of asset for owners, by type of asset and age of householder, 2001)

	total	under 35	35 to 44	45 to 54	55 to 64	65 to 74	75 or older
PERCENT OWNING ASSET							
Any financial asset	**93.1%**	**89.2%**	**93.3%**	**94.4%**	**94.8%**	**94.6%**	**95.1%**
Transaction accounts	90.9	86.0	90.7	92.2	93.6	93.8	93.7
Certificates of deposit	15.7	6.3	9.8	15.2	14.4	29.7	36.5
Savings bonds	16.7	12.7	22.6	21.0	14.3	11.3	12.5
Bonds	3.0	–	2.1	2.8	6.1	3.9	5.7
Stocks	21.3	17.4	21.6	22.0	26.7	20.5	21.8
Mutual funds	17.7	11.5	17.5	20.2	21.3	19.9	19.5
Retirement accounts	52.2	45.1	61.4	63.4	59.1	44.0	25.7
Life insurance	28.0	15.0	27.0	31.1	35.7	36.7	33.3
Other managed assets	6.6	2.1	3.1	6.4	13.0	11.8	11.2
Other financial assets	9.3	10.4	9.5	8.5	10.6	8.5	7.3
MEDIAN VALUE OF ASSET							
Total financial assets	**$28,000**	**$6,300**	**$26,900**	**$45,700**	**$56,600**	**$51,400**	**$40,000**
Transaction accounts	4,000	1,800	3,400	4,600	5,500	8,000	7,300
Certificates of deposit	15,000	4,000	6,000	12,000	19,000	20,000	25,000
Savings bonds	1,000	300	1,000	1,000	2,500	2,000	3,000
Bonds	43,500	–	13,600	60,000	60,000	71,400	35,000
Stocks	20,000	5,700	15,000	15,000	37,500	85,000	60,000
Mutual funds	35,000	9,000	17,500	38,500	60,000	70,000	70,000
Retirement accounts	29,000	6,600	28,500	48,000	55,000	60,000	46,000
Life insurance	10,000	10,000	9,000	11,000	10,000	8,800	7,000
Other managed assets	70,000	40,000	50,000	60,000	55,000	120,000	100,000
Other financial assets	4,000	1,300	2,000	5,000	10,000	8,000	17,500

Note: (–) means sample is too small to make a reliable estimate.
Source: Federal Reserve Board, results from the Survey of Consumer Finances; Internet site http://www.federalreserve.gov/pubs/oss/oss2/2001/scf2001home.html

Table 9.4 Stock Ownership of Households by Age of Householder, 1989 to 2001

(percentage of householders owning stocks directly or indirectly, median value of stocks for owners, and share of total household financial assets accounted for by stock holdings, by age of householder, 1989 to 2001; percent and percentage point change, 1989–2001 and 1998–2001; in 2001 dollars)

						percentage point change	
	2001	1998	1995	1992	1989	1998–01	1989–01
PERCENT OWNING STOCK							
Total households	**51.9%**	**48.9%**	**40.4 %**	**36.7%**	**31.7%**	**3.0**	**20.2**
Under age 35	48.9	40.8	36.6	28.4	22.4	8.1	26.5
Aged 35 to 44	59.5	56.7	46.4	42.4	39.0	2.8	20.5
Aged 45 to 54	59.2	58.6	48.9	46.4	41.8	0.6	17.4
Aged 55 to 64	57.1	55.9	40.0	45.3	36.2	1.2	20.9
Aged 65 to 74	39.2	42.7	34.4	30.2	26.7	–3.5	12.5
Aged 75 or older	34.2	29.4	27.9	25.7	25.9	4.8	8.3

						percent change	
	2001	1998	1995	1992	1989	1998–01	1989–01
MEDIAN VALUE OF STOCK							
Total households	**$34,250**	**$27,212**	**$16,875**	**$12,992**	**$11,700**	**54.6%**	**240.0%**
Under age 35	7,000	7,619	5,895	4,331	4,129	–8.1	69.5
Aged 35 to 44	27,500	21,769	11,558	9,280	7,089	26.3	287.9
Aged 45 to 54	50,000	41,362	29,986	18,561	18,100	20.9	176.2
Aged 55 to 64	81,200	51,158	35,831	30,934	25,327	58.7	220.6
Aged 65 to 74	150,000	60,954	39,298	19,798	27,942	146.1	436.8
Aged 75 or older	120,000	65,308	23,117	30,934	34,412	83.7	248.7

						percentage point change	
	2001	1998	1995	1992	1989	1998–01	1989–01
STOCK AS SHARE OF FINANCIAL ASSETS							
Total households	**56.0%**	**53.9%**	**39.9%**	**33.7%**	**27.8%**	**2.1**	**28.2**
Under age 35	52.6	44.8	27.2	24.8	20.2	7.8	32.4
Aged 35 to 44	57.3	54.6	39.5	31.0	29.2	2.7	28.1
Aged 45 to 54	59.1	55.7	42.6	40.8	33.5	3.4	25.6
Aged 55 to 64	56.1	58.4	44.2	37.3	27.6	-2.3	28.5
Aged 65 to 74	55.1	51.3	35.8	31.6	26.0	3.8	29.1
Aged 75 or older	51.4	48.7	39.8	25.5	25.0	2.7	26.4

Source: Federal Reserve Board, results from the Survey of Consumer Finances; Internet site http://www.federalreserve.gov/pubs/oss/oss2/2001/scf2001home.html; calculations by New Strategist

Table 9.5 Characteristics of Equity Owners by Generation, 2002

(selected characteristics of equity owners by generation, 2002)

	total	Generation X (born 1965 or later)	Baby Boom (born between 1946 and 1964)	Silent or GI (born in 1945 or earlier)
Percent of all equity investors	100%	25%	48%	27%
Median age*	47	30	46	65
Median household income	$62,500	$60,000	$70,000	$50,000
Median household financial assets**	100,000	35,000	125,000	350,000
Median household financial assets in equities	50,000	25,000	51,000	69,600
Median number of individual stocks and stock mutual funds owned	4	3	5	5
Percent of equity-owning households				
Married or living with partner*	71%	66%	76%	66%
College or postgraduate degree*	50	52	49	48
Employed*	77	93	91	38
Own individual stock (net)***	49	43	49	54
Inside employer-sponsored retirement plans	17	18	20	11
Outside employer-sponsored retirement plans	41	34	41	48
Stock mutual funds (net)***	89	86	92	88
Inside employer-sponsored retirement plans	66	69	76	43
Outside employer-sponsored retirement plans	56	48	53	68

* Refers to the household's responding financial decisionmaker for investments.
** Includes assets in employer-sponsored retirement plans but excludes value of primary residence.
*** Multiple responses included.
Note: Number of respondents varies.
Source: Investment Company Institute and the Securities Industry Association, Equity Ownership in America, 2002; Internet sites http://www.ici.org and http://www.sia.com

Nonfinancial Assets of Boomer Households Exceed $100,000

Since 1989, the value of nonfinancial assets owned by householders aged 45 to 54 has declined.

The median value of nonfinancial assets owned by the average American household stood at $113,500 in 2001, a gain of 22 percent since 1989, after adjusting for inflation. In contrast to the national trend, however, the value of the nonfinancial assets held by 45-to-54-year-olds declined 5 percent during those years, after adjusting for inflation. For those aged 35 to 44, the increase was less than 2 percent.

During the three-year period between 1998 and 2001, middle-aged householders saw a modest increase in the value of their nonfinancial assets, with a rise of 3 to 5 percent—or slightly less than the gain for the average household. Householders aged 45 to 54 owned a median of $141,558 in nonfinancial assets in 2001, while the figure was a smaller $117,806 for those aged 35 to 44.

Because housing equity accounts for the largest share of nonfinancial assets, delayed homeownership is the primary reason for the decline in the value of nonfinancial assets owned by older Boomers. The homeownership rate in the 45-to-54 age group fell 0.3 percentage points between 1989 and 2001. Among homeowners in the age group, their homes' median value stood at $135,000 in 2001. They owed on average $75,000 in home-secured debt.

■ As Boomers age and pay down their mortgages, their net worth will grow—but only if they can resist the lure of home equity loans.

The nonfinancial assets of Boomers are above average

(median value of nonfinancial assets of total householders and householders aged 35 to 54, 2001)

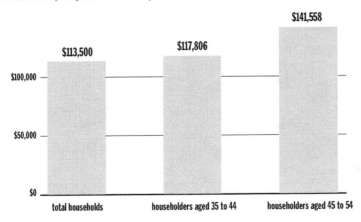

Table 9.6 Nonfinancial Assets of Households by Age of Householder, 1989 to 2001

(percentage of households owning nonfinancial assets and median value of assets for owners, by age of house-holder, 1989 to 2001; percentage point change in ownership and percent change in value of asset, 1989–2001 and 1998–2001; in 2001 dollars)

	2001	1998	1995	1992	1989	percentage point change 1998–01	percentage point change 1989–01
PERCENT OWNING ANY NONFINANCIAL ASSET							
Total households	**90.7%**	**89.9%**	**90.9%**	**90.8%**	**89.3%**	**0.8**	**1.4**
Under age 35	83.0	83.3	87.1	85.6	83.9	–0.3	–0.9
Aged 35 to 44	93.2	92.1	90.6	92.3	91.8	1.1	1.4
Aged 45 to 54	95.2	92.9	93.6	94.4	93.2	2.3	2.0
Aged 55 to 64	95.4	93.8	93.9	92.7	91.2	1.6	4.2
Aged 65 to 74	91.6	92.0	92.6	91.6	92.7	–0.4	–1.1
Aged 75 or older	86.4	87.2	89.9	91.3	85.4	–0.8	1.0

	2001	1998	1995	1992	1989	percent change 1998–01	percent change 1989–01
MEDIAN VALUE OF NONFINANCIAL ASSET							
Total households	**$113,500**	**$106,398**	**$96,050**	**$85,379**	**$92,911**	**6.7%**	**22.2%**
Under age 35	30,538	24,654	25,486	21,468	23,606	23.9	29.4
Aged 35 to 44	117,806	112,602	111,211	102,003	116,035	4.6	1.5
Aged 45 to 54	141,558	137,991	130,593	116,777	148,554	2.6	–4.7
Aged 55 to 64	147,863	138,154	124,830	131,687	129,249	7.0	14.4
Aged 65 to 74	149,211	119,568	109,631	97,474	86,717	24.8	72.1
Aged 75 or older	122,619	104,575	91,311	86,090	71,129	17.3	72.4

Source: Federal Reserve Board, results from the Survey of Consumer Finances; Internet site http://www.federalreserve.gov/pubs/oss/oss2/2001/scf2001home.html; calculations by New Strategist

Table 9.7 Nonfinancial Assets of Households by Type of Asset and Age of Householder, 2001

(percent of household owning selected nonfinancial assets, and median value of asset for owners, by type of asset and age of householder, 2001)

	total	under 35	35 to 44	45 to 54	55 to 64	65 to 74	75 or older
PERCENT OWNING ASSET							
Any nonfinancial asset	**90.7%**	**83.0%**	**93.2%**	**95.2%**	**95.4%**	**91.6%**	**86.4%**
Vehicles	84.8	78.8	88.9	90.5	90.7	81.3	73.9
Primary residence	67.7	39.9	67.8	76.2	83.2	82.5	76.2
Other residential property	11.3	3.4	9.2	14.7	18.3	13.7	15.2
Equity in nonresidential property	8.3	2.8	7.6	10.0	12.3	12.9	8.3
Business equity	11.8	7.0	14.2	17.1	15.6	11.6	2.4
Other nonfinancial assets	7.6	6.9	8.0	7.2	7.9	9.7	6.2
MEDIAN VALUE OF ASSET							
Total nonfinancial assets	**$113,200**	**$30,500**	**$117,800**	**$140,300**	**$147,900**	**$149,200**	**$122,600**
Vehicles	13,500	11,300	14,800	15,700	15,100	13,600	8,800
Primary residence	122,000	95,000	125,000	135,000	130,000	129,000	111,000
Other residential property	80,000	75,000	75,000	65,000	80,000	145,000	80,000
Equity in nonresidential property	49,000	33,300	39,500	56,400	78,500	50,000	28,000
Business equity	100,000	50,000	100,000	102,000	100,000	100,000	510,900
Other nonfinancial assets	12,000	10,000	9,000	11,000	30,000	20,000	15,000

Source: Federal Reserve Board, results from the Survey of Consumer Finances; Internet site http://www.federalreserve.gov/pubs/oss/oss2/2001/scf2001home.html

Table 9.8 Household Ownership of Primary Residence by Age of Householder, 1989 to 2001

(percentage of households owning primary residence, median value of asset for owners, and median value of home-secured debt for owners, by age of householder, 1989 to 2001; percentage point change in ownership and percent change in value of asset, 1989–2001 and 1998–2001; in 2001 dollars)

						percentage point change	
	2001	1998	1995	1992	1989	1998–01	1989–01
PERCENT OWNING PRIMARY RSESIDENCE							
Total households	**67.7%**	**66.2%**	**64.7%**	**63.9%**	**63.9%**	**1.5**	**3.8**
Under age 35	39.9	38.9	37.9	36.9	39.4	1.0	0.5
Aged 35 to 44	67.8	67.1	64.7	64.5	66.1	0.7	1.7
Aged 45 to 54	76.2	74.4	75.3	75.4	76.5	1.8	–0.3
Aged 55 to 64	83.2	80.3	82.0	77.5	80.1	2.9	3.1
Aged 65 to 74	82.5	81.5	79.5	79.3	77.7	1.0	4.8
Aged 75 or older	76.2	77.0	72.8	77.2	69.9	–0.8	6.3

						percent change	
	2001	1998	1995	1992	1989	1998–01	1989–01
MEDIAN VALUE OF PRIMARY RESIDENCE							
Total households	**$123,000**	**$108,847**	**$104,025**	**$98,990**	**$96,352**	**1.3%**	**27.7%**
Under age 35	95,000	91,431	87,843	85,379	83,964	3.9	13.1
Aged 35 to 44	125,000	109,935	109,804	111,363	110,117	13.7	13.5
Aged 45 to 54	135,000	130,616	115,583	111,363	116,999	3.4	15.4
Aged 55 to 64	130,000	119,732	100,557	105,053	103,234	8.6	25.9
Aged 65 to 74	129,000	103,405	98,246	85,379	75,705	24.8	70.4
Aged 75 or older	111,000	92,520	92,467	86,616	75,625	20.0	46.8

						percent change	
	2001	1998	1995	1992	1989	1998–01	1989–01
MEDIAN VALUE OF HOME-SECURED DEBT							
Total households	**$70,000**	**$67,485**	**$59,119**	**$53,207**	**$44,047**	**3.7%**	**58.9%**
Under age 35	77,000	77,281	71,662	63,106	60,564	–0.4	27.1
Aged 35 to 44	80,000	76,193	69,350	68,055	55,058	5.0	45.3
Aged 45 to 54	75,000	74,016	56,636	49,495	35,788	1.3	109.6
Aged 55 to 64	55,000	52,247	42,766	37,121	27,529	5.3	99.8
Aged 65 to 74	39,000	28,300	21,961	21,035	12,527	37.8	211.3
Aged 75 or older	44,800	23,106	13,523	34,646	9,635	93.9	365.0

Source: Federal Reserve Board, results from the Survey of Consumer Finances; Internet site http://www.federalreserve.gov/pubs/oss/oss2/2001/scf2001home.html; calculations by New Strategist

Debts Increase for Boomers

The biggest debtors are householders aged 35 to 44.

The debt of the average American household grew a substantial 88 percent between 1989 and 2001, to $38,775, after adjusting for inflation. Among Boomers, debt grew more slowly than average—up 49 percent for householders aged 35 to 44 and 67 percent for those aged 45 to 54. Between 1998 and 2001, the average household increased its debt load by 10 percent, while debt rose only 2 to 4 percent among householders aged 35 to 54. Nevertheless, householders aged 35 to 54 continue to be the biggest debtors. Those aged 35 to 44 owed a median of $61,539 in 2001, while those aged 45 to 54 owed $54,255.

Mortgages and home equity loans account for the largest share of debt for most households. Forty-five percent of households have mortgage debt, owing a median of $70,000. Householders aged 35 to 44 had mortgage and home equity debt of $80,000 in 2001, while those aged 45 to 54 owed a slightly smaller $75,000. The majority of boomers carry a credit card balance, the amount ranging from $2,000 to $2,300.

■ Although the debt of older boomers has been growing more slowly than that of the average household, it still outpaced their asset growth, causing a decline in net worth.

Boomers owe the most

(median amount of debt owed by total households and householders aged 35 to 54, 2001)

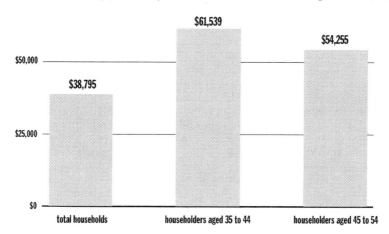

Table 9.9 Debt of Households by Age of Householder, 1989 to 2001

(percentage of households with debts and median amount of debt for debtors, by age of householder, 1989 to 2001; percentage point change in households with debt and percent change in amount of debt, 1989–2001 and 1998–2001; in 2001 dollars)

	2001	1998	1995	1992	1989	percentage point change 1998–01	percentage point change 1989–01
PERCENT WITH DEBT							
Total households	**75.1%**	**74.1%**	**74.5%**	**73.3%**	**72.3%**	**1.0**	**2.8**
Under age 35	82.7	81.2	83.5	81.5	80.0	1.5	2.7
Aged 35 to 44	88.6	87.6	87.0	86.4	88.6	1.0	0.0
Aged 45 to 54	84.6	87.0	86.3	85.4	85.3	–2.4	–0.7
Aged 55 to 64	75.4	76.4	73.7	70.1	70.8	–1.0	4.6
Aged 65 to 74	56.8	51.4	53.4	51.5	49.6	5.4	7.2
Aged 75 or older	29.2	24.6	28.4	31.6	21.0	4.6	8.2

	2001	1998	1995	1992	1989	percent change 1998–01	percent change 1989–01
MEDIAN AMOUNT OF DEBT							
Total households	**$38,775**	**$35,368**	**$24,987**	**$21,163**	**$20,647**	**9.6%**	**87.8%**
Under age 35	24,898	20,942	17,373	12,876	15,692	18.9	58.7
Aged 35 to 44	61,539	60,577	42,841	44,125	41,412	1.6	48.6
Aged 45 to 54	54,255	52,225	45,221	33,409	32,562	3.9	66.6
Aged 55 to 64	34,615	37,204	24,273	23,681	13,170	–7.0	162.8
Aged 65 to 74	13,100	12,964	8,146	5,974	6,882	1.1	90.3
Aged 75 or older	5,000	8,761	2,196	2,908	3,839	–42.9	30.2

Source: Federal Reserve Board, results from the Survey of Consumer Finances; Internet site http://www.federalreserve.gov/pubs/oss/oss2/2001/scf2001home.html; calculations by New Strategist

Table 9.10 Debt of of Households by Type of Debt and Age of Householder, 2001

(percent of householders with debt, and median value of debt for those with debts, by type of debt and age of householder, 2001)

	total	under 35	35 to 44	45 to 54	55 to 64	65 to 74	75 or older
PERCENT WITH DEBT							
Any debt	**75.1%**	**82.7%**	**88.6%**	**84.6%**	**75.4%**	**56.8%**	**29.2%**
Mortgage and home equity	44.6	35.7	59.6	59.8	49.0	32.0	9.5
Other residential property	4.7	2.7	4.9	6.5	8.0	3.4	2.0
Installment loans	45.2	63.8	57.1	45.9	39.3	21.1	9.5
Credit card balances	44.4	49.6	54.1	50.4	41.6	30.0	18.4
Other lines of credit	1.5	1.7	1.7	1.5	3.1	–	–
Other debt	7.2	8.8	8.0	7.4	7.4	5.0	3.6
MEDIAN VALUE OF DEBT FOR DEBTOR HOUSEHOLDS							
Total debt	**$38,800**	**$24,900**	**$61,500**	**$54,300**	**$34,600**	**$13,100**	**$5,000**
Mortgage, home equity	70,000	77,000	80,000	75,000	55,000	39,000	44,800
Other residential property	40,000	52,000	45,500	33,500	40,000	77,000	42,000
Installment loans	9,700	9,500	11,100	9,600	9,000	7,000	5,800
Credit card balances	1,900	2,000	2,000	2,300	1,900	1,000	700
Other lines of credit	3,900	500	700	5,300	20,500	–	–
Other debt	3,000	2,000	3,100	5,000	5,000	2,500	2,500

Note: (–) means sample is too small to make a reliable estimate.
Source: Federal Reserve Board, results from the Survey of Consumer Finances; Internet site http://www.federalreserve.gov/pubs/oss/oss2/2001/scf2001home.html

Pension Coverage Peaks in the 45-to-54 Age Group

Boomers worry about their economic security in retirement.

Only 43 percent of American workers were included in an employer's pension plan in 2001. Pension coverage peaks among workers aged 45 to 54, at 55 percent. The Current Population Survey data on pension coverage does not tell what kind of pension workers have, nor does it reveal how much money workers can expect to receive in retirement. The Bureau of Labor Statistics' 2003 National Compensation Survey reveals, however, that most workers with pension coverage are in defined-contribution (funded by the employee) rather than defined-benefit (funded by the employer) plans.

With workers now funding their own retirement, it's little wonder older Boomers (born between 1946 and 1954) are less confident than younger adults in their ability to live comfortably throughout retirement. Forty-one percent are "not at all" or "not too" confident, according to the 2003 Retirement Confidence Survey. Among younger Boomers, only 28 percent are this concerned about funding their retirement.

Few boomers expect an inheritance to help them out in retirement. In 2001, 17 percent had already received an inheritance, according to an AARP study of the Federal Reserve Board's Survey of Consumer Finances. Only another 15 expected to receive one, down substantially from the 27 percent who expected an inheritance in 1989. Of those receiving an inheritance, just 5 percent got $100,000 or more.

■ The substitution of defined-contribution for defined-benefit pension plans puts the burden of retirement savings on workers rather than employers. With Boomers finding it hard to save, millions will be forced to postpone retirement.

More than half of workers aged 45 to 64 have pension coverage

(percent of workers whose employer offers a pension plan who are included in the plan, by age, 2001)

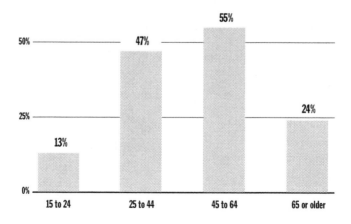

Table 9.11 Pension Coverage by Sex and Age, 2001

(total number of workers, number and percent whose employer offer a pension plan, and number and percent included in the plan, by sex and age, 2001; numbers in thousands)

	total	with employer offered plan		included in plan	
		number	percent	number	percent
Total workers	151,608	84,059	55.4%	65,445	43.2%
Aged 15 to 24	24,593	8,597	35.0	3,135	12.7
Aged 25 to 44	71,281	41,904	58.8	33,534	47.0
Aged 45 to 64	50,230	31,462	62.6	27,476	54.7
Aged 65 or older	5,504	2,096	38.1	1,301	23.6
Men	80,300	44,358	55.2	35,916	44.7
Aged 15 to 24	12,816	4,375	34.1	1,732	13.5
Aged 25 to 44	38,048	22,223	58.4	18,417	48.4
Aged 45 to 64	26,313	16,579	63.0	14,990	57.0
Aged 65 or older	3,123	1,181	37.8	776	24.9
Women	71,308	39,701	55.7	29,529	41.1
Aged 15 to 24	11,777	4,223	35.9	1,403	11.9
Aged 25 to 44	33,232	19,680	59.2	15,117	45.5
Aged 45 to 64	23,917	14,883	62.2	12,485	52.2
Aged 65 or older	2,382	915	38.4	525	22.0

Source: Bureau of the Census, 2002 Current Population Survey Annual Demographic Supplement, Internet site http://ferret.bls.census.gov/macro/032002/noncash/nc8_000.htm

Table 9.12 Retirement Confidence by Generation, 2003

(percent responding by generation, 2003)

	total	Gen X	younger Boomers	older Boomers	pre-retirees
Overall confidence in having enough money to live comfortably throughout retirement					
Very confident	21%	19%	23%	19%	29%
Somewhat confident	45	49	49	39	35
Not too confident	17	17	16	18	21
Not at all confident	16	15	12	23	14
Have saved for retirement					
Self	68	64	74	66	64
Household	71	68	78	69	68
Have done a retirement savings needs calculation					
Self	37	36	38	37	39
Household	43	41	45	41	42
Contribute to a retirement savings plan at work					
Yes	78	78	78	78	72
No	22	22	22	21	28
Expected retirement age					
Less than 55	6	8	7	4	–
Aged 55 to 59	10	11	10	11	0
Aged 60 to 64	21	19	22	22	24
Aged 65	25	28	28	21	17
Aged 66 or older	24	23	22	24	28
Never retire	6	4	5	7	10
Percentage expecting to work for pay in retirement	70	68	73	70	65

Note: Pre-retirees were born in 1945 or earlier; older Boomers were born between 1946 and 1954; younger Boomers were born between 1955 and 1964; Generation Xers were born in 1965 to 1978; (–) means data not available.
Source: 2003 Retirement Confidence Survey, EBRI/ASEC/Greenwald. Internet site http://www.ebri.org/

Table 9.13 Inheritance Receipt and Expectations by Generation, 1989 to 2001

(percent responding by generation and year, 1989 to 2001)

	pre-Boomers	Boomers	post-Boomers
Percent of households that have received at least one inheritance			
2001	24.0%	17.3%	11.0%
1998	29.1	16.9	11.8
1995	27.7	18.0	11.8
1992	27.1	15.5	9.9
1989	29.1	17.4	12.4
Percent of households that expect to receive an inheritance			
2001	5.8	14.9	18.4
1998	6.2	16.4	19.3
1995	6.4	18.1	20.7
1992	8.4	19.3	24.6
1989	10.8	26.9	20.6
Percent of households by amount inherited			
Total	**100.0**	**100.0**	**100.0**
No inheritance	76.0	82.7	89.0
$1 to $20,000	3.2	5.2	4.9
$20,001 to $50,000	3.8	3.6	2.4
$50,001 to $100,000	4.2	3.1	1.7
$100,000 or more	12.8	5.4	2.0
Median value of inheritances received (in 2002 dollars)			
2001	$108,885	$47,909	$22,167
1998	79,849	49,062	24,844
1995	78,499	41,833	20,325
1992	89,831	44,654	17,232
1989	105,165	44,692	27,635

Note: Pre-Boomers were born before 1946; Boomers were born from 1946 through 1964; post-Boomers were born after 1964.
Source: © 2003, AARP. Reprinted with permission. "Pennies from Heaven: Will Inheritances Bail Out the Boomers?" Mitja Ng-Baumhackl, John Gist, and Carlos Figueiredo, Data Digest, DD Number 90, AARP Public Policy Institute

For More Information

The federal government is a rich source of data on almost every aspect of American life. Below are the Internet addresses of federal and other agencies collecting the demographic data analyzed in this book. Also shown are phone numbers of the agencies and of the subject specialists at the Census Bureau and the Bureau of Labor Statistics, organized alphabetically by name of agency or specialty topic. A list of State Data Centers and Small Business Development Centers is also below to help you track down demographic and economic information for your state or local area. E-mail addresses are shown when available. Note: Telephone numbers at the Census Bureau change regularly. If the numbers below do not allow you to reach the specialists you need, go to http://www.census.gov/contacts/www/contacts.html for the most up-to-date lists.

Internet addresses

- AARP, http://www.aarp.org
- Agency for Healthcare Research and Quality, www.meps.ahrq.gov/Data_Public.htm
- Behavioral Risk Factor Surveillance System, http://apps.nccd.cdc.gov/brfss/index.asp
- Bureau of the Census, www.census.gov
- Bureau of Labor Statistics, www.bls.gov
- Centers for Disease Control and Prevention,www.cdc.gov
- Consumer Expenditure Survey, www.bls.gov/cex/
- Current Population Survey, www.bls.census.gov/cps/cpsmain.htm
- Employee Benefit Research Institute, www.ebri.org
- Federal Interagency Forum on Child and Family Statistics, http://childstats.gov/
- Higher Education Research Institute, www.gseis.ucla.edu/heri/heri.html
- Institute for Social Research, University of Michigan, http://monitoringthefuture.org
- Investment Company Institute, http://www.ici.org
- National Center for Education Statistics, http://nces.ed.gov
- National Center for Health Statistics, www.cdc.gov/nchs
- National Sporting Goods Association, www.nsga.org
- Securities Industry Association, www.sia.com
- Sourcebook of Criminal Justice Statistics,www.albany.edu/sourcebook/
- Sporting Goods Manufacturers Association, www.sgma.com
- Survey of Consumer Finances, www.federalreserve.gov/pubs/oss/oss2/scfindex.html
- U.S. Substance Abuse and Mental Health Services Administrations, www.samhsa.gov
- U.S. Citizenship and Immigration Services, http://uscis.gov/graphics/shared/aboutus/statistics/index.htm
- Youth Risk Behavior Surveillance System, www.cdc.gov/nccdphp/dash/yrbs/results.htm

Subject Specialists

Absences from work, Staff 202-691-6378
Aging population, Staff 301-763-2378
American Community Survey/C2SS Results, Larry McGinn 301-763-8050
Ancestry, Staff 301-763-2403
Apportionment, Edwin Byerly 301-763-2381
Apportionment and redistricting, Cathy McCully 301-763-4039
Business expenditures, Sheldon Ziman 301-763-3315
Business investment, Charles Funk 301-763-3324
Business owners, characteristics of, Valerie Strang 301-763-3316
Census 1990 and earlier, Staff 301-763-2422
Census 2000
- American Factfinder, Staff 301-763-INFO (4636)
- Annexations/boundary changes, Joe Marinucci 301-763-1099
- Apportionment, Edwin Byerly 301-763-2381
- Census 2000 Briefs, Staff 301-763-2437
- Census 2000 tabulations, Staff 301-763-2422
- Census 2010, Ed Gore 301-763-3998
- Census history, Dave Pemberton 301-763-1167
- Citizenship, Staff 301-763-2411
- Commuting and place of work, Clara Reschovsky/Celia Boertlein 301-763-2454
- Confidentiality and privacy, Jerry Gates 301-763-2515
- Count question resolution, Staff 866-546-0527
- Count review, Paul Campbell 301-763-2381
- Data dissemination, Staff 301-763-INFO (4636)
- Disability, Staff 301-763-3242
- Education, Staff 301-763-2464

- Employment/unemployment, Staff 301-763-3230
- Foreign born, Staff 301-763-2411
- Geographic entities, Staff 301-763-1099
- Grandparents as caregivers, Staff 301-763-2416
- Group quarters population, Denise Smith 301-763-2378
- Hispanic origin, ethnicity, ancestry, Staff 301-763-2403
- Homeless, Annetta Clark 301-763-2378
- Housing, Staff 301-763-3237
- Immigration/emigration, Staff 301-763-2411
- Income, Staff 301-763-3243
- Island areas, Idabelle Hovland 301-763-8443
- Labor force status/work experience, Staff 301-763-3230
- Language spoken in home, Staff 301-763-2464
- Living arrangements, Staff 301-763-2416
- Maps, customer services 301-763-INFO (4636)
- Marital status, Staff 301-763-2416
- Metropolitan areas, concepts and standards,
  Michael Ratcliffe 301-763-2419
- Microdata files, Amanda Shields 301-763-1326
- Migration, Carol Faber 301-763-2454
- Occupation/industry, Staff 301-763-3239
- Place of birth/native born, Carol Faber 301-763-2454
- Population (general information), Staff 301-763-2422
- Poverty, Alemayehu Bishaw 301-763-3213
- Race, Staff 301-763-2402
- Redistricting, Cathy McCully 301-763-4039
- Residence rules, Karen Mills 301-763-2381
- Small area income and poverty estimates,
  David Waddington 301-763-3195
- Special censuses, Mike Stump 301-763-3577
- Special populations, Staff 301-763-2378
- Special tabulations, Linda Showalter 301-763-2429
- Undercount, Phil Gbur 301-763-4206
  - Demographic analysis, Greg Robinson 301-763-2110
- Unmarried partners, Staff 301-763-2416
- Urban/rural, Ryan Short 301-763-1099
- U.S. citizens abroad, Staff 301-763-2422
- Veteran status, Staff 301-763-3230
- Voting districts, John Byle 301-763-1099
- Women, Renee Spraggins 301-763-2378
- ZIP codes, Staff 301-763-2422
Census Bureau customer service,
  Staff 301-763-INFO (4636)
Child care, Martin O'Connell/Kristin Smith
  301-763-2416
Children, Staff 301-763-2416
Citizenship status, Staff 301-763-2411
Communications and Utilities
- Current programs, Ruth Bramblett 301-763-2787
- Economic census, Jim Barron 301-763-2786

Commuting, means of transportation, and place of work,
  Clara Reschovsky/Celia Boertlein 301-763-2454
Construction
- Building permits, Staff 301-763-5160
- Economic census, Susan Bucci, Staff 301-763-4680
- Housing starts and completions, Staff 301-763-5160
- Manufactured housing, Lisa Feldman 301-763-1605
- Residential characteristics, price index, and sales,
  Staff 301-763-5160
- Residential improvements and repairs,
  Joe Huesman 301-763-1605
- Value of new construction, Mike Davis 301-763-1605
Consumer Expenditure Survey, Staff
  202-691-6900, cexinfo@bls.gov
Contingent workers, Staff 202-691-6378
County Business Patterns, Phillip Thompson
  301-763-2580
County populations, Staff 301-763-2422
Crime, Marilyn Monahan 301-763-5315
Current Population Survey, general information,
  Staff, 301-763-3806
Demographic surveys, demographic statistics,
  Staff 301-763-2422
Disability, Staff 301-763-3242
Discouraged workers, Staff 202-691-6378
Displaced workers, Staff 202-691-6378
Economic census 1997
- Accommodations and food services,
  Fay Dorsett 301-763-2687
- Construction, Staff 301-763-4680
- Finance and insurance, Faye Jacobs 301-763-2824
- General information, Robert Marske 301-763-2547
- Internet dissemination, Paul Zeisset 301-763-4151
- Manufacturing:
  - Consumer goods industries, Robert Reinard
    301-763-4810
  - Investment goods industries, Kenneth Hansen
    301-763-4755
  - Primary goods industries, Nat Shelton 301-763-6614
- Mining, Susan Bocci 301-763-4680
- Minority/women-owned businesses, Valerie Strang
  301-763-3316
- North American Industry Class. System,
  Wanda Dougherty 301-763-2790
- Puerto Rico and the Island Areas, Irma Harahush
  301-763-3319
- Real estate and rental/leasing, Pam Palmer
  301-763-2824
- Retail trade, Fay Dorsett 301-763-2687

Industry-occupation matrix, David Frank 202-691-5708

Projections:
- Computer, Chet Levine/Roer Moncarz
  202-691-5715/5694
- Construction, Doug Braddock/William Lawhorn
  202-691-5695/5093
- Education, Arlene Dohm 202-691-5727
- Engineering, Doug Braddock 202-691-5695
- Food and lodging, Theresa Cosca/Jon Kelinson
  202-691-5712/5688
- Health, Theresa Cosca/Alan Lacey/Terry Schau
  202-601-5712/5731/5720
- Legal, Tamara Dillon 202-691-5733
- Mechanics and repairers, Theresa Cosca
  202-691-5712
- Sales, Doug Braddock/Andrew Alpert
  202-691-5695/5754
- Scientific, Henry Kasper 292-691-5696
- Replacement and separation rates, Alan Lacey/
  Lynn Shniper 202-691-5731/5732

Older workers, Staff 202-691-6378

Outlying areas, Michael Levin 301-763-1444

Part-time workers, Staff 202-691-6378

Place of birth, Staff 301-763-2422

Population estimates and projections, Staff 301-763-2422

Population information, Staff 301-763-2422

Poverty statistics, Staff 301-763-3242

Prisoner surveys, Marilyn Monahan 301-763-5315

Puerto Rico, Idabelle Hovland 301-763-8443

Quarterly Financial Report, Yolando St. George
  301-763-3343

Race, concepts and interpretation, Staff 301-763-2402

Race statistics, Staff 301-763-2422

Retail trade
- Advance monthly, Scott Scheleur 301-763-2713;
  svsd@census.gov
- Annual retail, Scott Scheleur 301-763-2713;
  svsd@census.gov
- Economic census, Fay Dorsett 301-763-5180;
  rcb@census.gov
- Monthly sales and inventory, Nancy Piesto
  301-763-2747; retail.trade@census.gov
- Quarterly Financial Report, Yolando St. George
  301-763-3343; cad@census.gov

School enrollment, Staff 301-763-2464

Seasonal adjustment methodology, Richard Tiller/Thomas
  Evans 202-691-6370/6354

Services
- Current Reports, Ruth Bramblett 301-763-2787;
  svsd@census.gov

Economic census, Jack Moody 301-763-5181;
  scb@census.gov

General information, Staff 1-800-541-8345;
  scb@census.gov

Small area income and poverty estimates, Staff
  301-763-3193

Special censuses, Mike Stump 301-763-3577

Special surveys, Ron Dopkowski 301-763-3801

Special tabulations, Linda Showalter 301-763-2429

State population estimates, Staff 301-763-2422

Statistics of U.S. businesses, Melvin Cole 301-763-3321

Survey of Income and Program Participation (SIPP),
  Staff 301-763-3242

Transportation
- Commodity Flow Survey, John Fowler 301-763-2108;
  svsd@census.gov
- Establishments, James Barron 301-763-2786;
  ucb@census.gov
- Vehicle inventory and use survey, Thomas Zabelsky
  301-763-5175; vius@census.gov
- Wholesale trade, Donna Hambric 301-763-2725;
  svsd@census.gov

Undercount, demographic analysis, Gregg Robinson
  301-763-2110

Union membership, Staff 202-691-6378

Urban/rural population, Michael Ratcliff 301-763-2419

Veterans in labor force, Staff 202-691-6378

Veterans' status, Staff 301-763-3230

Voters, characteristics, Staff 301-763-2464

Voting age population, Staff 301-763-2464

Weekly earnings, Staff 202-691-6378

Wholesale trade
- Annual wholesale, Scott Scheleur 301-763-2713;
  svsd@census.gov
- Current sales and inventories, Scott Scheleur
  301-763-2713; svsd@census.gov
- Economic census, Donna Hambric 301-763-2725;
  wcb@census.gov
- Quarterly Financial Report, Yolando St. George
  301-763-3343; csd@census.gov

Women, Renee Spraggins 301-763-2378

Women in the labor force, Staff 202-691-6378

Work experience, Staff 202-691-6378

Working poor, Staff 202-691-6378

Youth, students, and dropouts in labor force,
  Staff 202-691-6378

Census Regional Offices

Information specialists in the Census Bureau's 12
regional offices answer thousands of questions each year.

If you have questions about the Census Bureau's products and services, contact the regional office serving your state. The states served by each regional office are listed in parentheses.

- Atlanta (AL, FL, GA) 404-730-3833 www.census.gov/atlanta
- Boston, MA (CT, MA, ME, NH, NY, RI, VT) 617-424-0510; www.census.gov/boston
- Charlotte (KY, NC, SC, TN, VA) 704-424-6430 www.census.gov/charlotte
- Chicago (IL, IN, WI) 708-562-1350 www.census.gov/chicago
- Dallas (LA, MS, TX) 214-253-4481 www.census.gov/dallas
- Denver (AZ, CO, MT, NE, ND, NM, NV, SD, UT, WY) 303-969-7750; www.census.gov/denver
- Detroit (MI, OH, WV) 313-259-1875 www.census.gov/detroit
- Kansas City (AR, IA, KS, MN, MO, OK) 913-551-6711; www.census.gov/kansascity
- Los Angeles (southern CA, HI) 818-904-6339 www.census.gov/losangeles
- New York (NY, NJ-selected counties) 212-264-4730 www.census.gov/newyork
- Philadelphia (DE, DC, MD, NJ-selected counties, PA) 215-656-7578; www.census.gov/philadelphia
- Seattle (northern CA, AK, ID, OR, WA) 206-553-5835 www.census.gov/seattle
- Puerto Rico and the U.S. Virgin Islands are serviced by the Boston regional office. All other outlying areas are serviced by the Los Angeles regional office.

State Data Centers and Business and Industry Data Centers

For demographic and economic information about states and local areas, contact your State Data Center (SDC) or Business and Industry Data Center (BIDC). Every state has a State Data Center. Below are listed the leading centers for each state-usually a state government agency, university, or library that heads a network of affiliate centers. Asterisks (*) identify states that also have BIDCs. In some states, one agency serves as the lead for both the SDC and the BIDC. The BIDC is listed separately if a separate agency serves as the lead.

- Alabama, Annette Watters, University of Alabama 205-348-6191; awatters@cba.ua.edu
- Alaska, Kathryn Lizik, Department of Labor 907-465-2437; kathryn_lizik@labor.state.ak.us
- American Samoa, Vaitoelau Filiga, Department of Commerce 684-633-5155; vfiliga@doc.asg.as

- Arizona*, Betty Jeffries, Dept of Economic Security 602-542-5984; betty.jeffries@de.state.az.us
- Arkansas, Sarah Breshears, University of Arkansas/ Little Rock 501-569-8530; sgbreshears@ualr.edu
- California, Julie Hoang, Department of Finance 916-323-4086; fijhoang@dof.ca.gov
- Colorado, Rebecca Picaso, Department of Local Affairs 303-866-3120; rebecca.picaso@state.co.us
- Connecticut, Bill Kraynak, Office of Policy and Mgmt., 860-418-6230; william.kraynak@po.state.ct.us
- Delaware*, Mike Helmer, Economic Development Office 302-672-6848; michael.helmer@state.de.us
- District of Columbia, Herb Bixhorn, Mayor's Office of Planning 202-442-7603; herb.bixhorn@dc.gov
- Florida*, Pam Schenker, Florida Agency for Workforce Innovation 850-488-1048; pamela.schenker@awi.state.fl.us
- Georgia, Robert Giacomini, Office of Planning and Budget 404-656-6505; girt@mail.opb.state.ga.us
- Guam, Isabel Lujan, Bureau of Statistics and Plans 671-472-4201; idlujan@mail.gov.gu
- Hawaii, Jan Nakamoto, Dept. of Business, Ec. Dev., and Tourism 808-586-2493; jnakamot@dbedt.hawaii.gov
- Idaho, Alan Porter, Department of Commerce 208-334-2470; aporter@idoc.state.id.us
- Illinois*, Suzanne Ebetsch, Dept. of Commerce and Community Affairs 217-782-1381; sue_ebetsch@commerce.state.il.us
- Illinois BIDC, Ed Taft, Dept. of Commerce and Community Affairs 217-785-7545; ed_taft@commerce.state.il.us
- Indiana*, Roberta Brooker, State Library 317-232-3733; rbrooker@statelib.lib.in.us
- Indiana BIDC, Carol Rogers, Business Research Center 317-274-2205; rogersc@iupui.edu
- Iowa, Beth Henning, State Library 515-281-4350; beth.henning@lib.state.ia.us
- Kansas, Marc Galbraith, State Library 785-296-3296; marcg@kslib.info
- Kentucky*, Ron Crouch, University of Louisville 502-852-7990; rtcrou01@gwise.louisville.edu
- Louisiana, Karen Paterson, Office of Planning and Budget 225-219-5987; kpaters@doa.state.la.us
- Maine*, Eric VonMagnus, State Planning Office 207-287-3261; eric.vonmagnus@state.me.us
- Maryland*, Jane Traynham, Office of Planning 410-767-4450; jtraynham@mdp.state.md.us

- Massachusetts*, John Gaviglio, Institute for Social and Econ. Research 413-545-3460; miser@miser.umass.edu
- Michigan, Daarren Warner, Library of Michigan 517-373-2548; warnerd@michigan.gov
- Minnesota*, Dona Ronningen, State Demographer's Office 651-296-4886; barbara.ronningen@state.mn.us
- Mississippi*, Rachel McNeely, University of Mississippi 662-915-7288; rmcneely@olemiss.edu
- Mississippi BIDC, Deloise Tate, Dept. of Ec. and Comm. Dev. 601-359-3593; dtate@mississippi.org
- Missouri*, Debra Pitts, State Library 573-526-7648; pittsd@sosmail.state.mo.us
- Missouri BIDC, Cathy Frank, Small Business Research Information Center 573-341-6484; cfrank@umr.edu
- Montana*, Pam Harris, Department of Commerce 406-841-2740; paharris@state.mt.us
- Nebraska, Jerome Deichert, University of Nebraska at Omaha 402-554-2134; jerome_deichert@unomaha.edu
- Nevada, Ramona Reno, State Library and Archives 775-684-3326; rlreno@clan.lib.nv.us
- New Hampshire, Thomas Duffy, Office of State Planning 603-271-2155; t_duffy@osp.state.nh.us
- New Jersey*, David Joye, Department of Labor 609-984-2595; djoye@dol.state.nj.us
- New Mexico*, Kevin Kargacin, University of New Mexico 505-277-6626; kargacin@unm.edu
- New Mexico BIDC, Beth Davis, Economic Development Dept. 505-827-0264; edavis@edd.state.nm.us
- New York*, Staff, Department of Economic Development 518-292-5300; rscardamalia@empire.state.ny.us
- North Carolina*, Staff, State Library 919-733-3270; francine.stephenson@ncmail.net
- North Dakota, Richard Rathge, North Dakota State University 701-231-8621; richard.rathge@ndsu.nodak.edu
- Northern Mariana Islands, Diego A. Sasamoto, Dept. of Commerce 670-664-3033; csd@itecnmi.com
- Ohio*, Steve Kelley, Department of Development 614-466-2116; skelley@odod.state.oh.us
- Oklahoma*, Jeff Wallace, Department of Commerce 405-815-5184; jeff_wallace@odoc.state.ok.us
- Oregon, George Hough, Portland State University. 503-725-5159; houghg@mail.pdx.edu
- Pennsylvania*, Sue Copella, Pennsylvania State Univ./ Harrisburg 717-948-6336; sdc3@psu.edu
- Puerto Rico, Lillian Torres Aguirre, Planning Bd. 787-727-4444; torres_l@jp.gobierno.pr
- Rhode Island, Mark Brown, Department of Administration 401-222-6183; mbrown@planning.state.ri.us
- South Carolina, Mike MacFarlane, Budget and Control Board 803-734-3780; mmacfarl@drss.state.sc.us
- South Dakota, Nancy Nelson, University of South Dakota 605-677-5287; nnelson@usd.edu
- Tennessee, Betty Vickers, University of Tennessee, Knoxville 865-974-5441; bvickers@utk.edu
- Texas*, Steve Murdock, Texas A&M University 979-845-5115/5332; smurdock@rsocsun.tamu.edu
- Texas BIDC, Ann Griffith, Dept. of Economic Dev. 512-936-0550; bidc@txed.state.tx.us
- Utah*, Sophia DiCaro, Governor's Office of Planning and Budget 801-537-9013; sdicaro@utah.gov
- Vermont, William Sawyer, Center for Rural Studies 802-656-3021; william.sawyer@uvm.edu
- Virgin Islands, Frank Mills, University of the Virgin Islands 340-693-1027; fmills@uvi.edu
- Virginia*, Don Lillywhite, Virginia Employment Commission 804-786-7496; dlillywhite@vec.state.va.us
- Washington*, Yi Zhao, Office of Financial Management 360-902-0592; yi.zhao@ofm.wa.gov
- West Virginia*, Delphine Coffey, West Virginia Dev. Office 304-558-4010; dcoffey@wvdo.org
- West Virginia BIDC, Randy Childs, Bureau of Business & Economic Research 304-293-7832; randy.childs@mail.wvu.edu
- Wisconsin*, Robert Naylor, Demographic Services Center 608-266-1927; bob.naylor@doa.state.wi.us
- Wisconsin BIDC, Dan Veroff, University of Wisconsin 608-265-9545; dlveroff@facstaff.wisc.edu
- Wyoming, Wenlin Liu, Dept. of Administration and Information 307-777-7504; wliu@missc.state.wy.us

Glossary

adjusted for inflation Income or a change in income that has been adjusted for the rise in the cost of living, or the consumer price index (CPI-U-RS).

American Housing Survey (AHS) The AHS collects national and metropolitan-level data on the nation's housing, including apartments, single-family homes, and mobile homes. The nationally representative survey, with a sample of 55,000 homes, is conducted by the Census Bureau for the Department of Housing and Urban Development every other year.

American Indians In this book, American Indians include Alaska Natives (Eskimos and Aleuts). In tables showing 2000 census data, the term "American Indian" may include those who identified themselves as American Indian and no other race (called "American Indian alone") or those who identified themselves as American Indian and some other race (called "American Indian in combination").

Asian The term "Asian" is defined differently depending on whether census or survey data are shown. In tables showing 2000 census data, Asians do not include Native Hawaiians or other Pacific Islanders unless noted. The term "Asian" may include those who identified themselves as Asian and no other race (called "Asian alone") or those who identified themselves as Asian and some other race (called "Asian in combination"). Asian estimates from the 2003 Current Population Survey include both those who identified themselves as Asian alone and those who identified themselves as Asian in combination. Asian estimates in earlier survey data do not include the multiracial option. Also, in surveys and other noncensus data collections, Asian figures include Native Hawaiians and other Pacific Islanders.

Baby Boom Americans born between 1946 and 1964.

Baby Bust Americans born between 1965 and 1976, also known as Generation X.

Behavioral Risk Factor Surveillance System (BRFSS) The BRFSS is a collaborative project of the Centers for Disease Control and Prevention and U.S. states and territories. It is an ongoing data collection program designed to measure behavioral risk factors in the adult population aged 18 or older. All 50 states, three territories, and the District of Columbia take part in the survey, making the BRFSS the primary source of information on the health-related behaviors of Americans.

black The black racial category includes those who identified themselves as "black or African American." The term "black" is defined differently depending on whether census or survey data are shown. In tables showing 2000 census data, the term "black" may include those who identified themselves as black and no other race (called "black alone") or those who identified themselves as black and some other race (called "black in combination"). Black estimates from the 2003 Current Population Survey include both those who identified themselves as black alone and those who identified themselves as black in combination. Black estimates in earlier survey data do not include the multiracial option.

central cities The largest city in a metropolitan area is called the central city. The balance of the metropolitan area outside the central city is regarded as the "suburbs."

Consumer Expenditure Survey (CEX) The Consumer Expenditure Survey is an ongoing study of the day-to-day spending of American households administered by the Bureau of Labor Statistics. The survey is used to update prices for the Consumer Price Index. The CEX includes an interview survey and a diary survey. The average spending figures shown in this book are the integrated data from both the diary and interview components of the survey. Two separate, nationally representative samples are used for the interview and diary surveys. For the interview survey, about 7,500 consumer units are interviewed on a rotating panel basis each quarter for five consecutive quarters. For the diary survey, 7,500 consumer units keep weekly diaries of spending for two consecutive weeks.

consumer unit *(on spending tables only)* For convenience, the term consumer unit and households are used interchangeably in the spending section of this book, although consumer units are somewhat different from the Census Bureau's households. Consumer units are all related members of a household, or financially independent members of a household. A household may include more than one consumer unit.

disability (*1997 Current Population Survey data*) People aged 15 or older were identified as having a disability if they met any of the following criteria: 1) used a wheelchair, cane, crutches, or walker; 2) had difficulty performing one or more functional activities (seeing, hearing, speaking, lifting/carrying, climbing stairs, walking, or grasping small objects); 3) had difficulty with one or more activities of daily living (or ADL, which include getting around inside the home, getting in or out of bed or a chair, bathing, dressing, eating, and toileting); 4) had difficulty with one or more instrumental activities of daily living (or IADL, which include going outside the home, keeping track of money and bills, preparing meals, doing light housework, taking prescription medicines, and using the telephone); 5) had one or more specified conditions such as a learning disability, mental retardation, or another developmental disability, Alzheimer's disease, or some other type of mental or emotional condition; 6) had any other mental or emotional condition that seriously interfered with everyday activities (frequently depressed or anxious, trouble getting along with others, trouble concentrating, or trouble coping with day-to-day stress); 7) had a condition that limited the ability to work around the house; 8) if age 16 to 67, had a condition that made it difficult to work at a job or business; or 9) received federal benefits based on an inability to work. People were considered to have a severe disability if they met criteria 1, 6, or 9, or had Alzheimer's disease, mental retardation, or another developmental disability, or were unable to perform or needed help to perform one or more activities in criteria 2, 3, 4, 7, or 8. Children under age 5 were identified as disabled if they had a developmental delay or a condition that limited the ability to use arms or legs or a condition that limited walking, running, or playing. Children aged 6 to 14 were identified as severely disabled if they met any of the following criteria: 1) had a mental retardation or some other developmental disability; 2) had a developmental condition for which they had received therapy or diagnostic services; 3) used an ambulatory aid; 4) had a severe limitation in the ability to see, hear, or speak; or 5) needed personal assistance for an activity of daily living.

disability (*2000 Census data*) The 2000 Census defined the disabled as those who were blind, deaf, or had severe vision or hearing impairments, and/or had a condition that substantially limited one or more basic physical activities such as walking, climbing stairs, reaching, lifting, or carrying. It also included people who, because of a physical, mental, or emotional condition lasting six months or more, have difficulty learning, remembering, concentrating, dressing, bathing, getting around inside the home, going outside the home alone to shop or visit a doctor's office, or working at a job or business.

disability (*2001 National Health Interview Survey data*) This survey estimated the number of people aged 18 or older who had difficulty in physical and/or social functioning, probing whether respondents could perform 12 activities by themselves without using special equipment. Physical functioning questions were grouped in two categories: mobility, and flexibility/strength. The mobility category comprised difficulties in performing the following activities: walking a quarter of a mile, standing for two hours, or walking up 10 steps without resting. The flexibility/strength category comprised difficulties in performing the following activities: stooping, bending, kneeling, reaching over one's head, grasping or handling small objects, carrying a 10-pound object, or pushing/pulling a large object. Social functioning questions probed the following: difficulty in sitting for two hours, going shopping, going to movies, attending sporting events, visiting friends, attending clubs or meetings, going to parties, reading, watching television, sewing, or listening to music. Adults who indicated that the activities were "only a little difficult" or "somewhat difficult" were considered to have a moderate difficulty, and those who indicated that the activities were "very difficult" or "can't do this activity" were considered to have severe difficulty.

disability, work (*2003 Current Population Survey data*) A work disability is a specific physical or mental condition that prevents an individual from working. The disability must be so severe that it completely incapacitates the individual and prevents him/her from doing any kind of work for at least the next six months.

Current Population Survey (CPS) The CPS is a nationally representative survey of the civilian noninstitutional population aged 15 or older. It is taken monthly by the Census Bureau for the Bureau of Labor Statistics, collecting information from more than 50,000 households on employment and unemployment. In March of each year, the survey includes the Annual Social and Economic Supplement (formerly called the Annual Demographic Survey), which is the source of most national data on the characteristics of Americans, such as educational attainment, living arrangements, and incomes.

dual-earner couple A married couple in which both the householder and the householder's spouse are in the labor force.

earnings A type of income, earnings is the amount of money a person receives from his or her job. *See also* Income.

employed All civilians who did any work as a paid employee or farmer/self-employed worker, or who worked 15 hours or more as an unpaid farm worker or in a family-owned business, during the reference period. All those who have jobs but who are temporarily absent from their jobs due to illness, bad weather, vacation, labor management dispute, or personal reasons are considered employed.

expenditure The transaction cost including excise and sales taxes of goods and services acquired during the survey period. The full cost of each purchase is recorded even though full payment may not have been made at the date of purchase. Average expenditure figures may be artificially low for infrequently purchased items such as cars because figures are calculated using all consumer units within a demographic segment rather than just purchasers. Expenditure estimates include money spent on gifts for others.

family A group of two or more people (one of whom is the householder) related by birth, marriage, or adoption and living in the same household.

family household A household maintained by a householder who lives with one or more people related to him or her by blood, marriage, or adoption.

female/male householder A woman or man who maintains a household without a spouse present. May head family or nonfamily households.

foreign-born population People who are not U.S. citizens at birth.

full-time employment Full-time is 35 or more hours of work per week during a majority of the weeks worked.

full-time, year-round Indicates 50 or more weeks of full-time employment during the previous calendar year.

Generation X Americans born between 1965 and 1976, also known as the baby-bust generation.

group quarters population The group quarters population includes all people not living in households. Two general categories of people in group quarters are recognized: 1) the institutionalized population, which includes people under formally authorized, supervised care or custody in institutions at the time of enumeration such as correctional institutions, nursing homes, and juvenile institutions; and 2) the noninstitutionalized population, which includes all people who live in group quarters other than institutions such as college dormitories, military quarters, and group homes.

Hispanic Hispanic origin is self-reported in a question separate from race. Because Hispanic is an ethnic origin rather than a race, Hispanics may be of any race. While most Hispanics are white, there are black, Asian, American Indian, and even Native Hawaiian Hispanics. On the 2000 census, many Hispanics identified their race as "other" rather than white, black, and so on. In fact, 90 percent of people identifying their race as "other" also identified themselves as Hispanic. The 2000 census count of Hispanics differs from estimates in the Current Population Survey and other noncensus data collections in part due to methodological differences.

household All the persons who occupy a housing unit. A household includes the related family members and all the unrelated persons, if any, such as lodgers, foster children, wards, or employees who share the housing unit. A person living alone is counted as a household. A group of unrelated people who share a housing unit as roommates or unmarried partners is also counted as a household. Households do not include group quarters such as college dormitories, prisons, or nursing homes.

household, race/ethnicity of Households are categorized according to the race or ethnicity of the householder only.

householder The householder is the person (or one of the persons) in whose name the housing unit is owned or rented or, if there is no such person, any adult member. With married couples, the householder may be either the husband or wife. The householder is the reference person for the household.

householder, age of The age of the householder is used to categorize households into age groups such as those used in this book. Married couples, for example, are classified according to the age of either the husband or wife, depending on which one identified him or herself as the householder.

housing unit A housing unit is a house, an apartment, a group of rooms, or a single room occupied or intended for occupancy as separate living quarters. Separate living quarters are those in which the occupants do not live and eat with any other persons in the structure and that have direct access from the outside of the building or through a common hall that is used or intended for use by the occupants of another unit or by the general public. The occupants may be a single family, one person living alone, two or more families living together, or any other group of related or unrelated persons who share living arrangements.

Housing Vacancy Survey The AHS is a supplement to the Current Population Survey, providing quarterly and annual data on rental and homeowner vacancy rates, characteristics of units available for occupancy, and homeownership rates by age, household type, region, state, and metropolitan area. The Current Population Survey sample includes 51,000 occupied housing units and 9,000 vacant units.

housing value The respondent's estimate of how much his or her house and lot would sell for if it were for sale.

immigration The relatively permanent movement (change of residence) of people into the country of reference.

in-migration The relatively permanent movement (change of residence) of people into a subnational geographic entity, such as a region, division, state, metropolitan area, or county.

income Money received in the preceding calendar year by each person aged 15 or older from each of the following sources: (1) earnings from longest job (or self-employment); (2) earnings from jobs other than longest job; (3) unemployment compensation; (4) workers' compensation; (5) Social Security; (6) Supplemental Security income; (7) public assistance; (8) veterans' payments; (9) survivor benefits; (10) disability benefits; (11) retirement pensions; (12) interest; (13) dividends; (14) rents and royalties or estates and trusts; (15) educational assistance; (16) alimony; (17) child support; (18) financial assistance from outside the household, and other periodic income. Income is reported in several ways in this book. Household income is the combined income of all household members. Income of persons is all income accruing to a person from all sources. Earnings are the money a person receives from his or her job.

industry Refers to the industry in which a person worked longest in the preceding calendar year.

institutionalized population See Group quarters population.

job tenure The length of time a person has been employed continuously by the same employer.

labor force The labor force tables in this book show the civilian labor force only. The labor force includes both the employed and the unemployed (people who are looking for work). People are counted as in the labor force if they were working or looking for work during the reference week in which the Census Bureau fields the Current Population Survey.

labor force participation rate The percent of the civilian noninstitutional population that is in the civilian labor force, which includes both the employed and the unemployed.

married couples with or without children under age 18 Refers to married couples with or without own children under age 18 living in the same household. Couples without children under age 18 may be parents of grown children who live elsewhere, or they could be childless couples.

median The median is the amount that divides the population or households into two equal portions: one below and one above the median. Medians can be calculated for income, age, and many other characteristics.

median income The amount that divides the income distribution into two equal groups, half having incomes above the median, half having incomes below the median. The medians for households or families are based on all households or families. The median for persons are based on all persons aged 15 or older with income.

Medical Expenditure Panel Survey MEPS is a nationally representative survey that collects detailed information on the health status, access to care, health care use and expenses and health insurance coverage of the civilian noninstitutionalized population of the U.S. and nursing home residents. MEPS comprises four component surveys: the Household Component, the Medical Provider Component, the Insurance Component, and the Nursing Home Component. The Household Component is the core survey and is conducted each year, and includes 15,000 households and 37,000 people.

metropolitan statistical area (MSA) To be defined as a metropolitan statistical area (or MSA), an area must include a city with 50,000 or more inhabitants, or a Census Bureau-defined urbanized area of at least 50,000 inhabitants and a total metropolitan population of at least 100,000 (75,000 in New England). The county (or counties) that contains the largest city becomes the "central county" (counties), along with any adjacent counties that have at least 50 percent of their population in the urbanized area surrounding the largest city. Additional "outlying counties" are included in the MSA if they meet specified requirements of commuting to the central counties and other selected requirements of metropolitan character (such as population density and percent urban). In New England, MSAs are defined in terms of cities and towns rather than counties. For this reason, the concept of NECMA is used to define metropolitan areas in the New England division.

Millennial generation Americans born between 1977 and 1994.

mobility status People are classified according to their mobility status on the basis of a comparison between their place of residence at the time of the March Current Population Survey and their place of residence in March of the previous year. Nonmovers are people living in the same house at the end of the period as at the beginning of the period. Movers are people living in a different house at the end of the period than at the beginning of the period. Movers from abroad are either citizens or aliens whose place of residence is outside the United States at the beginning of the period, that is, in an outlying area under the jurisdiction of the United States or in a foreign country. The mobility status for children is fully allocated from the mother if she is in the household; otherwise it is allocated from the householder.

Monitoring the Future Project (MTF) The MTF survey is conducted by the University of Michigan Survey Research Center. The survey is administered to approximately 50,000 students in 420 public and private secondary schools every year. High school seniors have been surveyed annually since 1975. Students in 8th and 10th grade have been surveyed annually since 1991.

National Ambulatory Medical Care Survey (NAMCS) The NAMCS is an annual survey of visits to nonfederally employed office-based physicians who are primarily engaged in direct patient care. Data are collected from physicians rather than patients, with each physician assigned a one-week reporting period. During that week, a systematic random sample of visit characteristics are recorded by the physician or office staff.

National Health Interview Survey (NHIS) The NHIS is a continuing nationwide sample survey of the civilian noninstitutional population of the U.S. conducted by the Census Bureau for the National Center for Health Statistics. Each year, data are collected from more than 100,000 people about their illnesses, injuries, impairments, chronic and acute conditions, activity limitations, and the use of health services.

National Home and Hospice Care Survey These are a series of surveys of a nationally representative sample of home and hospice care agencies in the U.S., sponsored by the National Center for Health Statistics. Data on the characteristics of patients and services provided are collected through personal interviews with administrators and staff.

National Hospital Discharge Survey This survey has been conducted annually since 1965, sponsored by the National Center for Health Statistics, to collect nationally representative information on the characteristics of inpatients discharged from nonfederal, short-stay hospitals in the U.S. The survey collects data from a sample of approximately 270,000 inpatient records acquired from a national sample of about 500 hospitals.

National Household Education Survey (NHES) The NHES, sponsored by the National Center for Education Statistics, provides descriptive data on the educational activities of the U.S. population, including after-school care and adult education. The NHES is a system of telephone surveys of a representative sample of 45,000 to 60,000 households in the U.S. It has been conducted in 1991, 1993, 1995, 1996, 1999, 2001, and 2003.

National Nursing Home Survey This is a series of national sample surveys of nursing homes, their residents, and staff conducted at various intervals since 1973–74 and sponsored by the National Center for Health Statistics. The latest survey was taken in 1999. data for the survey are obtained through personal interviews with administrators and staff, and occasionally with self-administered questionnaires, in a sample of about 1,500 facilities.

National Survey on Drug Use and Health *(formerly called the National Household Survey on Drug Abuse)* This survey, sponsored by the Substance Abuse and Mental Health Services Administration, has been conducted since 1971. It is the primary source of information on the use of illegal drugs by the U.S. population. Each year, a nationally representative sample of about 70,000 individuals aged 12 or older are surveyed in the 50 states and the District of Columbia.

Native Hawaiian and other Pacific Islander The 2000 census, for the first time, identified this group as a separate racial category from Asians. The term "Native Hawaiian and other Pacific Islander" may include those who identified themselves as Native Hawaiian and other Pacific Islander and no other race (called "Native Hawaiian and other Pacific Islander alone") or those who identified themselves as Native Hawaiian and other Pacific Islander and some other race (called "Native Hawaiian and other Pacific Islander in combination").

net migration Net migration is the result of subtracting out-migration from in-migration for an area. Another way to derive net migration is to subtract natural increase (births minus deaths) from total population change in an area.

net worth The amount of money left over after a household's debts are subtracted from its assets.

nonfamily household A household maintained by a householder who lives alone or who lives with people to whom he or she is not related.

nonfamily householder A householder who lives alone or with nonrelatives.

non-Hispanic People who do not identify themselves as Hispanic are classified as non-Hispanic. Non-Hispanics may be of any race.

non-Hispanic white People who identify their race as white and who do not indicate a Hispanic origin. The 2000 census classified people as non-Hispanic white if they identified their race as "white alone" and did not indicate their ethnicity as Hispanic. This definition is close to the one used in the Current Population Survey and other government data collection efforts.

noninstitutionalized population *See* Group quarters population.

nonmetropolitan area Counties that are not classified as metropolitan areas.

occupation Occupational classification is based on the kind of work a person did at his or her job during the previous calendar year. If a person changed jobs during the year, the data refer to the occupation of the job held the longest during that year.

occupied housing units A housing unit is classified as occupied if a person or group of people is living in it or if the occupants are only temporarily absent—on vacation, example. By definition, the count of occupied housing units is the same as the count of households.

other race The 2000 census included "other race" as a racial category. The category was meant to capture the few Americans, such as Creoles, who may not consider themselves as belonging to the other five racial groups. In fact, more than 18 million Americans identified themselves as "other race," including 42 percent of the nation's Hispanics. Among the 18 million people who claim to be of "other" race, 90 percent also identified themselves as Hispanic. The government considers Hispanic to be an ethnic identification rather than a race since there are white, black, American Indian, and Asian Hispanics. But many Hispanics consider their ethnicity to be a separate race.

outside central city The portion of a metropolitan county or counties that falls outside of the central city or cities; generally regarded as the suburbs.

own children Own children are sons and daughters, including stepchildren and adopted children, of the householder. The totals include never-married children living away from home in college dormitories.

owner occupied A housing unit is "owner occupied" if the owner lives in the unit, even if it is mortgaged or not fully paid for. A cooperative or condominium unit is "owner occupied" only if the owner lives in it. All other occupied units are classified as "renter occupied."

part-time employment Part-time is less than 35 hours of work per week in a majority of the weeks worked during the year.

percent change The change (either positive or negative) in a measure that is expressed as a proportion of the starting measure. When median income changes from $20,000 to $25,000, for example, this is a 25 percent increase.

percentage point change The change (either positive or negative) in a value which is already expressed as a percentage. When a labor force participation rate changes from 70 percent of 75 percent, for example, this is a 5 percentage point increase.

poverty level The official income threshold below which families and people are classified as living in poverty. The threshold rises each year with inflation and varies depending on family size and age of householder.

proportion or share The value of a part expressed as a percentage of the whole. If there are 4 million people aged 25 and 3 million of them are white, then the white proportion is 75 percent.

race Race is self-reported and defined differently depending on the data source. On the 2000 census, respondents identified themselves as belonging to one or more of six racial groups: American Indian and Alaska Native, Asian, black, Native Hawaiian and other Pacific Islander, white, and other. In publishing the results, the Census Bureau created three new terms to distinguish one group from another. The "race alone" population is people who identified themselves as only one race. The "race in combination" population is people who identified themselves as more than one race, such as white and black. The "race, alone or in combination" population includes both those who identified themselves as one race and those who identified themselves as more than one race. Other government data collection efforts included the multira-

cial option beginning in 2003. The tables in this book that include race data from government surveys or from censuses prior to 2000 do not include the multiracial option.

regions The four major regions and nine census divisions of the United States are the state groupings as shown below:

Northeast:
—New England: Connecticut, Maine, Massachusetts, New Hampshire, Rhode Island, and Vermont
—Middle Atlantic: New Jersey, New York, and Pennsylvania

Midwest:
—East North Central: Illinois, Indiana, Michigan, Ohio, and Wisconsin
—West North Central: Iowa, Kansas, Minnesota, Missouri, Nebraska, North Dakota, and South Dakota

South:
—South Atlantic: Delaware, District of Columbia, Florida, Georgia, Maryland, North Carolina, South Carolina, Virginia, and West Virginia
—East South Central: Alabama, Kentucky, Mississippi, and Tennessee
—West South Central: Arkansas, Louisiana, Oklahoma, and Texas

West:
—Mountain: Arizona, Colorado, Idaho, Montana, Nevada, New Mexico, Utah, and Wyoming
—Pacific: Alaska, California, Hawaii, Oregon, and Washington

renter occupied *See* Owner occupied.

rounding Percentages are rounded to the nearest tenth of a percent; therefore, the percentages in a distribution do not always add exactly to 100.0 percent. The totals, however, are always shown as 100.0. Moreover, individual figures are rounded to the nearest thousand without being adjusted to group totals, which are independently rounded; percentages are based on the unrounded numbers.

self-employment A person is categorized as self-employed if he or she was self-employed in the job held longest during the reference period. Persons who report self-employment from a second job are excluded, but those who report wage-and-salary income from a second job are included. Unpaid workers in family businesses are excluded. Self-employment statistics include only nonagricultural workers and exclude people who work for themselves in incorporated business.

sex ratio The number of men per 100 women.

suburbs *See* Outside central city.

Survey of Consumer Finances The Survey of Consumer Finances is a triennial survey taken by the Federal Reserve Board. It collects data on the assets, debts, and net worth of American households. For the 2001 survey, the Federal Reserve Board interviewed more than 4,000 households.

Survey of Income and Program Participation (SIPP) SIPP is a longitudinal survey conducted at four-month intervals by the Census Bureau. The main focus of SIPP is information on labor force participation, jobs, income, and participation in federal assistance programs. Information on other topics is collected in topical modules on a rotating basis.

two or more races People who identified themselves as belonging to two or more racial groups on the 2000 Census. *See* Race.

unemployed Unemployed people are those who, during the survey period, had no employment but were available and looking for work. Those who were laid off from their jobs and were waiting to be recalled are also classified as unemployed.

white The term "white" is defined differently depending on whether census or survey data are shown. In tables showing 2000 census data, the term "white" may include those who identified themselves as white and no other race (called "white alone") or those who identified themselves as white and some other race (called "white in combination"). White estimates from the 2003 Current Population Survey include both those who identified themselves as white alone and those who identified themselves as white in combination. White estimates in earlier survey data do not include the multiracial option.

Youth Risk Behavior Surveillance System (YRBSS) The YRBSS was created by the Centers for Disease Control to monitor health risks being taken by young people at the national, state, and local level. The national survey is taken every two years based on a nationally representative sample of 16,000 students in 9th through 12th grade in public and private schools.

Bibliography

AARP

Internet site http://www.aarp.org
—*Boomers at Midlife: The AARP Life Stage Study*, A National Survey Conducted by Princeton Survey Research Associates, November 2002
—"Pennies from Heaven: Will Inheritances Bail Out the Boomers?" Mitja Ng-Baumhackl, John Gist, and Carlos Figueiredo, *Data Digest*, No. 90, AARP Public Policy Institute
—*Staying Ahead of the Curve 2003: The AARP Working in Retirement Study*

Bureau of Labor Statistics

Internet site http://www.bls.gov
—1997 and 2002 Consumer Expenditure Surveys, Internet site http://www.bls.gov/cex/
—2002 Consumer Expenditure Survey, unpublished data
—2003 Current Population Survey, unpublished data
—*Characteristics of Minimum Wage Workers*, 2002, Internet site http://www.bls.gov/cps/minwage2002.htm
—*Contingent and Alternative Employment Arrangements, February 2001*, USDL 01-153, Internet site http://www.bls.gov/news.release/conemp.toc.htm
—*Employee Tenure in 2002*, Internet site http://www.bls.gov/news.release/tenure.toc.htm
—*Employment Projections, 2002–2012*, Internet site http://www.bls.gov/emp/emplab1.htm
—Labor force participation rates, historical, Public Query Data Tool, Internet site http://www.bls.gov/data
—*Workers on Flexible and Shift Schedules in 2001*, USDL 02-225, Internet site http://www.bls.gov/news.release/flex.toc.htm

Bureau of the Census

Internet site http://www.census.gov
—2003 Current Population Survey Annual Social and Economic Supplement, Internet site http://www.census.gov/hhes/income/dinctabs.html
—*Age: 2000*, Census 2000 Brief, 2001
—*American Housing Survey for the United States in 2001*, Internet site http://www.census.gov/hhes/www/ahs.html
—Census 2000, Internet site http://factfinder.census.gov/servlet/BasicFactsServlet
—*Children's Living Arrangements and Characteristics: March 2002*, detailed tables for Current Population Report P20-547, Internet site http://www.census.gov/population/www/socdemo/hh-fam/cps2002.html
—Current Population Surveys, historical data, Internet site http://www.census.gov/hhes/income/histinc/histinctb.html
—*Disability Status: 2000*, Census 2000 Brief, 2003
—*Educational Attainment in the United States: March 2002*, detailed tables (PPL-169), Internet site http://www.census.gov/population/www/socdemo/education/ppl-169.html

—*Foreign-Born Population of the United States, Current Population Survey—March* 2002, detailed tables (PPL-162), Internet site http://www.census.gov/population/www/socdemo/foreign/ppl-162.html

—*Geographic Mobility: 2003*, detailed tables for P20-549, Internet site http://www.census.gov/population/www/socdemo/migrate/p20-549.html

—Housing Vacancy Surveys, Internet site http://www.census.gov/hhes/www/housing/hvs/annual03/ann03ind.html

—National Population Estimates, Internet site http://eire.census.gov/popest/

—*School Enrollment—Social and Economic Characteristics of Students: October 2002*, detailed tables; Internet site http://www.census.gov/population/www/socdemo/school/cps2002.html

—*U.S. Interim Projections by Age, Sex, Race, and Hispanic Origin*, Internet site http://www.census.gov/ipc/www/usinterimproj/

Centers for Disease Control and Prevention

Internet site http://www.cdc.gov

—Behavioral Risk Factor Surveillance System Prevalence Data, Internet site http://apps.nccd.cdc.gov/brfss/index.asp

Employee Benefit Research Institute

Internet site http://www.ebri.org

—2003 Retirement Confidence Survey, EBRI/ASEC/Greenwald, Internet site http://www.ebri.org/

Federal Reserve Board

Internet site http://www.federalreserve.gov

—2001 Survey of Consumer Finances; Internet site http://www.federalreserve.gov/pubs/oss/oss2/2001/scf2001home.html

Investment Company Institute and Securities Industry Association

Internet sites http://www.ici.org and http://www.sia.com

—*Equity Ownership in America, 2002*; Internet sites http://www.ici.org and http://www.sia.com

National Center for Education Statistics

Internet site http://nces.ed.gov

—Adult Education and Lifelong Learning Survey of the National Household Education Surveys Program, Internet site http://nces.ed.gov/programs/coe/2003/section1/tables/t08_2.asp

National Center for Health Statistics

Internet site http://www.cdc.gov/nchs

—Births: Final Data for 2002, *National Vital Statistics Reports*, Vol. 52, No. 10, 2003

—Deaths: Leading Causes for 2001, *National Vital Statistics Report*, Vol. 52, No. 9, 2003

—Deaths: Preliminary Data for 2002, *National Vital Statistics Report*, Vol. 52, No. 13, 2004

—Health Behaviors of Adults: United States, 1999–2001, *Vital and Health Statistics*, Series 10, No. 219, 2004

—*Health, United States, 2003*, Internet site http://www.cdc.gov/nchs/hus.htm

—National Ambulatory Medical Care Survey: 2001 Summary, *Advance Data* No. 337, 2003

—National Hospital Ambulatory Medical Care Survey: 2001 Emergency Department Summary, *Advance Data* No. 335, 2003

—National Hospital Ambulatory Medical Care Survey: 2001 Outpatient Department Summary, *Advance Data* No. 338, 2003

—*Summary Health Statistics for U.S. Adults: National Health Interview Survey, 2001,* Series 10, No. 218, 2004

U.S. Citizenship and Immigration Services

—*2002 Yearbook of Immigration Statistics,* Internet site http://uscis.gov/graphics/shared/aboutus/statistics/index.htm

U.S. Substance Abuse and Mental Health Services Administration, Office of Applied Studies Internet site http://www.samhsa.gov/

—National Survey on Drug Use and Health, 2002

Index

cerebrovascular disease, as cause of death, 60–62
certificates of deposit, 300
child support, as source of income, 134–139
childbearing. *See* Births.
children, presence of in households, 179, 189–199
cholesterol, high, 40, 47
cigarette smoking, 21, 34–35. *See also* Tobacco
      products.
citizens, 227–228
college, as a reason for moving, 84–86
college enrollment, 5, 16–17
contractors. *See* Independent contractors.
coronary, 41, 43, 45
credit card debt, 307, 309

death, causes of, 21, 59–62
debt, household, 307–309
dental problems, 41, 43, 45
depression, 41–46
diabetes:
    as cause of death, 60–62
    health condition, 41, 43, 45
dieting, 24, 26
disability:
    benefits, as source of income, 134–139
    by education, 53
    by type, 49–52
    work, 21, 49–50, 53
dividends, as source of income, 134–139
divorce, 179, 204–215
drinking, alcoholic beverages, 34, 36
drugs:
    consumer spending by detailed category, 267,
        273, 288, 294
    consumer spending trends, 251
    illicit, use of, 34, 37
dual-income couples, 143, 152–153
earnings:
    as source of income, 133–139
    by educational attainment, 87, 120–132
    minimum wage, 172–173
    of full-time workers, 120–132
eating away from home. *See* Food.
education:
    adult, 5, 18–19
    consumer spending by detailed category, 269,
        273–274, 290, 294
    consumer spending trends, 251–252
    earnings by, 87, 120–132
educational assistance, as source of income,
    134–139
educational attainment:
    by race and Hispanic origin, 5, 10–13
    by sex, 5–13
emergency department visits, 55, 58
emphysema, 41, 43, 45
employment-based health insurance, 38–39

employment, long-term, 164, 166
employment status:
    by race and Hispanic origin, 148–151
    by sex, 146–151
entertainment:
    consumer spending by detailed category, 253,
        267–269, 273, 288–290, 294
    consumer spending trends, 248, 251–252
exercise, participation in, 24, 26–27

face pain, 41, 43, 45
families. *See* Households.
family, as a reason for moving, 84–86
female-headed household. *See* Households,
    female-headed.
financial services, spending on, 270, 291
food:
    at home, 249, 253–257, 271, 274–278, 292
    away from home, 248–249, 253, 257, 278
    consumer spending by detailed category,
        253–257, 271, 274–278, 292
    consumer spending trends, 248–249, 251
foreign-born population, 217, 227–229
full-time workers, 108–132, 160–161
furnishings and equipment:
    consumer spending by detailed category,
        261–263, 271, 274, 282–284, 292
    consumer spending trends, 250

geographic mobility:
    rate, 82–83
    reason for, 82, 84–86
gifts:
    consumer spending by detailed category,
        271–273, 292–294
    consumer spending trends, 248, 251–252

hay fever, 41, 43, 45
headaches, 41, 43, 45
health, as a reason for moving, 84–86
health care:
    consumer spending by detailed category,
        266–267, 273, 287–288, 294
    consumer spending trends, 247–248, 251–252
health conditions, 40–54
health insurance:
    consumer spending by detailed category,
        266–267, 287–288
    consumer spending trends, 248, 251
    coverage, 21, 38–39
health problems by type, 21, 40–54
health status, 21–23
hearing impairments, 40–41, 43, 45
heart disease:
    as cause of death, 21, 59–62
    health condition, 41, 43, 45

high blood pressure. *See* Hypertension.

high cholesterol, 40, 47

Hispanic-American men:
    educational attainment, 10–11
    employment status, 148–149
    full-time workers, 108, 112
    income, 108, 112
    living alone, 185
    marital status, 207, 212–213

Hispanic-American women:
    births to, 31–32
    educational attainment, 12–13
    employment status, 150–151
    full-time workers, 114, 118
    income, 114, 118
    living alone, 182, 185
    marital status, 207, 212–213

Hispanic Americans:
    by state, 237–245
    educational attainment, 10–13
    homeownership of, 72–73
    household income, 92, 95
    household types, 182, 185, 189, 193
    households with children, 189, 193
    in poverty, 140–141
    population, 223–225, 237–245

homeowners:
    by household type, 65, 70–71
    by race and Hispanic origin, 72–73
    by value of home, 80–81
    housing costs of, 65, 78–79
    in new housing, 76–77
    number of, 68–69
    trends in, 65–67

homes, as nonfinancial assets, 295, 303, 305

homicide, as a cause of death, 60–61

hospital emergency department visits, 55, 58

hospital outpatient department visits, 55, 57

household services:
    consumer spending by detailed category, 253,
        260–261, 271–272, 281–282, 292–293
    consumer spending trends, 250

households:
    by race and Hispanic origin, 182–186, 189,
        191–194
    by type, 179–186, 189–199
    income of, 87–104
    inheriting money, 310, 312
    single-person, 180–186, 200–203
    size, 179, 187–188
    wealth of, 295–313
    with children, 179, 189–199

households, female-headed:
    by race and Hispanic origin, 182–186, 189,
        191–194
    homeownership of, 70–71
    housing costs of, 79
    housing value of, 80–81

    income of, 97–104
    living alone, 181
    with children, 189–194, 198

households, male-headed:
    by race and Hispanic origin, 182–186, 189,
        191–194
    homeownership of, 70–71
    housing costs of, 79
    housing value of, 80–81
    income of, 97–104
    living alone, 181
    with children, 189–194, 199

households, married-couple:
    by race and Hispanic origin, 182–186, 189,
        191–194
    dual-income, 143, 152–153
    homeownership of, 65, 70–71
    housing costs of, 65, 78–79
    housing value of, 80–81
    income of, 87, 97–104
    with children, 189–194, 197

households, single-person:
    by race and Hispanic origin, 182–186
    by sex, 180–186, 200–203
    homeownership, 71
    housing costs of, 79
    housing value of, 80–81
    income of, 97–104

housekeeping supplies:
    consumer spending by detailed category, 261,
271, 282, 292
    consumer spending trends, 250–251

housing: *See also* Shelter *and* Homeowners *and*
        Renters.
    as a reason for moving, 82, 84–86
    by type of structure, 74–75
    costs of, 65, 78–79
    new, 76–77
    value of, 65, 80–81, 305–306

human immunodeficiency disease (HIV):
    as cause of death, 59–61
    people with, 49, 54

hypertension, 21, 40–41, 43, 45, 48

immigrants, 217, 230–231

income: *See also* Earnings.
    by household type, 87, 97–104
    by race and Hispanic origin, 92–96, 108–119
    household, 87–104
    men's, 87, 105–106, 108–113, 133–136
    of full-time workers, 108–119
    source of, 133–139
    trends in, 88–89, 105–107
    women's, 87, 105, 107, 114–119, 133, 137–139

independent contractors, 167–168

influenza, as cause of death, 60

inheritance, 310, 313

installment debt, 309
insurance, personal: *See also* Life insurance *and*
        Health insurance.
    consumer spending by detailed category, 270,
        291
    consumer spending trends, 251
interest, as source of income, 133–139

job: *See also* Occupation.
    as a reason for moving, 82, 84–86
    long-term, 143, 164, 166
    tenure, 164–65

kidney disease, 41, 43, 45

labor force: *See also* Workers.
    by occupation, 154–159
    by race and Hispanic origin, 148–151
    by sex, 143–151
    full-time, 160–161
    participation, 143–151
    part-time, 160–161
    projections, 143, 176–177
    self-employed, 133–139, 162–163
    trends, 143–145
life expectancy, 59, 63
life insurance:
    as financial asset, 300
    consumer spending on, 251, 270, 291
liver disease:
    as cause of death, 60–62
    health condition, 41, 43, 45
living alone, 180–186, 200–203. *See also*
        Households, single-person.
living arrangements, 179, 200–202

male-headed households. *See* Households,
        male-headed.
marital status:
    births by, 28, 32
    by race and Hispanic origin, 207–215
    by sex, 179, 204–215
married couples. *See* Households, married-couple.
Medicaid, 38–39
medical services, use of, 55–58
Medicare:
    coverage, 39
    spending on, 266–267, 287–288
men:
    disabled, 50
    drinking, 34, 36
    earnings by educational attainment, 87,
        120–126
    educational attainment, 5–8, 10–11

employment, long-term, 143, 164, 166
employment status, 146–149
exercise, participation in, 27
full-time workers, 87, 108–113, 120–126,
        160–161
high cholesterol, 47
hypertension, 40, 48
income, 87, 105–106, 108–113, 133–136
job tenure of, 164–165
labor force participation, 143–149, 176–177
labor force projections, 176–177
life expectancy, 59, 63
living alone, 180–181, 183–186, 200–201, 203
living arrangements, 200–201, 203
marital status, 200–201, 204–215
overweight, 24–25
part-time workers, 160–161
pension coverage, 311
physician visits, 56
population, 220
school enrollment, 14–15
self-employed, 133–136, 162–163
source of income, 133–136
unemployed, 146–149
union membership, 174–175
with AIDS, 49, 54
with flexible schedules, 169–170
mental problems, 41–46, 50
migraines. *See* Headaches.
military health insurance, 38–39
minimum wage workers, 172–173
mobile homes, living in, 74–75
mobility, geographic:
    rate, 82–83
    reason for, 82, 84–86
mortgage debt, 306–307, 309
movers. *See* Mobility, geographic.
multiracial population, 223–224, 226
mutual funds, 298, 300, 302

Native Hawaiians:
    by state, 237–245
    population, 224–225, 237–245
naturalized citizens, 227–229
neck pain, 41, 43, 45
nephritis, as cause of death, 62
net worth, household, 295–297

obesity, 21, 24–25
occupations, 143, 154–159
out-of-wedlock births, 28, 32
outpatient department visits, 55, 57
overweight problems, 21, 24–26. *See also*
        Weight loss.